Real Estate Brokerage

Real Estate Brokerage

A Success Guide

2nd Edition

John E. Cyr
Joan m. Sobeck

REAL ESTATE EDUCATION COMPANY
a division of Longman Financial Services Institute, Inc.

Executive Editor: Richard A. Hagle
Sponsoring Editor: Jeny Sejdinaj
Project Editor: Carole J. Bilina
Cover Design: Edwin Harris
Art: Paul R. Barnes

Published by Real Estate Education Company/Chicago, a division of Longman Financial Services Institute, Inc.

Printed in the United States of America

88 89 90 10 9 8 7 6 5 4 3

Library of Congress Cataloging-in-Publication Data

Cyr, John E.
  Real estate brokerage.

  Includes index.
  1. Real estate agents—United States. 2. Real estate business—United States. I. Sobeck, Joan m.
II. Title.
HD278.C95   1988   333.33′068   87-16650
ISBN 0-88462-674-1

This book is dedicated to the thousands of REALTORS®
and REALTOR-ASSOCIATES® who have participated
in the continuing effort to professionalize our industry.
If we have furthered that goal in any way,
this book has served its purpose.

Contents

PREFACE   **xi**

1 REAL ESTATE BROKERAGE IN PERSPECTIVE   **1**
    Economic Justification for Real Estate Brokerage   1
    Prospects for Real Estate Brokerage   3
    Evolution of a Brokerage Specialty   5
    Potential Earnings   7
    Response to Change   8
    Marketing Versus Professional Concept   10

2 REQUIREMENTS FOR SUCCESS   **17**
    The Need for Formal Professional Education   17
    What Experience Can Teach   19
    Legal Requirements for the Broker License   21
    Initial Financing Needs   22
    Psychological Traits and Social Skills   24
    The Need for Management Skills   25
    Integrity—The Most Important Psychological Trait   26

3 THE AGENCY RELATIONSHIP AND THE LAW   **31**
    The Law of Agency   31
    The Agency Relationship   32
    Responsibilities of Each Party in the Agency Relationship   35
    Types of Listing Agreements   43
    Protecting the Broker's Commission   46

4 ESTABLISHING AN OPERATING PHILOSOPHY   **51**
    Formulating a Business Plan   51
    Eight Basic Questions   52

Choosing a Specialty   53
Selecting the Right Size   54
Acquiring Sales Associates   59
Independent Contractors or Employees?   59
Tax Legislation Affecting Independent Contractor Status   60
Form of Ownership   66
Franchises and Some Alternatives   69
Vertical or Horizontal Growth—or Both?   72
Procedural Guidelines   73

5 ORGANIZING AND OPENING THE OFFICE   77
Small vs. Large   77
The Non-Owner/Manager   79
The Real Estate Sales Process   79
Location   80
Physical Layout   82
Equipment   86
Selection of Equipment   90
The Budget   91
Miscellaneous Considerations   97

6 NO-NONSENSE SALES MANAGEMENT   103
The Real Estate Sales Manager   104
Techniques for Motivating Sales Associates   107
Meetings that Matter   111
Evaluating Performance   114
Personnel Problems   119

7 RECRUITING AND SELECTING SALES ASSOCIATES   125
Some Early Decisions To Make   126
Recruitment Methods   127
The Selection Process   133

8 TRAINING SALES ASSOCIATES   139
Benefits and Objectives of a Training Program   140
Ingredients of a Good Training Program   141
A Time Management Plan   152
A Market Survey Questionnaire   154
A Training Manual for Each Sales Associate   155

9 ACCUMULATION AND CONTROL OF INVENTORY   163
The Importance of a Strong Listing Acquisition Program   164
Developing an Affirmative Listing Attitude   164
Sources of Listings   165

The Initial Interview   168
Preparing and Presenting the CMA   173
The Presentation   174
Communication and Control   185

10 ADVERTISING AND PROMOTION   **197**
Initial Exposure   198
Advertising   200
Advertising Control   207
Open Houses   215
MLS and the Cooperating Broker   217
Maintaining Contact   218

11 TURNING PROSPECTS INTO BUYERS   **221**
Finding Prospects   221
The Qualifying Process   222
Presenting the Property   226
The Close   229
The Offer   232
Presenting the Offer   235
Negotiating   237

12 FINANCING STRATEGIES   **241**
Real Estate and the Money Market   241
The Importance of Financing   242
The Broker's Role in Financing   243
Problem Examples   244
Financing Tools: Promissory Notes and Security Devices   244
Alternative Mortgage Instruments   250
Private Sources of Financing   252

13 A BLUEPRINT FOR CLOSING   **257**
Legal Requirements for a Valid Closing   257
Responsibilities for Title Closing   258
Satisfying Contingencies in the Contract   262
Searching and Certifying the Title   264
Settlement   267
The Federal Real Estate Procedures Act (RESPA)   271
Broker Follow-Up After the Closing   271

14 THE PUBLIC SECTOR'S IMPACT ON REAL ESTATE   **279**
The Concept of Social Property   280
Government Activities Affecting Real Estate Brokerage   281
Government Activities Affecting Property Financing   288

Government Activities Affecting Property Ownership   290
Industry's Answer—Involvement   293

15 BEYOND RESIDENTIAL BROKERAGE   297
The Nine Major Advantages of Investing in Real Estate   298
Five Possible Disadvantages of Real Estate Investing   303
The Exciting World of Investment Brokerage   305
Five Areas of Investment Expertise   308
Three Stages of Real Estate Investing   310
Investment Market Analysis   313
Alternative Marketing Methods   316
Counseling: The Ultimate Real Estate Profession   321
Responsibilities of the Broker to the Community   322

16 TRENDS AND IMPACTS: THE CHANGING INDUSTRY   325
Tax Reform Act of 1986 (TRA '86)   325
New Laws Regarding Consumer Protection   326
Increased Uses for the Computer   330
Trend Toward Appraiser Certification and Licensing   331
Development of Marketing Sessions by Professionals   332
New Developments in Finder's Fee Exceptions   332
Trend Toward Licensing Reciprocity Among States   333

POLICY MANUAL   335
GLOSSARY   345
INDEX   359

Preface

This is a practical book; it is a basic, no-nonsense, easy-to-read work written by two REALTORS® whose main occupation is real estate brokerage. They both enjoy what they do, having been successful at it, and are willing to share their experience and knowledge with others coming up in the profession. Between them they have experienced just about every situation that can be encountered or imagined in residential brokerage. These experiences have proved to be excellent material for composing a book of this sort.

Both authors feel that if such a book had been available when they started their businesses it would have saved them countless mistakes and misdirections of effort. Flying "by the seat of one's pants" may have been an accepted procedure in the early days of aviation training but it is a poor way of learning to compete in today's jet-age real estate business. A clear understanding of what lies ahead helps one to prepare and develop a game plan that affords a minimum number of mistakes and a maximum rate of progress.

Both authors know what it takes to start from scratch, persevere and eventually succeed. Neither knew the other before being approached for this subject, yet after they met and compared notes they found a great deal of common ground upon which to base a book.

Each author started as a residential salesperson and gradually grew into the broker role. Although each had only a high school education and started in business with relatively little capital, both acquired the expertise and knowledge needed to succeed through the educational opportunities provided by the National Association of REALTORS®,*together with its

---

*In 1987 the National Association of REALTORS® had a membership of more than 700,000, representing the 50 states, Puerto Rico and the Virgin Islands. The societies, institutes and councils are: American Institute of Real Estate Appraisers (AIREA), American Society of Real Estate Counselors (ASREC), the REALTORS®

local boards, state associations, societies, institutes and councils. They have consistently been highly visible in the activities of these organizations. In 1985 Cyr was President of the REALTORS® Land Institute of the National Association of REALTORS,® and Sobeck was President of the New Jersey Association of REALTORS®.

Both authors have attained the CRS (Certified Residential Specialist) designation from the REALTOR® National Marketing Institute (RNMI) as well as being Graduates of the REALTOR® Institute of NAR (GRI). Each has written about real estate subjects, a fact that undoubtedly led the publishers to choose them for this assignment.

Each author has two offices that engage between 15 and 24 salespersons, not large offices, but probably average in size. They do, however, exhibit certain basic differences, which makes for a well-rounded coverage of the subject. One lives on the east coast in a New Jersey suburban community close to the high-density area of New York; the other is from a semi-rural, agriculture-oriented city in central California. Joan m. Sobeck is the broker/owner of Joan m. Sobeck, Inc., REALTORS® of Hillsdale, New Jersey. Her business is primarily engaged in residential resales. John E. Cyr, the broker/owner of John Cyr, Inc., REALTORS® of Stockton, California, has a business somewhat more diversified, engaging in the sale and leasing of agricultural, residential, industrial and commercial properties.

While it may be said that experience is a good teacher, it may be further stated that learning from the experience of others is even better. It certainly is less painful. The foresight this book provides to the readers is derived from the hindsight of the two authors, and this is where the real value of this book lies. Its 16 chapters attempt to explain and describe the entire brokerage procedure from the perspective of experience.

Whether the reader is a newcomer to real estate brokerage or has been in it for some time, there is plenty of solid material offered here to assimilate and put into practice. This work will be a valuable addition to every practicing broker's library.

The authors would like to thank the following individuals for their valuable assistance in the development of the second edition of this text: Billy Crownover, American College of Real Estate, San Antonio, Texas; Andrew M. Gray, NIRE Schools of Real Estate, Vienna, Virginia; Eli A.

Land Institute (RLI), FIABCI/USA (the American Chapter of the International Real Estate Federation), Institute of Real Estate Management (IREM), Real Estate Securities and Syndication Institute (RESSI), REALTORS® National Marketing Institute (RNMI), Society of Industrial and Office REALTORS® (SIOR) and Women's Council of REALTORS® (WCR).

Naffah, North American College, Laguna Niguel, California; Vicki B. VanBuren, Forsyth Technical College, Winston-Salem, North Carolina; and Dick Ward, Harbour Associates, REALTORS®, Wilmington, North Carolina. Appreciation is also extended to the California Association of REALTORS® and the New Jersey Association of REALTORS® for permission to reproduce forms and to the National Association of REALTORS® for permission to quote from materials provided by the Economics and Research Division.

1 Real Estate Brokerage in Perspective

INTRODUCTION

A broker is defined as "one who offers to buy and offers to sell for another for compensation or arranges for the negotiation of contracts of various types." The definition sounds simple, yet even the briefest look at the real estate business will reveal that it fails to reflect the whole picture: The brokering of real estate can be stimulating, frustrating, rewarding, exasperating, stressful and exhilarating. The key word in the definition is *negotiation.*

It takes a special sort of person to become a successful broker—one who can cope with the frustrations and disappointments of nerve-wearing negotiation. Studies and experience have shown that many people do not have, nor can they ever hope to acquire, the necessary interpersonal skills to master this difficult art of bringing two parties together for their mutual satisfaction.

How can one determine who is capable of becoming a successful broker? This chapter examines some basic requirements.

ECONOMIC JUSTIFICATION FOR REAL ESTATE BROKERAGE

In earlier, simpler days in this country's history, an owner who had a property to sell merely set out a for-sale sign, found an interested purchaser, and then sold the property at fair market value with a minimum of fuss. Now, however, modern life has become far too complex for most people to handle all of their problems without professional help. Many people can hardly fill out their own tax returns or settle minor legal problems without the aid of attorneys. So it is with real estate. The many legal, technical, financing and tax problems in the consummation of a real estate transaction make the lawyer's old adage applicable to real estate: "The seller who represents himself has a fool for a client."

At this writing, almost two million people are licensed to sell real estate in the United States. Many of them earn substantial incomes. There must be many reasons for such an industry to exist and then to grow so dramatically.

As the population becomes denser and more mobile, the trend is away from families permanently residing in the same small community. No longer does everyone in town know when another family is about to sell a home and move, which would enable a direct transfer of ownership between two parties. If a modern family plans to move from Los Angeles to Phoenix, it will be virtually impossible for them to scout out and inspect every home for sale in Phoenix to find one that meets their needs. It will be more sensible and certainly easier for them to contact a brokerage firm in Phoenix that belongs to a multiple-listing service (MLS). The broker's salesperson can sift through all available properties for sale, and show only those that meet the buyer's needs.

Brokers in any community serve as the marketplace for real property sales in that community, just as stockbrokers are the marketplace for securities. The brokers and their associates collect information about every property for sale in their market area, gather together the data on those properties and correlate these data to have them available for the customer who is looking for a specific type of property. Brokers advertise and promote the property. The broker is the person who negotiates to solve real estate problems for buyers and sellers as well as for landlords and tenants, frequently at a lower cost than if the individuals did it themselves. The three basic functions of the real estate brokerage are to serve the sellers, the buyers and the community as a whole.

For sellers, the broker's exposure in the marketplace helps them set a fair market price and then obtain a buyer offering the highest price possible within the shortest time span. Most brokerage firms, through their knowledge of market conditions and area activity or, in many cases, by working with their MLSs, perform this function efficiently.

For buyers, using a broker or associate to search out the most suitable available property saves time and money and prevents mistakes. Working with a professional who knows real estate practice, who is familiar with the area and who is informed about values and prices, a buyer can obtain information that otherwise would be inaccessible to him or her. Although this arrangement has appeared to work well for both buyer and seller for many decades, in recent years the question "Whom does the agent represent?" has been asked. The problem of dual agency has already been resolved in some states by requiring a disclosure to the buyer or, in some cases, the seller that the broker is the agent of the other party. Dual agency will be covered in more detail in Chapter 3.

Finally, modern communities are beginning to realize the highly important contributions of real estate brokers to helping the community develop and grow, especially in times when mortgage money is expensive and hard to obtain. The role of the broker intensifies in importance in direct proportion to the increase in population density of the community. In other words, the larger and more urban the town or city becomes, the more opportunities there are for the broker of real estate. A knowledgeable broker is the first person to recognize the possible uses for various properties and point out these possibilities to potential users.

Brokers create a variety of transactions that probably would not take place without them. In these transactions they satisfy the needs of buyers and sellers as well as those of users. The real estate business is an "expandable" business and it is usually the real estate broker and/or developer who creates much of this expansion. The broker is trained to see opportunities for investments and to be aware of potential users' needs for space. By identifying these needs for the clients—the investors—the broker brings into existence the new apartment complex, office building or commercial venture. Through the planning and building of industrial parks, city growth accompanies new industry.

PROSPECTS FOR REAL ESTATE BROKERAGE

According to tabulations by the National Association of Real Estate License Law Officials (NARELLO) there are almost 2 million licensed real estate brokers and sales associates in the U.S. today.

According to economists for the National Association of REALTORS® (NAR) sales of existing single-family units reached 3.6 million in 1986. Add to that the 750,000 new homes that were sold, and you have an approximate sales volume of 4.4 million homes marketed in 1986. (This is higher than the figure for 1985 because of the lower interest rates experienced in most of 1986 and the pent-up demand caused by the higher interest in the immediately preceding years.)

Divide the 4.4 million homes sold by approximately 2 million licensees and you arrive at an average of 2.2 homes sold per licensee that year. If you multiply the December 1986 median sales price of $80,800 per unit nationwide by an arbitrarily chosen average commission of 5.5 percent, then those 2.2 sales result in $177,760 × 5.5 percent or $9,777 gross average commission per licensee.

After splitting the gross commissions with the brokerage firm, not much of a living wage is left for the average licensee. But there are a number of circumstances that account for such low average income figures.

TABLE 1.1   Prior Occupations of Brokers Who Pursued Another Career Before Entering Real Estate

Previous Allied Occupation	Percentage Distribution	Previous Nonallied Occupation	Percentage Distribution
Management	10.0	Retailing	5.7
Sales	9.9	Secretarial/bookkeeping	10.0
Insurance	4.4	Teaching	7.9
Banking/finance	5.4	Armed Forces	5.0
Building	2.7	Engineering	2.0
Law	.5	Government	3.6
Other	.8	Accounting	3.7
TOTAL	33.7	Farming	.9
		Communications	2.5
		Other	25.2
		TOTAL	66.5

SOURCE: Economics and Research Division, NATIONAL ASSOCIATION OF REALTORS®, *Membership Profile 1984.* (Washington, DC: NAR, 1984), 21.

1. During times of decreased sales volume the number of licensees tends to drop dramatically. For example, during the 1980 recession there was a sharp drop in licensee enrollment to less than 1.5 million licensed persons.

2. There is an old saying in the business that 20 percent of the practitioners do 80 percent of the business. (This has never been established as being factual; however, for the purposes of this discussion, let us assume it has some basis in fact.) If such were the case, then 20 percent, or 400,000, of the 2 million licensees would account for 80 percent, or approximately 3.5 million, of the 4.4 million sales. Carried a step or two further, 3.5 million sales divided by those 400,000 licensees would equal 8.75 sales per licensee. Those 8.75 sales multiplied by the $80,800 median sales price would equal $707,800 in gross sales volume and, at an average 5.5 percent commission rate, an average total commission of $38,885. (Authors' note: These figures can be somewhat misleading—one must keep in mind that there are as many who exceed the average as there are who fall short of it. Somewhere between the $9,777 figure and the $38,885 lies the true "average" production of the "average" licensee.)

3. Not all licensees work full time or even sell real estate. Many hold licenses "just in case I may need it someday when I retire." Others, such as appraisers, bank officers, and so forth, hold licenses as incidental to their main occupation.

4. The figure of 2 million licensees comprises a number of persons who sell and deal in other than single-family dwellings who are, therefore, not included in the foregoing projections. As shown in some subsequent

tables, many high producers are engaged in selling, developing and leasing industrial, commercial and agricultural properties.

All in all, after the boom years of the mid-1980s have passed, the ranks of licensees will once again shrink; only the most proficient will survive, while the less capable will fall by the wayside. But even as this attrition occurs, a constant stream of hopefuls will arise to obtain licenses and take the places of the fallen.

Attrition creates an increasingly proficient upper level of professionals who handle more of the business. They are proficient because they constantly take advantage of opportunities for education and in-service training to stay ahead of the newcomers. Those who are ill-prepared and who are not devoted to continual upgrading of their skills and knowledge will surely be among the first casualties.

EVOLUTION OF A BROKERAGE SPECIALTY

Real estate brokers evolve from three general sources:

- Successful real estate sales associates who "spin off" from an established brokerage firm;
- Individuals who transfer from another profession (see Table 1.1); and
- College graduates who major in real estate and go directly into brokerage.

In a recent survey, *Membership Profile 1984,* the NAR commented about the professional background of brokers:

> Few people enter real estate as their first career. Indeed, most brokers—over 83 percent—came into real estate from other occupations. The remaining 17 percent have spent their entire careers in real estate.

> Brokers who pursued a previous career before entering real estate worked in both allied and non-allied occupations. The most frequently cited occupation from fields related to the real estate business was management/administration. Secretarial/bookkeeping work was the most frequently cited prior non-allied occupation followed by teaching and retailing.

Whatever the broker's background may be, he or she becomes licensed by the state and is then empowered to solicit listings and offer real estate for sale or lease; he or she may then collect a commission or other compensation for providing such services.

While by far the largest segment of the business is the sale of residential property (single-family, condominiums and rental income units), many other fields of specialization are open. These fields can offer greater challenges, better income and often more interesting work.

TABLE 1.2   Brokers Engaged in Specialties and Their Median Annual Incomes

Primary Business Specialty	Percent	Median Income
Residential brokerage	68.5	$25,000
Commercial brokerage	8.3	$47,400
Industrial brokerage	0.8	*
Farm and land brokerage	3.6	$28,000
Property management	4.9	$43,200
Appraising	4.5	$30,000
Counseling	0.5	*
Building and development	4.4	$50,000
Mortgage finance	1.1	*
Syndication	0.4	*
Other	3.1	*
Total	100.1†	$35,000

*Not available.
†Column does not total 100 percent because of rounding.
SOURCE: Economics and Research Division, NATIONAL ASSOCIA-
TION OF REALTORS®, *Membership Profile 1984* (Washington, DC:
NAR, 1984), 28, 29.

In the smaller office or community the broker may find that the work includes a combination of specialties, requiring the broker to act as a general practitioner within the real estate industry. Larger cities, however, present ample opportunities for pure specialization in any of the following areas:

- Single-family residential marketing;
- Tract or subdivision sales (including condominiums);
- Multiple-family residential income units;
- Commercial property sales and leasing;
- Industrial properties;
- Property management;
- Small farms and rural properties;
- Large ranches and commercial farming operations;
- Land development;
- Recreational land development and sales;
- Sales management;
- Office administration;
- Appraising; and
- Consulting.

The NAR revealed, in its *Membership Profile 1984,* that nearly seven of every ten brokers (68.5 percent) indicated single-family brokerage as their principal business specialty (*see* Table 1.2). This proportion was a decrease from NAR's 1980 survey, which showed that 70 percent of brokers listed that specialty as their main activity.

POTENTIAL EARNINGS

Membership Profile 1984 also presented some interesting comparisons of past and current incomes of REALTORS® as well as those for associates.

The brokers in the survey had a median gross personal income after business expenses in 1983 of $30,000, a rise of $1,100 over the 1980 level. The median income of full-time salespeople was $18,000 compared with $14,700 three years earlier. The incomes of full-time and part-time salespeople were quite different; part-timers had a median gross personal income of only $6,400 in 1983.

Male brokers and sales associates received substantially higher earnings than females. (Female brokers showed an average of $20,000 compared with the $36,200 average of male brokers and the $30,000 median income.)

Generally, income of brokers and sales associates rises as greater levels of formal education are attained. But the relationship between formal education and income is not as strong as it is in most other professions.

The vast majority of brokers and salespeople have taken additional real estate education courses after licensure. Fully eight of every ten brokers and seven of every ten salespeople have enrolled in at least one real estate instructional program.

NAR's 1984 *Membership Profile* commented about licensing, length of service and other professional patterns.

> The experience in real estate of members as a whole has increased a bit over the last several years, reflecting the decline of new people entering the real estate industry. Brokers reported a median of 11 years of experience in the industry—an increase of one year from the 1981 survey—while salespersons have typically worked in real estate for five years—up from three years in 1981.

> Working in real estate is not a profession for someone who is afraid to put in long hours or work on weekends. Brokers work 50 hours a week, on average, but nearly one-quarter devote sixty or more hours a week to their profession. Salespersons (both part-time and full-time) typically put in 42 hours, on average, a shorter work week than brokers.

> Longer hours were generally rewarded with higher income for both brokers and salespersons. For example, brokers putting in a work week of less than

30 hours typically earned an income of $12,000 in 1983. In contrast, brokers who worked 65 hours or more earned a median income of $40,000.

While the majority of brokers have an ownership interest in their firm, a growing minority have no equity interest in the firm with which they are affiliated. In 1964 only 10 percent of brokers held no ownership interest in the firm with which they were affiliated but by 1984 over four out of ten brokers had no ownership interest in their firm.

Among brokers the highest median incomes of about $38,000 were reported by stockholders and corporate officers and individual proprietors, while those with no ownership role reported the lowest median income of $22,000.

The earning power of brokers varied according to their business specialty. The highest median incomes were reported by "builder/developers" ($50,000) and commercial brokers ($47,400). Brokers specializing in residential brokerage had a median income of $25,000.

RESPONSE TO CHANGE

Probably no other form of business enterprise has undergone such radical changes during the past ten years as real estate brokerage. Recent unprecedented swings in the mortgage interest rates have caused a considerable change in the volume of home sales and all building programs. Successful brokers make an effort to understand circumstances that cause profound changes in the manner in which they must conduct their business. These circumstances include such varied and unpredictable influences as inflation, new laws, energy availability, marketing versus professional concepts, taxation, franchise networks, referrals and even the ubiquitous computer. All have their effects on business policies.

Inflation

Inflationary pressures on the economy create the following cycle of real estate business activity: (1) high business activity creates inordinately high profits for a broker; (2) this activity is rapidly followed by a governmentally induced tight money policy, which creates high interest rates; (3) the tight money policy is followed by a business recession and the curtailment or even abandonment of long-term, fixed-interest-rate mortgages.

The inflationary spiral from 1975 to 1980 graphically illustrated the aforementioned cycle. Only after deflationary measures were taken by the government were the economy and the real estate business able to return to some semblance of normalcy. Hence, the low and relatively stable inflationary rates that began in 1982 created one of the biggest booms in real estate this country has ever experienced. The stock market, which generally follows real estate expansion, experienced a marked rise during the early months of 1987, reflecting investor confidence that inflation and the economy will remain relatively stable over the next few years.

In one sense, inflation itself is not injurious to the brokerage business because commissions increase with the sales prices of property. It also creates a sense of urgency. People are more likely to buy as much property as they can afford, as often as possible (especially with borrowed money). What hurts, however, is the antidote to inflation: the recession that must inevitably follow if the inflation syndrome is to be shattered.

New Laws

Almost every week one finds that some new law, rule or regulation affects the real estate industry. Most have nothing to do with changes in property tax law but are constraints that are lobbied for and passed at the instigation of environmentalists, preservationists and no-growth proponents.

Although certain controls may be needed and justified, many inequities are created by planning and zoning laws supposedly intended for the good of all the people. Some planning may be justified as the state's constitutional right through its police power to safeguard the people's health and welfare. Yet, in many cases, planning is used to create inequities. For example, consider zoning powers. "Exclusionary zoning" is sometimes used to keep multiple-family dwellings out of predominantly single-family neighborhoods, thereby keeping "undesirable" renters from mingling with homeowners and their children. In other cases, with "inclusionary zoning," cities require developers to provide a number of lower-priced units among their regularly priced homes. This action has the effect of costing buyers of regularly priced homes more money to subsidize lower-income buyers. All brokers who aspire to boost themselves out of the familiar field of residential sales into the more exciting arenas of commercial, industrial and urban land brokerage should strive to become competent in working around and with the legal red tape that is continually being produced.

Energy

The spiraling cost of energy used in the home has become increasingly important to home builders and home buyers. Even if a buyer can afford to heat a home that has a cathedral ceiling and floor-to-ceiling windows or to have the luxury of central air conditioning and a heated pool, homes with such features will become more and more difficult to market. Brokers must be knowledgeable about energy features in old and new homes to be of assistance to both buyers and sellers. Future buyers will select homes that offer cost-efficient energy features; in many cases, buyers will qualify for higher mortgages if a more energy-efficient home is chosen compared with other homes in the same market area. Sellers, therefore, must be advised how to compete with other sellers by seeing that their properties are properly insulated, fitted with double-paned windows, have efficient furnaces, and so forth. This is the type of information of which brokers must be aware to keep in step with the ever-changing real estate market.

MARKETING VERSUS PROFESSIONAL CONCEPT

There is an imperceptibly growing division in the conception of real estate brokerage. Perhaps it boils down to this: Is real estate a commodity to be bought, sold and exchanged in a commercial manner as stocks and bonds are, with marketing as the prime endeavor of the broker, or is real estate an instrument of investors that must be carefully manipulated under competent advice and direction from professional practitioners? Changes promulgated in the Tax Reform Act of 1986 lead one to believe that because the government is becoming more directly involved and more interested in how investors make money in real estate, the latter scenario will prevail.

To add another variable, many advanced thinkers in real estate believe that the industry will eventually evolve into three general categories of operation: large chains of proprietary firms, such as Coldwell Banker and Cushman Wakefield; individual firms banded together under the umbrella of franchise networks; and very small offices run on professional consulting principles. (Recently there have been new developments in this evolution: Coldwell Banker entered the residential franchise field by franchising smaller owner-operated firms under its name and the giant Merrill Lynch proprietary network announced that it wished to get out of its real estate business, which it found unprofitable.)

The dichotomy in the conception of real estate brokerage may be best exemplified by the two different methods used by the three groups to prepare their representatives for roles in brokerage. The large companies, as well as the franchise brokers, necessarily must operate *training* programs to instruct their agents in how to handle their limited fields of expertise extremely well. The little professionals will be distinguished by their *educated* knowledge in handling almost any form of transaction as "holistic" brokers.

Headway is being made in this latter direction through the efforts of such educational arms of the NAR as the REALTORS® Land Institute, the American Institute of Real Estate Appraisers, the Society of Industrial and Office REALTORS® and the American Society of Real Estate Counselors.

Perhaps the eventual outcome will be that the large companies with their multiple offices will be fighting for the bulk of the business with the franchise networks as the marketing goliaths. This will leave the small lone-wolf operators, those with only a few offices and less than a hundred sales associates, to specialize in certain geographic areas where they have strong footholds. Others, less brokerage-minded and more profession-oriented, will be content to specialize in appraising, exchanging properties, property management and development of income properties, as well as in solving problems of acquisition and disposition.

Taxation

Taxation policies that influence real estate brokerage strategies may be divided into two general categories: personal income taxes and real property taxation.

Probably no other set of government laws exerts as many far-reaching effects on real property investments as the Internal Revenue Code. Rental earnings (cash flow) and certain proceeds from real estate sales are subject to personal taxation; nevertheless, the code also provides means of alleviating, reducing and sometimes even deferring these taxes indefinitely.

During the past decade or so Congress has made a number of changes in the Tax Code; some of them have been beneficial to the real estate industry and, as in the Tax Reform Act of 1986, some of them less than helpful. As these laws become more complicated and more difficult to understand it is incumbent upon the broker to keep up with those changes so as to be of utmost service to the clients.

Franchise Networks

Often, the independent broker receives an invitation to join a new and promising real estate franchise. The NAR *Profile of Real Estate Firms: 1984* shows the changes in franchise penetration.

> Franchising is indeed a significant part of the real estate industry. Not only do franchise organizations account for 19 percent of all real estate firms, but they also encompass more than three out of every ten salespersons in the industry. With the recent increase in the affiliation of firms with 11 to 50 associates, the loss in large firms that are affiliated is more than offset. The net effect—franchise penetration in terms of the industry sales force stands at 32 percent and is up somewhat from last year's 28 percent.

This topic is covered more thoroughly in Chapter 4.

Referrals

As the people of the United States become more mobile and change their places of residence more frequently, brokers naturally wish to capitalize on the trend. For example, a broker who lists a home for people who are leaving a city notifies another broker in the destination city. The destination broker contacts the prospects to show them property in their new location. Upon a sale the destination broker remits a certain percentage of the commission to the referring broker.

This referral system works in reverse also. If a member of a brokerage firm in the destination city has a prospective buyer, he or she may learn that the prospect has not yet listed a present home in a different town. The enterprising broker contacts a firm in the family's hometown and alerts that firm to the prospect for a listing. Upon sale of the home, a referral fee is paid to the referring broker.

Large-chain brokerage firms usually use their own referral system, while franchise networks send all their referrals to another member of the same network, where available. Independents choose a cooperating broker from a variety of sources. They may belong to a referral system or service or may send the referral to another member of some organization to which they belong. They may use as sources the Women's Council of REALTORS®, the REALTOR® National Marketing Institute, the REALTOR® Land Institute or a NAR member who advertises his or her availability in the national roster. Referral fees usually range between 20 and 25 percent of the *actual amount* of commission received by the referred broker.

Careful consideration must be given before deciding to join a referral network. There are many advantages, not the least of which are the training programs for sales-associates, regional or national advertising and the creation of an identity one may not be able to attain on his or her own. However, most brokers place considerable emphasis on the prospect of increased clientele. A recent survey indicates that seven of ten firms affiliated with an intercity referral network derive five percent or less of their business from that affiliation. Major companies may also make beautiful sales presentations extolling the wonders of the affiliation when, in actuality, the broker's local economic sector may not be conducive to such an affiliation. One must consider if his or her market area is one that attracts transferees, the turnover ratio and whether or not the area is already blanketed by other networks.

A slightly different variation is developing among brokers who deal in properties other than residential. For instance, a farm broker in Iowa may list a farm there for people who want to sell it and buy a ranch in Montana. The Iowa broker may not know a Montana broker who specializes in ranches but he does know one in Wyoming. The friend in Wyoming then sets up a referral with a Montana broker with whom he or she works. The Wyoming broker functions as a "broker's broker" and is usually entitled to a referral fee should a sale result.

Another source of brokerage business closely akin to the referral business is the transferee market. Occupationally, transferees can be placed in one of several categories:

1. Those working for large "Fortune 500" type companies;
2. Those working for second-tier national or international entities and other large employers;
3. Those employed by regional firms; and
4. Those moving from a local employer in one area to a different local employer in another area.

To be most effective, the broker must know where the business comes from and who controls it:

1. The corporate relocation management companies (or, as they are known in the real estate industry, the third-party equity contractors);
2. The corporations who provide their own form of relocation assistance; and
3. The individual who shifts jobs within a company or from one employer to another without benefit of organized relocation assistance.

A number of corporate management companies enter into agreements with large corporations to handle their employee transfer problems for them. Such management companies usually team up with reliable independent local brokerage firms in each community in which their client has an office or plant. It is the experience of both authors of this book that by taking good care of such relocation companies' transferee relocating problems, brokers may generate a considerable source of added income. The key word is *service,* if a broker is to attract and keep the relocation company business. These companies demand and expect service above and beyond that usually required to keep a homeowner/lister happy. This service might entail such duties as providing gardening service, protecting the plumbing against freezing, supervising painting and other cosmetic repairs (and advancing the costs of same), sending in weekly or monthly reports on the status of merchandising efforts, and so forth. Any broker who aspires to acquire a large segment of the relocation business is well-advised to appoint and train a relocation director who can competently handle the myriad details such business entails.

Computers

By 1981 the use of computers by real estate firms had become widespread. According to *Profile of Real Estate Firms: 1984,* a Publication of the Economics & Research Division of the NAR, in that year just under one third of the firms reported having any type of computer capability—computer terminals, in-house computers or word processors. By 1985 this number had grown to just under the 60-percent mark. Real estate firms, both large and small, found ready application for this new technology. Computers are used in many tasks, including the following:

Information storage and retrieval.   Large companies with their own computer capabilities have been able to keep accurate records of their listings, both active and expired. A smaller company that belongs to an MLS equipped with a computer for providing listing information can have a terminal set up in the office with direct access to the MLS information. All expired listings and sold properties can be recorded for retrieval when needed to appraise properties or provide comparables for the competitive market analysis form.

Office records and word processing.   Bookkeeping, higher accounting, personal information and other records can be stored on computer. The computer is also ideal for such jobs as sending letters to individuals in areas on which the broker wishes to concentrate or to certain types of buyers, such as investors and users of specific categories of properties.

Closing statements.   The computer can be programmed to issue statements when a transaction is completed.

Mortgage amortization schedules.   Projections showing payments and loan balances at specified intervals can be generated from information storage.

Computations.   Internal rate of return on investment properties can be determined and printed out on a form. Yield from an investment property can be shown under various conditions of down payment, interest and length of loan.

All of these operations and many more can be performed by computers; some can be performed by sophisticated calculators. The real estate broker of today cannot be considered totally competent or efficient in this field unless he or she is at least somewhat conversant with the use of calculators and computers. Computers and their capabilities are covered in greater detail in Chapter 5.

SUMMARY

Real estate brokers serve as the marketplace for real property sales. A broker's familiarity with the marketplace helps sellers set a fair market price and helps buyers find the most suitable available property. Brokers also contribute to the development of their community by directing potential users to various properties.

The largest segment of the business is the sale of residential property. There are opportunities, however, for specialization in any number of areas, including commercial and industrial property, property management and farms and ranches, among others. Potential earnings for real estate professionals are influenced by factors such as advanced education, number of working hours, ownership interest in the firm and type of business specialty.

Various elements influence the real estate business. Inflation causes high levels of business activity with correspondingly high profits, as well as high interest rates and business recessions. New planning and zoning laws often constrain owners and brokers in the development of property. The cost and availability of energy affects the location of homes in relation to business centers and cost-efficient energy features are important to many homebuyers. Taxation policies regarding personal income and real property change frequently and affect every real estate transaction. The use of computers is continually growing and plays an important part in the function, organization and development of brokerage firms.

Brokers may choose either to remain independent or to belong to a chain or franchise; may decide what type of referral system to join, if any; or may elect to become involved in the relocation business. One must consider the facts from the past and trends predicted for the future before making the decision to embark on a career in brokerage.

DISCUSSION QUESTION

Compare the advantages and disadvantages to *you* as a broker (owner or manager) with the advantages and disadvantages of another field you could choose.

2 Requirements for Success

INTRODUCTION

To become successful, a real estate broker must meet certain minimal standards and then surpass them. It is no major accomplishment to remain only mediocre, practicing over a lifetime and attaining only a modicum of success.

The NAR *Profile* learned that the median income for brokers was $30,000; thus, half the people interviewed earned less than that amount while half earned more. What separates the two categories? What determines that one broker can barely eke out an existence while another becomes independently wealthy? These are some of the questions to be explored in this chapter.

Certain attributes, qualities and characteristics are known to increase chances for success. There also are legal and financial requirements to be met and complied with even to become a broker. The balance of the chapter discusses several ingredients of success, including education, experience and training; legal and financial requirements; psychological and social traits; and the importance of superb health.

THE NEED FOR FORMAL PROFESSIONAL EDUCATION

Formal education may not be absolutely necessary, but it certainly helps. Almost every state has some education or experience requirements for license qualification. Beyond the state requirements, other educational opportunities can be beneficial to a career in real estate. Considerable

TABLE 2.1   Median Income of Brokers by Educational Level: 1963–1983

Educational Level	1963	1969	1971	1974	1977	1980	1983
Some high school	$10,000	$15,500	$16,000	$18,000	$28,500	$25,100	*
High school graduate	$11,000	$17,300	$18,000	$20,000	$25,000	$23,500	$25,000
Some college but less than four years of college	$12,000	$17,800	$20,000	$23,000	$25,000	$25,100	$25,000
Four years of college— Bachelor's Degree	$14,000	$21,500	$24,000	$25,000	$30,000	$33,400	$35,000
Graduate study	$14,000	$24,100	$25,000	$27,500	$30,000	$34,500	$30,000
All brokers	$12,000	$18,000	$20,000	$24,000	$28,000	$28,900	$30,000

*Included in high school graduate.
SOURCE: Economics and Research Division, NATIONAL ASSOCIATION OF REALTORS®, *Membership Profile 1984* (Washington, DC: NAR, 1984), 17.

time and money can be saved by taking certain courses rather than by trying to obtain the same information through trial and error.

Academic education is necessary; it teaches the reasons *why* certain courses of action lead to success. *Professional training* teaches *how* to perform those tasks that result in success. The NAR *Membership Profile 1984* found that:

> While higher and higher levels of formal education may improve the chances of earning higher incomes, there is no guarantee that additional academic achievement will be translated into correspondingly greater monetary rewards. For example, brokers with a high school diploma increased their average earnings between 1980 and 1983. Similarly, brokers with a bachelor's degree increased their median earnings over the same period. However, brokers who had some college training and those who received a graduate degree did not fare as well in 1983 as they had in 1980.

Table 2.1 shows the results of the NAR study.

Real Estate's Higher Education

Occupations accepted as professions by the public generally require at least a four-year college degree; additional education beyond the bachelor's degree is not uncommon as a requisite. As yet, however, there does not seem to be a comfortable home for real estate education in the academic world. Many academicians view real estate as vocational training, not as a separate discipline. They feel that a general background of business education may successfully be fused with practical on-the-job training taught by experienced practitioners. Hence, most universities conceal their real estate education programs in the business school among courses in management, economics, finance and insurance. Few universities offer separate departments of real estate.

There is no doubt, as many experiences have shown, that formal academic education is of tremendous help in making a newcomer to the real estate business more successful in a shorter period of time. Those who have academic credentials also tend to rise higher on the economic ladder. This is not to say that the high school graduate cannot aspire to considerable success in real estate. There are many examples of people, including the authors of this book, who have shown that it can be done. But those people are the exception—not the rule. In our cases, success required heavy involvement in real estate educational programs and the completion of many college-level courses, seminars and in-service training programs. Educational achievement not only indicates the amount of accumulated "why" knowledge but is also an excellent indicator of the amount of motivation and drive it took to acquire this knowledge. For every high school graduate who has attained success, there are hundreds of college graduates who have made it.

Necessary Courses for Brokers

For those not fortunate enough to have acquired a formal college education with a specialization in real estate, there are many ways of obtaining the requisite knowledge. Community colleges, private schools, state colleges and universities offer many subjects, either through their regular programs or through their evening or extension divisions. Any or all of these courses are helpful in becoming proficient in the brokerage business.

Some of the most important of those courses are real estate principles and practice, real estate economics, legal aspects of real estate, appraisal, real estate finance (including taxation and exchange), introduction to real estate investments, office administration, escrow procedure and agency relationships.

WHAT EXPERIENCE CAN TEACH

Three types of knowledge are needed to sell real estate: technical knowledge, marketing knowledge and product knowledge. The first two types can be acquired through education and on-the-job training. The third can be gained only through exposure and experience.

Technical Knowledge

Technical knowledge provides the *tools* of the business, instruments and resource information that enable one to construct transactions correctly and process them efficiently. It means knowing how to use deposit receipts, sales contracts, listing agreements, financing devices, leases, escrow instructions and many other forms of paperwork.

Much of the technical knowledge comes from the formal academic sector; some is available in the vocational sections of community colleges. In-service training courses also help provide this kind of information. Technical knowledge includes the information needed to pass the state real estate examinations, as well as to comply with all other real estate laws.

Marketing Knowledge

Learning how to sell real estate includes not only an understanding of the psychology of buyers and sellers, it also encompasses obtaining listings, showing and presenting properties, qualifying buyers and closing sales. Marketing knowledge helps the broker handle clients and problems such as sales resistance.

Training and instructional courses in sales and marketing are provided through books, local board of REALTOR® courses and seminars, private school courses and courses given by the institutes, societies and councils of NAR.

Product Knowledge

This is the knowledge that one acquires in the marketplace. It is only through showing properties, studying all available listings for sale and attending sales meetings that one is able to acquire the necessary information to be thoroughly knowledgeable about the properties he or she must sell. It is perhaps the most important of the three types of knowledge.

The NAR *Membership Profile 1984* reports that:

> The real estate experience of brokers nationwide has increased slightly since the last survey. The median number of years in the business rose from 10 years in 1981 to 11 years in 1984. This reflects a decline in newer entrants into the field. The proportion of brokers with less than 10 years experience dropped from 56 percent of all brokers in 1981 to 46 percent in 1984. Conversely, the number of brokers with 11 or more years in the real estate field rose markedly from 44 percent in 1981 to 54 percent in 1984 [*see* Table 2.2].

TABLE 2.2 **Real Estate Experience of Brokers: 1964–1984 (Percentage Distribution)**

Years in Real Estate	1964	1970	1972	1975	1978	1981	1984
1	1.0	1.3	1.4	0.5	0.8	1.3	1.1
2	1.7	1.3	2.2	1.8	1.8	2.3	1.4
3	2.6	2.3	3.3	3.8	3.6	5.6	2.4
4	3.4	2.9	4.2	4.5	4.1	6.5	3.4
5	5.0	3.6	5.0	5.4	7.9	7.1	5.8
6–10	23.3	19.4	21.7	22.6	30.5	33.0	32.1
11–15	22.7	22.4	19.5	19.4	17.6	16.2	22.9
16–25	24.0	31.2	26.7	26.5	21.7	17.4	18.7
26–39	11.0	10.2	11.6	11.5	10.1	9.2	10.9
40 and Over	5.3	5.4	4.4	4.0	1.8	1.5	1.3
Total	100.0	100.0	100.0	100.0	100.0	100.0	100.0
Median Years	14 yr.	15 yr.	14 yr.	14 yr.	11 yr.	10 yr.	11 yr.

SOURCE: Economics and Research Division, NATIONAL ASSOCIATION OF REALTORS®, *Membership Profile 1984* (Washington, DC: NAR, 1984), 23.

LEGAL REQUIREMENTS FOR THE BROKER'S LICENSE

Each state has legislated certain requirements regarding examination, education and experience necessary to qualify for a broker's license. These requirements range from practically none to highly sophisticated demands.

Many states also require continuing education to retain one's broker's license. However, although they agree on its necessity, many states have experienced poor results in the administration of a meaningful continuing education program, due, in some cases, to the dilution of the syllabus as it travels through the legislative process or a lack of funds when it comes before the appropriations committee in a request for funding.

The National Association of Real Estate License Law Officials (NARELLO) is an organized group whose members are involved in enforcing state license laws. NARELLO has available a list of the education, experience and continuing education requirements of the various states and territories for a broker's license. However, because each state differs in its requirements and those requirements change from year to year, it would not serve any purpose to list them here. If one is interested in learning the requirements for obtaining a broker or salesperson license in a particular state, he or she can write to the regulatory body, either the Real Estate Commission or the Department of Real Estate, at that state's capital.

All 50 states have exercised their police power in an attempt to protect the public from incompetent real estate salespeople through the enactment of license laws. The constitutionality of real estate licensing has often been tested under the due process clause of the Fourteenth Amendment. Opponents have argued that licensing laws restrict entry by allowing only those individuals with special knowledge to enter the industry. In the majority of cases the courts have upheld the laws, stating that their purpose was to regulate in the public interest, not to restrict the number of applicants entering the field.

Almost all licensing laws contain provisions for creation of a commission to establish and implement the law's provisions. These commissions have enacted general prerequisites for prospective licenses in addition to any experience and educational requirements. These prerequisites usually include a good character documented by references, a residency requirement and passing an examination covering the real estate business.

INITIAL FINANCING NEEDS

How much money it takes to establish a real estate brokerage office depends on a number of variables. Chapter 4 covers establishing a philosophy of business, showing that overall philosophy is closely related to financial considerations. For example, it costs considerably less to start out with a one-person office in a spare room of one's home than to open a full-scale office complete with receptionist, secretary, bookkeeper and a number of sales associates—perhaps even a sales manager.

To help determine how much initial outlay is required, however, a form is presented in Figure 2.1. The user should fill in the blank spaces with the anticipated costs. All expense items should be estimated on the high side; anticipated revenues should be computed conservatively.

This form includes not only the one-time expenses required but also the estimated cost of operation for the first six months. After six months most new brokers are either out of business or well enough established to sustain their business without more reserves. This kind of projection illustrates the need for budgetary planning—a broker must have enough monetary resources to get an office well established.

Anyone who does not have the necessary cash, as indicated by the bottom line, "Minimum Cash Needed to Start," should perhaps postpone the project and continue saving. If one is willing to take chances and has enough confidence in his or her ability, some of the necessary cash may be borrowed from a bank or a private backer. The budget must then allow for repayment in installments.

Even with this suggested budget, not all possible expenses can be anticipated. It is wise to consult a good accountant, and perhaps a friendly broker or two, to review the budget and advise regarding any omissions.

FIGURE 2.1   Budget for Establishing a Real Estate Office

One-Time Expenses

Legal fees (to establish corporation or partnership)	$ _____
Accounting fees (advice, start-up, books)	_____
Telephone installation	_____
Initiation fees, board of REALTORS®, MLS	_____
License fees—state, city	_____
Office space costs—deposit, remodeling	_____
Office equipment—typewriters, files, desks	_____
Office supplies—stationery, cards, forms	_____
Automobile purchase or lease	_____
Artist work for logo, signs, stationery	_____
Advertising agency cost (if applicable)	_____
Stock of lawn signs	_____
Office sign—purchase or lease	_____

TOTAL ONE-TIME EXPENSES $ _____ $ _____

Monthly Expenses

Office rent	$ _____
Office salaries	_____
Legal and accounting fees	_____
Insurance premiums	_____
Automobile cost	_____
Utilities (if applicable)	_____
Office supplies	_____
Janitorial wages (if applicable)	_____
Telephone expense	_____
Newspaper advertising	_____
Your salary	_____
Miscellaneous dues and subscriptions	_____
Sign repair and replacement	_____
Entertainment	_____
Reserve for contingencies	_____

TOTAL MONTHLY EXPENSES $ _____ x 6 mo. $ _____

GROSS AMOUNT NEEDED $ _____

LESS PROJECTED INCOME FOR SIX MONTHS $ _____

MINIMUM CASH NEEDED TO START* $ _____

*In addition to the Minimum Cash Needed to Start, one must have either a cash reserve or an income to sustain himself or herself for at least three months (six is more comfortable) during the lag time between sales and closings.

This may well forestall some sleepless nights and perhaps even an embarrassing and costly failure.

PSYCHOLOGICAL TRAITS AND SOCIAL SKILLS

As stated in Chapter 1, it takes a special sort of person to become a successful broker—to be able to cope with the many frustrations in the real estate business. Although it is well known that no one can motivate anyone else but that the motivation must be within oneself, once the broker has reached the owner/manager level this is even more important to understand. What time these brokers spend or do not spend during each day or what they do right or do wrong will have a direct result on the success of their firms and their ability to pay their bills. But although a contact may bring immediate results, this is the exception rather than the rule. There will be times when even 14-hour days and doing everything "by the book" will not bring the return brokers might expect. These are the times when they will feel rejected; without the proper psychological traits they might not be able to overcome the feelings of rejection that could lead to ultimate failure.

Residential real estate sales require a great amount of emotional investment, not only in oneself but in clients and especially associates. For this reason, it is essential to try to understand the operations of the human mind.

The Psychology of Winning

It is difficult to say exactly what type of personality constitutes a winner. Is it the dynamic, hard-driving individual who constantly strives for perfection and is always working against time? Perhaps. But certain risks accompany this type of behavior, according to Doctors Friedman and Rosenman, two San Francisco heart specialists. In their book, *Type A Behavior and Your Heart,* published in 1974, they characterize three types of behavior. The first type, described above, they call the tough battler.

A second type of behavior is displayed by the friendly helper. This is the type who is easygoing, trying to help everyone, with no sense of urgency and only the desire to be of service. If persons of this type become real estate salespersons, they trust that some commissions will come their way if only they do the right things. Is this type a winner?

Or is the winner the objective thinker? This person is characterized as one who carefully thinks out all of the consequences before he or she makes any moves. Carefully calculating the results of contemplated actions, this type makes no overt move without considering the odds. Certainly these are admirable qualities.

FIGURE 2.2   The Successful Person

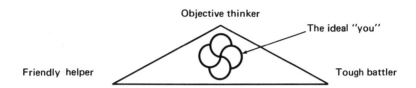

The authors conclude that the truly successful and happy person is one who combines all of the above characteristics in a balanced manner so that any single one is not too strong. The theory is illustrated graphically in Figure 2.2.

The real answer to being a winner is to become well adjusted. Being well adjusted does not mean having no worries, fears, anxieties, problems, difficulties—but it does mean knowing how to face them with courage, bear them with patience and deal with them intelligently. To be well adjusted means knowing how to win with modesty and lose with courage.

THE NEED FOR MANAGEMENT SKILLS

As pointed out in Chapter 1, most brokers opening their own offices have come up through the sales ranks. Most have had little or no exposure to the problems of management except for possible college courses in business administration. Progression from successful salesperson to broker-owner may take place when the person has one or all of several characteristics.

1. They are usually the best salespeople on the sales force. Consequently, they have earned and saved enough money to get started in the brokerage business.
2. They are sufficiently intelligent to pass the required broker's examination and other required courses; usually they have had the necessary experience.
3. They have the drive and motivation to succeed, as illustrated by their top earnings on the sales force.
4. They frequently have an all-consuming, egotistical desire to see their name displayed on the sign over the office.

Thus the combination of good sales abilities, intelligence, drive, motivation and egotism propels a majority of brokers into the business. Unfortunately this list does not include being a good manager, except possibly for the managerial quality of saving enough money to get started. In fact, good salespeople are notorious for their aversion to the confining details of management.

Most top salespeople have had little preparation for management. It is no wonder that many of them fall by the wayside or fail to attain respectable success when they open their own brokerage businesses. The chart in Figure 2.3 is a graphic display of the fate of salespeople who aspire to become broker-owners without the necessary training.

Although the percentages represented in the figure are only estimates, and there are certainly gray areas between the categories, one fact stands out. It is absolutely necessary for the salesperson who hopes to attain any degree of success in the business to have or to develop managerial capabilities. In the face of this great attrition rate, this is one powerful advantage.

There are alternatives. A broker who recognizes that he or she is a productive salesperson but lacks managerial capabilities may choose to hire an office manager. In some cases this decision makes good sense. The owner is able to be out selling properties and generating commissions, which can more than compensate for the manager's salary and overhead.

INTEGRITY—THE MOST IMPORTANT PSYCHOLOGICAL TRAIT

> Integrity without knowledge is weak and useless, and knowledge without integrity is dangerous and dreadful.   *Samuel Johnson*

Integrity is built of many things. A broker-owner of a firm must be constantly conscious of the need to maintain an image of integrity in the community. Whether the firm is small or large, the new role requires awareness of others' expectations.

First of all, a person may be the most sincere and upright of people but lack of knowledge to back up opinions will cause his or her integrity to suffer immeasurably. If the broker gives a wrong answer to a problem, whether to a customer or a sales associate, it will affect that broker's credibility (and, hence, integrity) with that person for years to come. It may also result in a lawsuit against the brokerage. It is far better to say, "I don't know but I will find out for you," than to give an answer that will later be proven wrong.

Second, a broker's image in the community is closely monitored by the public. Because the broker often handles the largest single asset in people's lives, their homes, he or she is closely scrutinized for any aberra-

---

FIGURE 2.3   Attrition Patterns of Salespeople Who Aspire to Broker-Ownership

---

Of salespeople who become brokers and open their own offices for the first time:

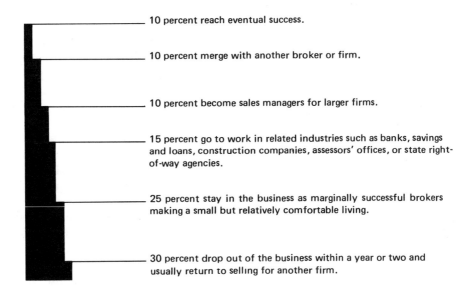

10 percent reach eventual success.

10 percent merge with another broker or firm.

10 percent become sales managers for larger firms.

15 percent go to work in related industries such as banks, savings and loans, construction companies, assessors' offices, or state right-of-way agencies.

25 percent stay in the business as marginally successful brokers making a small but relatively comfortable living.

30 percent drop out of the business within a year or two and usually return to selling for another firm.

SOURCE: Compiled by the authors from information collected by the California Department of Real Estate, 1966-76.

tions of character. Should the broker drink too heavily, gamble too much or be indiscreet in sexual activities, it will undoubtedly be noticed in the community and affect business. The adverse effect on the broker's image of integrity will no doubt carry over to the attitude of some salespeople toward their broker.

Third, the head of the firm will often be called upon to make some unpleasant decisions to maintain integrity. A decision of this nature may result in the loss of a commission to a sales associate or another broker. The alternative is to give an answer that he or she knows is not patently correct but saves the commission. Every wrong one of these small decisions takes away a little bit of integrity and self-image, and erodes public esteem when the community becomes aware of them.

Fourth, high self-concept is important in being a successful manager. Brokers who view themselves as short on knowledge, unsure of goals and needing strong support from family and associates, will probably become uncertain, weak and vacillating individuals with little integrity. When a manager vacillates in his or her decisions, associates often either have, or acquire, the same traits or are repelled by them to such an extent that they seek other, stronger leadership. However, the broker who considers himself or herself to be a well-prepared, strong, self-determining individual, confident in directing his or her own destiny, will attract and inspire others who have or aspire to the same traits.

Fifth, a sense of one's own integrity inspires the same feeling in others. This has the effect of creating an *esprit de corps* in the organization. While this is a nebulous feeling, it is still one of the most binding forces any company can have.

Emotional Health

The last, but not the least, of the psychological attributes a successful broker must have is good emotional health. This is the term used to describe the mental state in which one works. It means waking up in the morning looking forward to a day's work and feeling able to cope with any problems that might arise. Poor emotional health is frequently caused by domestic conflict with a spouse or children who resent the demands on time and energy the real estate business requires. Eventually, a broken marriage and divorce may result. If, on the other hand, the broker or associate neglects business because of the needs of spouse and children, the person's work and emotional health suffer, possibly to the destruction of an otherwise promising career.

These are not nebulous, theoretical situations. They do occur. They are part of the "real world" of real estate.

The Need for Good Health

Sometimes emotional health is tied to physical health. When the body is in poor physical condition, it naturally affects mental well-being. Few chores are more difficult than to work at selling real estate when in poor health. The requirements are obvious: being pleasant at all times, suffering exposure to the elements while actively showing outdoor properties, constant involvement in the stressful situations of extensive negotiations, meeting deadlines and appointments of all kinds. All these tasks require physical well-being.

Because of these demands, it makes good sense to observe those rules of good health that will keep one feeling fit, eager and energetic. To be success-minded at all times, it is absolutely imperative to observe the following regimen: exercise regularly, maintain a proper diet, keep weight down and get plenty of rest. One should also engage in a relaxing hobby of some sort.

There are many good books on the subject of healthful living; the aspiring broker should make it a practice to review them frequently.

Social Awareness

Social awareness is involvement in governmental affairs, community activities and professional associations. No longer can brokers simply pursue a career in real estate while ignoring what is happening in the outside world. They need to understand and keep up with those pressure groups that are legitimate and vigorously oppose those they deem against their principles. Those who make their living in the real estate profession must stay aware of these changing trends.

Perhaps the ideal social philosophy in real estate was stated most succinctly in the applicable portion of NAR's 1987 Statement of Policy:

> WE BELIEVE in equal opportunity in housing. No person of this country should have his rights to rent or purchase shelter of his choice abridged because of race, color, religion, sex, or national origin. Furthermore, these rights should not be limited because of existing or desired ethnic, racial or religious proportions in any defined area.

While brokers must realize that they have the responsibility to see that no person is discriminated against, they must also realize their duty to monitor and resist the erosion of private property rights caused through intrusion of governmental overregulating. Zoning and down-zoning, environmental impact reports, general plan requirements, requirements for multiple permits for developments, the concept of "social property" and ecological "overkill" laws are all examples of how the encroachment of government can hurt and often quash the right of brokers and their clients and customers to utilize their property for its highest and best use.

The role of the real estate broker today must include active participation in community affairs—through serving on city and county governing bodies, appointment to zoning and planning boards or commissions, being active on a community development committee and serving wherever else a voice may be needed to protect the rights of individual property owners.

The broker who is a member of the local board and the state and national associations of REALTORS® may benefit from their efforts in regard to these three areas, the principal reasons for their existence: ethics, legislative functions and education.

SUMMARY

In this chapter the topic under discussion is requirements for success with the main emphasis on *knowledge*. The need for formal professional education is emphasized and the statistics to prove that need are incorporated in the text. That other form of knowledge acquisition, *experience,* is broken down into the three basic forms of knowledge to be acquired: technical, marketing and product knowledge.

The legal requirements for obtaining a license, which basically involve studying for a comprehensive examination in all of the 50 states, are related to the acquisition of knowledge. The advent of continuing education requirements for the practitioner who wishes to renew his or her license is a newer requirement of legislation relating to real estate. Although continuing education is not yet required in all states, it is a requirement in some of the more progressive ones and probably eventually will be required in the others.

No chapter on requirements would be complete without some discussion of financial needs. A form entitled "Budget for Establishing a Real Estate Office" is included that will help the student project the cash needed to get started.

Some space is devoted to the psychological traits and requirements needed for coping with the stressful situations that arise daily in a business that consists mostly of negotiating contracts. It is pointed out that not all who aspire to being brokers are able to adapt to such demands.

No requirements list would be complete without addressing the need for management skills, a strong sense of integrity, and good health (both emotional and physical), as well as social awareness. The last four requirements are directly related to the image a broker must project in his or her community of being a stable, highly responsible individual.

DISCUSSION QUESTION

Using the form on page 23, determine what capital you would need to begin the operation you desire.

3 The Agency Relationship and the Law

INTRODUCTION

One of the most important things a broker must understand and impart to those he or she trains and manages is the relationship between the principal and the agent. There would be no sales or rentals consummated in a real estate office if there was not first an authorization on the part of an owner to a broker to sell or rent the owner's property. The various types of authorizations are discussed in this chapter, along with the obligations they entail.

In residential sales it is almost always the seller who hires the broker, while in commercial sales it is frequently the buyer who does so. Whoever the principal is, the broker has a fiduciary responsibility to that person. In the past decade, some have questioned if a broker, who is a fiduciary to the principal, could also be fair with the other party. This has raised the problem of "dual agency," as it is called, which also is explored.

THE LAW OF AGENCY

The so-called law of agency is not statutory law at all, because no specific statute established it; rather, it is the end result of common law, court decisions and local practices dating back to the seventeenth century. Over the years, however, governments have defined the law of agency and made certain parts of it statutory—by enacting statutes of frauds or by establishing administrative bodies to regulate the real estate industry and other professional enterprises. This area of real estate is in a constant state of flux and must be carefully watched for new legislation.

The statutes of frauds are based on an English law passed in 1677 during the reign of Charles II and intended to prevent fraudulent practices in certain types of contracts. In the real estate area, our present statutes of frauds require that all contracts of sale of an interest in land, as well as leases over prescribed time periods, be in writing. The law also covers deeds, mortgages and deeds of trust. The stipulation of writing does not mean that oral agreements can never be legal or valid. Should there also be a written contract, however, the courts are not likely to uphold the oral agreement over the written contract.

The administrative or regulatory bodies established within each state are frequently called real estate commissions. Under authority of acts passed by the legislature, they have adopted rules and regulations governing all phases of the industry, from licensing requirements to advertising of property to the handling of escrow money. In this way they regulate the performance of brokers and others who act as agents.

Regardless of the derivation of the laws of agency, they are the rules of the law that apply to all obligations and responsibilities the broker assumes when he or she accepts authorization to act for another. It is upon this authorization that agency relationships rest.

THE AGENCY RELATIONSHIP

An agency is created when the owner of a property authorizes a real estate broker to represent him or her in the sale, rental or leasing of property. It should be noted that nothing requires that the contracting principal in a listing agreement be the owner of the property being listed for sale. The principal could be the spouse of the owner, a relative, a partner or have no interest at all. A listing is a contract to perform something. The principal, who is not necessarily the owner, is the person who signs the contract and who becomes liable for any commission earned by the broker. Of course, the usual situation is that the owner signs a listing agreement; occasionally, however, situations dictate that a non-owner, such as the executor of an estate, enter into a listing contract. After a broker produces a purchaser who performs in accordance with the terms of the contract, the broker is entitled to the commission.

In the most common type of agency relationship in real estate, the owner is the principal and the broker becomes his or her agent. Although authorization can be either oral or in writing, most states require, by either statutes or licensing laws, that all agency agreements to sell real estate be in writing. A less common form of agency is created when a prospective buyer authorizes a broker to find a specific property for him or her to buy, rent or lease. In this case the broker is still the agent but the prospective purchaser becomes the principal. In either case the agency relationship should be in the form of a written contract stipulating all terms, conditions and compensation.

It is common for licensed salespeople to be called agents. Nevertheless, it must be remembered that it is the broker who is the agent of the principal, not the salesperson. The salesperson is not a part of the agency contract but is, in fact, the agent or subagent of the broker and the broker is the principal to the salesperson. These relationships will be covered more fully as we proceed.

It is, therefore, the broker (agent) who acts for the seller (principal). The duties of an agent can be divided into two very broad classes: the general agent, who performs continuing services for the principal, such as management, and the special agent, who is employed to accomplish a specific act, such as to sell a property. The relationship of the agent to the principal is known as a fiduciary relationship.

Fiduciary Responsibilities

A real estate broker who acts as an agent is also a fiduciary. This means that he or she has a legal duty to act in a confidential manner for another person, the principal. This fiduciary has five specific responsibilities to the principal: care, obedience, accounting, loyalty and notice. These responsibilities are spelled out in the REALTOR® Code of Ethics and we will review them here.

Regardless of how a broker conducts his or her own affairs, one who has accepted an agency must perform one's duties for the principal with utmost *care*. Failure to do so, if it results in loss or damage to the principal, could mean liability for any damage that results.

Obedience is another responsibility. The agent may refuse an agency; but if accepted, the specific instructions of the principal must be followed. It is the agent's obligation to advise the principal if the instructions given are not in the principal's best interest. If the principal still insists after being so advised, however, the broker must comply unless these instructions are known to be illegal. For example, the federal Civil Rights Act of 1968 and civil rights acts passed by most states make it illegal for a broker to comply if a seller asks that the house not be shown to members of a minority group. In addition, consumer protection laws passed in recent years require disclosure of known pertinent facts to a prospective buyer. For instance, the broker may not try to keep from a prospective purchaser the fact that there is a water condition in the basement, even if the seller requests that it be withheld.

The agent must *account* to his or her principal for all monies belonging to the principal that the agent handles during the term of the agency. Most state laws do not permit commingling of funds, stipulating that these monies be kept separate and apart from the broker's business accounts. Most states require a special trust account in which all deposit monies are kept. How to set up and keep records for such a trust account will be covered in Chapter 5.

There can be no excuse for anything less than total *loyalty* to the principal (except in the case of an illegal act), regardless of how many temptations a broker encounters. This is probably the most difficult of a broker's responsibilities. For example, a broker cannot accept a commission from anyone other than the principal in a transaction, unless the fact is made known and agreed to by all parties. It is also illegal to make any profit without disclosing it and the broker may not gain an interest in the property involved in the agreement unless he or she makes the fact known to the principal. The agent must make every effort to produce the highest and best offer for the principal. Even if an initial offer made by a prospective purchaser is agreeable to the client, if it does not represent fair market value, the agent must so advise the client!

Further, the broker as agent must anticipate any problems. For instance, the broker may know that the down payment the purchaser pledges is not fluid but is coming by way of a gift from a parent or equity in other property. The broker must make the seller aware of the possibility that this money will not be available when needed. Or the broker may know that a purchaser is a bad credit risk who will have difficulty obtaining financing. Even though the commission at the end of the transaction usually looks very good, the wise broker knows that there can be no wavering from the absolute fidelity and loyalty that was assumed when the agency was accepted.

The broker must provide *notice;* that is, he or she must reveal to the principal any information about the property that comes to his or her attention during the agency. For example, matters that might cause the property to increase in value, such as proposed zoning changes, must be revealed to the principal.

The Role of Subagent

Just as the broker is the agent of his or her principal, salespeople are actually subagents of their broker. Other brokers to whom an agent extends his or her listings are also subagents. These other broker subagents may be either members of an MLS, in which listings are shared automatically, or independent brokers to whom the agent extends cooperative listings.

The subagent has no rights or privileges concerning the listing except those given by the listing broker, the agent. The agent could be held responsible even if the subagent has been granted certain rights, such as advertising the property, making appointments or negotiating directly with the client. The agent should not lightly give away his or her rights under the law of agency to a subagent.

RESPONSIBILITIES OF EACH PARTY IN THE AGENCY RELATIONSHIP

Agent's Duties to the Principal

It is interesting to note that in the listing agreement the principal pledges payment of a fee to the agent if the agent produces a ready, willing and able buyer. The principal may condition the payment of the commission on actual passing of title but he or she does agree to pay a commission if the agent produces a buyer. The agent, on the other hand, does not promise to produce a buyer. This does not mean, however, that only the principal is under obligation. The agent's responsibilities under a fiduciary relationship are defined by law, as we noted earlier in this chapter. Under certain circumstances, for example, if the agent does not work diligently to find a buyer, the law permits the principal to revoke the listing agreement.

For the agent's own protection, therefore, good records are a necessity. Accurate and current notations should be entered on the listing file to indicate marketing procedures followed, number of times advertised, calls received on the ads or for-sale sign, number of showings of the property and reactions of prospects. Above all, the agent must communicate regularly with the principal. Without this contact it is understandable that a homeowner may feel his or her broker is not doing the job, when actually the broker has made diligent efforts to market the property.

Extension of this responsibility to subagents requires the broker to train his or her salespeople in their obligation regarding their own listings as well as those received by arrangement with other brokers. When salespeople get a signed listing agreement, the listing party becomes the broker's principal. Too often salespeople identify with the buyer and forget to whom they owe their loyalties. Of course, salespeople or brokers should not be dishonest with buyers, but their primary loyalty is to the principal. The relationship is defined clearly in Article 7 of the REALTORS® Code of Ethics:

> In accepting employment as an agent, the REALTOR® pledges himself to protect and promote the interests of the client. This obligation of absolute fidelity to the client's interests is primary, but it does not relieve the REALTOR® of the obligation to treat fairly all parties to the transaction.

An example of a situation that commonly arises to test the degree of loyalty the agent owes his or her principal is illustrated in the following case. A prospective purchaser offered $70,000 on a house listed at $72,500, telling the salesperson, "Try to get it for me for $70,000. If I have to go to $72,500, I will." Although the subagent was confident that the seller would accept the offer and a fast transaction would result, it was the salesperson's duty to tell the principal of the prospect's intention to pay full price if necessary.

Another responsibility the agent has to the principal is to counsel him or her about obtaining legal advice. Depending on the area, legal advice might mean consulting an independent attorney or the attorney for the title or escrow company. Whatever action is dictated by local tradition, the agent should not attempt to act as "attorney" if there is anything in the course of the transaction to indicate that legal advice is necessary. In such instances the agent should, if asked for a recommendation, offer more than one name so the principal can make a free choice rather than accept a specific referral of the broker.

To some extent, the broker's fiduciary obligation to the principal resembles that of an attorney to a client, a doctor to a patient or a priest to a penitent. Confidentiality is a very important part of the agency relationship and every legal matter between principal and agent must be kept in strict confidence by the agent. There is, however, no privileged communication between the principal and agent in a real estate matter that can be kept from a government investigation. All records and information in a broker's file, as well as information known to him or her that is not on file, are available to interested parties on appropriate demand. In some cases, this requires a court subpoena or order but it is available. This distinction has been created by statute. The right of privileged communication exists primarily as a creation of legislation. Therefore, it is strictly limited to those areas covered by statute.

The fiduciary relationship between the broker and principal extends through the settlement or closing, as Chapter 11 will show. It extends beyond the term of the listing and even beyond the closing date. The agent may not act to the detriment of the principal. This rule is limited only by the broker's obligation to deal fairly with all parties.

The broker's continuing fiduciary relationship is illustrated in the following case. A broker listed and sold a residential property. After the closing, the buyer discovered a water condition in the basement. The buyer, assuming the seller had guilty knowledge of the water condition, wished to arrange a confrontation to obtain a damaging admission and requested the salesperson to be a witness to the conversation.

The broker wisely advised the salesperson not to do this. The action would put the salesperson (subagent) in a position of taking an active step that would not be to the advantage of the client (principal). The obligation to act for the benefit of the principal continued even though the transaction had been closed.

Dual Agency

Originally a real estate broker was just that—a "broker," defined as "one who offers to buy and offers to sell for another for compensation or arranges for the negotiation of contracts of various types." In the early 1980s, however, the media and government regulators focused on what appeared to be confusion among buyers and sellers as to whom the broker actually represented. Unfortunately, too often real estate salespeople identify with the buyer more than the seller. They refer to the buyers as "my buyers" and sometimes try to negotiate a price in favor of the buyer rather than the seller. It is no wonder, therefore, that some buyers might have assumed that the broker was their agent when, in fact, if the seller and the broker had a listing agreement, the broker was actually the agent of the seller.

Lawsuits against brokers began to take place seeking rescission of contracts. These lawsuits were based on allegations that real estate brokers were breaching their fiduciary duties by acting as "undisclosed dual agents." In early 1985 an Agency Task Force was formed by the NAR to study the agency issue and to formulate policy recommendations designed to reduce real estate brokers' potential liability for damages or rescissions for breaches of their agency obligations and also to dispel, as much as possible, the confusion on the part of sellers and buyers as to the agency duties a broker has to a client.

The Task Force concluded that "dual agency" is an inappropriate agency relationship for brokers to create as a matter of general business practice and, to avoid confusion concerning the agency status, recommended that a program of disclosure by real estate brokers to buyers (or to the seller, if the buyer hires the broker) be established. Because of differing local and regional customs and practices, the Task Force further concluded that the decision whether to adopt and implement a disclosure program, as well as the form and content of any disclosure notice, should be determined on a state-by-state basis through legislation or regulation. It is important that the disclosure be government mandated for two reasons: (1) to keep the program competitively "neutral" and (2) to avoid or limit dispute over whether the notice was adequate.

Seller's and agent's duties of disclosure. Both the owner and the agent have a duty to disclose any and all known facts about the condition of the property, especially defects not readily apparent on perfunctory inspection.

A case in California in which the agent knew the house was built on fill and that erosion and settlement problems were likely to occur and did not disclose this to the buyer resulted in a lawsuit (*Easton* v. *Strassburger* 1984 152 CA 3rd 90) that found the agent responsible for damages, both actual and punitive.

The *Easton* case has resulted in a considerable change in the manner in which California agents now treat exclusive listings. Effective January 1, 1987, in the State of California a new law became effective that requires all sellers of residential property of from one to four units to fill out and sign a form titled "The Real Estate Transfer Disclosure Statement."

The document, drawn up by attorneys of the California Association of REALTORS®, has three major parts. The first asks sellers to check what features their homes have on a list of 50—ranging from burglar alarms to water softeners—and to tell whether they are in operating condition. Then they are asked to describe what is wrong with those that do not work.

The second portion addresses defects and malfunctions in plumbing and electrical systems; structural components, including ceilings, floors, walls and foundations; and sidewalks, fences and driveways.

The greatest potential for litigation, perhaps, is found in the final section that delves into general conditions that may adversely affect the property's value. These relate to problems with noise, drainage, settling, easements, deed restrictions and zoning violations, plus additions, alterations and repairs that may have been made without building permits in compliance with local building codes. (A sample is provided in this chapter as Figure 3.1, copyrighted by the California Association of REALTORS®. To order, write to the Association, 525 S. Virgil Ave., Los Angeles, CA 90020, and request Form TDS-14-1. LI.)

While the document makes the seller solely responsible for the information provided, it also requires the listing agent to declare in writing his or her assessment of the condition of the property. That assessment must be based not only on the information provided by the seller but also on the agent's own visual inspection.

Lest buyers become too complacent, however, the disclosure document cautions that the seller's statements about the condition of his or her property are based only on his or her knowledge and belief and do not constitute a warranty.

Listing or selling a property "as is" is no guarantee that the agent is relieved of any responsibility should the buyer discover some defects that had not been disclosed prior to close of escrow. An agent should be put on notice that there may be something seriously wrong with the property when the owner insists that the listing be offered "as is." The agent should then make a determined effort to discover all inherent defects of the property and make sure any potential buyers are made aware of such defects through written notice of same. One should never take an obligation to list a property without making a thorough visual inspection of the subject property.

Making inaccurate statements.   In real estate transactions it is quite easy to make an inaccurate statement. Such statements are usually innocent mistakes on the part of the seller or his or her agent or due to indifference on the part of either; or they could be made with the intention of trying to deceive or mislead the buyer. An inaccurate statement may involve the water supply, soil condition, building components, building code violations, zoning, expenses of sale, unrecorded but known liens, and many others.

After a buyer finds out about an inaccurate statement that he or she was not alerted to, the buyer may decide to file suit against the seller and/or the seller's agent. Damages, both compensatory and punitive, can be considerable if the jury is convinced of an actual attempt to defraud.

Principal's Responsibilities to the Broker/Agent

Much has been written about the agent's responsibility to his or her principal, but little is ever said about a principal's responsibility to the agent. The principal does have such responsibility. One of the ingredients in a contract is consideration, promises made by both parties to the contract. In the listing contract, the principal promises to pay a commission to the broker if the broker produces a buyer for the property. The principal, therefore, should do nothing that will interfere with the marketing process unless the action is valid and agreed upon before the broker agrees to accept the agency.

Owners may impose any legal restrictions they want before a listing is accepted by a broker, such as no for-sale sign, no key to be available, limited hours during which the property may be shown, and even that the broker take the milk in and let the cat out. If the broker feels uncomfortable with these restrictions, it is his or her right to reject the listing. Nevertheless, just as the broker must fulfill all fiduciary duties, so the principal may not put unreasonable restrictions upon the agent. If this is done, the agent has the right to rescind the agreement.

Unfortunately many homeowners think that once a property is listed, the broker should sell it as if by magic. Almost every licensee has experienced the principal who makes the marketing of his or her property difficult—the phone that is always busy, absence from home during normal hours without leaving a key, leaving a key and then locking the screen door or leaving a messy house. A client may request that the broker not present any offers less than the acceptable price. This stipulation prevents the agent from performing the art of negotiation, which is really one of the agent's most important responsibilities to the principal. The broker should encourage full cooperation from the principal; it is really in the principal's best interest. If this is understood at the beginning of the agency relationship, it will make for a faster and more profitable transaction for both the agent and the principal.

FIGURE 3.1 Listing Information Disclosure Statement

REAL ESTATE TRANSFER DISCLOSURE STATEMENT
(CALIFORNIA CIVIL CODE 1102, ET SEQ.)

CALIFORNIA ASSOCIATION OF REALTORS® (CAR) STANDARD FORM

THIS DISCLOSURE STATEMENT CONCERNS THE REAL PROPERTY SITUATED IN THE CITY OF _____, COUNTY OF_____, STATE OF CALIFORNIA
DESCRIBED AT _____ .
THIS STATEMENT IS A DISCLOSURE OF THE CONDITION OF THE ABOVE DESCRIBED PROPERTY IN COMPLIANCE WITH SECTION 1102 OF THE CIVIL CODE AS OF _____, 19____. IT IS NOT A WARRANTY OF ANY KIND BY THE SELLER(S) OR ANY AGENT(S) REPRESENTING ANY PRINCIPAL(S) IN THIS TRANSACTION, AND IS NOT A SUBSTITUTE FOR ANY INSPECTIONS OR WARRANTIES THE PRINCIPAL(S) MAY WISH TO OBTAIN.

I
COORDINATION WITH OTHER DISCLOSURE FORMS

This Real Estate Transfer Disclosure Statement is made pursuant to Section 1102 of the Civil Code. Other statutes require disclosures, depending upon the details of the particular real estate transaction (for example: special study zone and purchase—money liens on residential property).

Substituted Disclosures: The following disclosures have or will be made in connection with this real estate transfer, and are intended to satisfy the disclosure obligations on this form, where the subject matter is the same: _____
_____
_____

(list all substituted disclosure forms to be used in connection with this transaction)

II
SELLER'S INFORMATION

The Seller discloses the following information with the knowledge that even though this is not a warranty, prospective Buyers may rely on this information in deciding whether and on what terms to purchase the subject property. Seller hereby authorizes any agent(s) representing any principal(s) in this transaction to provide a copy of this statement to any person or entity in connection with any actual or anticipated sale of the property.

THE FOLLOWING ARE REPRESENTATIONS MADE BY THE SELLER(S) AND ARE NOT THE REPRESENTATIONS OF THE AGENT(S), IF ANY. THIS INFORMATION IS A DISCLOSURE AND IS NOT INTENDED TO BE PART OF ANY CONTRACT BETWEEN THE BUYER AND SELLER.

Seller ☐ is ☐ is not occupying the property.

A. The subject property has the items checked below (read across):

☐ Range	☐ Oven	☐ Microwave
☐ Dishwasher	☐ Trash Compactor	☐ Garbage Disposal
☐ Washer/Dryer Hookups	☐ Window Screens	☐ Rain Gutters
☐ Burglar Alarms	☐ Smoke Detector(s)	☐ Fire Alarm
☐ T.V. Antenna	☐ Satellite Dish	☐ Intercom
☐ Central Heating	☐ Central Air Conditioning	☐ Evaporator Cooler(s)
☐ Wall/Window Air Conditioning	☐ Sprinklers	☐ Public Sewer System
☐ Septic Tank	☐ Sump Pump	☐ Water Softener
☐ Patio/Decking	☐ Built-in Barbeque	☐ Gazebo
☐ Sauna	☐ Pool	☐ Spa ☐ Hot Tub
☐ Security Gate(s)	☐ Garage Door Opener(s)	☐ Number of Remote Controls _____
Garage: ☐ Attached	☐ Not Attached	☐ Carport
Pool/Spa Heater: ☐ Gas	☐ Solar	☐ Electric
Water Heater: ☐ Gas	☐ Solar	☐ Electric
Water Supply: ☐ City	☐ Well	☐ Private Utility ☐ Other _____
Gas Supply: ☐ Utility	☐ Bottled	

Exhaust Fan(s) in _____ 220 Volt Wiring in_____
Fireplace(s) in _____ ☐ Gas Starter
☐ Roof(s): Type: _____ Age: _____ (approx.)
☐ Other:_____
Are there, to the best of your (Seller's) knowledge, any of the above that are not in operating condition? ☐ Yes ☐ No If yes, then describe.
(Attach additional sheets if necessary.): _____
_____
_____

B. Are you (Seller) aware of any significant defects/malfunctions in any of the following? ☐ Yes ☐ No If yes, check appropriate space(s) below.
☐ Interior Walls ☐ Ceilings ☐ Floors ☐ Exterior Walls ☐ Insulation ☐ Roof(s) ☐ Windows ☐ Doors ☐ Foundation ☐ Slab(s)
☐ Driveways ☐ Sidewalks ☐ Walls/Fences ☐ Electrical Systems ☐ Plumbing/Sewers/Septics ☐ Other Structural Components
(Describe: _____
_____)

If any of the above is checked, explain. (Attach additional sheets if necessary.): _____
_____
_____

Buyer and Seller acknowledge receipt of a copy of this page, which constitutes Page 1 of 2 Pages.
Buyer's Initials (_____) (_____) Seller's Initials (_____) (_____)

OFFICE USE ONLY
Reviewed by Broker or Designee _____
Date _____

To order, contact—California Association of Realtors®
525 S. Virgil Avenue, Los Angeles, California 90020
Copyright© 1986, California Association of Realtors®

Page 1 of 2

TDS-14-1

SF-K6-SF

Reprinted with permission of the California Association of REALTORS®.

FIGURE 3.1 (Continued)

Subject Property Address _____

C. Are you (Seller) aware of any of the following:

1. Features of the property shared in common with adjoining landowners, such as walls, fences, and driveways.
   whose use or responsibility for maintenance may have an effect on the subject property. .... ☐ Yes ☐ No
2. Any encroachments, easements or similar matters that may affect your interest in the subject property. .... ☐ Yes ☐ No
3. Room additions, structural modifications, or other alterations or repairs made without necessary permits. .... ☐ Yes ☐ No
4. Room additions, structural modifications, or other alterations or repairs not in compliance with building codes. .... ☐ Yes ☐ No
5. Landfill compacted or otherwise) on the property or any portion thereof. .... ☐ Yes ☐ No
6. Any settling from any cause, or slippage, sliding, or other soil problems. .... ☐ Yes ☐ No
7. Flooding, drainage or grading problems. .... ☐ Yes ☐ No
8. Major damage to the property or any of the structures from fire, earthquake, floods, or landslides. .... ☐ Yes ☐ No
9. Any zoning violations, non-conforming uses, violations of "setback" requirements. .... ☐ Yes ☐ No
10. Neighborhood noise problems or other nuisances. .... ☐ Yes ☐ No
11. CC&R's or other deed restrictions or obligations. .... ☐ Yes ☐ No
12. Homeowners' Association which has any authority over the subject property. .... ☐ Yes ☐ No
13. Any "common area" (facilities such as pools, tennis courts, walkways, or other areas co-owned
    in undivided interest with others). .... ☐ Yes ☐ No
14. Any notices of abatement or citations against the property. .... ☐ Yes ☐ No
15. Any lawsuits against the seller threatening to or affecting this real property. .... ☐ Yes ☐ No

If the answer to any of these is yes, explain. (Attach additional sheets if necessary.): _____
_____
_____

Seller certifies that the information herein is true and correct to the best of the Seller's knowledge as of the date signed by the Seller.

Seller _____ Date _____

Seller _____ Date _____

III
AGENT'S INSPECTION DISCLOSURE
(To be completed only if the seller is represented by an agent in this transaction.)
THE UNDERSIGNED, BASED ON THE ABOVE INQUIRY OF THE SELLER(S) AS TO THE CONDITION OF THE PROPERTY AND BASED ON A REASONABLY COMPETENT AND DILIGENT VISUAL INSPECTION OF THE ACCESSIBLE AREAS OF THE PROPERTY IN CONJUNCTION WITH THAT INQUIRY, STATES THE FOLLOWING:
_____
_____
_____

Agent (Broker
Representing Seller) _____ By _____ Date _____
(Please Print)   (Associate Licensee or Broker-Signature)

IV
AGENT'S INSPECTION DISCLOSURE
(To be completed only if the agent who has obtained the offer is other than the agent above.)
THE UNDERSIGNED, BASED ON A REASONABLY COMPETENT AND DILIGENT VISUAL INSPECTION OF THE ACCESSIBLE AREAS OF THE PROPERTY, STATES THE FOLLOWING:
_____
_____
_____

Agent (Broker
obtaining the Offer) _____ By _____ Date _____
(Please Print)   (Associate Licensee or Broker-Signature)

V
BUYER(S) AND SELLER(S) MAY WISH TO OBTAIN PROFESSIONAL ADVICE AND/OR INSPECTIONS OF THE PROPERTY AND TO PROVIDE FOR APPROPRIATE PROVISIONS IN A CONTRACT BETWEEN BUYER AND SELLER(S) WITH RESPECT TO ANY ADVICE/INSPECTIONS/DEFECTS.

I/WE ACKNOWLEDGE RECEIPT OF A COPY OF THIS STATEMENT.

Seller _____ Date _____ Buyer _____ Date _____

Seller _____ Date _____ Buyer _____ Date _____

Agent (Broker
Representing Seller) _____ By _____ Date _____
(Please Print)   (Associate Licensee or Broker-Signature)

Agent (Broker
obtaining the Offer) _____ By _____ Date _____
(Please Print)   (Associate Licensee or Broker-Signature)

A REAL ESTATE BROKER IS QUALIFIED TO ADVISE ON REAL ESTATE. IF YOU DESIRE LEGAL ADVICE, CONSULT YOUR ATTORNEY.

┌─── OFFICE USE ONLY ───┐
Reviewed by Broker or Designee _____
Date _____

To order, contact — California Association of Realtors®
525 S. Virgil Avenue, Los Angeles, California 90020
Copyright© 1986, California Association of Realtors®

SF-K6-SF

Page 2 of 2
TDS-14-2

Broker's Duties to Other Brokers

If a broker belongs to an MLS, his or her listings are usually automatically shared with the other MLS participants. An MLS is defined as a means by which the participant makes a blanket unilateral offer of subagency to the other participants, and as a facility for orderly correlation and dissemination of listing information among the participants so that they may better serve their clients and the public. There are times, however, when the broker might send a "co-op" listing to non-MLS members to give the listing more exposure. In either case the cooperating broker becomes a subagent, as discussed previously. In fact, a non-MLS broker will frequently request a co-op from the listing broker. If it is in the best interest of the client to give this added exposure, and it usually is, the broker must do so. Article 22 of the REALTOR® Code of Ethics requires this cooperation expressly. A cooperative listing in effect is an assignment by a broker of his or her rights under a listing contract. The assignment does not relieve the listing broker of obligations under the contract but continues them, and makes him or her responsible as well for the acts of the subagent (the cooperating broker). Laypeople and many licensees erroneously speak of "giving" a listing to or "listing with" the MLS. In fact, MLSs are not licensed brokers; they function merely as information clearinghouses. The listing broker retains his or her primary fiduciary responsibilities at all times until title actually transfers, even if the property is sold by another (cooperating) broker.

In some states, the real estate commission rules are very specific on this matter of cooperating. For example, under the New Jersey Real Estate Commission, Rules 11:5-1.23 (c):

> Every licensee shall fully cooperate with any other New Jersey licensee, utilizing his customary cooperation arrangements which shall protect and promote the interest of the licensee's client or principal and which shall not constitute unreasonable practices within the real estate brokerage business. This obligation shall be a continuing one unless the client or principal, with full knowledge of all relevant facts, expressly relieves his agent from all or any portion of this responsibility. Should the client or principal direct the licensee not to cooperate with other licensees, evidence of this intent shall be in writing and signed by the client or principal. However, no direction or inducement from the client or principal shall relieve the licensee of his responsibility of dealing fairly and exercising integrity in his business relations.

Any co-ops that are requested should not be given on a different commission split arrangement than that indicated on the listing as it was submitted to the MLS or other independent brokers, unless there is a valid reason. Some states require documentation in such cases.

From the viewpoint of the fiduciary relationship with the principal, any request for a co-op should be granted and complete assistance offered. It might result in a sale for the client, and the sale is what the broker has been hired for. Brokers should always remember that the fiduciary relationship requires a subordination of their own interests to those of the clients. Obviously, not even one opportunity must be overlooked to fulfill the agency agreement.

TYPES OF LISTING AGREEMENTS

Three types of listings are commonly in use: the open or general listing, the exclusive agency listing and the exclusive-right-to-sell listing. A fourth type, the net listing, is not so common. We will discuss each in turn.

Open Listing

The open listing is one in which the owner of the property gives a listing to any number of brokers who can work simultaneously to try to sell the property. The owner can sell the property independently to a buyer not introduced to the property through a broker without having to pay a commission. It is the least desirable type of listing for both the owner and the broker for several reasons. From the broker's point of view, it enables the property to be sold by the owner or another broker without a commission being due to the listing broker. From the owner's point of view, no agency has been created; therefore, no one broker has a fiduciary relationship to the owner. Although the broker who sells the listing gets the entire commission, which many homeowners think is an advantage to the brokers, brokers rarely advertise these properties or perform any other service for the owners under this arrangement. The open listing can be oral or written and terminates on notification by the seller of the sale of the property or of its withdrawal from the market by the owner.

Exclusive Agency Listing

In this type of listing the owner and the broker (agent) enter into a written contract (agreement) with a termination date. The broker, as agent for the seller, will receive a commission if the property is sold during the term of the listing by that broker or any other but not if the owner sells the property independently.

This type of listing also is less than fully satisfactory. Obviously, the broker might expend money and time and earn no commission. Even more important, this type of listing creates competition between the agent and his or her own principal. If both agent and principal advertise the property simultaneously and (even worse) at different prices, a careful buyer will see that the price of the house can be negotiated. If the advertised price is the same, the public will still think the seller is trying to save the commission; offers will tend to be much lower than those made through a broker. Most homeowners are not experienced in the art of negotiation and are not able to induce a buyer to raise an offer to an acceptable figure, as the broker would be able to do.

The following actual case illustrates how the exclusive agency listing can harm the seller. During the term of an exclusive agency a couple was shown a house that was listed at $69,500. They told the salesperson they would review the matter that evening and would most likely make an offer on the property the next day. The offer they considered making was $65,000.

That evening the principal advertised the house in a local paper at $64,000. The same couple, scanning the classified ads that night, saw the ad and thought it sounded like the type of home they were looking for. On calling the advertised number they were astonished to learn it was the same house they had seen earlier that day. Of course they did not know—nor, unfortunately, did the listing salesperson know—that the owner had decided to put his rock-bottom price in the paper to try for a fast sale. The prospects rightly thought the homeowner was trying to save commission, and they further deducted the commission from the $64,000.

Fortunately, the buyer really did want this particular house and the sale was finally consummated, but not before all parties reluctantly made adjustments. The salesperson adjusted the commission. The seller sold for less than he would have if the buyers had made the original $65,000 offer through the salesperson, because negotiation might have been able to raise that offer somewhat. The buyers paid more than the $60,000 they thought they could get away with when they read the principal's ad.

Exclusive-Right-to-Sell Listing

Under the exclusive-right-to-sell contract, also known as the exclusive authorization to sell, the principal authorizes the agent to represent him or her and agrees to pay a commission if the property is sold during the term of the listing. Commission is paid regardless of who makes the sale—agent, cooperating agent or owner. Remember that it is the wording of the listing contract that determines what type of listing is established. It is not enough to have *exclusive right* written across the top of a listing if the words in the agreement establish it as an exclusive *agency*. Certain key phrases appear in the different types of agreements; the phrase *agree to pay a commission if sold by you* creates an exclusive agency; the phrase *agree to pay a commission if sold by anyone* creates an exclusive right to sell.

Both the exclusive agency listing and the exclusive-right-to-sell agreement supersede an open or general listing. To avoid potential problems the owner should give notice of termination to the open or general listing broker. Remember, however, that an exclusive-right-to-sell agreement cannot supersede an exclusive-agency agreement. This is because the exclusive agency is a contract with a termination date that has been signed by all parties (the principals and the agent).

As we saw in the case just presented, misunderstanding, wasted time and money, frustrations and possible lost sales for the seller can easily result from exclusive-agency agreements. The broker should do everything possible to secure an exclusive right to sell. Assuming the broker is willing to do the selling job completely and fulfill his or her fiduciary relationship, it is the best listing agreement for both the principal and the broker (agent).

The REALTOR® Code of Ethics, Article 6, also emphasizes the importance of the exclusive-right agreement: "To prevent dissension and misunderstanding and to assure better service to the owner, the REALTOR® should urge the exclusive listing of property unless contrary to the best interest of the owner."

Net Listing

Under a net listing, the owner agrees to accept a net figure and the broker receives as commission any monies above that amount. Net listings are illegal in many jurisdictions and should not be used unless required by local custom and their *legality is verified*. The net listing is considered unsatisfactory because it does not tie the agent's benefits to the client's benefits. For example, a seller indicates he wants to net $86,000. The broker has determined that fair market value for the client's property is $93,500. (Fair market value should include the broker's commission.) Assuming the broker's commission is seven percent, that would give the seller a net of $86,955, or $955 more than the seller indicated he wanted. If the commission is a percentage of the selling price, the broker is more likely to work diligently to bring in the highest offer because this would afford not only a higher net for the client but also a greater commission for the broker. However, if the agreement was that the broker's commission would be any amount over the $86,000 net, the broker might be tempted to offer the property at an unrealistic price above the fair market value in an attempt to get a larger commission. This, as in all overpriced listings, would delay the sale and perhaps there would be no sale at all for the client. In any case an agent owes it to the client to advise him or her of the highest probable fair market value the property will sell for and not base the list price on what the owner wants to net.

If a broker wants to compute the list price based on a net figure, the following formula can be used: 100 percent minus the percentage of commission, balance divided into the net. For example, if the seller wants a net of $85,000 and the rate of commission is six percent, subtract .06

from 1.00. Divide the balance, .94, into the net of $85,000. The answer is $90,426. Rounded off to the next highest $100 or $500, this would suggest a listed price of $90,500 or $91,000.

Other Principal-Agent Agreements

In the operation of a real estate business, the broker will find certain other agreements that also create principal-agent relationships, such as representing a buyer in search of a specific type of property, property management agreements, mortgage placement and others not readily classified. These relationships, while not established by listing agreements, are still governed by the general principles relating to principal-agent relationships set forth earlier in this chapter.

PROTECTING THE BROKER'S COMMISSION

A listing agreement signed by all parties setting forth the rate of commission, whether it is an open, exclusive agency or an exclusive-right-to-sell listing, together with a sale is sufficient evidence to earn a commission. The payment may be subject to other conditions, such as the actual passing of title but if those conditions are met, the commission should be paid.

Statutory Letter

In cases where the listing is given orally, it is possible for a broker to produce a contract to purchase that meets every requirement the owner has—full price, agreeable closing date and all cash (no mortgage contingencies)—and the owner may pass title to that purchaser with no requirement to pay the broker a commission. In at least one state, New Jersey, the legislature has created a Statute of Frauds (N.J.S.A. 25:1–9) under which, when an oral open listing exists, the owner is required to pay a commission if a document known as the statutory letter has been delivered. The statutory letter is a notice; it must be sent by registered mail or hand delivered to the owner within a fixed number of days (usually five) after the oral authorization is given to the broker. It must furthermore include these facts: the date the authorization was given, who gave the authorization and who accepted it, a description of the property, the price at which to offer the property and the rate of commission to be paid. If the owner does not repudiate the letter before the broker actually produces a buyer, the broker's commission is protected.

If no statutory letter exists, but the owner enters into a contract with the purchaser that defines the commission, a commission must be paid.

At one time it was generally agreed that if a broker brought a buyer who was ready, willing and able to buy the property, the seller was bound to pay a commission; in recent years, however, some courts have determined that a commission is not due and payable until passing of title, unless the seller defaults.

Sometimes a clause is put into the listing agreement that says, in effect: "commission due and payable when, as, and if title passes"; even if this clause is not in the listing agreement, however, it is often assumed because of prior court decisions.

Signed Agreement

There is an additional method available to a broker to protect his or her commission that is usable on both open and exclusive agency listings. The prospective purchaser acknowledges in writing the properties that the broker will be offering. This affords the broker additional protection if the purchaser attempts to negotiate directly with the seller.

Courtroom Challenges

The broker's right to a commission has been the subject of much recent litigation in an effort to define what is required for a commission to be earned. The function of the broker is still to produce a purchaser ready, willing and able to buy in accordance with the authorization to sell given in the listing agreement or on other terms acceptable to the seller. Recent opinions, however, have redefined the legal meaning of "ready, willing and able."

This change has occurred because it seemed unjust that a broker could earn a commission when a buyer was unable or unwilling to close the transaction as agreed. The court in a 1967 landmark case said, "A new and more realistic approach to the problem requires that the seller be extended a right to expect that a buyer will perform in accordance with the contract of sale before the broker's commission is earned" (*Ellsworth Dobbs, Inc. v. Johnson*, 92 *NJ Super* 271,223 A2d 199, rev'd 50 NJ). This opinion, which has been indicated as the likely trend around the country, takes into consideration the "realities of the relationship created between owner and broker" and the fact that the seller's expectation of a completed transaction is a reasonable one.

Therefore, the true test of whether the broker has performed is demonstrated when title is transferred. If the buyer unjustifiably refuses or is unwilling to perform, the broker has not produced a willing buyer and the seller cannot be held liable for the commission. Stated simply, the broker's right to a commission from the seller comes into existence only when the buyer performs in accordance with the contract.

The right of the broker to a commission generally is still preserved when the seller defaults. That is, the broker is entitled to his or her commission if the seller refuses to complete the transaction and is not prevented from doing so by circumstances beyond his or her control.

There are other circumstances in which the broker may seem to have earned a commission. For example, if the buyer defaults and the seller retains an earnest money deposit (assuming a usual proportion of amount of deposit to purchase price), the broker is not entitled to a commission. This is considered salvage only and no liability ensues. In contrast, when the seller demands and receives a substantial amount above the deposit in exchange for a release or sues the buyer and receives damages for breach of contract, the broker is entitled to a commission from the seller. Note, however, that there is no duty on the seller to sue.

The broker is usually entitled to a commission from the buyer in the event of the buyer's unwillingness or inability to perform, provided that the inability was not known to the broker prior to entering into the contract or did not occur afterward due to circumstances beyond the buyer's control.

This new trend in the law is not a blow to the broker's efforts at earning a livelihood, as it might first appear. The enlargement of the rights of brokers against defaulting purchasers in conjunction with the new legal concept of the duty of a broker should foster the growing attitude of professionalism among licensees and create a new and greater public respect for brokers, their function and their right to full protection under the law.

A final point of importance to brokers: the brokerage fee or commission is not a lien on property. It need not be paid out of the proceeds of the sale unless agreed to by the seller in advance. If the seller is insolvent, the broker stands in line with the grocer, the butcher and other general creditors to share in any proceeds of the sale left over after liens (mortgages, judgments, and so on) are satisfied. It is recommended that a broker, faced with a seller who seems to be insolvent or a property title search that reveals substantial liens that were not disclosed at the inception of the listing, should consult a knowledgeable attorney to protect his or her interests. The principal-agency fiduciary relationship does not require the broker to "take it lying down."

SUMMARY

This chapter points out that the entire legal basis for real estate brokerage comes under the authorizations provided by the "law of agency," as expressed in the Statutes of Frauds.

The agency relationship comes in two forms: the broker acting as agent for his or her principal, i.e., seller or buyer of a property, and as agent for another broker or brokers.

Accompanying the agency relationship is a strict necessity for observing the fiduciary relationship inherent therein. This area of real estate brokerage is probably the cause of more censure for brokers who violate it than any other activities.

A recent development in the legal aspects of brokerage is the subject of "dual agency." This refers to the fact that there is often confusion as to which party—the buyer or the seller—the broker represents in a transaction. It appears there will be some legislative developments in the near future that will try to regulate more closely the responsibilities of brokers representing the buyer, the seller or both parties.

Another recent change in the brokerage picture is the greater interest displayed by regulatory bodies in how much disclosure should be required by the owner/seller and his listing broker concerning the condition of the offered property. A brand-new form required in California is included.

This chapter delineates the various forms of listing authorizations and briefly explains how each is used.

Finally, there is some discussion of the most important aspect of the authorization process, the commission agreement. Emphasis is placed on the need for a clear-cut agreement on how the commission is to be calculated and how it is to be paid.

DISCUSSION QUESTION

Keeping in mind the potential problems to the broker/owner if proper disclosure is not made (inherent defects in a property, dual agency, etc.), outline how you would cover the topic "Disclosure" in either your policy manual or a training program for your associates.

4 Establishing an Operating Philosophy

INTRODUCTION

Planning for a real estate brokerage operation may be broken down into six steps:

- Establishing an operating philosophy;
- Setting goals;
- Determining policies;
- Setting up procedures;
- Developing a timetable of objectives; and
- Evaluating accomplishments.

In this chapter we will discuss the all-important first steps, setting goals and establishing an operating philosophy. Following chapters will discuss policies and procedures.

FORMULATING A BUSINESS PLAN

This may be a good place to stop and consider the basics of going into business for oneself. Perhaps the best place to start is by answering the following questions:

1. WHAT? In what type of real estate do you wish to specialize? The usual transition from sales associate to broker is in the single-family residential field. However, one should not become "locked into" thinking

that this is the only option. By studying your community and the brokerage offices that serve it you may determine that there is a kind of property that is not being adequately served. For example, the community may be developing a number of apartment houses or condominiums and your competition may not be particularly adept at handling sales or resales of this kind of property. Here is an opportunity to specialize where the competition is limited. Of course, you must learn more than anyone else about selling this kind of property if you want to gain the reputation of being the expert.

2. WHERE? Next in line for planning is to determine where most of the type of property in which you wish to specialize is located. It may be in a specific residential area in which you live and have prospered as a sales associate or it may be in a suburb that is growing fast and has no adequate brokerage office serving it. Wherever it is, make sure to make a market study to determine the feasibility of opening an office there.

3. WHEN? One can delay a move into the ranks of brokerage firms indefinitely by always trying to determine the "very best time" to make the move. There is never a "best" time! If you can survive when economic conditions are bad and your competition is going broke, think of what you can do when economic conditions improve. If you move into your own office when times are at their best, then be careful not to overspend on equipment and fixtures; maintain a liquid position for the day when economic conditions turn down.

4. HOW? After you have determined the what, where and when of going into business, the most important question of all is raised—HOW? Find a suitable location, formulate a budget for the next six months, hire a secretary, devise an advertising program, make the necessary arrangements with your local MLS and/or board of REALTORS®, stock up on your signs and other supplies and then open your doors. Next comes the question of whether to engage associates and, if so, how. That question will be explored in great detail in subsequent chapters.

EIGHT BASIC QUESTIONS

Success in any venture may be simply defined as *reaching stated goals.* Before discussing an operating philosophy, therefore, it is appropriate first to examine the difference between goals and objectives. *Goals* are the hoped-for, long-term results to be derived by striving toward previously defined accomplishments. Clearly, the first step in attaining a goal is to define it. *Objectives,* on the other hand, are the short-term tasks one must accomplish to achieve goals. Objectives may change daily but goals do not. *Goals are achieved through the accomplishment of short-term objectives.*

To establish a business philosophy, a broker must answer eight basic goal-related questions. They are:

1. Which specialty of the business will be pursued?
2. Should the business stay small or expand?
3. Will sales associates be engaged?
4. If the plan includes sales associates, will they be employees or independent contractors?
5. Will the broker act as selling broker, selling and managing broker, sales manager or administrator? (An alternative might be to plan for dynamic progress up a ladder, as will be shown later.)
6. Will the firm operate as a proprietorship, partnership, corporation or S corporation?
7. Which form of operation should the broker choose?
8. Will the business grow horizontally or vertically?

CHOOSING A SPECIALTY

In real estate there are specialists as well as general practitioners, to use the medical profession as an analogy. In practice, the larger the city in which a broker operates the better chance he or she has of specializing successfully. Conversely, the smaller the community, the more the broker should consider being a general practitioner.

In the larger cities of North America it is not unusual to find brokerage firms that confine their businesses to such activities as industrial brokerage, commercial property sales and leasing, commercial or apartment-house property management, multiple-family residential property brokerage (apartment-house sales) or land sales and development.

In smaller and rural communities some large offices may specialize in farm and land sales, leasing and managing, or possibly land development and sales. Most firms in these areas, however, are devoted to the business of general brokerage. That is, they do whatever is necessary to provide the services their clients and customers demand. One day, for example, a small-town broker may be called upon to find a suitable site for an apartment house, while the next day he or she may be finding a home for a newly transferred executive. The same broker might also be called upon to lease a commercial store building, sell a small industrial plant or find a larger farm or ranch for a successful farmer.

While the specialist is required to accumulate considerable knowledge about his or her chosen specialty, the generalist must have considerable knowledge about many areas.

SELECTING THE RIGHT SIZE

In the evolution of a real estate brokerage business, a single-person operation can easily become an unwieldy group of offices while the broker hardly realizes what is happening. In making the decision whether to grow larger or stay small, the broker must first be aware of the four general categories of office sizes:

- The one-person office;
- The office with one to ten associates;
- The monolithic office with ten or more associates; and
- The multiple-office firm.

The One-Person Office

Most Americans have been reared on the big-is-better theory; they believe the bigger a company is, the better it must be. However, the small single-proprietor office with only one selling and managing broker can be attentive to the clients' needs while at the same time being lucrative and relatively trouble-free. This broker usually specializes in one specific field or area of real estate.

Advantages and Disadvantages

The one-person office carries certain advantages. For one thing, it is not necessary to split commissions with associates. For another, these brokers are not responsible for all the demands usually made on owners of large staffed offices. The brokers' time is their own and they may come and go at will without sales management responsibilities. Such a broker may work as much or as little as he or she wishes, perhaps even closing down the office to take a pleasure trip when business is slack. Finally, the initial investment is small.

Nevertheless, the one-person office is not without its disadvantages. When the broker is away, for example, no one is available to follow up on calls, prospects or problems with transactions in process. If the broker dies or is unable to conduct the business, the firm dies too. Further, there may be little prestige attached to being a lone-wolf businessperson in a community. The broker does not experience the satisfaction of having built a large, permanent organization. In cases of personality clash between the broker and either a buyer or seller, there is no other person, perhaps with a more amiable personality, to whom the broker may turn over that client. Finally, profitability and growth are limited to the broker's own production.

The One- to Ten-Associate Office

In this type of real estate office the broker usually acts in all four capacities: selling broker, selling-managing broker, sales manager and administrator.

Essentially, the best ratio for a sales force is ten associates plus a sales manager and a combination secretary-receptionist to one broker. When the broker engages the first sales associate, he or she has entered the world of sales management. The broker must then be prepared to devote at least one tenth of his or her time, taken out of personal production, to aid and supervise the new associate. Progressively, as each new associate is added to the staff, personal production will be reduced by another tenth. When the full staff of ten associates is reached, the broker may become a full-time sales manager with little time for further personal production.

Advantages and Disadvantages

The one- to ten-associate office carries certain advantages, including complete control of the business and the ability to make business decisions quickly. In addition, possibilities exist for developing substantial income with no division of the net income. Someone is always available to take care of clients when the broker is away or when the broker and client are incompatible. There is ego satisfaction in owning a substantial business in the community and more opportunities occur for vacation or attendance at conventions, self-improvement courses or seminars. The flow of productive income is relatively even, and opportunities exist for growth into larger forms of operations.

Disadvantages of the ten-associate office include considerably more overhead expense than in the one-person office, more responsibility for the actions of others and for the results of those actions, more time needed for problem solving and the need for continual development of management skills. Further, until the full complement of ten associates is acquired, the operation is not normally large enough to employ full-time sales management help. The broker must also make provisions for the company to continue after his or her retirement or death.

The Monolithic Office

This firm has ten or more associates located under one roof. In theory there is no upper limit on the number of associates a broker may engage. This category, usually confined in a single office structure, is described as monolithic because it is *single* and (potentially) *immense,* as opposed to the multiple-office or branch-office concept.

In the monolithic office arrangement, a number of principals are usually involved. Each principal is a partner, a corporate officer or a stockholder, or each may be the head of a department. The business may be managed by a board of directors or executive committee headed by the president. In a monolithic form, the broker may engage 100 or more sales associates assigned to various departments, such as residential, commercial, industrial, investments and even farms and ranches. The business may also have satellite business departments, such as property management, insurance, loan brokerage, leasing and land development. Each department generally has its own supervising managers or sales managers, often with several sales managers overseeing various segments of the residential sales force.

Besides a number of sales managers and department managers, the firm's operation is usually under the control of an administrative broker, who is the president or general manager. A table of organization for larger companies appears in Figure 4.1.

Advantages and Disadvantages

The monolithic company structure has both advantages and disadvantages over the forms already discussed. Among the advantages are:

1. Central control comes from a close-knit management team.
2. Overhead cost per associate is lower than in the multiple-office structure because all operations are under one roof, which saves duplication of equipment and facilities.
3. Few communication problems exist among the staff; all concerned can attend their indicated meetings.
4. A central-city location provides easier access for the various types of clients the company serves—commercial, industrial, investment, residential and income.
5. The broker can spread the cost of overhead among a number of departments.

Disadvantages of the monolithic office may be summarized as follows:

1. Space limitations usually restrict growth. They generally create overcrowding of facilities and expansion necessitates expensive remodeling.
2. It is difficult to keep the residential sales associates close to the residential market without opening branch offices. As the suburbs keep growing away from the central city, the residential market gets farther and farther away.
3. Residential sales associates may be reluctant to work in a central-city office.

FIGURE 4.1 Table of Organization

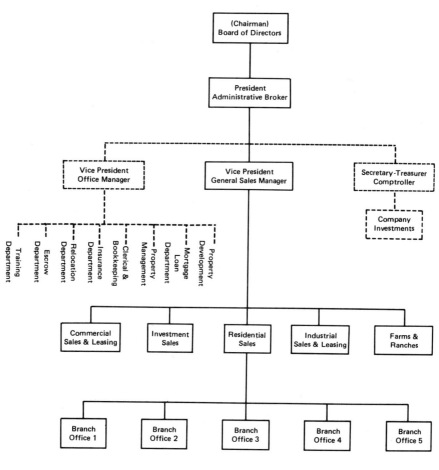

Key: Vertical growth _____
        Horizontal growth - - - - - - - - - - - - - - - -

4.   The mixing of the various specialties of brokerage in the same office can result in confusion of responsibilities and division of commission, as when a residential salesperson obtains a commercial or industrial listing or sells a property from that department.

5.   A large central office requires considerable investment in time and money, both for building and providing facilities and for finding and training managerial help.

The Multiple Office Firm

"Multiple office" is the term used to describe the establishment of several branch offices that parallel a city's residential growth into the suburbs. The ten-associate ratio described earlier may be used as the basis for expansion.

The theory behind this business concept is that as a neighborhood or community of 10,000 or more people develops in a suburb, the firm situates a residential sales office within that area. Each office functions as a profit center. Ideally, such an office is composed of ten associates, a sales manager, and a receptionist-secretary. This is not to say that the office must be as large as ten associates or limited to ten. In an office with fewer than ten sales associates the sales manager usually sells part-time to round out his or her income.

This system of expansion works well around a dynamic, growing city where the broker can follow the exodus of dwellers and homebuyers from the central city. The growth of a company following this pattern is limited only by the amount of growth the area experiences. The same format may be followed to expand into neighboring cities or even throughout the state, should the broker be so motivated.

Advantages and Disadvantages

The firm with multiple offices has certain advantages:

1.   The company can follow the residential market as it grows outward from the perimeter of the city.

2.   Residential sales associates, who probably make up as much as 85 percent of the sales force, are drawn to companies that maintain an office in the community in which they wish to specialize.

3.   Branch offices provide both easier access to and wider dispersion of the company's profit centers. Customers need not travel as far to use the company's services.

4.   There is ego satisfaction in building a large, successful business that will continue after the broker's retirement or death.

5. The opportunity for monetary gain is great.

6. Multiple offices tend to free the broker's personal time to pursue other avenues of interest because the firm can afford to hire experienced management.

The disadvantages of the multiple-office firm are:

1. Considerable investment in time and money is required.

2. There is a greater chance of going bankrupt in a falling market; the broker has more to lose in more individual markets.

3. It takes a great deal of preparation to handle complex management chores. With the growth of bureaucracy, business decisions usually are made more slowly.

4. Imagination as well as the gambling instincts of the broker must be on target.

5. Extremely high overhead is incurred because of the many different locations.

6. There is greater risk of losing money through poor choice of locations, managers and sales associates and through other variables.

ACQUIRING SALES ASSOCIATES

Along with the question of whether to stay small or grow, the broker must decide whether to acquire sales associates. The broker who chooses not to remain a one-person office must proceed up the ladder. The broker then is committed to acquiring sales associates and must, inevitably, become a sales manager. These associates may or may not act as employees. The broker who opts for sales associates must be prepared to recruit, select, train and supervise these people. All of this will be covered in detail in subsequent chapters.

INDEPENDENT CONTRACTORS OR EMPLOYEES?

Whether sales associates will be engaged as independents or as employees is probably the most important decision the broker must make. It will affect the philosophy of the business and the form of operation. Either relationship has both advantages and drawbacks. It is up to the broker to be thoroughly familiar with both forms to make an intelligent decision.

A sales associate who acts as an independent contractor is under only limited supervision. That salesperson contracts with the broker to produce certain results—real estate sales and leasing commissions. The manner in which these commissions are produced cannot be controlled by the broker except within the guidelines of the contract. Although a written contract between each independent contractor and the broker must clearly state the responsibilities of both parties, the broker may not be unduly restrictive as to the methods the associate may choose.

The employer-employee relationship is more limited. In this situation the broker has the normal powers inherent in any employer-employee relationship—he or she can hire, direct activities, require certain standards of conduct or terminate the employee at will.

The major reason for this difference is financial. When associates are employees, the broker is required to withhold federal and state income taxes from commissions, pay the employer's share of Social Security taxes, and withhold state unemployment insurance. The broker may also choose to provide fringe benefits, such as pension plans and health insurance. When the associates are independent, however, these deductions are neither required nor allowed. Clearly, it is less expensive and requires less bookkeeping to engage independent contractors than to hire employees.

TAX LEGISLATION AFFECTING INDEPENDENT CONTRACTOR STATUS

The Tax Equity and Fiscal Responsibility Act (TEFRA) of 1982 established that under a safe harbor provision contained in Section 3508 of the Internal Revenue Code of 1954, real estate salespeople were to be treated as independent contractors and not as employees for federal tax purposes. To meet the criteria, three requirements had to be met:

1. The salesperson must be a licensed real estate agent.

2. Substantially all of the salesperson's remuneration (whether or not paid in cash) for the services performed as a real estate agent must be directly related to sales or other output rather than to the number of hours worked.

3. A written agreement must exist between the salesperson and the person for whom he or she works that must provide that the salesperson will not be treated as an employee with respect to such services for federal tax purposes. *Note:* It is *essential* that the written agreement include this statement: "The salesperson may not be treated as an employee with respect to the services performed by such salesperson as a real estate agent for *federal tax purposes.*"

For salespeople to meet the statutory definition of independent contractor, it was mandatory that such written agreement be effective as of

January 1, 1983. Contracts entered into before January 1, 1983, required a separate written notice to the salesperson by February 28, 1983.

Proposed regulations published in January 1986 attempted to clarify certain aspects of the three requirements. For example, the proposed regulations addressed advances and draws and what constitutes "substantial" remuneration. At this writing, final regulations have not been approved; although it is not known if the final regulations will deviate to any great extent from the proposed regulations, history has proved that they probably will not be altered to any great extent.

It must be noted that the three-part statutory test clarifies the independent contractor status for federal tax purposes only, and does not control whether a salesperson is an employee or an independent contractor under various state laws governing workers' compensation, unemployment compensation or state income taxation. Therefore, although a broker's control over a salesperson does not jeopardize the independent contractor status for federal tax purposes, it might very well establish an "employee" relationship under state rules and laws.

Advantages and Disadvantages of Independent Contractor Status

It is sometimes difficult for the veteran broker to maintain an independent contractor relationship with salespeople. Over the years, the broker becomes accustomed to designating floor time, requiring attendance at sales meetings and generally controlling not only the direction of a salesperson's efforts but also the means and methods used. It is not unusual to hear such a broker, when asked if he or she has an independent contractor office, exclaim, "Oh yes, all my employees are independent contractors!"

To justify the relationship as a legally independent one, both parties should sign an agreement, to be kept on file in the broker's office. See Figure 4.2, which serves as an example of such an agreement. Further, maintaining professional independent contractor status with sales associates requires that the broker follow certain behavior guidelines.

The independent sales associate must pay his or her own license fees and board dues. This individual is also responsible for car and transportation expenses, including insurance. Entertainment expenses and expenses incidental to obtaining clients or customers are the salesperson's responsibility, and no drawing account may be provided.

The independent associate must not be required to follow any set schedule, procedure or policies, such as adhering to established working hours, vacation schedules or dress codes. Sales training programs, attendance at sales meetings and quotas must not be enforced by the broker. The broker must not instruct the independent associate as to which property he or she may or may not sell.

FIGURE 4.2   Independent Contractor Agreement

NJAR-585

**BROKER-SALESPERSON
INDEPENDENT CONTRACTOR AGREEMENT**

1 THIS AGREEMENT, is made and entered into this _____ day of _____, 19 ____, by and between
2
3 _____ (hereinafter referred to as the "Broker"), having its principal office at _____
4
5 _____, and   _____
6
7 (hereinafter referred to as the "Salesperson"), residing at _____
8
9 _____
10
11 **WITNESSETH:**
12 WHEREAS, Broker is engaged in business as a real estate broker trading as _____, with its
13 principal office at _____, and as such is duly licensed to engage in activities including, but not
14 limited to, selling, offering for sale, buying, offering to buy, listing and soliciting prospective purchasers, and negotiating
15 loans on real estate, leasing or offering to lease, and negotiating the sale, purchase or exchange of leases, renting or
16 placing for rent, or managing real estate or improvements thereon for another or others; and
17 WHEREAS, Broker has and does enjoy the goodwill of the public, and has a reputation for fair and honorable
18 dealing with the public; and
19 WHEREAS, Broker maintains an office in the State of New Jersey equipped with furnishings, listings, prospect
20 lists and other equipment necessary, helpful, and incidental to serving the public as a real estate broker; and
21 WHEREAS, Salesperson is duly licensed by the State of New Jersey as a real estate salesperson; and
22 WHEREAS, it is deemed to be to the mutual advantage of Broker and Salesperson to enter into this Agreement.
23 NOW, THEREFORE, in consideration of the foregoing premises and the mutual convenants herein contained, it is
24 mutually convenanted and agreed by and between the parties hereto as follows:
25
26 1. **SERVICES.** Salesperson agrees to proceed diligently, faithfully, legally, and with his best efforts to sell, lease,
27 or rent any and all real estate listed with Broker, except for any listings which are placed by Broker exclusively with
28 another salesperson(s), and to solicit additional listings and customers for Broker, and otherwise to promote the business
29 of serving the public in real estate transactions, and for the mutual benefit of the parties hereto.
30
31 2. **OFFICE SPACE.** Broker agrees to provide Salesperson with work space and other facilities at its office
32 presently maintained at _____, or at such other location as determined
33 by Broker at which Broker may maintain an office. The items furnished pursuant to this Paragraph 2 shall be for the
34 convenience of the Salesperson.
35
36 3. **LISTINGS.** Broker agrees to generally make available to Salesperson all current listings maintained by its
37 office. Notwithstanding the foregoing, Broker reserves the right to place any of its listings, in the exclusive possession
38 of one or more salesperson(s) other than Salesperson.
39
40 4. **RULES AND REGULATIONS.** Salesperson and Broker agree to conduct business and regulate habits and
41 working hours in a manner which will maintain and increase the goodwill, business, profits and reputation of Broker
42 and Salesperson, and the parties agree to conform to and abide by all laws, rules and regulations, and codes of ethics
43 that are binding on, or applicable to, real estate broker and real estate salespeople. Salesperson and Broker shall be
44 governed by the Code of Ethics of the NATIONAL ASSOCIATION OF REALTORS, the real estate laws of the State
45 of New Jersey, the Constitution and By-Laws of the _____ Board of Realtors, the rules and
46 regulations of any Multiple Listing Service with which Broker now or in the future may be affiliated with, and any
47 further modifications or additions to any of the foregoing. Salesperson acknowledges receipt of a copy of said Code of
48 Ethics, the Local Board Constitutions and By-Laws and the rules and regulations of any Multiple Listing Service with
49 which Broker is now affiliated. Salesperson agrees also to abide by the rules, regulations, policies and standards
50 promulgated by Broker.
51
52 5. **LICENSING AND ASSOCIATION MEMBERSHIP.** Salesperson represents that he is duly licensed by
53 the State of New Jersey as a real estate salesperson. Salesperson acknowledges that Broker is a member of the _____
54 _____ Board of Realtors, the New Jersey Association of Realtors and the NATIONAL ASSOCIATION OF
55 REALTORS, and as a result thereof, Broker is subject to the rules and regulations of those organizations. Salesperson
56 agrees to be subject to and act in accordance with said rules and regulations. If Broker requires Salesperson to become
57 a member of any real estate organization, then Salesperson agrees that he shall become a member thereof and shall pay
58 all applicable fees and dues required to maintain said membership. As a result of Broker being a member of the aforesaid
59 groups, Broker and Salesperson agree to abide by all applicable rules, regulations and standards of such organizations,
60 including, but without limitation, those pertaining to ethics, conduct and procedure.
61
62 6. **COMPENSATION.** Salesperson's sole compensation from Broker shall be in the form of commissions. The
63 commissions for services rendered in the sale, rental, or leasing of any real estate and the method of payment, shall be
64 determined exclusively by Broker. Commissions, when earned and collected by Broker, shall be divided between
65 Broker and Salesperson after deduction of all expenses and co-brokerage commissions in accord with the Salesperson's
66 Commission Schedule attached hereto.
67
68 7. **MULTIPLE SALESPEOPLE.** In the event that two (2) or more Salespeople under contract with Broker
69 participate in a sale and claim a commission thereon, then and in that event the amount of commissions allocable to
70 each salesperson shall be divided in accordance with a written agreement among said salespeople. In the event that the
71 salespeople shall be unable to agree, the dispute shall be submitted to and be determined by Broker, in his sole discretion.

Reprinted with permission of the New Jersey Association of REALTORS®.

FIGURE 4.2 (Continued)

8. **RESPONSIBILITY OF BROKER FOR COMMISSIONS.** In no event shall Broker be liable to Salesperson for any commissions not collected, nor shall Salesperson be personally liable for any commissions not collected. It is agreed that commissions collected shall be deposited with the Broker and subsequently divided and distributed in accordance with the terms of this Agreement.

9. **DIVISION AND DISTRIBUTION OF COMMISSIONS.** The division and distribution of the earned commissions as provided for in this Agreement which may be paid to or collected by the Broker, but from which Salesperson is due certain commissions, shall take place as soon as practicable after collection and receipt of such commissions, but in no event more than ten (10) days after receipt by the Broker.

10. **RESPONSIBILITY FOR EXPENSES.** Unless otherwise agreed in writing, Broker shall not be liable to Salesperson for any expenses incurred by Salesperson or for any of his acts, nor shall Salesperson be liable to Broker for Broker's office help or expenses, or for any of Broker's acts other than as specifically provided for herein.

11. **ADVANCES.** Broker may from time to time and in its sole discretion make advances to Salesperson on account of future commissions; it being expressly agreed, however, that such advances are temporary loans by Broker for the accommodation of Salesperson which are due and payable on demand or as otherwise agreed to by the Broker, and are not compensation. Upon notice to Salesperson, Broker shall have the right to charge interest on any and all advances made to Salesperson, either at the time of making the advance or thereafter, at a rate chosen by Broker in its sole discretion, but not in excess of the maximum rate permitted by law. Upon receipt of payment of commissions, Broker shall credit the account of Salesperson (first toward interest, if any, and then toward principal) with the portion of such commissions due Salesperson. If at any time, the advances made to Salesperson together with interest thereon, if any, exceed the credits to his account for his share of commissions collected, then such excess shall be owing by Salesperson to Broker and shall be due and payable upon demand. After such demand, interest at the maximum rate permitted by law shall accrue upon the amount due Broker, notwithstanding the fact that any or all of the advances made to Salesperson have initially been interest free or at a reduced rate of interest.

12. **REAL ESTATE LICENSES, BONDS, DUES AND FEES.** Salesperson agrees to pay the cost of maintaining his real estate license, dues for membership in the NATIONAL ASSOCIATION OF REALTORS, the New Jersey Association of Realtors, the local Board of Realtors and other dues and fees related to the rendering of services by Salesperson as a real estate salesperson.

13. **AUTHORITY TO CONTRACT.** Salesperson shall have no authority to bind, obligate or commit Broker by any promise or representation, either verbally or in writing, unless specifically authorized in writing by Broker in a particular transaction. However, in accordance with his duties under this Agreement, Salesperson shall be and is hereby authorized to execute contracts of sale, leases, and listing agreements for and on behalf of Broker as agent.

14. **CONTROVERSIES WITH OTHERS.** In the event any transaction in which Salesperson is involved results in a dispute, litigation or legal expense, Salesperson shall cooperate fully with Broker. Broker and Salesperson shall share all expenses connected therewith, in the same proportion as they normally would share the commission resulting from such transaction if there were no dispute or litigation. It is the policy to avoid litigation wherever possible, and Broker, within his sole discretion may determine whether or not any litigation or dispute shall be prosecuted, defended, compromised or settled, and the terms and conditions of any compromise or settlement, or whether or not legal expense shall be incurred. Salesperson shall not have the right to directly or indirectly compel Broker to institute or prosecute litigation against any third party for collection of commissions, nor shall Salesperson have any cause of action against Broker for its failure to do so.

15. **OWNERSHIP OF LISTINGS.** Salesperson agrees that any and all listings of property, and all actions taken in connection with the real estate business and in accordance with the terms of this Agreement shall be taken by Salesperson in the name of Broker. In the event Salesperson receives a listing, it shall be filed with Broker no later than twenty four (24) hours after receipt of same by Salesperson. All listings shall be and remain the separate and exclusive property of Broker unless otherwise agreed to in writing by the parties hereto.

16. **DOCUMENTS.** Broker and Salesperson agree that all documents generated by and relating to services performed by either of them in accordance with this Agreement, including, but without limitation, all correspondence received, copies of all correspondence written, plats, listing information, memoranda, files, photographs, reports, legal opinions, accounting information, any and all other instruments, documents or information of any nature whatsoever concerning transactions handled by Broker or by Salesperson or jointly are and shall remain the exclusive property of the Broker.

17. **COMMUNICATIONS.** Broker shall determine and approve all correspondence from the Broker's office pertaining to transactions being handled, in whole or in part, by the Salesperson.

18. **FORMS AND CONTRACTS.** Broker shall determine and approve the forms to be used and the contents of all completed contracts and other completed forms before they are presented to third parties for signature.

19. **INDEPENDENT CONTRACTOR.** This Agreement does not constitute employment of Salesperson by Broker and Broker and Salesperson acknowledge that Salesperson's duties under this Agreement shall be performed by him in his capacity as an independent contractor. Nothing contained in this Agreement shall constitute Broker and Salesperson as joint ventures or partners and neither shall be liable for any obligation incurred by the other party to this Agreement, except as provided herein. The Salesperson shall not be treated as an employee for Federal, State or local tax purposes with respect to services performed in accordance with the terms of this Agreement. Effective as of the date of this Agreement, Broker will not (i) withhold any Federal, State, or local income or FICA taxes from Salesperson's commissions; (ii) pay any FICA or Federal and State unemployment insurance on Salesperson's behalf; or (iii) include Salesperson in any of its retirement, pension, or profit sharing plans. Salesperson shall be required to pay all Federal, State, and local income and self-employment taxes on his income, as required by law, and to file all applicable estimated and final returns and forms in connection therewith.

20. **NOTICE OF TERMINATION.** This Agreement, and the relationship created hereby may be terminated by either party hereto with or without cause, at anytime upon three (3) days written notice. However, in all events this Agreement shall immediately terminate upon Salesperson's death. Except as otherwise provided for herein, the rights of the parties hereto to any commissions which were accrued and earned prior to the termination of this Agreement, shall not be divested by the termination of this Agreement.

FIGURE 4.2   (Continued)

154 155 156 157 158 **21. SERVICES TO BE PERFORMED SUBSEQUENT TO TERMINATION.** Upon termination of this Agreement, all negotiations commenced by Salesperson during the term of this Agreement shall continue to be handled through Broker and with such assistance by Salesperson as is determined by Broker. The Salesperson agrees to be compensated for such services in accordance with the schedule attached hereto.

159 160 161 162 163 164 165 **22. LIST OF PROSPECTS.** Upon termination of this Agreement, Salesperson shall furnish Broker with a complete list of all prospects, leads and foreseeable transactions developed by Salesperson, or upon which Salesperson shall have been engaged with respect to any transaction completed subsequent to termination of this Agreement in which Salesperson has rendered assistance in accordance with the terms of this Agreement. Except as expressly provided for in Paragraph 21 of this Agreement, Salesperson shall not be compensated in respect of any transaction completed subsequent to termination of this Agreement unless agreed to in writing by the Broker.

166 167 168 169 170 171 172 173 174 **23. DUTY OF NON-DISCLOSURE.** Salesperson agrees that upon termination of this Agreement, he will not furnish to any person, firm, company, corporation, partnership, joint venture, or any other entity engaged in the real estate business, any information as to Broker or its business, including, but not limited to, Broker's clients, customers, properties, prices, terms of negotiations, nor policies or relationships with prospects, clients and customers. Salesperson, shall not, after termination of this Agreement, remove from the files or from the office of the Broker, any information pertaining to the Broker's business, including, but not limited to, any maps, books, publications, card records, investor or prospect lists, or any other material, files or data, and it is expressly agreed that the aforementioned records and information are the property of Broker.

175 176 177 178 179 180 **24. OPTIONS EXERCISED SUBSEQUENT TO TERMINATION.** Upon termination of this Agreement, Salesperson shall not be compensated in respect of any sale or lease option contained in any then existing sale or lease agreements, or in any sale or lease agreement consummated under the terms of a termination agreement and Broker shall thereafter perform all necessary services in connection with the foregoing, unless compensation and performance of services by the Salesperson shall be specifically agreed to in writing by Broker and Salesperson.

181 182 183 184 185 186 **25. ESCROW DEPOSIT.** All contracts of sale shall be accompanied by an escrow deposit in an amount as determined by Broker. Salesperson will, at all times, require purchaser or prospective purchasers, to put up such escrow deposit unless a higher or lower sum shall be mutually agreed to by Broker and Salesperson. Salesperson is expressly prohibited from accepting a smaller escrow deposit, a post-dated check, or agreeing not to deposit an escrow check, unless such action has been expressly authorized by Broker.

187 188 189 190 191 192 193 194 **26. AUTOMOBILE.** Salesperson agrees to furnish his own automobile, pay all expenses in connection with the operation and maintenance of said automobile, and that Broker shall have no responsibility therefor. Salesperson agrees to carry throughout the terms of this Agreement public liability insurance upon his automobile with minimum limits not less than _____ ($ _____) for each person and _____ ($ _____) for each accident, and property damage insurance with a minimum limit of not less than _____ ($ _____). Upon request, Salesperson agrees to furnish to Broker certificates certifying as to such insurance prepared by the insurance company.

195 196 197 **27. ASSIGNABILITY AND BINDING EFFECT.** This Agreement is personal to the parties hereto and may not be assigned, sold or otherwise conveyed by either of them.

198 199 200 201 202 **28. NOTICE.** Any and all notices, or any other communication provided for herein shall be in writing and shall be personally delivered or mailed by registered or certified mail, return receipt requested prepaid postage, which shall be addressed to the parties at the address indicated herein, or to such different address as such party may have fixed. Any such notice shall be effective upon receipt, if personally delivered, or three (3) business days after mailing.

203 204 205 **29. GOVERNING LAW.** This Agreement shall be subject to and governed by the laws of the State of New Jersey, including the conflicts of laws, irrespective of the fact that Salesperson may be or become a resident of a different state.

206 207 208 **30. WAIVER OF BREACH.** The waiver by the Broker of a breach of any provision of this Agreement by the Salesperson shall not operate or be construed as a waiver of any subsequent breach by the Salesperson.

209 210 211 212 **31. ENTIRE AGREEMENT.** This Agreement constitutes the entire agreement between the parties and contains all of the agreement between the parties with respect to the subject matter hereof; this Agreement supersedes any and all other agreements, either oral or in writing, between the parties hereto with respect to the subject matter hereof.

213 214 **32. GENDER.** When used in this Agreement, the masculine shall be deemed to include the feminine.

215 216 217 218 219 **33. SEPARABILITY.** If any provision of this Agreement is invalid or unenforceable in any jurisdiction, the other provisions herein shall remain in full force and effect in such jurisdiction and shall be liberally construed in order to effectuate the purpose and intent of this Agreement, and the invalidity or unenforceability of any provision of this Agreement in any jurisdiction shall not effect the durability or enforceability of any such provision in any other jurisdiction.

220 221 222 **34. MODIFICATION.** This Agreement may not be modified or amended except by an instrument in writing signed by the parties hereto.

223 224 225 **35. PARAGRAPH HEADINGS.** The paragraph headings contained in this Agreement are for reference purposes only and shall not affect in any way the meaning or interpretation of this Agreement.

226 227 **36. SURVIVAL OF PROVISIONS.** The provisions of this Agreement shall survive the termination of the Salesperson's services under this Agreement.

228 229 IN WITNESS WHEREOF, the undersigned have set their hands and seals, or if a corporation, has caused this Agreement to be signed and sealed by its duly authorized corporate officer, the day and year first above written.

230 231 232 WITNESS:

233 234 _____   _____

WITNESS: (Broker)

235 236 _____   _____

(Salesperson)

The agreement between broker and independent agent is terminable at the will of either party; in most states, in the event of termination the sales associate must not be divested of any earned commissions.

Reports to the broker concerning business activities or status of sales must not be required and no commissions may be paid until they are paid by the seller to the broker. The salesperson is responsible for his or her own state and federal income taxes as well as Social Security taxes. The broker may not withhold taxes from an independent contractor's commission, even as a favor.

Independent contractors may not be compensated by any means other than by the commissions specified in the contract. The broker may not pay any bonuses, fringe benefits or retirement plans for those not under contract as employees. Further, any title, such as sales manager or vice president, automatically suggests an employee relationship and should be avoided.

No contract may forbid an independent from having an outside job, except with another real estate firm.

It may seem that the broker loses all control if he or she wants to maintain a sales staff of independent contractors but the contrary is true. The following paragraphs explain what the broker *may* do and still avoid an employee relationship.

The broker may hold meetings for the purposes of communication and information and invite associates to attend; however, attendance must be at their own volition only.

The broker may provide for those expenses called for in the contract or those that are important to normal business operation, such as office space, telephone, secretarial help and sales management advice and counsel.

The broker may, and should, furnish listings generated by the people in the firm as well as any MLS membership privileges to which the broker is entitled.

Assistance may be offered on a voluntary and advisory basis only.

The broker may require that the associate work diligently in complying with his or her portion of the contract.

The broker may produce an office guideline manual and offer it as "suggested procedures" for sales associates.

Advantages of Employee Status

Under some circumstances an associate may wish to switch from independent contractor to employee. Although such a change is possible, only by carefully studying the advantages and disadvantages and communicating them to the associates will the broker bring about a successful switch.

There are certain advantages of employee status that can accrue to both the broker and the sales associate. For instance, the broker has considerably more control over the working procedure of the associate. He or she can require attendance at sales meetings, observance of definitely appointed floor days, adherence to a required dress code and canvassing of certain areas of a "farming" territory. Also, by withholding state and federal income taxes from the associate's commissions, the broker is assured that the salesperson will not get in trouble with the IRS, with all its attendant problems; however, this arrangement creates additional bookkeeping expense for the employer.

Most states require that all employees be protected by workers' compensation insurance, which would cover a job-related injury or death; employers must make contributions to this fund. In most states the law does not *specifically* require a broker to provide workers' compensation insurance for independent contractors, although in actual practice it is considered a necessity. The uninsured broker risks being exposed not only to court costs but to penalties, sanctions and numerous losses if an associate is injured on the job. As a precaution to avoid the possibility that providing workers' compensation might jeopardize an associate's independent contractor status, the broker should include a paragraph such as this one in the contract: "Purely as a matter of business judgment, the broker is providing workers' compensation insurance for the mutual benefit of all parties, and this is not intended to reflect any relationship except that of independent contractor."

FORM OF OWNERSHIP

With regard to the firm's ownership, the broker's choices are closely allied to other business goals and objectives. The two general forms of ownership are sole proprietorship and joint ownership with others. If the broker intends to stay small with not more than one or two sales associates, sole proprietorship or sole ownership may be adequate. The broker who intends to grow, expand operations and perhaps join with other individuals in the ownership of the business, however, would be wise to plan ahead for a different form of ownership. Each broker should seek counsel from an attorney, accountant or business consultant to choose the form of ownership most appropriate to other goals.

The four primary forms of multiple ownership used in business today are:

- Corporation;
- S corporation;
- General partnership; and
- Limited partnership.

The license laws of each state define the ownership position of the responsible broker (broker of record); these will help a broker determine which form to use. A corporation usually has one responsible broker, an officer of the corporation who has the responsibility for the corporation's adherence to state real estate laws.

Corporation

The main disadvantages to the corporate form of ownership involve taxation and losses. Profits are taxed twice: once on the corporate level, before dividends are distributed, and once on the individual level, as the dividends are distributed to stockholders. Salaries paid to the officers of a corporation, however, are not considered profits; they are taxable only to the individuals receiving them. In addition, losses of a corporation may not be passed on to the stockholders but may be applied only to the corporation's future earnings. Also, if the corporation enjoys any capital gains (profits resulting from the sale of capital assets), such gains are passed on to the individual stockholders as ordinary income.

On the other hand, there are five major advantages of the corporate form of ownership.

Limited liability. Any liability the corporation may incur, through actions for damages, judgments or bankruptcies, is limited to the investment of the stockholder in the corporation and does not affect that individual's personal assets (unless he or she has signed a personal guarantee of corporate obligations).

Continuity of life. Because a corporation is a legal entity that technically never dies, the officers may be continually replaced, should they die, retire or resign.

Centralized management. The stockholders elect a board of directors who, in turn, elect a slate of officers. The officers manage the company in general, leaving (by state law) the licensed broker-officer directly responsible for the real estate brokerage operations.

Transferability. The corporate stock may be transferred freely from one stockholder to another, usually with no strings attached.

No income limitations. There is no upper limit on the number of stockholders a corporation may have or the amount of income it may earn.

Generally speaking, if a company is earning considerable profits it is better to be structured as a corporation. This is because the income tax brackets can be divided between the officers and the corporation. In a high-income situation, the corporation's upper tax bracket is often lower than the brackets the owners would be in if they were to hold ownership as a partnership or S corporation. Therefore, it is better to let the corporation pay some of the income tax at a lower rate and thus reduce the owners' tax brackets and tax liabilities.

S Corporation

In many ways the S corporation is an ideal form for a real estate brokerage operation, despite two important disadvantages. First, no more than 35 stockholders may be owners. Second, not more than 20 percent of the income may be from so-called passive investments. Passive investments are those that are income-related, such as stock dividends, rentals from investment properties and interest from money deposits. Nevertheless, these two disadvantages will not be unduly restrictive if the purpose of the entity is primarily to be active in a real estate brokerage.

There are at least three advantages of an S corporation. First, there is no double taxation—the income, losses and capital gains are passed directly to the stockholders. The second advantage is centralized management and continuity of life, as with the ordinary corporation. Third, liability is limited, as in a regular corporation, and stockholders' interests are freely transferable.

Under no circumstances should the foregoing explanation of the use of the S corporation be interpreted as a recommendation that one should structure his or her business in such a form without expert advice. While it appears on the surface to be an ideal vehicle by which to avoid double taxation for a corporation, a certified public accountant or tax attorney may point out alternate ways of achieving the same results.

General Partnership

Some disadvantages of owning a real estate business as a general partnership involve problems that occur if one of the partners dies, goes bankrupt or becomes liable in a lawsuit. The ownership also is not completely free for transfer.

The advantages are financial. Income is directly taxable to each partner with no double taxation; losses or capital gains pass directly to the partners.

Limited Partnership

The limited partnership, used primarily to acquire investments, is seldom used in an active brokerage firm. In this form of ownership one or more general partners are responsible for the operation of the business and have unlimited liability. There may be a number of limited partners who may have no say in the operations of the business and whose liability is limited only to the amount of their investment. Because the limited partnership form of ownership is used mostly for joint ventures and syndicates and has been badly abused at times, it is closely regulated by state and federal agencies. Anyone considering limited partnerships is well advised to consult an attorney who specializes in them.

FRANCHISES AND SOME ALTERNATIVES

After choosing the form of ownership the business should take, the broker must decide whether to become a landlord-broker, to become a broker-associate or to affiliate with another organization, such as a franchise or a network.

It is only natural that the franchise type of operation, so popular in the fast-food industry, should grow and prosper in the real estate business. Brand-name merchandising is the principal philosophy behind real estate franchises. Attributes of this type of marketing include instant identification, consumer confidence, recognition of a level of expertise and loyalty to a name with which clients have had favorable prior experience.

Before discussing these alternatives, we will review the eight choices open to the broker when choosing a mode of operation. He or she can:

- Remain as an independent operator;
- Join a referral system;
- Sell the business to a corporate chain;
- Become part of a full-franchise system;
- Become part of a quasi-franchise system;
- Belong to a broker cooperative;
- Be a part of a broker association; or
- Become a landlord-broker through the 100-percent commission concept.

Remaining Independent

Operating as an independent broker involves pride of individuality and a trustworthy company name. Many independent brokers are active in their community and support local businesses. They are familiar with local land values. They tend to believe that people want to do business with others who totally own and operate their own firms. Independents recognize the importance of quality service that brings in repeat and word-of-mouth business. These brokers may be members of the NAR as well as of local boards of REALTORS®.

Joining a Referral Service

One big advantage of membership in a franchise system is the referral of prospects and listings among offices. To counteract these advantages, a number of independent referral firms have come into operation throughout the nation. These firms offer independent brokers the advantages of nationwide referrals without the disadvantages inherent in a franchise operation.

Joining a Franchise

As mentioned earlier, many brokers join a franchise for the potential referrals. However, the main advantages of joining such full-franchise organizations are their approaches to management and marketing. Each is designed to increase the profits of members in exchange for a percentage of these profits. Most charge an initial fee in return for exclusive rights to a specific territory. Thereafter, a percentage of either gross or net income is assessed. In return the franchisor offers a "bundle of expertise," such as techniques for recruitment, selection, training and supervision of sales associates, as well as methods and tools for obtaining listings. Other advantages include economies that result from large-quantity purchase of equipment, signs and supplies; an effective client referral system and an aggressive corporate transferee department; wider mortgage financing capabilities; and group advertising and promotions through national newspaper, magazine and television advertising.

Disadvantages include expensive initial cash outlay plus high franchise fees (usually five to six percent), loss or subordination of the broker's own identity and limited geographical exclusivity. The franchise affiliation appeals primarily to new, younger brokers without long-term or proved reputations.

Profile of Real Estate Firms: 1985, a publication of the Economics and Research Division of the NAR, reports that after continuous and rapid growth of franchises in the 1970s, growth stopped during the poor real estate markets of the early 1980s, with fewer firms becoming affiliated. Since then, however, the trend has reversed. In 1985, 18 percent of all real estate firms were affiliated with national franchise organizations and one percent with regional or local organizations. Franchises are most attractive, the report indicates, to firms with 21 to 50 sales associates, but there is little attraction for firms of ten salespeople or less and for the large firms. Although a majority (86 percent) of firms affiliated with franchises have expressed overall satisfaction with their arrangement, 12 percent see room for improvement.

The question to ask when considering whether or not to become a part of such a franchise is this: What can it do for me that I can't do for myself? If the answer is "Nothing," then the broker should forget it. If the answer is "Many things," the broker probably should join.

Joining a Quasi-Franchise

The term quasi-franchise may be applied to such networks as The Real Estate Network, Home Guide, Better Homes and Gardens, Gallery of Homes, and (in Southern California) the Herbert Hawkins Organization. A number of smaller organizations probably fall into this category as well. Each offers a slightly different variation on the "bundle of expertise" but all have in common the right to retain one's own name as part of the firm identification. Real estate magazines regularly carry ads from full franchises and quasi-franchises urging brokers to join.

Selling to a Corporate Chain

Another form of real estate business organization is currently gaining prominence. Huge corporate chains buy up real estate firms and merge them into their own operations, often retaining the same management. Coldwell Banker Company is such a chain. A California-based corporation that has gone national as part of Sears, it also owns the giant Forest E. Olson Company of Southern California and the Henry Broderick Company of Seattle. There are undoubtedly many other burgeoning chains in the market for representative firms in any given area. With a little investigation and inquiry, a broker who has the inclination to become part of a corporate operation can probably find a purchaser for the business.

Joining a Broker Co-op

A broker co-op is a hybrid organization that is not a merger, not a sellout to a chain, not a franchise, not even a quasi-franchise; it is an incorporated group of companies that have joined together for their mutual benefit. Usually the group incorporates in the regular manner, electing a board of directors who, in turn, elect their own officers. They charge an initiation fee for joining the co-op and assess a monthly charge to cover such group expenses as office rent, telephones, secretarial help, advertising and promotions. Sometimes each firm retains its own offices but pools advertising costs and shares in corporate profits.

Joining a Broker Association Group

A broker association group is another step removed from the concentrated, centralized control of a regular company. This type of organization may be described best as a single office comprising a group of brokers. These groups are composed mostly of single brokers who have banded together to share office space and secretarial, telephone and advertising expenses. Actually another form of broker co-op, these groups lack the formal structuring of incorporation, a board of directors and officer elections.

Becoming a 100 Percent Commission Office

The terms *100 percent commission office* and *landlord-broker* may not be entirely accurate, but unfortunately there is no terminology that fits. In this situation the broker owns an office and all of its facilities, but rents those facilities to other brokers and associates on a per-desk basis. Each broker or associate pays a stipulated monthly fee to cover all of the landlord's office expenses and gives a small percentage of his or her commissions for the common benefit of all the brokers.

For instance, suppose Joe Smith is a broker who is tired of nursing fledgling sales associates. He decides to rent available desk space to a number of fellow brokers or sales associates. Each broker or associate pays a monthly fee, say $500 per month, which covers his or her share of the housing, staffing and equipping expense. In addition, the participating brokers each contribute a certain percentage of their commissions to an advertising pool administered by a committee of their members. Participating brokers, after paying these expenses, may keep all commissions they earn from sales. Legal liability for any associate member is borne by the landlord-broker; legal responsibility for his or her own actions is borne by each individual member-broker.

Certainly there are other variations of the 100 percent commission office. For example, a broker can charge each sales associate a flat amount for the desk space and then take a percentage of the associate's gross commissions, with the sales associate paying his or her own advertising and long-distance telephone call charges. It is up to the individual broker/owner to devise the plan that best suits the practice in his or her specific area of operations.

VERTICAL OR HORIZONTAL GROWTH—OR BOTH?

The table of organization in Figure 4.1 graphically illustrates the difference between vertical and horizontal growth with regard to real estate companies. The word vertical is used to describe upward growth in a straight line, confining one's efforts to the brokerage business only and devoting all growth efforts in that direction. Horizontal growth, on the other hand, means branching out into related, so-called satellite businesses, such as property insurance, property management, loan brokerage and perhaps even a separate property investment and development program.

As a brokerage firm grows, it can begin to feel the horizontal expansion pressures. The inclination is to become a full-size real estate business with departments in all the related fields. This path can become very lucrative, as each department can feed from the others. For example, a land development and building department not only will make money from its own operation but also will provide listings for the brokerage department. The property management department can be there as a service to clients who purchase investment properties from the brokerage operation; it also can provide listings of managed properties later to the selling department. And so it goes. Each department should be set up not only to show a profit from its own type of service or production but also to provide business for the other departments. One enterprising broker in California has five such departments organized as separate corporations, in each of which he owns 51 percent and the managing president owns 49 percent. This ensures him of complete ownership control but saddles his minority stockholder with the responsibility for showing a profit. Needless to say, he has made provisions to replace the minority stockholder with another if one of the corporations is not profitable.

PROCEDURAL GUIDELINES

No chapter on establishing the philosophy of a business would be complete without providing some guidelines to policies that the broker may expect his or her associates to observe. Nevertheless, the broker who engages independent contractors as associates should avoid any statement the IRS could interpret as asserting domination or control over those associates. The broker may not tell independents what to do or how to do it; in most cases, he or she may only *suggest* the proper procedure.

Policy guidelines should include some indication of how to handle problems that may arise in connection with the following items:

- Membership in the local board of REALTORS® (also state and national associations);
- Membership and observance of the MLS regulations;
- Sales meetings;
- Caravan tours;
- Opportunity (floor) time;
- Servicing listings;
- Advertising;

- Cooperating with fellow associates and outside offices;
- Appearance and demeanor;
- Policy on keys and lockboxes;
- Insurance: automobile, errors and omissions and workers' compensation;
- Desk space;
- Telephone facilities and techniques for answering;
- Policy on long-distance calls;
- Stenographers;
- Drinking on the job;
- Legal expenses;
- Commissions: rates and splitting arrangements;
- Settlement of disputes;
- Associates' buying and selling for their own accounts; and
- Termination.

These are just a few of the many areas where problems can occur; therefore, problems should be anticipated. By establishing clear-cut policies on how they should be handled, the broker can eliminate 95 percent of the problems before they arise. More information on suggested policies and procedures will be found in the following chapters.

SUMMARY

This chapter gets into the fundamental elements of establishing a viable brokerage business. It asks, and attempts to answer, the eight basic questions needed to be considered by the neophyte broker before making the first move.

Should the broker specialize in any particular aspect of brokerage or geographic area? And if so, what and where?

What size operation does he or she envision as being the right size that can be efficiently handled? A list of the various options from which to choose as well as the advantages and disadvantages of each is provided.

Along with the operating philosophy is a discussion of proposed relationships with sales associates. How many, if any, and how they should be contractually established are questions that are explored.

Another important question for a planned brokerage operation is Which form of ownership should be utilized? The different types of ownership vehicles that can be chosen from as well as the advantages and disadvantages of each are delineated.

Finally a discussion of the various forms of franchising that one can become affiliated with is provided, along with information that may help the aspiring broker make either choice or no choice, as the case may be.

DISCUSSION QUESTION

In making a decision whether to join a franchise, list the advantages and disadvantages as you see them and come to a conclusion as to what you would do.

5 Organizing and Opening the Office

INTRODUCTION

Rarely does the broker take care of every office detail personally. Even one who wishes to be the only licensee in the office usually finds need for a secretary to answer the phone, type letters, do filing, keep a simple set of books, follow up on the transaction details and attend to all the other office chores. Already the neophyte broker has become involved in *office administration*.

If the broker should decide to acquire one or two sales associates to help in listing and selling, a crucial career decision has been reached. The individual is starting to become involved in the art of *sales management*, truly a crossroads in the evolution of a broker's business. The evolution, from small to large, will be studied in this chapter.

SMALL VS. LARGE

A broker who decides to remain as a single-broker operation, employing only a secretary, has responsibilities to no one except customers and clients. As soon as an associate is acquired, however, the broker must think about providing additional desk space, another telephone, training and supervision, secretarial service, more advertising, a policy manual, a sales associate contract, insurance, workers' compensation and coverage against errors and omissions suits. Now is the time to decide whether one really wants to be burdened with this new area of responsibility—sales management.

Having made this choice, many brokers decide that if they are to have one sales associate they may as well hire several more to help defray the expenses of the new and larger office they intend to rent. With each additional associate, the manager finds personal production suffering more and more. The broker-owner, spending more time training and supervising associates, is getting deeper and deeper into sales management and office administration. Often this happens without the broker realizing it, wanting it or being prepared for it.

At this stage, the broker-owner does not have time to take care of personal clients and begins to refer them to the associates. But old clients may not be satisfied with that arrangement. They insist on dealing with that broker or they will go elsewhere. The broker who does help the new associate complete the transaction finds that the commission must be shared.

As the business expands, some of the associates may become involved with properties and specialties in which neither broker nor associate has any expertise or experience—farms, ranches, commercial or industrial properties, land development or mobile home parks. But the broker must provide those associates with answers to their questions; the broker then decides to take some courses in those fields. The broker also joins one or more of the specialized institutes, societies or councils of the NAR that provide specialized training; he or she enrolls in college courses to correct these deficiencies. In any case, attending to education takes the broker farther still from personal production and into the new tasks of office manager and sales manager.

More overhead comes when the broker decides to hire a manager to do these tasks and help out when he or she is gone. Searching for a manager, the broker chooses one of the top sales associates as the most logical candidate. After all, she was successful at selling, wasn't she? That should qualify her as a sales manager, shouldn't it? Unfortunately, there are two things wrong with this picture: One of the best salespeople is taken out of production and the best producers are not necessarily the best managers because the jobs require two different types of personalities.

Nevertheless, the broker then puts pressure on the new sales manager to find a competent sales associate to replace herself. And, incidentally, to hire a few more sales associates.

Success for this broker-owner means there is not enough office space to accommodate all these new people. The next decision is whether to expand present quarters, move to larger and more suitable space or open a branch office for new staff members in a faster-growing sector of the city. Whatever the broker decides will surely increase the overhead.

The climax comes when the accountant, whom the broker had to hire because the secretary could no longer keep such a complex set of books, presents the profit-and-loss statement for the year. The thought slowly dawns: *I am not making as much take-home pay from the business as I earned last year as a lone broker!* This realization can be painful for a broker who builds an organization with a big overhead expense only to see the real estate market take a turn downward. There are high expenses and little income to support them.

As the real estate industry grows it becomes more competitive and sophisticated, thus requiring changes in business practices. These changes involve selecting an appropriate location, determining the physical setup of the office and choosing the equipment needed. Sophistication is not limited to the conglomerates and franchises but affects even the one-person office in rural areas. It is true that in a one-person operation a broker might want to adapt only some of the suggestions made in this chapter to his or her individual needs; nevertheless, all should be carefully considered before the broker tries to establish an office.

THE NON-OWNER/MANAGER

As more and more multioffices are opened, many brokers who would have normally opened their own offices now opt to become managers of other brokers' offices. Owners of multioffice firms must depend on their managers to run their offices with the same care as the owners themselves would. Therefore, the responsibilities of a non-owner/manager parallel those of an owner/manager.

THE REAL ESTATE SALES PROCESS

Now more than ever it is true in this business that the firm that controls the listings controls the business.

The real estate sales process is based on the concept that every function and aspect of a real estate firm's makeup should be organized and directed with one major objective in mind—attracting and obtaining good-quality, marketable and exclusive listings. Those objectives should be implemented by the following policies, as shown in Figure 5.1.

1. A major objective of the broker-owner is to build a favorable image and untarnished reputation in his or her community and within the firm's sphere of influence to attract local people to the broker's firm. The broker's integrity must remain high, his or her honesty unquestioned and competence in the brokerage business universally acknowledged. Activity in community, religious, club, civic and political affairs indicates sincerity and generates influence—clients will be attracted to the firm and listings to the office.

2. The image and public relations aspects of operations, such as advertising and promotion, office exterior and interior and office personnel should create an aura of confidence, stability and competence to which the public can relate easily. These elements, which are discussed later in this chapter and also in the chapter on advertising, include tasteful sign design, advertising logos, stationery, billboards, newspaper ads, brochures, business cards and anything else that consciously or subconsciously influences the buying and selling habits of the public.

3. The broker must be an expert on property values and market conditions of real estate in his or her trading area, and must have the ability to impart that knowledge to sales associates.

4. Sales associates must be professional—properly trained, tastefully dressed and well mannered—to instill confidence in the client. Such associates create a foundation of mutual respect as well as a pleasant and harmonious working relationship.

5. Financial controls of the business must also be carefully budgeted and continually monitored. The well-managed brokerage business maintains a name for responsible fiscal management and an impeccable record for meeting its obligations promptly.

Property owners of the community will be more willing to trust the sale of their property to the broker who follows these guidelines. As a bonus, potential sales associates looking for an office to join will be attracted to the broker's office for the same reasons.

LOCATION

The geographic area chosen for an office will depend primarily on the broker's goals and objectives relating to specialization. If one's speciality is commercial, a downtown location or location on a major highway would be preferable to a quiet suburb. On the other hand, a residential specialist would most likely choose a location in close proximity to a residential area. In identifying the area from which prospects will be drawn, the broker must make certain the area shows trends that will support the business. Is the community growing? Does it attract industry and commerce? Is residential turnover high? Answers to these questions can be obtained from chambers of commerce, banks, utility companies and schools. The local MLS statistics are also a valuable source of population and business trends.

When opening a new branch, the broker must consider the proximity of the firm's established offices. It is generally advisable to choose an adjacent area or at least one that is covered by present advertising. This

FIGURE 5.1 The Real Estate Sales Process

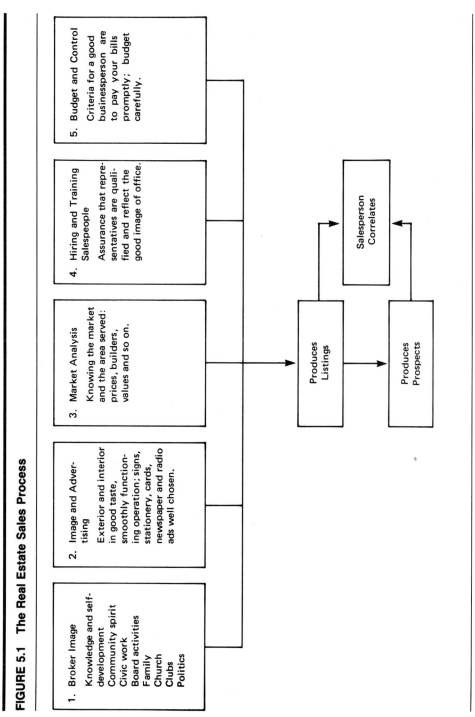

1. Broker Image

    Knowledge and self-
    development
    Community spirit
    Civic work
    Board activities
    Family
    Church
    Clubs
    Politics

2. Image and Adver-
    tising

    Exterior and interior
    in good taste,
    smoothly function-
    ing operation; signs,
    stationery, cards,
    newspaper and radio
    ads well chosen.

3. Market Analysis

    Knowing the market
    and the area served:
    prices, builders,
    values and so on.

4. Hiring and Training
    Salespeople

    Assurance that repre-
    sentatives are quali-
    fied and reflect the
    good image of office.

5. Budget and Control

    Criteria for a good
    businessperson are
    to pay your bills
    promptly; budget
    carefully.

Produces
Listings

Produces
Prospects

Salesperson
Correlates

SOURCE: Developed by John Cyr.

ensures that the firm already has some degree of recognition. In addition, it eliminates the need for a major increase in advertising expenditures.

Once the broker has chosen a general geographic location that can support the new office, he or she has to decide on the actual site. The broker should determine what is most important—building exposure, traffic, parking or a combination of all three. If a firm's reputation is established and is supplemented by an ongoing advertising and public relations program, good office front exposure might not be a priority; prospects will seek the company wherever it is located. If the firm is new to the area, however, top priority might be given to a site where maximum exposure can reduce the cost of the advertising needed to attract attention to the firm. A main street initially might appear to offer the most traffic, but an office in a shopping center or enclosed mall should not be overlooked. This alternative often provides more traffic at less cost. A corner location might give the office good exposure but parking might be severely limited.

PHYSICAL LAYOUT

Having chosen a location, the broker must plan both the interior and exterior layout and decor of the office. Whether it is in a rented storefront, a renovated gas station or a three-story office building, both functional and cosmetic aspects are important to success.

Some functional needs are obvious: a restroom, adequate parking and wide enough driveways so that a car driving in can pass one driving out at the same time. Some needs are not so obvious. For example, glass exposure should be kept to a minimum in areas that are frequently vandalized. One REALTOR® in Texas built a round office and kept it off the ground, not only to be seen better and provide more parking but also to withstand hurricanes.

Cosmetics are important, too, because the office image is frequently the first and most important form of advertising. A later chapter will review many different types of advertising but the first and most lasting advertising impression is the image reflected in office surroundings. Repetition and consistency are two of the most important things to remember in advertising; therefore, whatever theme you choose for layout and decor, keep in mind that additional offices should look like the original.

Market Identification

The first decision the broker must make is what identification is to be projected in the marketplace. The marketplace is that area from which the broker expects to draw clients and buyers and in which the inventory will be marketed. Also called the service area, it usually is a certain geographic area, the size of which is determined by the firm's ability to service (the number of brokers and associates) and the extent of the firm's advertising and public relations programs.

Market identification is reflected in the name chosen, the type style and logo and the colors to be used. Although this can be done by the broker, it probably would be wise to use a professional to design the logo, choose the colors and coordinate all materials. Whether this is for a brand-new office or a face change for an established office, the proper choice should have an impact on the community that will be profitable for the broker for many years. It must also be remembered that if one is changing existing logos and colors, all old materials must be discarded. Once these new identifying marks have been decided on, they should then be used as much as possible in the exterior design of the office, right through to lawn signs and business cards. In this way, by constant repetition, the public will begin to recognize the firm not only by name but by logo or even color used. Uses of color will be explored in more depth in Chapter 10; it is well to remember, however, that the first opportunity the broker has to establish identity in the marketplace is in the building exterior.

Space Ratios and Desk Cost

Wherever possible, the theme that has been established should be carried into the office interior. It is here, in the interior space, that the broker has some hard decisions to make. By now the broker has set goals relating to size and rate of growth: whether it will be a one-person, ten-person or larger office; how many secretaries, bookkeepers and others will be employed; how much rent can be realistically budgeted. Then more questions arise. Where will desks and phones be placed? Where will the broker's office and manager's office be? Where will the secretary sit? What is the best place to put the coat rack or the kitchen? Where should signs, frames and extra stationery be stored?

From a managerial point of view, the sales staff should be accessible for supervision by the manager and for client consultation. Aside from those conveniences, space also must be used productively. That is, it must be apportioned to accommodate the number of salespeople needed to cover the broker's *desk costs,* the cost of providing the opportunity for salespeople to do business. Desk cost is computed by dividing the total operating expenses of the firm—including salaries, rent, insurance, supplies, and so forth—by the number of salespeople. It has nothing to do with the number of desks, unless coincidentally each salesperson has an assigned desk and every desk is occupied by a salesperson. For example, if the broker's annual overhead is $20,000 and there are two desks, each accommodating one salesperson, the desk cost for each desk is $10,000 annually. On a 50/50 split, each salesperson does not begin to earn a profit for the broker until each has brought in a total of $20,000 in gross commissions for the year. Once the broker determines the number of salespeople he or she needs to cover overhead and bring in a profit, the broker must decide how best to set up the facilities to provide for those salespeople.

A popular arrangement, personally recommended by one of the authors who has used it for many years, allows private or semiprivate space for customers or clients to meet with the salesperson in an area separate from the desks of the rest of the sales staff. This layout offers a degree of privacy to customers and secludes them from office conversations and other distractions. The staff is seated in an open area known as a bull pen. (*See* Figure 5.2.) A comfortable amount of space to provide in a bull pen is 30 to 35 square feet for each salesperson, including aisles. If space permits, the broker may provide private or semiprivate offices or cubicles for sales desks, as well as a conference area for customers.

Furniture style and arrangement in the conference area should be planned to put customers and clients at ease. Chairs can be placed so that the salesperson can look at all customers while the customers cannot look at each other. The broker must be aware of how best to arrange the office to make closing and other operations simple and natural.

The broker should begin by listing the space allocations needed for all office functions and then listing space areas that are desirable although not absolutely necessary. Table 5.1 is a checklist of possible space allocation.

If the broker is moving into quarters previously used as an office, space already may be arranged appropriately. It will be easy to spot what changes are needed. However, if the broker is planning extensive renovations or is building from scratch, there are many other considerations besides space allocations. The following environmental checklist should be studied before knocking down walls and installing carpeting:

- Traffic patterns;
- Lighting;
- Ventilation;
- Noise pollution;
- Heating and cooling systems;
- Power sources;
- Parking;
- Snow removal and lawn maintenance;
- Interior and exterior cleaning; and
- Waste disposal.

FIGURE 5.2   A Popular Office Arrangement

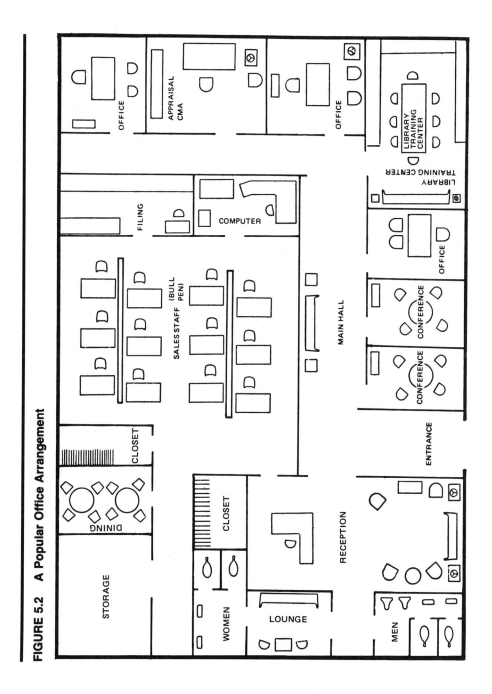

EQUIPMENT

In today's real estate office there are many operations. Major ones include advertising, accounting, sales processing and communication—equipment is available to support all of them.

TABLE 5.1   Space Area Checklist

Necessary	Optional	
Desk space	Reception area	Storage
Salespeople	Conference or	Supplies
Managers	closing room(s)	Signs
Broker	Coffee bar/kitchen	Records
Restroom	Coat closet	Children's play area
File cabinets	Library	Display lobby
	Training room/	Photocopying
	audiovisual	Bookkeeping
		Appraisal and research

There is no doubt that a broker who wants to use all the equipment available on the market today could spend hundreds of thousands of dollars to set up an office. This expenditure would be neither wise nor necessary. It *is* necessary to accept the fact that competitors are using some of these new devices. When used properly they can make operations more efficient and save more time than ever before.

Any list of equipment should be reviewed with three questions in mind.

1. Will any of these items provide better service to client and customer?

2. Will it save time and thereby make each day more productive?

3. Most important of all, is the cost-benefit ratio such that it is worth the money?

Communication

The most important method of communication is the telephone. Any telephone company or private communications expert can provide a list of gadgets they think will be useful in your operation. The question is: Are any of those gadgets absolutely necessary? Do you need an office intercom or internal paging equipment? Will automatic dialing save time? Is conference calling or a "no-hands" speaker really worth the extra expense? Will an automatic answering device be helpful in salvaging important prospect calls? A call diverter is often useful to ensure that evening calls to the office are diverted to the broker's or associate's home.

The second most important means of communication is the letter. Is dictating equipment necessary, or can the secretary handle the load efficiently? If one needs dictating equipment, then which is the best mode? The kind of letter an office produces is important to the company's image. Is the appearance of the letters clean and crisp? Sometimes spending the extra money for a typewriter with interchangeable type elements is well worth it for the professional look it gives letters. Would an investment in word-processing equipment be practical? For offices with, or considering, a computer, many word-processing software packages are available or one can buy a machine that does nothing but word processing. A good "letter-quality" printer is essential to produce professional office letters. The benefits of word processing are many: You can compose a letter on the screen, make all necessary corrections before it is printed, press a key to print the letter in perfect condition and preserve a copy of the letter on a disk for recall at any time. These are all questions that must be studied and answered if the office communications are to project a professional image.

The third most important equipment for presentable office communication is copying equipment. Today's real estate offerings as well as transaction documents require so many copies that a machine providing clean, easy-to-read copies is absolutely essential. Consider your need for the following capabilities before buying or leasing a copier:

- Copies that look as if they were originals;
- Copies on both sides of the paper;
- Copies on colored graphics, maps or charts;
- Speed of operation; and
- Cost of paper, ink, powder or repairs.

We have mentioned just a few basic pieces of equipment an office requires. From here a broker can accumulate as little or as much sophisticated equipment as his or her operation justifies. For example, there are various types of calculators, cameras, tape recorders, chalkboards and computers to choose from. All have a definite use in most real estate offices, but how important is that need?

Computers

According to a report issued by the Economics and Research Division of the NAR in 1985, just under 60 percent of real estate firms have computer capability. This is an impressive growth since 1981, when less than one third had any type of computer capability—computer terminals, in-house computers or word processors.

Today the computer is used for things never dreamed of a few decades ago. Here is a partial list of what a computer is capable of doing for brokers; remember that this list will grow longer and longer as the years go on.

MLS printouts
New listings
Available listings for waiting buyers and sellers
Comparable listings
Settlement (closing) information
Sales activity reports by salesperson
Area
Office
Price
Property management
List all financing possibilities
Determine cash flow
Analyze values
Record and report rents and costs
List vacancies
Bookkeeping and accounting
Prepare payrolls and commissions
Keep accounts payable
Issue appropriate checks
Prepare tax returns
Prepare financial statements and balance sheets
Advertising
Analyze and compare expenditures and results
Make projections
Store mailing lists
Produce labels or addressed envelopes
Commercial investment
Compute cash flow
Compute depreciation
Analyze tax shelters
Escrow closings
Prepare closing statements
Office management
Maintain records and analysis to assist in management decisions
Follow-up
Maintain client information
Print and mail follow-up literature

A computer terminal for MLS access is the most frequently found piece of data-processing equipment in a real estate office, with nearly four of ten real estate firms using a terminal for that purpose. However, the growth in use of in-house office computers has been so great that their level of importance is almost equal to the computer terminal used for MLS access.

Additional equipment adds to a computer's capacity. According to the NAR *Profile of Real Estate Firms 1985,* 93 percent of firms with an in-house computer have a printer. About half of these firms have additional disk drives for greater storage flexibility and 49 percent have a modem to communicate with other systems, such as those of an MLS.

The actual computer itself and its components are called *hardware.* The written programs fed into it to provide information storage and retrieval are called *software.* Three basic costs involved when a broker gets an office computer are purchase or lease of the hardware, design or purchase of software and costs for services provided by the central processing facility.

There are several recommended ways to keep costs down. Leasing rather than buying hardware is one step that should be considered. Another is sharing time on a system rather than owning an in-house computer. Time-sharing means that many users share a single, centrally located computer, and each office has its own terminals. Costs for each participant as based on amount of use. Because of the development of smaller and smaller computers, which will perform all the necessary operations at comparatively low cost, time-sharing is becoming obsolete. Terminals tied to a central core are still useful, however, when the stored information is used by all of the participants, as in the computerized MLS.

As for the software, it is generally advisable for small operations to purchase prepackaged programs, which are less trouble and a lot cheaper than custom-designed programs. The most frequently used source is the off-the-shelf package sold by the hardware manufacturer or outside suppliers. Some firms write their own software; others obtain a turnkey system with software and hardware combined in one package.

Making the Decision

In making the decision whether or not to own a computer or even to use computer capabilities, as in evaluating any other piece of equipment, the broker must carefully calculate the benefits and disadvantages. The benefits, along with all the intricacies of the computer, can best be explained by the representatives of the many companies that produce and sell (or lease) them. The broker must weigh the advantages against the disadvantages, including the cost of space used, amount of operator salary, the cost of changes in other procedures needed to adapt current operations (such as additional phone lines), the prospect of obsolescence of equipment and procedures and the need for tight control over input. The computer-related cliche known as GIGO—"garbage in, garbage out"—is true; no data processing method, automated or otherwise, is any better than the information fed into it.

After the decision to use a computer has been made, the broker should carefully plan the place for it when designing the interior floor plan. The reason is that the computer serves two functions. Not only does it have the capability to come up with answers and solutions in seconds or minutes that would take hours or days to compute with paper, pencil and human brain but it is great for public relations and is a superb piece of institutional advertising for the firm. The computer should be given a place of honor where customers and clients can see it, touch it and—if it is programmed for customer use—use it.

SELECTION OF EQUIPMENT

In choosing the appropriate computer the broker has several considerations. First, exactly what will the computer be expected to do? Second, is the cost within the broker's budget? Third, can all personnel learn to operate it easily?

Nothing is more frustrating to a broker or manager than to invest in a costly piece of equipment, only to have it gather dust in the storeroom because the sales staff refuses to use it. It may be too difficult to use or the language may be too complicated for salespeople to learn. Computers may speak either basic English or a mnemonic language. The latter requires less storage capacity but may be more difficult for users to learn than the basic English mode.

Economic Factors

It is always important to separate the value in dollars of any new equipment from the ego satisfaction its ownership brings. The latest ideas are not always the best; the most expensive gadget is not always the right one for a particular situation. Economic justification should always dominate the decision to purchase equipment. The broker must be certain the uses will be ultimately productive—not only in more information available from a computer, or faster and better copies from a copy machine, but in greater profits resulting from either larger business volume or lower costs.

Standardization

When ordering equipment one should always make certain it is standardized, both within one office and among other offices. If there are three typewriters, for example, each a different make with different type styles, it may be impossible for the broker to shift unfinished work or corrections from one typist to another.

THE BUDGET

Usually a broker has a set amount of capital with which to open an office and support the business through the first lean months. He or she must design the office and decide on the number of salespeople and the type of equipment, based on that capital amount. If, however, one has a predetermined idea of the type of office desired, as well as the possibility of obtaining the necessary amount of capital to realize those desires, one must still be aware of factors already discussed in this chapter. In that way, ideas and dreams can be converted into dollars. In either case, the broker is now at the point of measuring the capital available and apportioning it in the best way.

The NAR has promoted the use of a standard term, the *company dollar*. The NAR defines the company dollar as the amount that remains after subtracting all commissions from gross income. Gross income includes money earned from all sources: sales, appraisals, management fees, etc. Commissions include MLS fees as well as all commissions—the broker's own and those paid to salespeople and cooperating brokers. Even if the broker does not draw his or her own commissions but keeps them in the business account, the broker's commission should be deducted to calculate the company dollar.

A survey conducted by the Economics and Research Division of the NAR in 1985 indicates the distribution of gross income and the income and expenses of residential brokerage firms in the United States. (*See* Figure 5.3).

There is no doubt that the majority of real estate offices in this country do not operate on a budget, and the success stories, while heartwarming and inspirational, are exceptional. The following steps should be taken when setting up a budget:

1. Determine capital available to open the office and carry through for a set period of time.
2. Determine sources of income and forecast income based on current conditions.
3. Determine amount of operating expenses, both fixed and variable.
4. Create individual budgets for such main variables as advertising.

FIGURE 5.3   Distribution of Gross Income

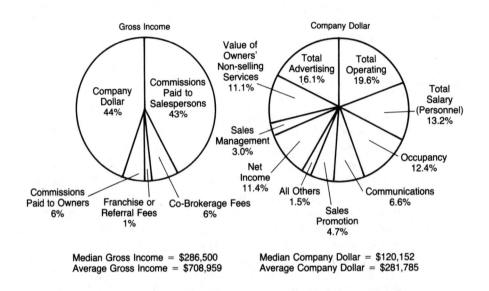

Median Gross Income = $286,500
Average Gross Income = $708,959

Median Company Dollar = $120,152
Average Company Dollar = $281,785

SOURCE: Economics and Research Division, NATIONAL ASSOCIATION OF REALTORS® *Real Estate Brokerage 1985: Income, Expenses, Profits* (Washington, DC: NAR, 1985), 8–10.

Capital

The amount of money the broker has available to set up the office determines if it is better to rent or to buy office space; to lease or to buy equipment; to hire one, two, or no secretaries. It also determines how much capital the broker should allocate for office expenses during the first few months. If one allows three months before the first transaction takes place and two months to close it, no income can be anticipated for five months. The broker must, therefore, have enough capital to cover opening costs and full operating costs for five months, as well as some funds to cover operating losses until income catches up with expenses. It is wise to be conservative when estimating income and expenses. Too often a business fails because of a broker's overoptimistic estimate of cash flow.

To cover an operating desk cost of $9,000 per year on a 50/50 split, each salesperson must bring in $1,500 of earned commissions each month. The broker must have funds available to make up the difference between the $750 monthly cost and what each salesperson actually brings in. It is wise to hold enough capital in reserve to cover operating costs for a period of at least six months. In a slow market, it is better to allow for even more. (*See* Figure 2.1 to project office expenses.)

Income

Although the main source of income in most real estate offices is from the sale and leasing of property, other sources also exist. Sources of income include commissions earned on sales, listings and leases; appraisal fees; insurance; speaking and instructor's fees; guaranteed sales program fees; title commissions and insurance commissions (where permitted); and management fees.

With no previous year in business by which to judge, a new broker can only estimate what he or she will earn from these sources; the guess can be fairly accurate if it is reduced to the time input necessary to achieve the desired income. Chapter 8 covers how a salesperson can earn his or her desired income through time planning and goal setting. If the broker discovers that the average salesperson's income, multiplied by the number of allocated desks, does not equal anticipated expenses, he or she must either increase staff or cut expenses.

Operating Expenses

Fixed operating expenses are easily determined, but the variable expenses require an intelligent estimate. The greatest single expense in most real estate offices is usually advertising; therefore, advertising is used here as an example of creating a budget. National surveys indicate that the advertising dollar spent in a real estate office may be as low as five percent of the company dollar or as high as 25 percent. In the average office it is around 16 percent. Not having a previous year's company-dollar figure to go by, the new broker has to rely on projections. Based on a projected gross income of $240,000, therefore, the company dollar may be in the range of $110,000:

$240,000	Gross income
130,000	Paid out in commissions and MLS fees
$110,000	Company dollar

This projection would be considered realistic for an office whose brokerage fee is six percent if total sales were $8 million. Assuming a 50/50 commission split, that yield would come from 100 transactions at an average sales price of $80,000.

Under some circumstances a broker may decide the advertising outlay should be high. A new office, for example, can benefit by advertising exposure. Unusual commercial activity, such as the influx of major industry, may also call for heavy advertising exposure. An average advertising outlay, however, would call for 16 percent of the company dollar, or $17,600, to be spent on advertising.

$$\$110,000 \times 0.16 = \$17,600 \div 100 = \$176/\text{transaction}$$

Assuming 100 transactions, this budget costs $176 per transaction. On the low side, or five percent of the company dollar, $5,500 would be required for advertising.

$$\$110,000 \times 0.05 = \$5,500 \div 100 = \$55/\text{transaction}$$

This budget costs $55 per transaction.

Keeping Records

The broker has two available methods of keeping financial records: the cash method and the accrual method. The decision of which method to use should be made by an accountant, with tax liabilities as a major consideration. The basic difference is that the cash method records income as it is received and disbursements when made, while the accrual method records income when earned and expenses when incurred. It is somewhat more complicated to set up accrual books, so most beginning firms operate under the cash system.

To keep track of how your budget is working, a simple yet effective group of bookkeeping records is required. These should be set up in conference with an accountant, since he or she will have to use the information for many purposes. It is suggested that the accountant be provided with a copy of the NAR "Financial Analysis," which can be obtained from the association. It provides a standardized method of classification of income and expenses. If records are kept using a matching breakdown, it will be possible to compare one's percentage of expenses in each category with those of other offices. Each salesperson's average income can also be matched with those of salespeople in other offices of similar size and type around the country. Statistical data are furnished by a large sample of REALTOR® offices that contribute information annually.

Once the expense categories are established and income categories are assigned, it is possible, by entering a coded identification number on each check written and on each deposit slip, to provide further information from which an accountant's computer service can prepare financial statements, balance sheets and profit-and-loss statements quickly and inexpensively. A sample bookkeeping system requires only a few types of records, including income, expenditures, accounts payable, payroll and commissions.

Record of income.   This information can be entered on a ledger page or in a checkbook register.

Record of payments.   A duplicate of the check or a carbon copy of the entries is sufficient.

Accounts payable.   In a file or book, one should list in one column all bills received and in a second column the date of payment. In this way the length of time a bill is unpaid can be easily ascertained. The sample in Figure 5.4 is drawn from a system where each account is kept on a separate page. In a small beginning office, this might not be necessary, depending on how many separate accounts are involved.

Payroll card.   The record should show gross and net salary as well as federal and state tax deductions for all employees (but not for independent contractors). From this record it is easy to fill out the necessary forms for forwarding quarterly tax payments.

Commission records.   These books should indicate the amounts of all commissions paid to each salesperson, with each transaction identified. They can also be used to record any temporary payments and reimbursements from salespeople for such items as business cards, dues or other fees. This is useful in establishing proof of the independent contractor relationship.

Trust accounts.   In most states commingling of business monies with escrow monies (money held in trust) is forbidden by law; even if it is not, however, it is wise to keep two separate accounts for these monies. In some states where it is required by law, setting up a trust account requires immediate attention, as the broker's records may be called for review without notice.

The minimum requirement for a trust account is that a record be kept of the names of the parties for whose benefit the trust account is created (in most instances a matched pair of seller and buyer or landlord and tenant), a notation of the date of receipt of any sum and a record of the date and manner of disbursement of the funds held in trust; this notation should include the check number and the name of the payee. The funds, of course, should be deposited in a checking account maintained especially for this purpose.

A simple but useful way to keep a trust account record is in a bound ledger that contains an indexed section followed by numbered pages with two columns for figures. Each escrow record may be established with minimum identification. There is no need, for example, to know the address of the property or the date of receipt of the escrow to find the account; the name of one of the parties will suffice.

FIGURE 5.4 A Sample Ledger Page

XYZ Coffee Service, Inc.
151 Hudson Street NY NY 10013   212-925-8607

	CHECKS PAID					INVOICES RECD.		
1988				1988				
Aug 19	6710	191 00	July 1	6710	Pd✓	42 70
Sept 2	6860	128 05	15	6710	Pd✓	34 50
Sept 30	7135	157 80	23	6710	Pd✓	77 50
Nov 9	7475	154 10	29	6710	Pd✓	36 30
Dec 5	7591	219 05	Aug 12	6860	Pd✓	4 30
Feb 24 (1989)	8169	323 30	20	6860	Pd✓	45 10
May 5	8727	281 25	26	6860	Pd✓	78 65
June 14	9046	450 55	Sept 9	7135	Pd✓	37 90
			18	7135	Pd✓	41 60
			29	7135	Pd✓	78 30
			Oct 7	7475	Pd✓	34 50
			13	7475	Pd✓	43 60
			21	7475	Pd✓	41 90
			29	7475	Pd✓	34 10
			Nov 4	7591	Pd✓	113 60
			12	7591	Pd✓	34 80
			18	7591	Pd✓	70 65
			25	8169	Pd✓	42 20
			Dec 4	8169	Pd✓	40 40
			12	8169	Pd✓	7 70
			19	8169	Pd✓	33 70
			30	8169	Pd✓	34 90
			Jan 13 (1989)	8169	Pd✓	77 30
			21	8169	Pd✓	38 10
			27	8169	Pd✓	49 60
			Feb 10	8727	Pd✓	8 10
			17	8727	Pd✓	38 35
			24	8727	Pd✓	34 20
			27	8727	Pd✓	77 80
			Mar 4	8727	Pd✓	17 70
			13	8727	Pd✓	75 00
			19	8727	Pd✓	30 10
			24	9046	Pd✓	63 50
			April 2	9046	Pd✓	31 20
			7	9046	Pd✓	42 25
			20	9046	Pd✓	43 60
			28	9046	Pd✓	25 80

Useful Economies

Keeping costs down in a real estate office can be a real challenge, especially when the size of the office and the number of salespeople reaches a proportion where control seems impossible. The following are a few ideas on how to avoid waste.

Phones.   Salespeople should avoid making outgoing personal calls. Each call on a business phone costs company money, whereas the same call made on a residence phone would not. Family or friends should be asked to call in if necessary. A patch-in system for incoming calls can relay calls to the salesperson at home if he or she is not in the office. This economy saves twice. It saves the cost of returning the call and the time required by the salesperson who fields the call to relay the message.

Advertising.   Ads should be charted to keep track of calls received. In this way ads that do not pull can be revised. Each classified ad should be carefully checked for errors and "widows" (one or two letters alone on a line), as newspapers usually will give credit for these mistakes. The number of lines in the classified ad should be counted and compared with the linage charge on the bill. There will be more advice on how to do this quickly and easily in the chapter on advertising, but it is sufficient for now to report that one of the authors has saved more than $200 in some months in credits for errors.

Supplies.   Lawn signs, frames, stakes and lockboxes can be costly if not returned to the office when no longer needed on the property. A sign-in and sign-out sheet, controlled by the secretary, will keep track of where these items are; the salesperson can then be reminded to return them.

MISCELLANEOUS CONSIDERATIONS

A few other things should be considered before one throws open the door to a new office.

Licensing requirements.   Although all 50 states require licensing of salespeople and brokers, specific requirements differ in each state. Additional minimum legal requirements to open an office vary from state to state. Brokers are advised to check the requirements of their particular state. Certain information must be posted. This may include minimum wage rates for employees, existence of workers' compensation insurance coverage and civil rights and equal housing opportunity notices for the public.

Contracts with managers, salespeople and others. Whether one maintains the independent contractor relationship or the employer-employee relationship, a contract with each person should be signed. In the case of the independent contractor, a contract is essential; it is one of the criteria the IRS needs to establish the relationship. It is incumbent on each broker to be familiar with those state rules that govern his or her license. Contracts with managers detailing their responsibilities are also a good idea.

Office inspections. Inspections of the office are often required by state regulations or by local boards of REALTORS® before the business can open.

Certificate of occupancy. This document certifies compliance with local building codes and zoning ordinances.

Policy manual. While not required by law, it is highly advisable that an office policy and procedures manual be ready at the time a real estate brokerage office is opened.

Legal contacts. Because our society has become very litigious, brokers constantly face potential lawsuits, frequently over matters that, until recently, were not even considered to be within the realm of a broker's responsibility. However, times have changed. Even though the wise broker suggests to buyers that they retain an attorney and have an expert of their choice inspect the property (usually structural and termite inspections, but more recently inspections for toxic waste and radon gas), should a problem arise, the broker often finds himself or herself involved in a lawsuit. It is wise for brokers to retain good attorneys that they and their salespeople can call on for sound legal advice on short notice.

Insurance Coverage Needed

Insurance coverage is a major cost item in operating a brokerage business. The cost of each type of coverage should be weighed against the risk factors that are to be protected against. If the broker is not personally qualified as a licensed insurance agent (many real estate licensees are), it is wise to establish a relationship with a qualified agent. The relationship can provide new business for the broker as well as necessary advice about insurance. The broker should always be frank with his or her insurance counselor as to available funds to get good advice about priorities. Some coverage is required, some essential, some advisable and some nice to have if one can afford it.

Workers' compensation, frequently required by state law, provides staff members with protection against loss for injuries sustained on the job. Many states require either disability insurance for staff or payment into a state fund. In the case of workers' compensation, all employees and independent contractors must be included. Disability coverage, which pays for time lost from work for any illness or injury (job-related or not), is required only for employees.

Liability insurance, which comes in many forms and variations, is legally optional but really essential. Automobile liability is the most common. The broker should insist that each associate carry an adequate amount. In today's economy, minimum coverage should be $100,000/ $300,000—meaning $100,000 per person with a total of $300,000 per accident. The broker, who usually has the greatest exposure to loss, can get an "umbrella" policy, which provides protection over and above that of each associate in the event an accident occurs in an associate's car. Liability coverage can also be obtained covering injuries to clients or customers on the broker's premises.

Other desirable forms of protection include fire and comprehensive coverage for equipment; records replacement coverage; business interruption insurance; glass breakage; hospitalization, including medical, dental and major medical coverage; and errors and omission coverage.

Errors and omission coverage is highly desirable as protection against lawsuits for mistakes made in the course of business. It protects the broker and the sales staff from claims. In addition to the financial protection afforded, it is an important item in attracting and retaining a top-level sales staff.

Hospitalization insurance in many forms, errors and omission coverage and life insurance and disability income protection insurance are available at reduced cost through REGIT, the Real Estate Group Insurance Trust of the NAR, and through many state and local REALTORS® group insurance programs.

Establishing Bank Connections

Once a salesperson becomes a broker, he or she ceases to work under the direction of a manager or broker who can serve as a referral to the best source for the particular type of financing needed. The new broker then must establish his or her own connections. This action helps assure that mortgage money will be available to finance those properties sold through the office.

The new broker can begin by listing all sources within the market area, breaking them down generally into three categories: savings and loans, commercial banks and mortgage brokers. Of course, there are many more types of banks, as well as insurance companies, pension funds, and so forth, that lend money for real estate financing, just as there are numerous types of financing available through these lending sources. These tools will be discussed in detail in Chapter 12. The broker needs to get to know and be known by those persons in the surrounding area who will be instrumental in financing properties sold by the firm. The best way to accomplish this is for the broker to visit each of these banks and meet personally the president, vice president or whoever else is in authority. In larger banks the mortgage officer will usually be the most direct contact. Mortgage brokerage companies, on the other hand, have field representatives to cover designated areas. These representatives are usually available on short notice to answer the broker's financing questions as well as to pay regular visits to the offices and, when necessary, meet with buyers to fill out mortgage applications and offer advice on the method of financing.

It is usually advisable to use many financing sources rather than one. In tight money markets, some banks and mortgage companies dry up; the broker's chances of getting financing from other sources that might have some cash fluidity are slim if the broker has never done business with them before. Depending on locality, the broker might also find that some banks are not knowledgeable about government-secured loans, such as FHA and VA, or privately insured mortgages, such as MGIC. Where this is true, mortgages are better processed through a mortgage company. On the other hand, service charges on mortgages obtained through mortgage brokers are sometimes higher than those obtained through banks.

It is important to determine, therefore, in choosing a financial source the crucial opening phase of a brokerage business, whom the broker's contact will be, what services are offered and how competitive one source is with another. Since lending institutions vary in rates of interest and required down payments, as well as in the terms of a loan, these data should be kept available in the office for salespeople's use. They should be constantly updated because they change so quickly.

Another important reason to establish bank connections is so the broker can obtain a *line of credit,* a prearranged commitment by a bank to advance up to a specific amount of money to a borrower as requested. Therefore, while visiting these sources of mortgage money, the broker should also make certain that he or she meets with whoever can assist in this regard. A line of credit will enable the broker to get through low cash periods as well as make money available for worthwhile investment opportunities.

Establishing an Identity in the Community

The broker's personal involvement in the community probably does more to establish his or her identity than any other single thing. Creating this identity costs time or money, depending on the chosen vehicle. In many cases, it will cost both. It is important, therefore, for the broker to remain in control of the situation. One should never become involved just because, when asked to do something, one did not know how to say no. It is also important that whatever the broker does is done to the very best of his or her ability and with sincerity. If the broker does a poor job, or does something because of what he or she can get out of it, it will show and it will destroy any potential goodwill. Although most brokers probably will want to lend moral and financial support to good causes in the market area, each one should choose to become actively involved in only those things that he or she wants to do, and limit involvement to no more interests than may be adequately handled.

Some services a broker may render to the community include participation in chambers of commerce; fund drives; political or religious organizations; the League of Women Voters; PTA; groups such as Rotary, Kiwanis, Lions or Optimists; local planning boards; baseball teams; Red Cross; rehabilitation of neighborhoods; Meals on Wheels; hospital aid groups—the list is endless.

Another way to establish identity as a knowledgeable leader in the community is through publicity releases, personal appearances and community education through direct mail newsletters or newspaper columns. The latter will be covered in Chapter 10, on advertising and promotion.

SUMMARY

When it comes to the actual start of business, considerable thought and planning should go into organizing and opening one's office.

The first thing to consider is whether one wants eventually to have a large operation or to remain small. Pros and cons of each side of this question have been discussed thoroughly, so the prospective broker should have most of the information needed to make an informed decision.

One should thoroughly understand the real estate sales process as presented in this chapter because it is the basis from which all operating decisions are made.

Location, market identification strategies and planning of the office itself are areas that probably will require the help of outside experts to make the right decisions. Today, one can find firms that specialize in advertising, marketing and space planning and that offer excellent professional perspectives to help make some serious selections, if engaged.

Because computers are becoming a necessary and integral part of real estate business operations, it is important that the prospective broker start his or her office planning with all the latest computer capabilities. Computers are so adaptable to the real estate business that a broker is remiss today in not using them.

Another extremely important aspect of sensible business planning is the budgetary process. So much information is available from professional real estate organizations today that one has no excuse for not knowing how to prepare and follow a *realistic* budget. Emphasis is placed on the term *realistic* because that is where so many businesses fail, by not being realistic enough.

Other considerations in establishing a viable operation are the careful selection of banking connections, professional insurance and accounting firms and community-based organizations to join for personal involvement.

DISCUSSION QUESTION

Visit a real estate brokerage office in your area and ask the broker if you can make a sketch of the layout. Then bring the layout plan back to class and discuss it with the other members of the class. After such discussions try to choose the one office that best suits the needs of the business.

6 No-Nonsense Sales Management

INTRODUCTION

A common misconception when one starts a brokerage business is that all one has to do after opening the office doors is to let it be known that one now has openings for sales associates; to engage anyone who applies; and then to sit back and reap the rewards of one's efforts.

Not so. If it were as simple as that there would be no need for the job classification of sales manager. If one thinks the job of sales manager is somewhat superfluous in an organization, that opinion may change considerably after reading this chapter, because the day the broker engages the firm's first sales associate is the day he or she becomes a sales manager, like it or not! Sales management may be defined as *the ability to attain predetermined company sales goals through the studied direction of other people's efforts.*

A good sales manager should be able to motivate sales associates to perform tasks that they might not do if left to their own resources. A real estate sales manager's job description might read: "to recruit, select, train, supervise, motivate, retain and (sometimes) terminate real estate sales associates."

Sales managers have distinct and important responsibilities. In fact, the sales manager of any organization with something to sell may well be the most important person in that operation. In real estate especially, without a sales manager there can be no planned, organized or systematic sales production effort—only scattered and sporadic individual attempts by sales associates to list and sell property with little direction, motivation or guidance.

THE REAL ESTATE SALES MANAGER

When a brokerage firm grows to the point where the broker can no longer handle all the tasks required to manage a sales force, it becomes necessary to add a sales manager to the staff. This frees the broker to spend more time on other important activities, such as office administration and the general management duties that can include future growth planning, personal production and community involvement or public relations, as well as the task of developing a personal investment portfolio.

This transformation from broker/sales manager to administrative broker generally takes place around the ten-sales-associate level.

What It Takes

Just because a person has set an exemplary record as a salesperson, it does not mean that he or she will necessarily be a good sales manager. The attributes of a successful sales manager are altogether different from those required for successful selling. For example, most good sales types are very poor at maintaining detailed records; a sales manager must be able to supervise the production and maintenance of sales records to track production. Successful salespersons also are often notorious for underestimating the problems that can arise in a transaction; a sales manager must be constantly on the alert for developing problems that will cause a headache further along in the transaction.

The sales manager's role should be supportive and strong without coddling, a role that sometimes is difficult to maintain. A sales manager must be able diplomatically to point out some of the legal and ethical implications that an associate may be facing, without constantly throwing cold water on the sales associate's enthusiasm for a possible sale.

In other words, a sales manager must be stern but understanding; helpful but not dictatorial; highly knowledgeable regarding real estate matters but not imperious about it; and, finally, patient with ineptness and what sometimes appear to be idiotic questions, avoiding caustic and sarcastic remarks at all times.

Basic Functions

The sales manager in a real estate office should function somewhat like the coach of a football team. It is his or her responsibility to develop a team that will work together harmoniously as a group. Yet the sales manager should be able to recognize the idiosyncrasies, peculiar talents, weaknesses and strengths of each team member.

It is a wise policy for the broker who is acting as sales manager to watch the people in the sales force for any signs of leadership ability; for someone who can assume the position of sales management as the firm thrives and grows.

Good sales managers do not compete with sales associates. The sales manager who is required to contribute a certain amount of personal production should limit it to the minimum needed and confine it only to those who have specifically requested the manager. Nothing disrupts and discourages a sales force more quickly than a sales manager or broker who grabs all the best leads and listings before others have a chance at them.

Specific tasks include recruiting, training, setting goals, motivating and evaluating salespeople's performance.

Recruiting.   The sales manager should be able to recruit promising sales associates who have the necessary selling ability and will fit comfortably into the organization. Recruitment and selection techniques are discussed in Chapter 7.

Training.   One of the sales manager's most important functions is training. Some larger companies consider this function so important they employ a training officer or consultant solely for this task. If the sales manager does a good job of training, the duties of supervising, retaining and motivating salespeople will be much easier. Through proper training the sales manager should be able to encourage sales associates not to consult the manager at every turn, thus making the associate more self-reliant in handling everyday transactions. Good training also dramatically reduces the need for terminating associates.

To train associates properly, the sales manager must be able to impart three kinds of knowledge—technical knowledge, product knowledge and marketing knowledge. In addition, the sales manager needs a good background in management. Chapter 8 covers this technical, product and marketing knowledge in detail and shows how all three are combined in the training process.

Setting realistic goals.   Goal setting is a primary function of any manager. However, before the manager can help associates set their own personal goals, he or she must know what the company goals are. With this knowledge the manager can "orchestrate" staff members so as to generate the production needed to attain company goals. If the staff's production falls short of the company's goals, three things must be considered: The company goals might not be realistic and might have to be adjusted, more sales help might be required to raise the level of production or the manager might not be generating the maximum production of which the staff is capable.

One way to encourage top production is for the manager to guide each associate into working in the certain field or locality that is best suited to that person's skills. It might be something as general as recommending a particular neighborhood in which the associate lives or is successful in selling or it might be as specific as convincing the associate to concentrate on the type of real estate sales for which he or she has shown a particular talent. For example, a sales associate who was reared on a farm probably would be well suited to farm brokerage; one who has sold industrial supplies might find success in selling industrial property.

Motivating. There are different opinions about whether one person can truly motivate another. Certain types of motivating techniques are discussed later in this chapter. Sales meetings, however, provide a frequent opportunity for motivating. At the very least, a first-rate sales manager must be able to conduct meetings that are so interesting and educational that the associates feel that they cannot afford to miss them. Such sales meetings take time and effort to prepare; they should not be treated lightly by either managers or associates.

Evaluating. Accurate records of the listings and sales that associates are producing will ensure that both manager and staff know each person's output. The manager should prepare and use a listing production form, a sales production form, a sales associate progress sheet and a company monthly recap of production. Samples of these forms appear later in this chapter. If necessary, the sales manager must also be able to perform the distasteful task of terminating those sales associates who do not show an aptitude for the work. These records are essential before making this final decision.

Compensation

The sales manager's title and description of duties virtually ensures his or her employee status in the eyes of the IRS. Because this is the case, the broker must be prepared to withhold taxes, pay the employer's share of the Social Security tax, and provide disability insurance. With employer status, however, the broker gains the privilege of directing the manager's work and demanding certain standards of work habits. The individual must then be compensated accordingly by the broker. There are a number of methods of compensation; each broker should choose the most appropriate use for the company's form of operation.

Salary only. The main drawback of this arrangement is the lack of incentive for the sales manager to keep increasing production.

Override of sales associates' commissions. This payment may be based on a percentage either of the gross commission (before the associates' shares are deducted) or of the net company dollar. It is wise to base any override on a percentage of the *net profits,* to ensure the sales manager's awareness that his or her compensation is directly related to the expenses involved. For instance, a sales manager who is only expected to build volume without regard to net profits might run up some astronomical advertising expenses while building that volume.

Here is how an override plan works: If the broker pays five percent of a gross income of, say, $250,000, the sales manager would earn five percent of the $250,000, or $12,500. If the override is ten percent of the company dollar and the broker is on a 50/50 split, the compensation would be based on one half of $250,000, that is, ten percent of $125,000, or $12,500. The type of override used depends on the commission split arrangement with sales associates. The sales manager's compensation rises with office productivity.

Salary plus override.   The sales manager working under this plan has the best of two worlds. He or she is assured of a salary large enough to take care of living expenses, while also receiving an incentive to increase the production of the sales force.

Sales commissions plus percentage.   A selling sales manager or branch office manager might be allowed to earn the same commission as an associate but be additionally rewarded with a percentage of the profits from that office. (A 50-percent split with a branch office manager is not unusual.) Here again, the sales manager is cautioned not to run up expenses.

Commission plus override.   This method is similar to the previous one. The sales manager is allowed to list and sell in competition with the associates but is also responsible for assisting the associates, for which an override is paid commensurate with ability and the time spent. Because providing a sales manager is the responsibility of the broker or company, any override should come out of the company's share of the commissions.

TECHNIQUES FOR MOTIVATING SALES ASSOCIATES

Motive can be defined as an emotion or desire operating on the will and causing action. The sales manager as motivator creates and nurtures an emotion or desire in the associate that causes the associate to act.

Talk of motivating generally calls up pictures of pep talks, sales rallies or counseling sessions. While these motivational techniques are effective for a short period of time, they do not sustain a salesperson indefinitely. Internal motivators seem to be the most effective and longest-lasting kind;

the sales manager must recognize the forces that motivate each particular salesperson, and then stimulate that internal motivator to encourage increased production.

The noted psychologist Abraham Maslow propounded the theory that all human beings have specific basic needs that motivate them.

Survival—the need for food, clothing, and shelter;

Security—the need to be safe and secure and to provide for future security;

Belonging—the need to be accepted and loved and to belong to a certain stratum of society;

Esteem and prestige—the need to be looked up to by one's peers;

Self-fulfillment—the need to have lasting and creative goals and to realize one's fullest potential.

Maslow's theory, very simply stated, was that as a person satisfies one level of need, he or she has an urge to progress upward to satisfy the next level. In other words, as a person satisfies the immediate survival needs of food, clothing and a place to live, he or she will then begin to look around for some means of providing safety and security. With that need satisfied he or she will then become interested in belonging to the community by taking part in church work, lodges and clubs or professional organizations.

In relation to real estate selling, people who are satisfied with fulfilling only their immediate survival needs do not make good salespeople. It takes an inner motivation to satisfy the more sophisticated needs that spur a person to greater accomplishments.

Maslow and other psychologists who promote his theories say that a person tends to strive to fulfill the lowest unmet need. Among such professionals as real estate brokers, only a few continue trying to research and do extended studies on the many unknown areas of the profession. Nevertheless, there is much to learn. It is safe to say that no one has learned all there is to know about real estate—or anything else, for that matter.

The sales manager's role in this process is to assess each associate's needs and help him or her progress from one level to the next. This can be done by helping associates plan their personal investing for future security; by pointing out the advantages and opportunities of joining certain civic clubs and real estate organizations; by encouraging participation in quasi-governmental activities (for example, planning commissions, zoning boards and economic advisory committees) or even encouraging them to run for public office.

Empathy and Ego-Drive as Motivators

The salesperson who needs to feel a sense of belonging to the organization and to be well liked by colleagues and customers alike invariably displays a great deal of empathy toward both.

Herbert M. Greenberg and Ronald L. Bern conducted extensive studies of what motivates successful salespeople for their book *The Successful Salesman* (1972). They found that successful salespersons displayed much more than the average amount of empathy and ego-drive. If we relate these findings to Maslow's hierarchy-of-needs theory, it would seem that the desire to belong, be liked and be respected is evidenced by an intense display of empathy by the more successful. In addition, the ego-drive syndrome suggests that people who have a stronger-than-average need to succeed are the ones who sell more property and close more difficult transactions to win the approval of their peers. This satisfies the need for esteem and prestige.

Goals and Quotas as Motivators

Firms that keep in close consultation with their associates and help them set goals are generally the best producers. A firm that has an independent contractor relationship with its associates, however, cannot require them to meet any specific sales goals or earnings quotas because that indicates too much control. Nevertheless, there is still no reason brokers cannot at least counsel associates and help them set their own nonmandatory production goals. Sales associates may be more highly motivated by *receiving attention,* rather than being left strictly on their own.

Sales goals affect the lives of everyone in the organization—the rate of growth the company sustains, and sometimes even its future existence, depends on meeting these goals. Goals must be monitored to enable the broker to project future earnings. In addition, goals provide standards by which performance may be evaluated. The chart in Figure 6.1 shows how to determine the sales goals for a given period by adding up the goals of all associates and projecting the total as the company's objective. This chart is based on a 50/50 commission split between sales associates and the company, so that the total of the bottom lines for the associates equals the bottom line for the company (at the lower right-hand corner). For different splits the company's share must be adjusted proportionately.

The Personal Success Plan

Another form of goal setting is known as personal success planning. Most people talk vaguely about becoming successful but few make the specific plans needed to attain success, nor do they set up a sequence of minor

FIGURE 6.1   Annual Company Production Goals, 1989–1990

Name	1st Quarter 1989 Actual	1st Quarter 1990 Goal	2nd Quarter 1989 Actual	2nd Quarter 1990 Goal	Total Year 1989 Actual	Total Year 1990 Goal
FORD	3,500		4,700		21,850	
		6,000		6,000		24,000
SMITH	7,500		3,250		20,950	
		5,500		5,500		22,000
ADAIN	4,500		5,100		24,000	
		7,000		7,000		28,000
DINKEL	6,800		7,200		34,000	
		10,000		10,000		40,000
FRANKS	4,200		3,600		16,800	
		4,000		4,000		18,000
RIGGS	8,700		7,600		37,100	
		10,000		10,000		40,000
KEAST	12,600		0		39,800	
		10,000		10,000		40,000
JONES	650		210		6,035	
		1,000		2,000		10,000
COSTA	4,700		3,300		25,600	
		5,000		5,000		22,000
BOWERS	0		3,000		13,000	
		6,000		6,000		24,000
COMPANY		64,500		65,500	239,139	268,000

objectives they hope to accomplish on the road to their major goal. To obtain a broker's license in almost any state today requires completion of additional courses of study and passing difficult examinations. The attainment of a broker's license could be a highly worthwhile step in any associate's plan. All nine of the NAR's societies, institutes and councils now offer courses of study and other requirements leading to a professional designation in a specific field—these are desirable goals for any ambitious associate.

Further, it can be shown that going through a rigorous regime of study is beneficial to anyone in the business, even those who do not aspire to become brokers. Salespeople everywhere can and should make a determined effort to take as many educational courses as are available because the technical and marketing knowledge they gain eventually leads to higher income. Fortunately, many salespeople do follow such a plan on their way to success.

The sales manager can help the new associate become organized for success by selecting meaningful personal objectives and establishing a timetable and a method for achieving these objectives. In the same way the sales manager may also aid those individuals who once showed promise but now are foundering.

MEETINGS THAT MATTER

The term *sales meeting* is often misunderstood. Actually the term is used to describe three separate and distinct intended functions: The sales meeting motivates by imparting marketing knowledge, the staff meeting informs by giving product knowledge and the training meeting increases technical knowledge.

Some meetings, of course, may contain elements of all three functions. Others may be divided into three separate segments, depending on the broker's choice and the time available.

Sales Meetings

The function of sales meetings is to motivate by imparting marketing knowledge. Sales contests, sales rallies, motivational speakers, information on latest techniques and discussion of goals and quotas all are excellent methods for motivating associates. Sales meetings should be used as a means for improving marketing knowledge.

Staff Meetings

Staff meetings are usually employed to improve the product knowledge of associates. This is done by sharing knowledge with them about new listings, discussing the latest information about recent sales and imparting knowledge about changing financing conditions and other developments. These meetings may or may not include caravan tours of new listings.

Training Meetings

While training's main purpose is to develop the technical knowledge of inexperienced sales associates, it is also used to provide continuing education for more seasoned associates or for management trainees. Meetings should be structured to discuss the many tools available in real estate marketing and to develop ways to use them efficiently.

Training means and methods are discussed in considerably more detail in Chapter 8.

How to Plan Meetings for Maximum Benefits

As with all meetings, there are four important points to keep in mind:

1. Do not schedule the meetings so they conflict with other events the associates must attend, such as board functions and MLS tours.

2. Carefully prepare an interesting and informative agenda ahead of time to ensure a willing and receptive audience.

3. Be prompt; start the meetings at the agreed time.

4. Do not let the meetings drag on too long! A long meeting is not necessarily a successful meeting—any meeting lasting more than one hour had better be highly necessary or informative. Training meetings, however, frequently run several hours or even all day.

The days and hours the broker should choose to hold meetings are naturally those best suited to each specific type of operation and section of the country. However, one might consider Monday or Thursday mornings at either eight or nine o'clock as logical times, depending upon local conditions, accessibility of the meeting place and the weather. Monday morning is good because it gets associates out of bed and to the office early on the first day of the week. While independent contractors cannot be required to attend, they will want to attend if they can see that the meetings are provided for their benefit. Another reason for Monday meetings is that weekends are generally the busiest time for people in residential sales; showings, open houses and listing appointments are all best held on weekends when all prospects may participate. On Monday morning salespeople can bring their new listings and sales contracts to the office for discussion and processing. Monday is also a good day for the new-listing caravan.

Thursday is also a good day. Sales associates can coordinate their plans for the weekend in regard to who will hold which home open for inspection and who will take office floor time; they can get ads in the open-house section of the newspapers for the Saturday and Sunday editions.

A Suggested Meeting Format

Combining elements of the ideal meeting, the following sequence is by no means the only meeting format, but it is suggested for a start.

First, the sales manager calls upon associates to present their newly negotiated sales contracts and exclusive listings, allowing listing salespeople a few minutes to describe the property and then answer any questions that fellow salespeople may ask. The manager then reviews the contracts for the assembled associates. This review, along with some sort of daily "flash" bulletin, such as the one illustrated in Figure 6.2, serves to inform associates immediately of all new developments: listings acquired overnight or over the weekend, changes in prices or terms, expiration or renewal of current listings, which properties have been sold, who bought them, who sold them, the prices for which they were sold and the terms of the sale. If there are any questions about customers or splitting commissions, this may be the time and place to bring them up. By reading the contracts, the sales manager also reveals prices and terms the sellers found acceptable, which may be valuable information in pricing other listings in the same neighborhood. Sometimes the contracts have contingencies written into them that must be met before the sale can be officially consummated, such as "subject to the undersigned buyers qualifying for and obtaining a maximum FHA loan." In cases where there is any doubt that the purchaser can obtain the specified financing or meet other contingencies, associates should be encouraged to bring in backup offers. Board and MLS regulations and state laws should be checked first because they sometimes prohibit presenting a second offer.

Finally, the sales manager focuses on financial information, reading any news articles, news releases, local board of REALTORS® announce-

FIGURE 6.2   Sample "Flash" Listing Notice

```
                              ! ! ! FLASH ! ! !

Sellers _____      ____ New listing _____ % _____ / ____
Full names _____      ____ Dabo @ _____
Prop. address _____      ____ BOM _____
Price _____ Phone no. ____     ____ Price reduced to $ _____
BR _____ Bath _____ Type ____      ____ Listing extended to _____
Buyers name _____      ____ Sign*
Listing office _____      Source of buyer:
   Salesperson _____         Sign (subject property) _____
   Selling office _____          Sign (other) _____
   Salesperson _____         Ad (subject property) _____
Inception date _____         Ad (other) _____
Expiration date _____
Flashed by _____  to _____ at _____ Office
```

ments or letters from banks or financing agencies. These matters may pertain to the money market and involve such issues as interest rate changes, point charges and policy changes.

Following a Monday morning meeting the sales force may visit the new listings in a caravan for a few hours. Following a Thursday morning meeting, a motivational speaker may be invited or experienced salespeople may be asked to provide an hour's training session for the new people. The training portion of the sales meetings will be covered in a subsequent chapter. When appropriate, an update on any sales contests or goals should be incorporated into the meetings.

Ideas for keeping sales meetings interesting and refreshing are found in many sources. These sources include trade magazines, such as *Real Estate Today,* and books that are written specifically to provide sales meeting formats.

EVALUATING PERFORMANCE

To properly evaluate performance, a manager should have an understanding of why some salespeople fail while others succeed. Criteria for evaluating, along with record keeping, are also necessary.

Turnover and Termination

Real estate salespeople may leave an office for many reasons, including:

1. Insufficient organization and office system of the broker;
2. Move to a more promising area;
3. Too much competition from the broker;
4. Insufficient assistance from the broker;
5. Conflict with the broker or other salespeople;
6. Lack of integrity on the part of the broker;
7. Inadequate commission scale;
8. Conflict with family activities;
9. Insufficient training; and
10. Insufficient earning potential.

Seven of the ten above reasons are under the broker's direct control; possibly another one of the reasons might qualify. All in all, the list gives a good background as to what it takes to retain sales associates.

Why Salespeople Fail

One of the most significant reasons for failure is the broker's selection of a salesperson who is unsuited to the field. Some people are simply uncomfortable with selling because they have a *low level of natural aggression.* The desire to make money is not sufficient to ensure an agent's success. Agents must have an affinity for selling, along with a natural interest in real estate. Without these traits, they will never be really proficient selling real estate—or anything else.

Going beyond that point, many sales hopefuls cannot communicate well. Since selling is a persuasive art, a salesperson must be able to communicate the advantage of a product and be able to persuade the customer to buy it. Unless salespeople learn how to communicate properly, their days in sales are limited.

Many salespeople do not learn from their experiences. An agent who makes 100 unproductive sales calls should have 100 experiences from which to learn something. Unfortunately, these 100 failures often represent only one experience repeated 99 times.

Another reason why salespeople fail is that they lack a personal success plan. They talk about success but do not actually go to the trouble of making the necessary plans to achieve that success.

To increase the likelihood of retaining salespeople, a broker should:

1. Make sure the right people are selected and that they are coming into the business for the right reasons;

2. Make sure selected associates can communicate effectively; and

3. Make sure the associates form correct working habits, including setting sales goals and personal success planning objectives.

Criteria for Evaluation: The MAP

Criteria to measure each individual's production relate to the desk cost of the firm in which he or she operates. Desk cost, calculated by dividing the total expenses of the firm by the number of salespeople, does not include a profit margin. A sales associate who merely returns his or her desk cost is not producing a profit for the broker.

To determine whether an associate is producing a profit, the broker must establish the MAP (*minimum average production*) needed from each sales associate. In other words, the broker takes his or her desk cost and adds a percentage that represents the *minimum profit* expected from the operation, then divides that figure by the number of associates. The resultant figure represents the MAP, which is then compared with the sales associate's actual production record.

A sales associate who consistently produces less than the required MAP is considered as *below average,* or type 1. The sales associate who barely meets his or her MAP may be considered an *average,* or type 2, producer. An associate who consistently exceeds his or her MAP may be considered *above average,* or type 3. One who consistently exceeds the minimum required by a wide margin is a *superstar,* or type 4.

If an associate exceeds his or her MAP by a considerable amount, the broker or the company may decide to allow that person to share in the overage. As pointed out previously, if sales associates are on independent contracts, theoretically they may not be rewarded with such incentives as bonuses, overrides or sliding-scale commission splits. It would seem that the IRS should look on the broker and sales associate as partners and should agree that as partners they might logically split profits that accrue over and above operating costs. However, it is strongly advised that a broker consult with a tax accountant before instituting such a bonus system. If a broker has been advised that this type of bonus system will not jeopardize the high producer's independent contractor status, then it is probably worthwhile to reward the above-average and the superstar associates for producing more than the required MAP.

For example, suppose the annual budget is $360,000, including the sales manager's expenses as well as *a profit on the broker's investment* and, further, suppose there are ten sales associates. Dividing ten "desks" into $360,000 gives a MAP of $36,000 per associate or $3,000 per month per associate. If an above-average associate on a 50/50 split takes home $20,000 and produces $20,000 for the broker, a logical step would be to pay that associate a bonus of $1,000 as his or her half share of the profit. This amount represents half of the excess of this person's MAP. Both parties would thus prosper from the associate's extended efforts.

To install such a system of incentive payment, the broker must be able to answer these three questions:

1. Are the records adequate to establish operating costs, desk costs and, finally, the MAP? (In a new business the broker must devise a realistic budget that can be revised and updated from time to time.)
2. Are there accurate records on each sales associate's production?
3. Which sales associates are type 1, 2, 3 or 4?

If a sales associate is below average, a type 1, the broker must decide whether there is any chance of bringing his or her production up to type 2 level or whether the only alternative is to terminate that individual. In most cases it is not wise to give up on the type 1 too quickly. It may take some individuals a year or two to prove their ability. If the associate is type 2, the broker must ask whether installation of the suggested incentive plan might increase the associate's production.

For a type 3 or 4 associate the broker should anticipate whether the suggested incentive plan is enough to retain that associate or whether any offer short of an ownership interest will retain the superstar. If not, and if the broker does not wish to relinquish any ownership status, he or she must be prepared to lose the superstars.

Keeping Records for Evaluation

To determine whether the company is making any progress toward the attainment of its goal (making a profit), it is absolutely necessary for the broker and/or sales manager to have an accurate measurement of the results of sales efforts. Standardized forms should be provided to each associate to measure production and compare actual production with the goals that were set. The sample reports in Figures 6.3 through 6.6 are reprinted with permission from the workbook for *Real Estate Office Administration,* a course developed by Dave Conger, MAI, for the State of California Department of Real Estate in 1976. Unfortunately that workbook is not available to the general practitioner; it was prepared solely for the use of instructors teaching that course in the community colleges of California.

Although standardized forms are the basis for good record keeping, the broker cannot require independent contractors to file regular call reports such as might be required from an employee. One alternative is to incorporate a production report into an expense account form to be turned in weekly or monthly when the associate seeks reimbursement. Information requested should include number of listings for each period and their total value; results in sales or deposits accepted also should be shown. The manager then uses a form to recap listing production, as shown in the example in Figure 6.3, summarizing the totals for all associates.

Sales production figures can be recapped similarly in a form such as the one shown in Figure 6.4.

Aggressive, self-motivated sales associates are not usually willing record keepers by nature. They would rather be out getting listings and closing sales than filling out reports about them. These salespeople, however, are likely to welcome standardized forms that help them keep accurate track of income and expenses when tax time comes around, especially if an IRS audit is a possibility. Inventory sheets such as Figures 6.5 and 6.6 will probably inspire their cooperation; Figure 6.5 summarizes monthly activity and Figure 6.6 compares goals to actual production. The daily activity log shown in Figure 6.7 also should be readily available; all associates should be expected to contribute to the log when on floor time.

FIGURE 6.3   Listing Production and Results

NAME	PRODUCTION					RESULTS	
	Listings To	Listings This Month	Total This Year	Total Value of Listings	% of Total Office Listings	Deposit or Sold	(% Deposit) (or Sold)
1.				$	%		(%)
2.							(%)
3.							(%)
4.							(%)
5.							(%)
6.							(%)
7.							(%)
8.							(%)
9.							(%)
10.							(%)
11.							(%)
12.							(%)

How Much Time Do You Give an Associate To Become Productive?

This is a difficult question to answer. Some associates are fast learners and become highly productive within a very short time but some of those on the so-called fast track tend to "burn out" at an early date; they either drop out of the business or move on to become brokers and open their own offices.

Other associates may be much slower in learning the art of making money in brokerage but have a tendency to stay with one office and become loyal producers for many years.

It appears that even the slowest learner should not take more than a year to reach his or her MAP. An associate who cannot become fully productive and carry his or her share of the necessary production in that space of time should be asked to leave; it is not fair to either the associate or the broker to continue with such an unprofitable relationship.

FIGURE 6.4   Sales Production

NAME	Deposit To	Deposit This Month	Total Account Deposit	Account Deposit That Fell	Net Account Deposit	Gross Volume	Co-op Volume	Net Volume
Date _____								
1.						$	$	$
2.								
3.								
4.								
5.								
6.								
7.								
8.								
19_____ 19_____ TOTALS						$	$	$
cc: Manager Secy.								

PERSONNEL PROBLEMS

Another area of concern for the sales manager is that of settling problems that arise among sales associates. Such problems can be caused by petty jealousies, commission disputes, personality conflicts and charges of pirating prospects. Conflicts such as these are part of the real world of sales management and should not be treated lightly. They should be handled with dispatch whenever and wherever they crop up.

Related situations that arise concerning the deportment of sales associates must be dealt with occasionally. All of these problems can be either avoided or substantially curtailed if the sales manager or training officer has a specific policy and procedures manual and goes over it with new sales associates as they arrive. (In the case of independent contractor affiliates, the manual can be known as the "suggested procedures guide.")

FIGURE 6.5   Monthly Activity Sheet

Name _____ Month_____

Sales . . . .
      1.
      2.
      3.
      4.
      5.
                                                            _____

Listings Sold . . . .
      1.
      2.
      3.
      4.
      5.
                                                            _____

New Listings . . . .
      1.
      2.
      3.
      4.
      5.
                                                            _____

Total Activities . . . .   _____

Current Listing Inventory
1.
2.
3.
4.
5.
6.
7.
Total Current Listing Inventory . . . .   _____

FIGURE 6.6   Self-Imposed Goals and Actual Evaluation

198___	INVENTORY LISTINGS		GOALS				ACTUAL			
	Goal	Actual	Sales	Listings	Total Activities	Earnings	Sales	Actual Listings	Total Activities	Earnings
JANUARY										
FEBRUARY										
MARCH										
1st QUARTER TOTALS										
APRIL										
MAY										
JUNE										
2nd QUARTER TOTALS										
JULY										
AUGUST										
SEPTEMBER										
3rd QUARTER TOTALS										
OCTOBER										
NOVEMBER										
DECEMBER										
4th QUARTER TOTALS										
YEAR-END TOTAL										

SIGNED

FIGURE 6.7 Daily Activity Log #_____

SALESPERSON A.M. P.M.	AD (ADDRESS)	SIGN (ADDRESS)	WALK-IN	OTHER	RENTALS

The manual should cover the subjects of office hours, floor time and professional dress standards expected of associates. Office procedures relating to record keeping, listings and telephone procedures (discussed in Chapter 9) should be included. Advertising policies should be covered. In addition, company policies relating to compensation and reimbursement of expenses should be detailed.

By developing and disseminating a comprehensive guide of what is expected from each associate, the broker can avoid many problems. If the salespeople become involved in some form of dispute and cannot settle it according to the rules established by the manual, then the sales manager must step in and adjudicate the controversy.

The policy and procedures manual developed and used by one of the authors is at the end of this book. Each broker/owner is encouraged to provide such a guide, composed to fit each particular circumstance, for his or her firm.

SUMMARY

The sales manager gives direction to the productive efforts of the sales force. Whether the broker/owner or managing broker/sales manager handles the job, he or she must be aware of the basic functions that the job demands, such as ability to recruit promising sales associates, see they are adequately trained and then directed to meeting realistic sales goals. Along with these tasks goes the responsibility to motivate associates, evaluate their efforts and techniques and see that they are amply rewarded and commended for successes reached.

How the sales manager is compensated depends a great deal on the extent of his or her responsibility. Some managers act merely as assistants to the owners and/or brokers, while others are allowed full charge of the sales force. This chapter has offered a number of ways for compensating the sales manager.

The authors believe that successful sales management begins and ends with the right selection of sales associates. In other words, a person who applies for the job must be carefully screened for attitude and self-motivating qualities. Salespersons who have had success in selling in other fields, who aspire to the real estate field because they know they can make more money there and who come to the firm determined to be successful usually have the attitude required to succeed.

It is important for the manager to understand the various kinds of meetings and their function so as not to be wasting his or her time, as well as the associates' time. Evaluation of associates' sales results not only tells how well they are doing but also reflects the ability of the sales manager.

DISCUSSION QUESTION

Interview five sales associates of other offices and ask them the following questions:

1. Does your company hold sales meetings?
2. If so, how often?
3. Do you feel those meetings are productive for you?
4. What topics are discussed in your meetings? What topics would you like to see discussed?

After your interviews, bring the results back to class and compare notes with the other members of the class. What is the consensus on how much sales meetings are used in the industry? What could be done to improve the practice?

7 Recruiting and Selecting Sales Associates

INTRODUCTION

Certainly one of the most critical aspects of the real estate brokerage business is whom you hire to represent your firm. The conduct of the agents in the field determines how a firm is judged. Poorly trained or uneducated associates result in an expectation of poor performance by the public. It behooves the owner/broker to engage only those people who will be most amenable to following the precepts of good training and competent guidance.

If one were to ask which attribute in a human being is the single most important one to look for in hiring a sales associate, the answer would have to be attitude! Attitude is manifested in many ways: the willingness to take and act on instruction, the ability to take criticism without feeling rancor, the initiative to see when some task needs doing and then doing it without being asked, the treating of the company's interest as if it were his or her own. These and many other signs point to the type of attitude a company wants to see in its associates.

The job of sales management is made eminently easier if the right choice of sales associates is made early in the formation of the sales force. There are two general methods of recruitment: the shotgun approach and the rifle method. In the shotgun approach a firm tries to attract as many applicants as it can and then begins the process of culling out those that do not measure up to the firm's standards, until only the select few remain.

In the rifle approach the sales force is composed of eight to ten experienced high-producers who work under the personal direction of the broker/owner. Each is an expert in his or her chosen field. Such fields may encompass high-priced residential sales, industrial sales and leasing, farms and ranches, business opportunities, and commercial sales and leasing, as well as office buildings and leasing.

After a firm acquires the image of offering expert services in most real estate specialties, then prospective sales associates and clients will gravitate to that firm. In this kind of an operation, recruitment is not so much of a problem as the careful selection process, and company image is paramount.

SOME EARLY DECISIONS TO MAKE

The broker's budgetary decision of income needed balanced by desk cost, available space and necessary number of salespeople must precede any thoughts about methods of recruitment and selection. The broker must also set other goals and objectives, including what image is to be projected by the firm and whether the staff will consist of full-timers, part-timers, or a combination of both. In addition, the broker must decide upon the criteria for selection and apply them consistently.

After these initial decisions, the broker must choose whether to run short-term, concentrated recruiting campaigns or to recruit continuously. Realizing that inexperienced salespeople need training before going into the field and that even experienced salespeople need orientation to office policies and procedures, the broker should see the need to coordinate recruiting campaigns with the necessary follow-up training. To hold a recruiting campaign in May, for example, when the next training program is scheduled for October, would result in potential producers having to wait six months for the training required before going into the field. If personnel are permitted to work before acquiring the proper training, poorly handled transactions and development of bad working habits can result.

The choice between continuous or short-term recruitment will depend on the brokerage size, the availability of trainers and the budget. Continuous recruiting requires nearly constantly rotating training courses and orientation programs. It is usually impractical unless money and trainers are available on a continuous basis and sufficient office space is available. Sporadic recruiting requires appropriately spaced training and orientation programs for recruits. This method does not create a constant drain on available trainers, space and cash. One possible compromise between these two choices allows for the continuous recruitment concept without the expense of trainers and space; training and orientation can be done on a one-to-one basis by the broker or manager or by a senior salesperson. Properly organized, one-to-one training can work well in a small office. It is not advised for a large office.

RECRUITMENT METHODS

Once the broker has decided on the frequency of the recruiting campaign, the choice of technique can be made from one or more methods: advertising, career nights, licensing courses, sponsorship, "trial" training sessions, scholarships and direct mail. Not included on the list is direct solicitation of another broker's salespeople. This is bad business practice, as a salesperson who can be pirated often is already working at a full potential that rarely is more than mediocre. The recruiting broker would be wise to concentrate instead on the talents available among the huge, untapped field of potential salespeople. The opportunities to develop star salespeople from outside sources are far greater than those for developing superstars out of another broker's mediocre salespeople.

Company Image as a Recruiting Factor

There are occasions where a sales associate from one firm may be attracted to your firm as a direct result of its image-building program. An aggressive, ambitious person may become disillusioned with his or her first firm because he or she has discovered flaws in its operation. It may not have a training program, there may be too much dissension within the company or the company's image in the community may be found to be wanting. There may be a dozen different reasons, any one of which would cause potentially good sales associates to want to make the move. Perhaps they have observed your operation, decided it is more to their liking and come to you for a position. After you evaluate their attitudes and motives for changing, you may discover that you have found some diamonds in the rough. It is the image a firm projects that will attract some of the best people.

Advertising

High on the list of effective recruiting methods is advertising. All media may be used, including radio and TV. Newspaper advertising is the most utilized medium and the one likely to bring the best return for the least money. The most common placement is in the help-wanted section, in which an ad only a few lines long can announce that the office is looking for salespeople. Sometimes the ad may offer attractive inducements, such as a luxury car, 90-percent commissions or a paid trip to Hawaii or some other exotic place. Unfortunately, the tendency for these ads to be misleading has increased alarmingly. The general public, including clients and customers, reads these ads; thus the broker must remember they are a public statement of office policy.

New applicants also can be invited by an appropriate message added to the broker's institutional advertising, such as, "Interested in a career in real estate? Sincere, service-minded individuals, regardless of age, experience or background, are welcome, with no obligation, to discuss with us training for this exciting profession."

Two important things must be kept in mind when using any type of advertising medium. First, one should be sure to draw from all available talent. To do this, the broker should design the ad to induce a response from the greatest cross section of readers. Potential salespersons, including potential top producers, may come from any walk of life. Brokers may lose out on superstars by not directing their recruiting ads to the total readership.

Second, brokers must make certain that the advertising is not discriminatory. The law requires that recruitment advertising must not discriminate by race, color, religion, sex, national origin or disability. For example, an ad that appears valid to the broker when it is written might be misinterpreted as discriminating. Take as an example the phrase "experienced salespeople only." In areas where minorities have not yet entered or are just beginning to enter the real estate field, that phrase could be interpreted as racial discrimination because minority members have had no opportunity to become experienced. Similarly, the phrase could be condemned as sex discrimination if it precluded the entry of a housewife. The woman who has spent many years rearing her family has not been able to acquire experience and is excluded from the recruitment pool.

The many thousands of REALTORS® who are signatories to the Affirmative Marketing Agreement (AMA), designed by the Department of Housing and Urban Development (HUD) and the NAR, have a responsibility under the agreement not only to provide equal service and housing opportunities to the public but also to reach out and attract salespeople, brokers and employees to the industry. Therefore, to abide by the law and the AMA, brokers should carefully scrutinize all recruitment advertising to make certain that the wording does not exclude minorities. They can further reinforce this intention not to discriminate by including in the advertising a phrase such as "equal employment opportunity," "previous training not necessary," or "experienced or inexperienced invited." It is permissible to say "prior experience and/or training desirable, but will train other qualified individuals."

The choice of radio or television as an advertising medium is determined by cost. In some market areas, the cost of television time is prohibitive; in others it is more reasonable. Radio time, while less expensive generally, becomes costly because a message needs repetition to be effective.

Those who sell radio advertising time are able to identify audiences for particular stations or programs so that the advertising message will reach a balanced audience. Advertising only during morning hours for the purpose of selling household products to a housewife is acceptable; advertising only during certain hours for employment purposes could be considered an attempt to discriminate.

Career Nights

In recent years career nights have become a popular recruiting tool. They are often sponsored by franchises or run independently by community colleges and licensing schools with brokers invited. If a broker belongs to a national or regional franchise, guidelines and support on undertaking such an endeavor will be made available by the franchise.

Any broker can run a career night for his or her individual office. Attendance can be limited to as few as ten people or open to hundreds, depending on space, money and other considerations. Only a small percentage of those present might have the requisite desire and ability to become salespeople; therefore, the group should be large enough to produce some results. It should not be too large for the broker to answer individual questions, however, or the personal approach will be lost.

Whether the group is small or large, the program must be planned step by step with no detail overlooked to produce the desired results. The following procedure is suggested for setting up an individual office career night.

1. Select a central location that is convenient to the area from which the broker will draw potential applicants. The facilities should be able to accommodate a range of group sizes; hotels and motels offer this flexibility. It is advisable to have, whenever possible, an agreement with the facility that the actual room size can be determined at a later date when the number of guests can be verified.

2. After a location has been chosen, promote the career night in advertising and by press releases. Press releases are more likely to be used if they reach the papers through the same channels as the advertising. Radio and TV can be used where economically feasible. It is best to use a reservation system in the announcements, giving a phone number to call for reservations and information. The person who will receive the calls must always be thoroughly briefed on how to handle the inquiries. Follow up by sending tickets and perhaps calling to verify attendance a day or two before the program night.

3. Choose a room that is large enough to handle the reservations plus about ten percent. This space will accommodate any who arrive without advance reservations and will leave a little breathing space. Beware of the too-large hall, which will create a feeling of poor attendance. Needed equipment should be available, such as chalkboards, projectors

and screens, tables, a podium, sound amplifiers and easels. Heating and air conditioning equipment should be checked for effectiveness and noise. The time, money and effort invested by the broker in a career night are extensive; one neglected detail could spoil the effect.

4. Light refreshments, such as coffee and cake, are useful either for a break or after the program to provide an opportunity for selected staff members of the sponsoring firm to mingle with the guests. The use of name tags makes people feel comfortable quickly.

5. Provide literature in packet form for each guest, including general information about careers in real estate and specific information about the host firm. The NAR pamphlet *Careers in Real Estate* is an excellent piece to include.

6. Begin the program with a welcoming statement, including a brief history of the private ownership of real estate, its economic importance, some statistics on current market conditions and the opportunities for real estate sales careers. Stress the importance of real estate as a service business; what is to be sold is not just a product but a valuable service as well. Follow this topic by a discussion of the sources and opportunities for income, a straightforward analysis of income that can reasonably be expected and an explanation of ways a desired income level can be attained by setting goals for listings and sales. Explain the firm's training program to reassure prospective applicants that it is complete and effective and describe the status that can belong to a salesperson who has achieved success.

Conclude the program with a brief history of the office and a projection of anticipated future growth. The reason for holding the career night should be explained, whether it is to fill vacancies, to expand staff in existing locations to handle current business or to staff projected new offices. Invite attendees to make an appointment at the end of the meeting for an interview. Prompt follow-up should include a thank-you letter to each guest and a phone call to extend a second invitation for an interview.

Licensing Courses

Licensing schools sponsored by individual brokers and franchises often have a hidden agenda outside the noble purpose of education. A broker who is able to observe students over a period of time, looking over their talents, dress, personality and academic abilities, naturally has the pick of the field. A broker who is interested in setting up a licensing school should contact the real estate licensing authority in the state to ascertain what requirements must be met.

Brokers who decide not to sponsor their own licensing course may instead choose to contact independent real estate schools or community colleges that sponsor such courses. Brokers may offer licensing sponsorship of a student or invite one or more students for an interview.

Sponsorship

Some states require that a candidate for a sales license be sponsored by a broker before the candidate can take the examinations required by the state's licensing rules. A broker may offer "sponsorship without strings" to those about to take the state examinations as a means of reviewing the talent pool. Some amount of work is involved in processing the papers necessary to take the examinations. This effort and time is well spent if an occasional sponsored applicant actually becomes a superstar. Sponsorship usually involves a character reference but does not require a commitment of continued employment.

Trial Training Sessions

As will be described in Chapter 8, a broker's training program may be continuous or sporadic, led by a member of the organization or an outside trainer, with supplementary or total use of audio cassettes, films or videotapes. Whatever the format, a segment may be extracted and used to attract recruits. Newspaper advertising or direct mail to public or licensing schools that offers a preview of the company's training course normally brings a good response. The response usually comes from three main sources: members of the public who are curious about the field of real estate as a career, those who are in the prelicensing process and salespeople who are already licensed and either working or inactive. Many salespeople who joined an organization because of the promise of training have been disappointed when the training did not match their expectations. By previewing segments of the training program, the potential recruit is able accurately to judge the benefits of joining the sponsoring organization.

Scholarships

High schools and junior colleges are usually pleased to participate in the awarding of designated scholarships. A scholarship program, consisting of tuition to a real estate licensing school, can be awarded annually in the name of the broker and can carry benefits beyond those enjoyed by the recipient. Others take notice when they see the publicity generated. The cost of acquiring qualified prospective salespeople by this method is often lower than that of most other methods. The awarding of scholarships, if amply promoted, carries substantial public relations benefits that produce listings and sales. An office representative, possibly the salesperson working the territory where the school is located, may often be permitted to make the presentation at a public graduation or awards ceremony. Choice of the recipient should be left to the school, even though the broker should review all applications and eventually interview all who look promising. This procedure may avoid the development of negative attitudes toward the office by unhappy losers.

Direct Mail

On a per-reader basis the use of direct mail often appears costly when compared with newspaper advertising. A $33 classified help-wanted/real estate ad in a paper with 100,000 circulation costs $1/30$ cent per paper. If the paper is read by three people in each household, the cost per reader becomes $1/90$ cent, or 90 readers per penny. This totals 9,000 readers per dollar expended. A professional piece of direct mail, sent first class, with artwork, copywriting, printing and the use of a mailing list bought from a professional source, can cost between 35 cents and $1.15 per recipient.

The expense of this method is well justified if the list is selected with care and imagination. As a rule of thumb, direct mail companies state that one response from every ten pieces mailed is good; but response to a random mailing of an invitation to a career in real estate is not likely to be that productive. If it were, the average cost would be about $57 per response. This cost is not unreasonable, even if one allows that perhaps only one in ten respondents is qualified, bringing the cost per qualified applicant to $575. When measured against the cost of business lost because of a staff vacancy, the cost of $575 for a productive salesperson is reasonable. On the other hand, if an appropriate mailing is directed to a large, select group of salespeople and middle-level executives of a local industry whose product has suddenly become obsolete, the response could be very productive and much less costly.

Direct mail is often used as an effective means of contacting students about to graduate from high school or college. Lists are usually available from commercial sources that may be found in the Yellow Pages under "Mailing Lists." It is generally wise to compare costs and list content of at least two companies, if possible. The services available from direct mail houses usually include writing and designing the mailing piece as well as printing, inserting, addressing and mailing.

The "King Arthur" Technique

Potential salespeople often become known to the broker because of the quality of their performance in other occupations. The service station attendant, waiter or waitress, store clerk, neighbor or customer the broker sees from day to day may show fitness for a real estate career through their attitude, poise and obvious intelligence. The alert broker should respond to these potential successes just as King Arthur did. Arthur recruited his Knights of the Round Table by saying, "I dub thee knight." The broker can ask the simple question, "How would you like a career in real estate?" The uninterested will at least be flattered; the interested may become leaders in the profession.

THE SELECTION PROCESS

Several stages are usually involved in selecting a salesperson to affiliate with the company. They could include application forms, interviews and aptitude tests. Although it is not necessary that these stages be conducted in any particular order, it is advisable that the broker determine which order is the best for him or her and always follow the same format when selecting salespeople. The most important requirement is that the first stage be one that makes possible quick elimination, with more than a fair degree of accuracy, of those applicants in whom the broker is not interested.

The Application

Some brokers require application forms as the first stage. These forms also are useful if a prospective salesperson seeking a position walks into the office without a prior appointment. The application serves several purposes. It gives basic information such as name, telephone number and address with which to start a file on the applicant. It lists former employers, to determine if those positions were sales-oriented, and it asks for references. Finally, it reveals whether the applicant can write legibly and answer questions thoroughly—not a minor detail where real estate paperwork is required. The broker can also discover if the applicant is already licensed and has had experience.

However, one should be careful not to use the application form to discriminate illegally. It may not ask for such information as age (except to meet licensing minimums), race, spouse's employment, maiden name of females, religion or political affiliation.

As a result of the Civil Rights Act of 1964, Title 7, federal law governs equal employment opportunity. The Equal Employment Opportunity Commission enforces the law. Each state may have stricter laws that supersede the federal law, but none may have less-strict laws regarding employment. Information requested on an application must be for a bona fide occupational qualification (BFOQ). For example, a request for information regarding education must be a BFOQ, as it is in states requiring, for example, a high school diploma to be licensed in real estate. However, to satisfy the age discrimination requirement, the dates of elementary and high school graduation may not be asked because they pinpoint the age of the applicant. (College graduation dates may be asked because people often attend and graduate from college at various points in their lives.)

The content of the application form should be reviewed by an attorney to be sure is does not violate state or federal laws.

The Interview

If the first contact between the salesperson and the office is an appointment made for the broker to meet with the potential salesperson, an interview is most likely to be the first step, usually combined with filling out an application.

The interview is probably the single most important aspect of recruiting. This is the big opportunity for the broker to get to know the applicant to some degree. If the broker plans to use an aptitude test, initial personal contact between broker and applicant need not exceed 15 or 20 minutes. If no testing is to follow, the broker should probably make the interview long enough so that at its conclusion he or she has a reasonably good idea of whether this particular salesperson is right for the firm or not.

As with the application, brokers should avoid asking an applicant questions that might be construed as discriminatory. Brokers should take advantage of resources that can provide guidelines to assist them in doing the job correctly and meeting regulatory guidelines in the hiring process. The federal government has reference material available that provides guidance for subject matter and types of questions that should be avoided—all designed to protect equal employment opportunity.

With these guidelines in mind, the broker might begin by stating company policies and asking the applicant if these policies pose any problems. For a more thorough type of interview, the broker should design a list of questions to ask during the interview to determine as quickly as possible if the applicant fits the company's image of the type of salespeople it wants. These are sometimes called shock questions because they are intended to jolt the applicant out of any preconceived ideas he or she might have about real estate being the way to a fast buck and into the reality of what the profession is all about: hard work, long hours and service to the public.

For example, if only full-time salespeople are wanted, the broker might ask:

- How many hours and what evenings and weekends are you available to work?

- Do you have any other part-time or full-time jobs?

If the desk cost is $10,000 a year, the broker could ask, "How much money do you want to earn from your real estate endeavors?" This simple question can provide insight into the applicant's goals. Many potential salespeople feel they will not be hired if they expect too much money, and therefore answer, "Oh, I don't need too much; I can live on very little," or "I only need enough to pay my oldest child's college tuition each year." An applicant who truly needs only a little to live is hardly a promising candidate if the broker needs $10,000 or $15,000 a year just to cover desk costs. If an applicant says this merely because he or she is afraid of the broker's reaction to a higher figure, this points to another flaw. A salesperson should not tell people what he thinks they want to hear but what is actual and true. Another revealing question the broker might ask during this initial interview is, "What would you say to a client who puts a restriction on a listing requiring that you not bring a person of a certain minority group to the house?" The wise broker should eliminate at this point any applicant who indicates in the slightest way that he or she would be tempted to discriminate in dealings with buyers and clients.

Other questions should be formed to get responses about:

- Ability to live for a minimum of three months without income;
- Willingness to knock on doors (cold canvass);
- Feelings about emptying a wastebasket or pencil sharpener, making coffee and generally tidying up around the office;
- Automobile ownership;
- Feelings about proper dress;
- Loyalty, that is, attitude toward necessity for loyalty to the firm;
- Team spirit, that is, willingness to share responsibility and credit with others and work as part of a team;
- Reactions under pressure and ability and style of handling failure and objections; and
- Ethics: the attitude toward a code of ethics.

There are certain qualities a person must have to be a good salesperson, the most important of which are ego-drive and empathy. Ego-drive is a person's inner need to persuade another person for the personal pleasure and gratification derived. A salesperson can have tremendous ambition, need money desperately, and work tirelessly 18 hours a day but the work will be in vain if he or she does not have a fair amount of ego-drive. Empathy is the ability to perceive another person's feelings. Too often confused with sympathy, which can be a negative quality in a salesperson, empathy means understanding another's feelings objectively without getting personally (emotionally) involved.

A common mistake made by brokers and others during the interview is to "sell" the company's image and completely forget the purpose of the meeting, which is to decide if they want to "buy" this particular product, the interviewee. Although it is true that a valuable or potentially valuable salesperson who is being wooed by other companies might eventually have to be sold on this particular company, the first interview is not the place to do it.

After an application or an interview has been completed, the applicant should always be told when he or she can expect to hear from the broker regarding the next step; the broker should *always* fulfill that commitment. It must be remembered that applicants who are eliminated are still a part of the broker's public and should be treated with respect. In this way the company will not be adversely affected by the ill will of someone who might become a client or a competitor.

The Test

Because the broker usually pays for tests, it can be expensive to have all applicants take them in the first stage. This is one reason why testing is sometimes done during the second or even the third stage in the broker's selection process. Other reasons for variations in the order of the steps include the size of the office operation and the number of people who will review the applicants. Nevertheless, the broker should be aware that not giving the tests to all applicants could be considered discriminatory. In addition, tests are under scrutiny because of possible cultural and verbal biases built into them.

The essential qualities of ego-drive and empathy are categorized in various ways by many of the testing services available. In some cases, characteristics are further categorized under such terms as aggression, confidence, dominance, determination, responsibility and sociability.

It is a very rare broker or manager who can determine, during one or two interviews, if the person being interviewed has these qualities. Furthermore, since ego without empathy or empathy without ego does not produce a good salesperson, the interviewer must not only determine if the potential salesperson possesses a sufficient balance between the two but also if the applicant possesses the other inner dynamics essential to becoming a good real estate salesperson. A well-designed objective psychological or occupational evaluation instrument can be a reliable measure of these qualities and might well be step three in the broker's selection process. Any such test *must* be validated so that the broker is not left open to a charge of discrimination.

The evaluation techniques used are at least as important as the test itself. All of the tests use a *model*, some kind of personality or skill profile compiled from the results of tests given to groups of successful and unsuccessful salespeople. When the subject's answers resemble those of the "success" model, the subject is graded a success; if the answers match those of the "failure" model, the subject is graded a failure.

If the profile of the model is carefully drawn from an appropriate sample and the test is administered accurately and evaluated with skill and knowledge, the results will be useful. The cost of the test is not the only cost wasted if the test is not effective. The broker also will have wasted time and perhaps either turned away a qualified prospect or spent time and money training an ineffective salesperson.

Brokers should always remember two facts: (1) the decision to hire a person is only the beginning of a major time and financial commitment and (2) the finest training in the world will be wasted on the person who is not sales-oriented. Extreme care should be taken in this selection.

Not only must the broker feel confident that the applicant possesses a balance of ego and empathy but also the person must have a sense of responsibility to, loyalty to and cooperation with those he or she will have to work with. The image projected should be compatible with the overall office image sought by the broker. Although the undesirable actions of a superstar may be more readily overlooked than those of a mediocre salesperson, there comes a time when even a million-dollar producer can cause so much dissent in an office that the commissions generated by him or her become secondary. An office can usually digest a small percentage of salespeople who barely meet or perhaps do not even meet the desk cost, provided those persons have qualities that are in other ways beneficial to the overall office pattern, such as image, responsibility and detail ability.

Pitfalls of Selection

Throughout the selection process the broker is constantly plagued by pitfalls. A relative or friend may want a job and it may be very difficult, because of the relationship, to refuse. The "windfall" salesperson may come to the broker with four listings "ready to be signed up" and three "hot" buyers just waiting for this salesperson to hang up a license somewhere. Finally, and probably most understandable of all, is the temptation to shortcut the process. If recruiting and selecting are not made as much a part of the broker's time plan as reading the mail, paying the bills and training associates, he or she will fall into the trap of taking shortcuts in the hiring process.

Final Selection

The final selection, therefore, must be based on a well-thought-out and consistent recruiting and selecting process, preceded by decisions on desk costs, available space, image to be projected and whether salespeople will work full time or part time.

Whether the broker depends solely on his or her own evaluation of the applicant or accepts outside recommendations and evaluations, the broker alone will have to live with the decision in the months and, sometimes, years ahead.

SUMMARY

The job of sales management is made eminently easier if the right choice of sales associates is made early in the formation of the sales force. There are two general methods of recruitment: the shotgun approach and the rifle method. In the shotgun approach a firm tries to attract as many applicants as it can and then begins the process of weeding them out through an extensive selection procedure until the select few are chosen.

The so-called rifle approach is used most of the time by one of the authors, who has a sales force of no more than ten experienced high producers who work under his personal direction. He reports that he has a waiting list of experienced sales associates and brokers who would like to become associated with his firm, but he only chooses the best. Each member of the force is an expert in his or her chosen real estate field.

This chapter offers many suggestions about how to build a large and a good sales force and how, after the selection mechanism is in place, it is almost an automatic process for the most logical sales candidate to emerge at the end.

In the final analysis, however, it is the broker or sales manager who has to live with his or her choice of final selection. A poor choice can mean many hours of wasted effort, not to mention the lost production that a better choice would have avoided.

DISCUSSION QUESTION

Given the information in this chapter, how would you go about organizing a real estate sales force in your community? Make a list of the steps you would take and explain how you would put them into practice.

8 Training Sales Associates

INTRODUCTION

If the real estate broker expects to prosper and grow through wise utilization of sales associates, one of the most important functions he or she can perform is to see that those sales associates receive proper training before they are released on the public.

Most sales managers agree that it is far easier to recruit, select and train newcomers to the field than to try to retrain people who come from another firm. Although there are exceptions to this rule, it should not be dismissed lightly. Salespeople who lack training or who have been poorly trained by other brokers may have developed bad habits, poor attitudes or ill-conceived theories about the real estate business. These patterns are very difficult to change. Nothing is more injurious to the morale of a sales force than one person who constantly repeats, "That's not the way we did it in my other office." An old adage may be rephrased to make this point: It is far easier to teach a new dog old tricks than it is to teach an old dog new tricks.

A broker engaging newcomers for the sales force should realize the responsibility he or she is taking on. In some ways it is like bringing a new baby into the world. The broker must provide enough knowledge and training to enable a real estate newcomer to be able to produce a livelihood as quickly as possible.

It is difficult for the broker/owner in a small office to maintain an ongoing training program for new associates. Because of this, several brokers may form a cooperative training program in which they share the teaching chores. Although the purpose of the course is to develop skills and confidence in new salespeople, veteran salespeople may find it beneficial as a refresher. A thorough presentation of the fundamentals of the real estate business can be provided, yet leave each broker with more time to devote to other pursuits because teaching responsibilities are shared.

This chapter addresses the various types of training programs, their objectives and benefits and a schedule of 50 topics to be included in the course content.

Because the success of any training program is a direct result of its trainer, the qualifications of a competent trainer are also included. Practical suggestions for the associate, including time management and improving product knowledge, are given, along with actual excerpts from the Associate Training Manual of John Cyr, Inc., REALTORS®.

BENEFITS AND OBJECTIVES OF A TRAINING PROGRAM

Benefits of offering a well-organized training program can be summarized as follows:

1. *Reputation.* A broker's reputation for good training attracts new sales associates to the firm. A smart person who has just obtained a real estate license looks first for a firm that offers a training program that will help him or her start producing as fast as possible. A broker who does not offer training is at a distinct disadvantage in competing for new associates.

2. *Selection.* An established training program helps the trainer or broker select the most competent associates. The trainer has every opportunity to observe people during the training process, when undesirable traits can be spotted early. The trainee then either learns to correct the faults or is terminated.

3. *Supervision.* Training reduces the need for close supervision of the new salesperson. Through the process of training, the individual should have received basic instructions on how to handle almost any normal situation.

4. *Morale.* Good training helps retain sales associates. The intense training they receive helps them get into production early and overcomes the feeling of despair that may descend when commissions are not generated immediately.

5. *Motivation.* Effective training motivates new sales associates and makes them anxious to go out and try the methods they have just been taught. They have fewer doubts of their own success because the trainer-expert has assured them they will succeed and they have no reason to believe otherwise.

6. *Less turnover.* Training reduces the chance of having to perform the unpleasant task of terminating the unproductive. If the trainer has imparted sufficient knowledge and training, associates are not as likely to founder.

An in-house training program should include the following objectives:

1. *Good habits.* The first objective of a training program should be to instill good working habits in the trainee. Any bad working habits that have been acquired should be replaced with good ones. This is the time to correct any misinformation about real estate a trainee may have.

2. *Better production.* A measurable objective of a good training program can be seen in the Hawthorne effect, named for a 1939 study at Western Electric Company's Hawthorne Plant in Illinois. The findings showed that by giving personnel a certain amount of time, attention and beneficial instruction, an employer makes them feel that someone really cares about whether they succeed or not. Production rises accordingly.

3. *Increased profits.* Most basic is the objective of making money. Effective training readily translates into money. The formula might be written like this: Carefully selected salesperson + Good training = Money in pocket.

4. *Better time management.* A good training program helps to wean a salesperson away from brokers or sales managers early, thereby freeing their time for more productive work.

5. *Learning from mistakes.* Another objective of training should be to teach the principle that even failure in a transaction can sometimes be beneficial. Salespeople should learn a lesson from failure and know enough to prevent a recurrence of the same mistakes in the future.

INGREDIENTS OF A GOOD TRAINING PROGRAM

The five essential ingredients that produce the best quality training program include a consistent format, a competent instructor, suitable location, pertinent instructional materials and proper equipment and teaching aids. Each of these five ingredients is discussed in this chapter.

Consistent Format: Methods and Timetables

Once a presentation format has been established and begun, it is crucial that both schedule and format be maintained until the trainees have completed the course. This is the first step in teaching the trainees good working habits. In addition, it lets them know how important the trainer considers the process.

Three basic methods.   Only three general methods of training real estate sales associates are in use today. Any other method that may be described is usually a variation of one of these three, which include on-the-job training (OJT), sales meetings and formal classroom instruction.

One-on-one, or on-the-job, training is used primarily by the broker who has a small office with only a few associates. As each new person is added, the broker takes the new associate under his or her wing, teaching the fundamentals of the business through day-to-day observations and explanations of current transactions.

One drawback is inherent in this form of training, however; it is necessarily limited in scope to what the broker knows or has had experience in handling. Frequently, many necessary areas of knowledge and expertise are neglected. Therefore, OJT limits the newcomer's level of knowledge to the broker's level, unless the new associate has the intelligence and initiative to seek additional instruction from supplementary sources.

The sales-meeting method of training is usually employed by the firm with from 10 to 25 sales associates. It consists of the broker/owner/sales manager conducting periodic training sessions coupled with sales meetings and extends over a prolonged period of time. This type of training must be carefully planned so that the trainer goes into the sessions well prepared and organized and covers the material in an efficient manner. The program may take years to cover completely all important facets of the business.

Organized classroom instruction is the form of training usually employed by the large multiple-office or franchised firm. It consists of daily, intensified sessions conducted by a designated trainer whose main duty is to recruit, select and train new associates before releasing them to the sales manager. In a smaller firm, this duty is usually assumed by the broker and/or the sales manager. This method is by far the most efficient and effective one and partially accounts for the success of multiple-office and franchise firms.

Timetables for sales training courses.   The size of the firm, the number of associates that must be trained and the available training facilities determine the timetables for these sessions. For example, in the one-on-one situation the broker may relegate the training period to hours not normally needed for general business activities. These hours could be from 7:00 to 8:30 six mornings a week, from 5:00 to 6:00 or 6:00 to 9:00 five evenings a week or all day Saturday.

In the sales-meeting method the material may be presented in a variety of ways: in two one-hour classes per week, as a portion of the weekly or semiweekly sales meeting or in weekly evening sessions of three hours each night, much as an adult course at a community college is conducted.

If the firm is large, well staffed and well equipped, the trainer may devise a more intensified sales training program. The material may be presented in a planned sequence over several weeks, involving lectures, role playing, field trips, guest speakers and the use of audiovisual equipment or audio cassettes in a classroom environment. Such training classes are generally held from 9:00 A.M. to 5:00 P.M. daily for five or six days per week for as many weeks as it takes to cover the required material.

Factors in planning a training program.   The first thing a broker should do in planning the training program is to formulate and write down the *objectives* trainees are expected to accomplish by the end of *each* training session. This gives the trainer a clear perspective of what each session aims to accomplish.

The *timetable* for completion of the course should be announced at the beginning of the first session, and include the hours of each session, any special instructions and the number of sessions it will take to complete the program. The broker should impress on trainees the importance of attending every session. The training director should be prepared to start the sessions *on time* and hold them regularly as specified. The first step in teaching new salespersons how to be prompt and dependable is for the trainer to exhibit those qualities.

The trainer should establish a *pattern* for each session by adhering to a format such as the following:

1. Call for and answer any questions regarding the previous session;
2. Call for homework or research projects assigned, if any;
3. Present the objectives of the current lesson;
4. Conduct the lesson; and
5. Assign the homework (or research project).

The sessions should be kept interesting by allowing *discussion* of the material. It is important to see that no one participant monopolizes the conversation. Personal experiences and references must be kept to a minimum, and then used only for illustration. Good trainers avoid lengthy lecturing, encourage feedback and draw the students into discussions by asking questions. It is an excellent idea to invite guest lecturers on subjects such as financing, escrow, pest control regulations and procedures, or new laws.

Student involvement should be encouraged. The best training is learning by doing. Some suggestions to accomplish this are:

- Appoint a trainee to conduct a discussion on a new phase of the real estate business.
- Employ "brainstorming" techniques as a method of instruction.
- Use role-playing among students.
- Utilize case studies.
- Try class problem solving.
- Assign market research studies—send the salespeople into the field to make market surveys, apartment vacancy surveys and demographic studies. (An example of a market survey questionnaire is offered on pages 154-155.)
- Ask each trainee to write down and describe his or her personal success plan and the timetable for accomplishing it.
- Conduct field trips to appraise a listing, visit an escrow or title company office or visit the local board of REALTORS® office and/or the MLS office.
- Tour one of the residential listings. Then ask each trainee to submit an ad that could sell the property.

In addition, periodic general staff meetings should include the trainees. One suggestion might be to hold a breakfast or luncheon meeting at least once a month to introduce new sales associates, announce the start of or winners of a sales contest or discuss a new company policy. The broker might consider holding an annual two-day seminar out of town in a relaxing atmosphere for brainstorming sessions, improvement of morale and inviting new suggestions and ideas for better management.

Competent Instructor

Any training program is only as good as the instructor. If the instructor is dull, uninteresting or ignorant of the subject matter, participants are likely to lose interest and attendance will fall off. Worse yet, they may transfer to another firm where they hope to get better instruction.

A competent instructor should be completely familiar with the instructional material and be articulate enough to present it properly. If the broker is either too busy or otherwise not qualified to do a good job, he or she should hire a consultant or assign someone else in the organization who is better qualified.

A list of do's and don'ts for the instructor.   Many brokers have the mistaken impression that teaching is not very difficult and that they can do it without much preparation or personal effort. Such is not the case, as any good teacher will testify. The following list shows the many things a good instructor must keep in mind.

- Do exhibit a positive mental attitude: "You can do it, Mr. or Ms. Associate!"
- Do display personal integrity: "We don't cut corners, lie, cheat or misrepresent at any time, in any form!"
- Do provide an example of appropriate appearance by dressing as the salespeople are expected to dress—clean, neat, tasteful ensemble.
- Do show resourcefulness—impress upon the trainees that they too must develop this quality.
- Do show the trainee "how to"—use examples of actual case studies pulled from the files of the office: a well-written listing, a sales agreement, contracts and other documents.
- Do be tactful—be aware of the trainees' feelings!
- Do be fair and objective with all personnel.
- Do give recognition and a pat on the back for a well-deserved accomplishment.
- Do use a variety of teaching methods to prevent the sessions from becoming boring.
- Do use self-analysis examinations whenever possible.
- Do give an accurate picture of the income opportunities—cite examples without giving names of the actual producers; be factual and describe the work involved.
- Don't *tell* them how to do it—*show* them!
- Don't gossip, be a bigot or slander anyone—especially competitors.
- Don't tell off-color or ethnic jokes.
- Don't waste your time and theirs in unproductive "bull sessions."
- Don't allow any individual to monopolize the discussions—there is usually one in every class.
- Don't promise what cannot be delivered—for instance, dangling the bait of a sales manager's job.
- Don't brag about yourself and your personal accomplishments.
- Don't exaggerate potential earnings.

The person who does the training has an important duty to set the example for newcomers by keeping regularly scheduled hours and by being prompt and dependable. A training director should be continually trying to increase his or her knowledge by taking advanced courses whenever possible, by attending timely seminars on current topics and by bringing that information back for dissemination to the sales force.

The trainer should also constantly strive to upgrade the training program with current developments that occur with changing times and conditions. Management should keep in mind at all times that *training is the sum total of all communication between management and sales staff.* It is essential, therefore, if the trainer is other than the broker or manager, that he or she be made a part of the management team and have some authority both in the choice of course material and in the selection of new associates. If communication between the trainer and management is infrequent or poor, salespeople will most likely receive inferior training, whereas if the lines of communication are open between the broker/manager and the trainer, associates will undoubtedly receive good training. Measurable results will be seen.

It must be noted, however, that the trainer should not be expected to work miracles with every potential salesperson. If the trainer is competent, prepared, knowledgeable and able to communicate effectively, he or she will be able to diminish failure but should not be expected to eradicate it altogether.

Suitable Location

The next necessary ingredient for a worthwhile training program is a suitable location. Probably the least desirable environment in which to conduct an effective training program is a working office during business hours with phones ringing and constant interruptions. A suitable location is one that is away from the working part of the office and where no interruptions are tolerated. A back room in the office building or a rented classroom in another part of town is infinitely preferable to the working office.

The training method used generally dictates the size of room needed. In the one-on-one situation the sessions may be conducted in the broker's home or private office or even in the associate's home. In the sales-meeting method, the meeting room must be large enough to accommodate everyone comfortably and still provide for the use of such teaching aids as slide or movie projectors, chalkboards or flip charts.

When the classroom method is used, the closer the environment is to a true classroom, the better are the results. One broker in California relates that for years he taught a real estate course for a business college in his community, tailoring the course to fit the needs of new and prospective sales associates. He paid the tuition for his own new salespeople. That broker had all the advantages: a suitable location, pertinent instructional materials, modern teaching equipment and aids and a consistent format for presentation.

Pertinent Instructional Materials

Probably the most important ingredient of a top-notch program is the course content. A nice classroom, a well-developed format and a competent instructor mean nothing unless the material is relevant and useful.

Literally dozens of topics must be covered if a sales training course is to be of any value. The goals and objectives of each firm should determine what to emphasize in the program. Selection of material also depends on the type of locale (urban, suburban or rural), the chief field of specialization (residential, investment, commercial, industrial or farm) and the degree of education and business sophistication of the trainees.

Course content.   A schedule of 50 topics that should be included in a complete training program follows. While much of the material needed to conduct these sessions is covered in this book, there is still a considerable amount that must be researched and presented to trainees from other sources.

1. The philosophy of the firm regarding ethics, board of REALTOR® membership, MLS participation, cooperation with other firms, the real estate sales process.

2. The jobs and duties of the broker and sales manager and what the new associate should expect of them; the jobs, duties and responsibilities of other employees of the firm; what the trainees may ask of fellow employees and tasks they cannot expect other employees to perform for them; the office layout and organizational chart.

3. The job description of a professional salesperson; what is expected of the trainee in the way of objectives, goals, working habits, demeanor, dress, attitude toward fellow associates.

4. The contract between the broker and the sales associate, what it contains and why; independent contractor versus employer-employee relationship, with an explanation of the different responsibilities of each party; why the company has chosen this specific form of contract and what it entails.

5. Reviewing the policy and procedures manual (if employer-employee relationship) or the suggested procedures guide (if independent contractor status).

6. How the associate can plan and manage time wisely. (This topic is expanded later in this chapter.)

7. Explanation of the company referral system; how referrals from other firms, former customers and clients are handled.

8. The importance of communicating properly: handling letters, telephone calls, brochures and other communication devices.

9. The law of agency and the exclusive listing; the various kinds of listings and the company's attitude toward each type.

10. The MLS to which the firm belongs, its rules and regulations, how it works, how best to use it.

11. Prospecting for listings, sources, methods.

12. The farm method of obtaining listings—setting up a market and research program.

13. Handling objections from the "for sale by owners" (FSBOs), using role playing.

14. Planning the listing presentation—use of the listing kit.

15. The first listing interview—role playing between trainees.

16. Pricing the listing; the dangers of overpricing; how to use the competitive market analysis form.

17. The appraisal process for residential properties.

18. The listing agreement: gathering the data, measuring the house, computing the square footage, filling out the form properly.

19. Processing the listing by compiling the in-house records needed to service it adequately; installing the sign; lockboxes; counseling the seller about showings.

20. Servicing the listing: advertising (all types—newspaper, radio, TV, brochures, etc.), touring the property, holding open house for inspection, callback reports, obtaining new loan commitments.

21. How to write compelling and attention-getting classified and display ads about the listing.

22. Renewing expiring exclusives.

23. Touring the listings and competing properties (improving product knowledge).

24. Prospecting for Buyers, Part One: advertising policy and techniques.

25. Prospecting for Buyers, Part Two: how to answer ad calls, getting the name and pertinent information, making the appointment, the use of "switch" sheets.

26. Prospecting for Buyers, Part Three: the use of open houses, how to conduct an open house properly, separating the buyers from the lookers.

27. Arranging for and conducting the showings correctly: cooperating with other firms, making the appointments, picking up and returning the keys, office policy regarding lockboxes.

28. Learning how to qualify buyers through role playing for the trainees.

29. Techniques for obtaining the offer: countering prospects' objections, when and how to close.

30. The Civil Rights laws (state and federal), the Affirmative Marketing Agreement, Equal Opportunity in Housing.

31. Handling offers and counteroffers, closing techniques, contingency clauses, the art of negotiating.

32. The deposit receipt or purchase agreement: how to fill it out correctly, pitfalls to avoid.

33. Follow-through on the transaction: setting up an escrow account; obtaining required inspections, permits, appraisals.

34. Estimating buyer and seller closing costs: how to prepare for the settlement, prorating customary charges in the locality.

35. The importance of after-sale servicing. (This is a good subject to "brainstorm.")

36. Financing, Part One: investigating and verifying the existing loan(s), obtaining the correct principal balance and interest rate; finding out if a loan is assumable and at what rate of interest; explaining the due-on-sale clause and use of the amortization book.

37. Financing, Part Two: finding out if the owner will carry back part of the purchase price, use of the contract of sale, first and second deeds of trust or mortgages, wraparound or all-inclusive mortgages.

38. Financing, Part Three: explaining government-supported financing—FHA, VA, Farm Home Administration loans, local state-supported loans.

39. Financing, Part Four: creative financing; the various sources coupled with the right tools.

40. Clauses in loans to watch for, such as subordination clause, "lock-in" loans, due-on-sale (alienation), notice of default, request for notice of default, acceleration clauses of various types, release clause.

41. Income tax implications in the sale of single-family residence, the avoidance or postponement of capital gains tax, the one-time after-55 credit, new laws affecting same.

42. The use of the installment sale method to spread out the capital gains tax on the sale of a home or farm.

43. Explanation of terms regarding the sale and exchange of real property; meaning of such terms as basis, depreciation, "like-kind" property, tax shelter, leverage.

44. IRS rules and regulations affecting the exchange of property; mechanics of effecting a tax-deferred exchange.

45. Exchanges: two-party, three-party, multiparty.

46. Listing and selling small-income properties.

47. Analyzing a Real Estate Investment, Part One: arriving at the NOI (net operating income).

48. Analyzing a Real Estate Investment, Part Two: basic knowledge.

49. Analyzing a Real Estate Investment, Part Three: advanced knowledge.

50. Discussion about and commitment to a personal success plan for each trainee.

Sources of instructional material.   In recent years, with the multitude of people entering the real estate field and rapid changes of the industry, it has become apparent that the new licensee should have the advantage of a quick, yet complete, program to prepare him or her for work in the field. Unfortunately, most licensing courses cover the technical but not the practical aspects of real estate. The NAR, as well as some state associations and regulatory bodies, has addressed this need and offers the broker of today sources of instructional material and teaching aids not available before.

The New Jersey Real Estate Commission appointed an ad hoc committee to review the requirements for obtaining a broker's license. The commission recommends adding five, 30-hour segments to the basic 90 hours and increasing the apprenticeship from two to three years. Commission approval would require an act of the New Jersey legislature to become final. The New Jersey Association of REALTORS® developed the "Smart Start" Program in 1986. The program was designed for new salespeople to be led by a professional instructor. It was designed to be held in each of the state's seven districts, on a repeating basis every seven weeks. This enabled brokers to enroll their new salespeople in a program held on a regular basis in close proximity to their offices.

On the national level, NAR designed the RITE™ (REALTORS® In-House Training and Education) Program, a comprehensive training package designed to meet the immediate educational needs of the newly licensed real estate agent. It is primarily a print-based program supplemented by audiovisual elements and can be used in the classroom, as a self-teaching program or as a combination of self-teaching with an instructor.

However, if brokers choose not to use such newly developed programs, they still can present a complete training program to their new salespeople. A method used by one of the authors of this book is to collect and develop a library of information concerning all of the projected topics. The source of pertinent information can be as mundane as a daily newspaper article on a new type of financing or an interest rate change or as sophisticated as an IRS bulletin dealing with income tax changes as they affect real property transactions. Whatever the source, the trainer must be constantly on the alert for current material.

One method of collecting these data is to buy 50 manila folders, labeling each one with one of the topics listed under "Course Content." Every article the trainer sees that refers to one of those topics should be clipped out and inserted into the proper folder. Prior to the class on a specific topic the trainer can get the folder out and review these pertinent articles. The item may sometimes refer to pages in a book or magazine that is in the firm's library. If possible, these should be copied and filed. If not, it is wise to include a note in the folder showing the reference source and pages to be reviewed. This requires having a well-stocked library of such reference materials. The trainer can thus be assured of a continuing, up-to-date supply of information to present to the new salespeople.

Proper Equipment and Teaching Aids

The variety of teaching aids a trainer uses to impart knowledge in an interesting and professional manner depends on how sophisticated he or she wishes to get. Certainly a chalkboard is a must in almost any size training class. Other methods and aids may include a flip chart, an overhead projector, an audio cassette recorder, a slide or movie projector, a video cassette recorder, a computer, closed-circuit TV or readings from trade publications.

Every office should collect and provide a selection of books, magazines and other trade publications that associates may check out and study at their leisure.

Supplementary Training

The trainer may want to vary the classroom environment by having the trainees participate in REALTOR®-sponsored events, such as the local board membership meetings, or other educational events, seminars, Graduate REALTOR® Institute (GRI) courses and the conventions of the state associations and the NAR.

The trainees also should be encouraged to attend the more advanced courses offered by the institutes, societies and councils of NAR. Many private real estate schools and book publishers also offer valuable courses and books for the real estate trainee. In addition, the salesperson may pursue his or her personal success plan by attending real estate courses at the local community college or university extension facility.

A TIME MANAGEMENT PLAN

Because of the nature of the work, especially if associates are engaged as independent contractors, many associates take a laissez-faire attitude toward the real estate business. Salespeople are left to their own resources most of the time; however, some need constant prodding to increase their production. Others have what has been described by author Dave Conger as an "economic thermostat." After earning a certain amount of money, some associates are inclined to relax, take it easy and quit applying themselves strenuously until the pressure for more income builds up again.

To anticipate and ward off such reactions, the new associate should be well grounded in work habits that will sustain him or her through such times. Following are some ideas the broker should suggest to the new associate regarding time and client management.

Draw up a daily work plan for each working day. Examples of such plans are available in many of the trade publications on training. (*See* Figure 8.1.) Efficient time management is the key to selling success. Considerable discipline is required for an associate to establish a daily work plan and faithfully adhere to it. Without such a plan, an associate cannot ever hope to achieve more than a fraction of his or her potential. The first step in organizing a work plan is to establish priorities of objectives and goals. Daily, weekly and monthly objectives lead to the eventual attainment of long-range goals.

The time-worn slogan of "Plan your work—and work your plan" is still as meaningful today as it was when first expounded years ago. All this advice must be impressed upon the trainee-associates the first day they report to work and must be continually emphasized during their early careers.

Schedule at least one day off each week. Spend it completely away from the office to have time set aside for self or family. A day in the middle of the week is often the best time because of the need to work on Saturday or Sunday.

Do not waste time. When office time is spent in socializing, drinking coffee, unproductive luncheon engagements, long telephone conversations with friends or other forms of nonproductive effort, income of the individual and the firm suffers.

FIGURE 8.1 Plan a Good Day Today and a Better One Tomorrow

DAY:_____ DATE:_____

GOALS: Today _____

This Month _____

Long Term _____

APPOINTMENTS TO KEEP	PRIORITIES BETWEEN APPOINTMENTS
7:30	○
7:45	○
8:00	○
8:15	○
8:30	○
8:45	○
9:00	○
9:15	○
9:30	○
9:45	○
10:00	○
10:15	○
10:30	○
10:45	○
11:00	○
11:15	○
11:30	○
11:45	○
12:00	○
12:15	○
12:30	○
12:45	○
1:00	○
1:15	○
1:30	○
1:45	
2:00	**PHONE CALLS TO MAKE**
2:15	○
2:30	○
2:45	○
3:00	○
3:15	○
3:30	○
3:45	○
4:00	○
4:15	○
4:30	○
4:45	○
5:00	○
5:15	○
5:30	○
5:45	○
6:00	○
6:15	○
6:30	○
6:45	○
7:00	○
7:15	○
7:30	○
7:45	○
8:00	○

Improving Product Knowledge

Spend free time previewing all homes in the area of specialization. When a call from a prospect comes in, the associate knows exactly what homes are on the market.

Screen potential listings thoroughly to make sure they are salable as to price, terms, possession and motivation of the sellers. Do not take unsalable listings.

Work on exclusive listings only, if working solely on residential property. Too much time may be wasted on properties that might be sold by the owner or a competitor without the knowledge of the sales associate.

Qualify buyers thoroughly before starting to show them homes. Hours or days may be spent in showing them properties only to find out they have neither the intention nor the resources to buy. Use the MLS advantage. Prospects should be informed that any property listed for sale in the community can be shown to them no matter what broker's sign is on the property. It is heartbreaking to spend several days showing homes to prospects only to find they have purchased from another broker.

Evaluate clients regularly. If a couple has been shown homes over three or four days and they have not made an offer on at least one house, then perhaps they should be dropped. The salesperson can then go on to someone or something else more productive.

Consider the return on time invested (ROTI) on every prospect, every listing and every transaction. By becoming intensely aware of ROTI, the sales associate can begin to cut down on wasted motion and continuously increase the time value of his or her hours.

A MARKET SURVEY QUESTIONNAIRE

The following market survey questionnaire form has three important purposes. It may be adapted to individual use as an icebreaker to help new associates overcome their aversion to door-to-door selling or prospecting. At the same time, its use can give both the associates and the broker valuable product knowledge about homeowners in a given district; in addition, as associates become more visible in the community they spread market identification for the office.

Good Morning! I'm John Jones of Edgerton Realty and I'm making a survey of property owners in this area to get an idea of the housing market, and to determine how I may be of service to you. Do you mind if I take a few minutes of your time and ask you a few questions? Thank you.

I see by the records that this property is owned by Joseph and Suzanne Dinero. Is that you? Yes_____ No_____. If not, may I ask your name? _____ How long have you lived

here?_____ Are you quite comfortable here?_____ If not, why not?_____
Have you ever considered moving to another area?_____ If so, where? _____ Are there any amenities this home does not have that you would like to have?_____ If so, what are they?_____
Is your husband subject to transfer?_____ [or] Is he thinking of retiring? _____ Would you be interested in trading for another home of a different style or setting?_____ If so, where?_____
Have you ever heard of our firm?_____ Do you know where our nearest office is?_____ Would you call upon our firm if you had need of our service?_____ If not, why not?_____
Thank you for your time, Mrs. Dinero, and here is a little token of our appreciation [potholder, calendar, ballpoint pen] for being so kind and cooperative. Also, here is my card if you ever have need of my services. Good Day!

Compiling a file of such questionnaires accumulated in a specific area gives a broker a good idea of who the property owners are, how long they have been there and if any of them are thinking of moving in the future. A good reading also is obtained of the office image in that area.

A TRAINING MANUAL FOR EACH SALES ASSOCIATE

One of the most valuable adjuncts to a successful training program is the training manual. This can be a loose-leaf binder in which the sales associate going through the training process can keep all pertinent material and handouts presented during the sessions for ready reference later.

Following is the prologue to the training manual used by John Cyr, Inc., REALTORS®. It can be used verbatim (except for the firm name change) or it can be redone to conform to the particular style of a broker's firm.

JOHN CYR, INC., REALTORS®

ASSOCIATE TRAINING MANUAL
PROLOGUE

First—let's level with one another . . . We know what concerns you! You are here because you have looked around and decided that the firm of John Cyr, REALTORS® is your best bet for receiving the necessary training and aid to make you a success in the real estate brokerage business.

We are here because, in order to ensure the success of our business, we need you! So, we must live up to your expectations. In a sense, we are partners in this enterprise with mutually compatible goals in mind. Let's define what are each of our responsibilities under this arrangement. First, John Cyr, REALTORS® must provide the following:

A pleasant working environment conducive to maximum production

The facilities required to operate a real estate office efficiently, such as telephones, desks, forms, typewriters, and secretarial help

Sales management—competent direction of your efforts. (Our definition of *sales management* is: the attainment of predetermined company sales goals through the successful direction of other people's efforts.)

A good reputation together with a valid broker's license so that we can continue in business together

Expertise and technical knowledge to help you put your transactions together—and *keep them together!*

Financial responsibility so that our bills are paid—and you receive your share of the commissions fairly and promptly

Adequate advertising—both institutional and merchandise—signs, newspaper ads, and brochures all cost money, which we are prepared to pay for out of our share of the commissions

What are you expected to provide towards this partnership?

Besides your license and your car, you mainly provide your time and your physical efforts.

Your time may be divided into three main thrusts: Organization, Discipline, and Education. *Those are the three secret keys to your success!* Once you understand that, you will be on your way to attaining your *objectives* and your *goals*.

But first, let's both understand what we mean by *GOALS* and *OBJECTIVES*. A GOAL is a statement that proposes a certain position in life you wish to attain, at some future time, through a calculated program of OBJECTIVES. An OBJECTIVE is a short-range achievement you will strive for as one more step toward your major GOAL.

Hence the goal is the top of the mountain you are attempting to climb, while objectives are the necessary steps it takes to get there. Now let's get back to ORGANIZATION, DISCIPLINE, and EDUCATION.

Organization

As stated above, to work towards your goals in life you must plan on completing objectives—as you plan these objectives and map out a strategy for accomplishing them you are providing *ORGANIZATION* to your life.

For example, although your long-range goal may be to become independently wealthy in life, a short-range objective is to earn $36,000 for the coming year.

How are you going to accomplish this? *PLAN FOR IT.* Realize the value of your time, and make the most of it! Plan to work 40 hours a week for the 50 weeks of the year. That's 40 × 50, or 2,000 hours for the year—your Golden Hours, as we call them. Your $36,000 objective divided by the 2,000 Golden Hours results in a value of $18 per hour. That's what your time is worth. Don't waste it!

Consider those 40 hours you work to be, not 8 hours a day from 8 a.m. to 5 p.m. for 5 days a week, but those hours of the day best suited to your prospects' life-styles and your own.

Some people are morning people and some are evening people. Decide which you are and what time of the day you do your best work, then make the most of it!

Another *objective* in the *organization* of your time should be to obtain at least ONE LISTING PER WEEK! This is necessary if you are to accomplish a third objective, *COMPLETING THREE UNITS OF PRODUCTION PER MONTH!*

To explain: a unit of production is either your listing sold, or a sale of someone else's listing.

If one of your listings is sold by another associate that's one unit of production.

If you sell someone else's listing that's another unit of production.

If you sell your own listing that's *two units of production.*

To explain further: Imagine the average sales price of a home to be $70,000. Six percent of $70,000 is $4,200. One-half of that is $2,100, which is split between the listing salesperson and the selling salesperson, so each receives $1,050. The *average* unit of production then equals $1,050.

Three units, or $1,050 × 3, equals $3,150 per month, if attained.

$3,150 × 12 months equals $37,800 per year—exceeding your yearly objective.

So—see how *organization* is tied to *objectives!*

1. Your time is worth $18 per hour—don't waste it!

2. Your first *objective* is to obtain one exclusive listing per week.

3. Your next *objective* is to accomplish at least three units of production per month.

4. Your yearly objective is to earn $36,000 for the year.

Remember—the more monthly units of production you accomplish, the higher your earnings will rise!

4 units × $1,050 = $4,200 × 12 months = $50,400 annual earnings
5 units × $1,050 = $5,250 × 12 months = $63,000 annual earnings

Discipline

As for company discipline you are provided here with a copy of our Policy and Procedures Manual. It gives you direction in how to conduct yourself in this business and this company.

But, in addition, you must learn to discipline yourself into good working habits so that you can make the best use of your Golden Hours. Figure 8.1 is a Daily Planning Form that can help you do just that. You will note at the top of the page your *objectives* for the day, month, and year. Also, there is a space for your long-term goal. By filling these forms out each day you will be keeping objectives and your goal in front of you at all times. On the right is a list of priority items you must accomplish that day in order to meet your objective. Also, there are schedules for appointments and phone calls.

Keep this Daily Planning Form in a loose-leaf binder so you can refer back every once in a while to see how well you are doing. Also, you can make daily notations of progress in your quest for your objectives. For example, your yearly objective is to earn $36,000, so each time you receive a commission check you can subtract its amount from the yearly objective figures. It will remind, and motivate, you constantly. You can also do the same with your monthly objectives of four listings and three units of production per month. As a further suggestion, if you should fail to attain any objective for the month then add it to your objectives for the next month.

What should be your priorities?

As for your priorities for the day—they should be closely allied with your monthly objectives. For example, a list of priorities should look something like this:

1. Check on your unclosed transactions—is anything holding them up? If so, take steps to clear it.
2. Write ads for the newspaper on your new listing.
3. Check the MLS book to see if any of the new listings may fit your customers. If so, arrange an appointment to show.
4. Check for any of your listings that may be expiring. Make an appointment with the owner to get it renewed. Do this at least a week in advance of the expiration date.

5. Discuss with owners of current listings any recent developments—such as customer reaction to recent showings, loan commitment obtained, and other news.

6. Check the MLS book to see if there are any new listings in your farm area you have not recently inspected. Make an appointment to do so.

7. Call on 10 homeowners in your farm area and make notations of each visit in your farm records.

8. Attend class in real estate course at Delta College this evening.

Education

The third key to success is *education*. This is a never-ending process. It is part of your *Personal Success Plan*. The following are the courses we suggest you take (in order of their priority).

Real Estate Practice
Real Estate Finance
Appraisal I
Legal Aspects of Real Estate
Real Estate Principles
Escrow I
Real Estate Investments
Appraisal II

As you accumulate knowledge you will find your income increasing and your work load decreasing—because you will be working SMARTER instead of HARDER!

Take the REALTOR® Institute courses as soon as you can—this involves taking three one-week courses that lead to your GRI (Graduate REALTOR® Institute) designation.

Eventually take those courses being offered by the various institutes of the National Association, depending upon the specialty of the real estate business you have chosen by then. Such specialties and institutes are:

Residential—REALTOR® National Marketing Institute (RNMI) courses leading to the Certified Residential Specialist (CRS) and Certified Residential Broker (CRB) designations

Commercial-Investment—RNMI courses leading to the Certified Commercial Investment Member (CCIM) designation

Land—REALTORS® Land Institute courses leading to the Accredited Land Consultant (ALC) designation

Property Management—Institute of Real Estate Management courses (IREM) leading to the Certified Property Manager (CPM) designation

Appraisals—American Institute of Real Estate Appraisers (AIREA) courses leading to the Member of the Appraisal Institute (MAI)

Industrial—Society of Industrial and Office REALTORS® (SIOR)

In addition to the foregoing there are often other, specialized courses, seminars and workshops offered by your local board of REALTORS® and the California Association.

So much for the *three secret keys to success:* Organization, Discipline, and Education. There are also two other necessary characteristics of the successful real estate salesperson:

CAN DO

WILL DO

Neither characteristic is any good without the other—we get many, many CAN DO's in this business but only a few WILL DO's! *ONLY THE WILL DO'S SURVIVE!* Make a resolution, as you enter this business, you are going to be both a CAN DO and a WILL DO!

HERE'S YOUR GAME PLAN FOR SUCCESS

1. Obtain a salable listing
2. Advertise, show, and service that listing
3. Write offers for that listing
4. Close the sale of that listing
5. Follow up with buyer on that listing

Let's close this session with:

Don't look—you might see!
Don't think—you might learn!
Don't walk—you may stumble!
Don't run—you may fall!
Don't try—you may fail!
Don't live—you might die!

SUMMARY

As one can see from this chapter, the training process is neverending, as long as one hopes to keep a top-notch sales force in existence. The person responsible for training also should be involved in the selection process, as the two functions go hand in hand. One also should be aware that no matter how selective one is in recruiting associates and no matter how much effort is put into training associates, there are always going to be failures. Good selecting and training cannot entirely eradicate failure, they can only hope to diminish it as much as possible.

While there are a number of good videotapes on training available on the market today that are of considerable value in helping trainees understand the overall picture of what is expected of them, there is nothing like the personal touch of on-the-job training by the broker/owner or his or her assigned local trainer.

DISCUSSION QUESTION

Evaluate the three basic training course methods as they relate to your firm and decide which would be most effective for you.

9

Accumulation and Control of Inventory

INTRODUCTION

A "listing" in the parlance of the real estate profession means a right to sell someone else's real estate. There are different types of listings: exclusive-right-to-sell, exclusive agency, open. For the purposes of discussion in this chapter, reference to a listing will mean the exclusive-right-to-sell listing contract.

The reason for this is that the exclusive-right-to-sell listing gives the broker the exclusive right to represent the property in question. The seller must pay a commission regardless of who sells the property if it is sold while the listing is in effect. Unless the broker has an exclusive-right-to-sell listing, the property cannot be considered an item in the broker's inventory. It is unwise to spend any considerable time or expense in trying to market a property when there is no assurance that one will be compensated for efforts expended.

The exclusive-right-to-sell listing is to a broker's firm what money is to a bank, food to a restaurant or groceries to a supermarket. It is the inventory; without it, there is nothing to sell.

Where an MLS is active it may seem unimportant for a broker to concentrate on maintaining an inventory of listings in the office. The pool of listings provided by the member brokers of the MLS may seem to be a sufficient source of sales, but the broker and his or her sales staff should avoid depending on other brokers' listings and concentrate on accumulating his or her own office inventory.

THE IMPORTANCE OF A STRONG LISTING ACQUISITION PROGRAM

There are several important reasons for having one's own listing inventory. First is the commission split arrangement. In most cases, 50 percent of the commission earned on the sale of a property is retained by the listing broker. If the property is an office listing, however, 100 percent of the commission stays in house.

Second, it is the listing contributions of all member brokers of an MLS that keep the MLS functioning. If every member only sold listings without replenishing them, the MLS inventory would soon be depleted.

Third, unless the broker quickly acquires a track record as a good listing office where listings are marketed and sold quickly and profitably for clients, potential clients will not be attracted to the firm. Because of the commission split, this lack of new clients can reduce potential income by 50 percent or more.

Finally, obtaining the listing, servicing the listing and selling the listing are the heart of the business; salespeople should be continually encouraged to expand this inventory.

DEVELOPING AN AFFIRMATIVE LISTING ATTITUDE

As a business grows and acquires a good name, a broker usually finds that most listings result from personal referrals of business associates, past customers and clients and an earned reputation for doing a good job. The new broker in the community, however, has not yet proved his or her ability to market properties successfully and does not have a long list of satisfied customers and clients. Obtaining listings is more difficult for this broker. The broker must truly believe that he or she can do a better job for the client than the client could possibly do alone. He or she must feel confident of bringing the client a qualified buyer who will pay fair market value for the property in the shortest time. This confidence will spring naturally from the possession of knowledge about the market, the ability to qualify the buyer, the existence of an advertising and marketing plan, the additional exposure through the multiple-listing service and access to the necessary financing. Few clients have this expertise.

The broker must maintain an affirmative attitude toward listing and foster it among the staff. Salespeople are frequently heard to say, "Oh, I can't list. I'm a 'selling salesperson.' " Or, "I tried to get that listing but the owners really want to sell the property themselves and save the commission. They need every penny they can get." This salesperson does not believe he or she can do a better job for the clients than the clients can do for themselves. This is the salesperson who will sell other salespeople's listings but will not replenish the broker's shelf with inventory.

SOURCES OF LISTINGS

Leads for obtaining listings come from many directions, sometimes unexpected. Perhaps the best way to describe the general sources from which one can expect his or her best listings is from what is called "centers of influence."

Centers of Influence

Wherever one comes in contact with people, one can begin to solicit the "right to sell" another person's property. Here's a list of the so-called centers of influence:

Personal friends and relatives

Social and civic groups to which one may belong

Neighbors

Previous customers

Zone Marketing or "farming," as it is sometimes called

Referral companies of which one may be a member

Getting the Leads

A real hindrance to obtaining listings from prospects in these centers of influence is the reluctance of the sales associate (or broker) to specifically ask those people for leads or listings. The most important way to get leads is to *ask*. Salespeople should learn to ask friends, neighbors, business associates, visitors to the open house, callers on home-for-sale newspaper ads and anyone who walks into the office for directions or information. They should be asked if they have a house to sell or if they know anyone who is thinking of moving. The telephone repairer, the letter carrier, the plumber, the babysitter, the person who plows the snow or cares for the lawn—the listing lead can come from anyone.

It is important to remember that techniques have been mastered for use in every phase of the business, from soliciting for listings to closing the sale, from answering the telephone to qualifying buyers. There are week-long seminars, 40-minute tapes and hundreds of books describing methods to use for all these selling activities. Competitors are learning to use them and the new associate also must learn them and use them if he or she hopes to compete successfully. It is extremely important to expose salespeople to these techniques at the beginning of their careers before sloppy habits take over. Even though many salespeople have natural selling abilities, real estate stars are not born, they are made. They become stars only with dedication to long hours, well-planned days and polished techniques.

It should be noted here that the words *closing* and *qualifying* have double meanings. "Closing the sale," or "the close," used as above, means getting the signature on the listing or sales contract. This is not to be confused with the transfer of title, known as the *settlement* in some areas, but the *closing* in others. The term *qualify* means to most people to qualify a person financially; in the above usage, however, it refers to determining a person's needs, whether customer or client.

Personal Contact

Turning leads into sales may mean turning customers into clients. In common usage a home buyer is referred to as the customer. The seller, because of the contractual relationship with the broker, is the client. Every customer should be seen as a potential client.

The cold canvass is another opportunity for personal contact. Walking up and down a street, the salesperson stops at every home or possibly every second or third home and asks if the occupant knows of anyone in the neighborhood who is thinking of moving. This method is an excellent way to get listing leads. In some companies this activity is a suggested procedure for all new salespeople as part of their training.

Advertising

Listings can be solicited by newspaper advertising in which the public is advised that buyers are waiting for homes of a particular style, price or location. Newspaper listings of existing homes for sale, as either classified or display advertising, are fine sources for obtaining listing leads.

In responses to ads in the for-sale section, every caller should be treated as a listing prospect because the caller may own a home. Even though the customer may not buy the house in question, he or she eventually will want to sell the currently owned house.

Institutional advertising will be covered in depth in Chapter 10; it is worth noting, however, that a major reason for institutional advertising is to attract listings to the office. It often takes time for this type of advertising to have an impact on a new market area. If handled properly, however, it can be a highly productive source of listings.

For Sale by Owner

Salespeople should take note of every for-sale-by-owner (FSBO) sign as they drive through their market area. Owners should be contacted either personally or by mail or phone. Principal-only advertisements in newspapers, referred to as POs or FSBOs, should also be followed up in an attempt to convert them into exclusive listings.

Direct Mail

As soon as the office opens for business, the broker and the salespeople should send announcements to family, friends, neighbors and business contacts informing them that the new office is available to serve all their real estate needs. Once a house is sold by the office, notes can be sent to neighbors telling them of the sale and explaining that in the process a list of qualified buyers for other homes in their area has been acquired. The notes should ask the neighbors if they or others they know are thinking of selling their homes.

Zone Marketing or Farming

These terms describe the process by which a sales associate develops a geographic area where the associate thinks he or she can most effectively obtain listings. It may be the general neighborhood in which the associate resides or it may be a neighborhood of property owners in the economic stratum in which the associate works best. However, whatever the choice, it should be an area with a history of high turnover. Whichever it is, the associate should become known as the real estate expert in that area. The system should be supplemented by mailings and handouts. The farm does not have to be a geographic area but may be a company, club, corporate firm or any group of people that will be followed up by regular contact. The purpose is to create recognition of the salesperson as the one person with whom to do business when real estate services are needed.

Open Houses

Whenever possible, an open house should be held on each new listing. Open houses often result in a sale of the particular property but they are even more effective in bringing new prospects to the office. These customers are usually homeowners themselves and, if they do buy, will have houses to sell.

Referral and Relocation Companies

One recent phenomenon in the development of the real estate business and a rich source of residential listings is the advent of the so-called referral or relocation companies. There are at least two dozen such "networks" now in existence in the United States; each of them is always looking for new members to represent it in most of the major communities in the country.

The objective of such a company is to put relocating homeowners in touch with its REALTOR® members for the purpose of selling the homeowners' existing homes and helping them purchase other homes in the area to which they are moving.

Usually the financial arrangements are such that part of the commission is paid to the referral company, part is paid to the referring brokerage house and the remainder is kept by the referred-to broker. The amount of such commission division depends upon the individual policy of each company.

THE INITIAL INTERVIEW

If all of these recommendations on how to obtain listings are diligently followed, it will not be long before the new broker hears someone say, "I was thinking of selling and looking for a larger home," or "My neighbor just told me that her company might transfer her to another state." This is a lead that must be converted into an appointment. And the only way to get an appointment is to ask for it.

There are two methods of obtaining listings, one using a one-appointment approach and the other using a two-appointment approach.

The one-appointment approach is used when the salesperson is confident that he or she will be able to gather sufficient information about the subject property and about comparable sold and currently listed properties to be able to prepare a competitive market analysis (CMA) in advance. This is usually not possible unless the subject property is one of a development of like properties for which comparable statistics are available; the only adjustment the salesperson has to make on the CMA after seeing the house is an adjustment for its general condition. If the interior layout of the house is not known to the salesperson in advance, numerous adjustments probably will have to be made. For example, improvements, taxes, age, area, appreciation and amenities are just some of the items that have an influence on adjustments of the base price.

The two-appointment approach affords the salesperson several opportunities he or she does not have in the one-appointment approach, such as the necessary time to thoroughly research comparable sold and currently listed homes, thereby enabling the broker to present a fair market value to the homeowner that is supported by all available facts. In addition, it gives him or her the opportunity to assess the owner's motivation and any demands the owner might want to impose on the listing agent. Finally, it very often makes it easier to get the appointment because the salesperson does not ask for the listing on the initial contact with a potential client, merely for an appointment to visit with the homeowner to inspect the property. An example of an incorrect approach would be, "I understand you might be selling your home. Would you list it with my office?" The correct approach is to say "I understand you are contemplating a move" or "thinking of moving" or "going to be transferred"—whatever is appropriate. "I'm associated with ABC REALTORS® and am knowledgeable about the real estate market in this area. I'm sure the first thing you'll want to know is today's market value of your house. Would you like me to help you establish that? There's no obligation, of course."

Few homeowners can resist an offer of this kind. After all, they have not been asked to do anything at this point. They have been asked neither for an appointment nor for the listing and they have been told there is no obligation. An offer has merely been made to help them establish a value. When the homeowner answers in the affirmative, the salesperson says, "Fine, first I'll have to inspect the home. Shall I come over this evening or tomorrow morning?"

There are dozens of possible ways to conduct this conversation. Each sales trainer has his or her own method and each is acceptable if it accomplishes the desired results—getting the appointment. It is important to develop a comfortable style, remembering three basic points:

1. Offer assistance without obligation.
2. Offer the owner a choice of two different times for the inspection appointment.
3. Do not discuss specific data, such as value of the house, types of listings or marketing techniques, until the house has been inspected and the homework done.

Some salespeople may object to the two-appointment approach because they fear that the listing will be given to another office before the second appointment takes place. It should be noted at this point that one of the authors has used the two-appointment approach for nearly 20 years, in the "hottest" of markets and with very keen competition, and has never lost a listing because the client would not wait for the second appointment. Remember that the two-appointment approach is explained to the prospective client at the beginning and that the span between the first and second appointments need be only long enough to prepare the CMA, which could be only a few hours from the time of the first appointment.

Background Research

The most important strategy to follow in following up a lead for a listing probably is to *do your homework!* Regardless of which approach is used, whether it is either of the two mentioned before or any other developed by your firm, as much information as possible should be gathered on the property prior to the first appointment. Having obtained the owner's name and address, the salesperson can then check tax books for full legal names, lot and block description, lot size, taxes, assessed values, zoning, easements and any other information useful in preparing the listing contract. If there is to be a second appointment, this information will not be discussed in any detail during the first inspection. In any case, it provides a certain advantage. Instead of asking "What are your taxes?" the salesperson can say, "My records indicate that taxes on this property are $1,245.89. Is that correct?" This evidence of professionalism imparts to the homeowner a feeling of confidence in the salesperson's ability.

For the same reason, comparable homes that have sold in that neighborhood should be identified. Not only will they be needed to prepare the CMA but it is wise to be familiar with them in case the owner mentions a house that recently sold and asks for information about it. To be able to say "Yes, that was a two-bath home and it sold for $75,500" is better than "Oh, I didn't know the house next door sold last month."

The Presentation Binder

After gathering as much information as possible about the property and the area, the salesperson should compile all the information he or she will want to show or leave with the homeowner. It is advisable to present all information in a binder or an office brochure or both. Salespeople may prepare presentation binders (listing kits) for themselves or the company may prepare them. Many salespeople prefer to prepare their own because they can include material about themselves as well as the company. The company brochure is best prepared by the broker; it should reflect company image, policy and attitudes.

The presentation binder may be a simple three-ring binder or a complex flip chart. The flip chart is an excellent tool because it enables the salesperson to read the textual material on the reverse side while the homeowner is concentrating on the visual presentation in front. Regardless of form, the following information should be included:

- Personal résumé;
- History of the office;
- Pictures of the office;
- Press releases;
- Facts and figures showing performance record;
- Copies of advertising;

- Information on referral networks and other services;
- Sample listing forms;
- Sample offer to purchase and/or contract;
- Awards earned by the office and salespeople; and
- Picture of sold homes with sign.

It is not necessary to go over all the contents of the binder with every homeowner. It only is necessary to establish familiarity with and confidence in the salesperson and the office. In the remaining time, answer any questions the potential client has.

Objective of the Interview

The first appointment should be organized to accomplish five tasks:

1. Obtain all data (interior and exterior) about the property to enable the homeowner to establish a fair market value for the home;
2. Qualify the homeowner as to motivation for selling;
3. Establish confidence in the salesperson and the firm;
4. Set the time for the second appointment; and
5. Determine whether or not one really *wants the listing*. Sometimes the seller's motivation is not strong enough to ensure complete cooperation in effecting a sale or the price asked is completely beyond reason with no hope of a compromise. In this case, the listing may be considered unsalable. It often is better to let some competitor waste his or her time and resources in attempting to sell the unsalable than to waste your own.

These five tasks can be accomplished in many ways, depending on personal style and other factors. It is easier for a salesperson to inspect property with an actual listing form on a clipboard so that pertinent data will not be overlooked. Unfortunately, some homeowners become very nervous when they see anything that in any way suggests a contract. Therefore, it is usually advisable, if this is the first appointment, to take notes on a pad and transfer the information to a listing form later on, either back at the office or in the car. If the homeowner invites the salesperson to sit down, the salesperson should decline, saying, "Thank you, we can sit down later. First, I'd like to walk through the house and take notes. Would you like to come with me so you can answer any questions I have?"

This procedure has several objectives. One can gather a wealth of information about the owner while walking through the house together.

The homeowner's comments and actions will indicate if he or she is happy or sad about the move, nervous or relaxed, anxious or calm. A number of questions can be asked in an easy, conversational manner. Questions that are asked in this fashion will elicit significant reactions that might not be forthcoming during a structured formal interview. For example, while walking from the den to the bedrooms, or from the first floor to the second, the salesperson can ask over his or her shoulder such questions as these: "How long have you lived here, Mrs. Jones?" "Has your company given you a firm date for the transfer?" "Will the company be paying any of the expenses involved in the sale or purchase?" The answers enable the salesperson to better understand the homeowner's position and attitude concerning the move. The technique should be continued throughout subsequent appointments, so that when the listing is signed the salesperson knows all he or she needs to know about the seller's motivation to close the eventual sale properly. When an offer is presented by a prospective buyer, the salesperson will be better able to negotiate for the seller's best interests.

It is important to end the visit inside the house so that conversation can take place and questions can be asked and answered. Therefore, if possible, the broker should inspect the exterior of the property first. Because the interior of the property is usually inspected first and the exterior later, however, it is important to create an opportunity to get back into the house. One useful technique is to leave the attaché case in the living room.

After inspecting the interior and exterior, the salesperson should accept the homeowner's invitation to sit down. At this time the homeowner should be told about the salesperson and the company. Impatient homeowners may not want to take the time, but it is important at this stage to build client confidence in the salesperson and the firm. The prospective client should be told in advance how long the appointment will take. The time specified should be a bit more than the time actually needed to inspect the home and take notes to allow time for "pitching" the salesperson and the firm.

Back in the house and seated with the owner, the agent should use the presentation binder. The CMA should be explained so that the owner will see how the salesperson arrives at a value for the home. A price for the home should *not* be suggested until the CMA is complete. If it is lower than the owner anticipates, the salesperson may never get the listing or the second appointment. If it is higher, the completed CMA may not support it.

The salesperson must be very firm about this. One way to answer a plea for a price is to say, "Of course, I'm very familiar with market values in this area, and I could give you a ballpark figure, but that would be very unfair to you. Sometimes, an entirely different price is indicated on the

CMA from what one would normally expect on the first inspection. That is why we prepare a CMA on every listing. When I come back, I'll have copies for you and I'll explain just how the price will be arrived at. May I come back tomorrow night or would late afternoon be better?" The salesperson always presents a choice between two positive alternatives.

The salesperson should allow enough time before the next appointment to prepare a thorough CMA, but not so much time that the seller loses interest or calls another office. If the first appointment has been handled properly, there is little danger that the homeowner will take any further action until he or she has heard the results of the CMA. If not confidence, at least curiosity will be on the side of the salesperson.

PREPARING AND PRESENTING THE CMA

As in all office procedures, the broker should provide a consistent method for salespeople to use when establishing the fair market value of a property. Although value can be determined on the basis of cost, income or market data, the basis most often used in determining the value of single-family residential properties is the market data approach. This approach requires comparing features of the subject property to those of similar (comparable) properties in the area. It is also the approach that can be learned most quickly by an observant, serious salesperson.

The forms provided on the following pages are the authors' adaptations of similar forms designed for NAR and distributed through RNMI, the REALTORS® National Marketing Institute.

The CMA form shown in Figure 9.1 provides space to list features of the subject property for easy comparison with those of similar homes recently sold and currently for sale, as well as for homes that were not sold before the listing expired. Figure 9.2 is an adjustment worksheet for CMA computation.

For Section 1, comparables closest to the subject property in area, style and amenities should be chosen. They should have closed as recently as possible (six months or less preferred, up to one year acceptable), showing that they sold in generally the same market conditions under which the subject property will be for sale.

Sections 2, Similar Homes for Sale Now, and 3, Expired Listings, although not essential to the preparation of the CMA, are helpful tools that serve a purpose. In the second section, the homeowner can readily compare the competition, thereby enabling the salesperson to price the home competitively. Section 3 shows the owner what happens to overpriced listings: They expire without having been sold.

In the adjustment process it is important to remember that *only* the feature being adjusted should be considered when determining the amount of the adjustment. One must assume that everything else about the two properties is identical, even though this is not entirely true. The subject property and the comparable property should be "seen" through the eyes of future buyers; for example, how much more a buyer would pay for subject property because it has one more bedroom than the comparable or how much less he or she would pay for subject property because it lacks the fireplace that is in the comparable must be determined.

Note that no formula or percentage system has proved absolutely effective in deciding on the amount of an adjustment. Although the salesperson might assume that a $50,000 house would be worth three percent more ($1,500) because it has central air conditioning, it does not hold that a $150,000 house would be worth three percent more ($4,500) because it has central air conditioning.

After entering the adjustments for each feature on the worksheet, the total of the *subtract* column should be subtracted from the base price, which is the dollar amount at which the comparable property sold, and the total of the *add* column should be added to the resulting subtotal. The final figure represents the adjusted price, which should be entered on the CMA form.

Not every adjusted price will be the same, although they should be fairly close if good comparables were used and the adjustments properly made. In the final decision, the salesperson should take the comparable most like the subject property and enter that figure on the CMA (his or her copy only) under fair market value. The fair market value is the suggested price at which the property will probably sell. The reason for not entering the fair market value on the homeowner's copy just yet is psychological. This approach keeps the salesperson in control of the presentation and the timing; it allows the salesperson ample time to explain the process by which fair market value is computed; it prevents the homeowners from prematurely putting an end to the presentation if their reaction to the figure is less than pleased.

Property is often listed at a price slightly higher than the fair market value to provide negotiating room; therefore, the salesperson should make the difference between fair market value and listed price clear to the seller during the second appointment.

Figures 9.3, 9.4 and 9.5 illustrate how information from a listing contract is pulled for use on the CMA and then adjusted on the adjustment chart to arrive at the fair market value and suggested list price.

THE PRESENTATION

If the two-appointment approach is used, the presentation is made at the second appointment. If the listing is to be obtained in one interview, then

FIGURE 9.1 Competitive Market Analysis

Date: _____

Competitive Market Analysis for _____

Sugg. list price
$ _____

Address	Style	Const	Age	No. of Rms	No. of Bdrms	No. of Baths	Gar	Fplc	Pool	C/A	Size Prop	Assess Value	Taxes	Comments & Extras	Fair Market Value

1. SIMILAR HOMES RECENTLY SOLD: These tell us what people are willing to pay . . . for this kind of home . . . in this area . . . at this time

Closed Price   Date   Adjustd Price

2. SIMILAR HOMES FOR SALE NOW: These tell us what we are competing against. Buyers will compare your home against these homes.

Askg Price   Days On Mkt.

3. EXPIRED LISTINGS — SIMILAR HOMES UNSOLD FOR 90 DAYS OR MORE: These illustrate the problems of overpricing.

PROBLEMS OF OVERPRICING:

A. HARD to get salespeople excited.
B. HARD to get people to make an offer.
C. HARD to get good buyers to look.
D. HARD to get financing.

JOAN m. SOBECK, INC.
Prepared by:

FIGURE 9.2   Adjustment Worksheet for CMA Computation

Subject Property:	COMP #1		COMP #2		COMP #3		COMP #4	
	In subj. not in comp	In comp not in subj.	In subj. not in comp	In comp not in subj.	In subj. not in comp	In comp not in subj.	In subj. not in comp	In comp not in subj.
FEATURE	Add	Subtract	Add	Subtract	Add	Subtract	Add	Subtract
Style								
Construction								
Age + if favors subject – if favors comp								
No. Rooms								
No. bedrooms								
No. baths								
No. garage spaces								
Fireplace								
Pool								
Central air								

Extra property size																	
Appreciation or Depreciation { of Comp since date of sale }																	
Area																	
Other																	
TOTALS																	
Base price																	
SUBTRACT																	
SUBTOTAL																	
ADD																	
ADJUSTED PRICE																	

FIGURE 9.3 Listing Form

SINGLE FAMILY

Style				List Date			Ex Date			Price	
Address							Town			ML#	

Directions

Fuel	Heat	Rms	BRs	Bths	Age	Gar	FPL	Area#	Commission
Taxes		Block	Lot	Lot Size		Sewer		A/C	Possession

Grnd Flr	
1st Flr	
2nd Flr	
3rd Flr	
Bsmt	
Exterior	S&S	Easmts/Assess
Items Incl.	
Not Incl.	
Mortgage	
Owner	Phone
Address	Bus Ph
LB	LB#	Key at
LS	LS#	
Remarks	

OPEN HOUSE ☐ Yes ☐ No DATE: TIME:

Listing Date _____ Expiration Date_____

To: _____ Broker
In consideration of your listing and endeavoring to procure a purchaser for the property described above at a price of

$_____, with a possession date of _____, We the Owners, hereby grant to you, Broker, the sole and exclusive rights to sell the above described property at the price and terms as herein stated and we,

Owners, further agree to pay you, Broker, a commission of_____ . If the commission is %, it shall be % of the said sales price or of any other sales price accepted by us, Owners. The said commission shall be earned if said property is sold or rented by us, Owners, or you, Broker, or through any other source, before the expiration of this agreement. We, Owners, represent that this property is not exclusively listed with any other broker.

"As seller you have the right to individually reach an agreement on any fee, commission, or other valuable consideration with any broker. No fee, commission or other consideration has been fixed by any governmental authority or by any trade association or multiple listing service." Nothing herein is intended to prohibit an individual broker from independently establishing a policy regarding the amount of fee, commission or other valuable consideration to be charged in transactions by the broker.

Authorization is hereby granted by us, Owners, for submission of this listing to the Bergen County Multiple Listing Service for dissemination to its particpants.

In the event the property described is sold or rented by us, Owners, or through any other source within _____ days after the expiration of this agreement to anyone to whom a broker or a broker's representative has shown the property, the said commission provided herein shall be paid to you, Broker, except in the event that we execute another Exclusive Right to Sell Agreement.

We, Owners, represent that we are the owners of the above described property and have full authority to enter into this agreement, or, if we are not the owners of the above described property, that we have full authority in writing from the owners to enter in this agreement, and no terms or conditions exist other than those contained herein.

In addition, we acknowledge that we have read this agreement, the New Jersey Attorney General's Memorandum, and Lock Box Agreement printed on the reverse side and have received a fully executed copy of this Agreement and information contained herein is accurate.

ACCEPTED BY:

Salesperson: _____

Owner Signature

Accepted by: _____
Broker/Manager's Signature

Owner Signature

Owner _____

Realtor Phone No. _____
Owner(s)
Residence Phone No. _____

Owner _____
Print

REVISED 1/84

FIGURE 9.4 Competitive Market Analysis

ADDRESS	STYLE	CONST.	AGE	#RMS	BRMS	#BATHS	GAR	FPLC	POOL	C/A	SIZE PROPERTY	AREA	TAXES	COMMENTS & EXTRAS	SUGGESTED LIST PRICE 209,900 / FAIR MARKET VALUE 201,000-205,500
274 CALVIN St. W.TWP.	CAPE	ALUM	30	6	4	2	2	NO	NO	NO	125×100	GOOD	2856.96	SEE EMPLOYMENT AGREEMENT	

1. Similar homes recently sold: These tell us what people are willing to pay . . . for this kind of home . . . in this area . . . at this time.

ADDRESS	STYLE	CONST.	AGE	#RMS	BRMS	#BATHS	GAR	FPLC	POOL	C/A	SIZE PROPERTY	AREA	TAXES	COMMENTS & EXTRAS	CLOSED PRICE	DATE	ADJUSTED PRICE
126 WALNUT ST.	CAPE	CEDAR	32	6	4	1½	NO	NO	NO	NO	75×100	GOOD	2673	NEW FURNACE, NEW H/W HEATER, FIN. BASE	192,500	12/86	202,500
311 FERN ST.	CAPE	ALUM	30	6	4	2	1	NO	NO	YES	100×100	GOOD	2711	NEW KIT, NEW SIDING, NEWER ROOF - NEW	196,000	2/87	201,000
254 HOWARD ST.	CAPE	VINYL	27	6	4	1	1	NO	NO	NO	100×100	GOOD	2402	MINT COND. - NEW KIT. & BATH	194,500	1/87	204,000
304 HICKORY ST.	CAPE	ALUM	30	6	4	2	1	NO	NO	NO	100×100	GOOD	2748	NEWER SIDING + WINDOWS-NEW KIT.	201,500	3/87	205,500

2. Similar homes for sale now: These tell us what we are competing against. Buyers will compare your home against these homes.

ADDRESS	STYLE	CONST.	AGE	#RMS	BRMS	#BATHS	GAR	FPLC	POOL	C/A	SIZE PROPERTY	AREA	TAXES	COMMENTS & EXTRAS	ASKING PRICE	DAYS ON MARKET
188 WALNUT ST.	RANCH	VINYL	30	6	3	1	NO	NO	NO	NO	75×100	GOOD	2185	FIN. BASE. - NEW ROOF - NEW STEPS	209,900	41
142 COSMAN St.	CAPE	CEDAR	32	6	4	1½	1	NO	NO	NO	75×100	GOOD	2468	TIRED - NEEDS UPDATING	212,500	62
422 BERGEN ST.	CAPE	ALUM	29	6	4	1	NO	NO	NO	NO	100×100	GOOD	2516	DECK - FIN. BASE. NEW H/W HEATER	212,900	37
321 CALVIN ST.	CAPE	CEDAR	30	6	4	2	1	NO	NO	YES	100×100	GOOD	2769	FULL DORMER - NEWER KIT.	214,900	56

3. Expired listings — Similar homes unsold for 90 days or more: These illustrate the problems of overpricing.

															ASKING PRICE	DAYS ON MARKET
NOT APPLICABLE AT THIS TIME																

Problems of Overpricing: A. HARD to get sales people excited.
B. HARD to get people to make an offer.
C. HARD to get good buyers to look.
D. HARD to get financing.

Joan M. Sobeck Inc.
Prepared by: _Wendy R. Green_

Date _MARCH 11, 1987_

FIGURE 9.5 A Completed CMA Worksheet

Subject Property: 235 CUSTER ST. NILES TWP.

FEATURE	COMP #1 700 BURKE ST. — In subj. not in comp (Add)	COMP #1 — In comp not in subj. (Subtract)	COMP #2 679 PINE LAKE DR. — In subj. not in comp (Add)	COMP #2 — In comp not in subj. (Subtract)	COMP #3 919 PINE LAKE DR. — In subj. not in comp (Add)	COMP #3 — In comp not in subj. (Subtract)	COMP #4 827 RIDGEWOOD BLVD. — In subj. not in comp (Add)	COMP #4 — In comp not in subj. (Subtract)
Style	—	—	—	—	—	—	—	—
Construction	—	—	—	−2000	—	—	—	−2000
Age + if favors subject − if favors comp	—	—	—	—	—	—	—	—
No. Rooms	—	−5000	—	—	—	−3000	—	−4000
No. bedrooms	—	—	—	—	—	—	—	—
No. baths	—	—	—	—	—	−1500	—	−1500
No. garage spaces	—	—	—	−2500	—	−2500	—	−2500
Fireplace	—	—	—	—	—	—	—	—
Pool	—	—	—	—	—	—	—	—
Central air	—	—	—	−3000	—	—	—	—

Extra property size	—	—	—	—	—	—	—	—
Appreciation or Depreciation — of Comp since date of sale	+8,000	−5,000	+5,000	—	+8,000	−5,000	+5,000	—
Area								
Other								
NEW KITCHEN		−5,000		−7,500		−3,000		−10,000
FIN. BASE		−5,000		—		−2,000		—
GAS HEAT	+2,000		—		—		—	
TOTALS	+10,000	−15,000	+5,000	−7,500	+8,000	−17,000	+5,000	−10,000
Base price	109,900		104,500		113,250		112,000	
SUBTRACT	−15,000		−7,500		−17,000		−10,000	
SUBTOTAL	94,900		97,000		96,250		102,000	
ADD	+10,000		+5,000		+8,000		+5,000	
ADJUSTED PRICE	104,900		104,000		104,250		107,000	

the presentation is made after the CMA is completed. The presentation to the homeowner has four important objectives:

- Present and explain the CMA;
- Get the seller to agree to the fair market value and list price;
- Get the listing signed; and
- Prepare the client for the first stages of the marketing process.

A copy of the CMA, complete except for the fair market value and listed price, should be made for each person to whom it will be presented. Value and price should not be entered on the seller's copy for the reasons mentioned earlier. The fair market value and suggested list price should be on the salesperson's copy but covered so the seller cannot see them, to avoid the possibility that the salesperson will be influenced by the seller's reaction and change the fair market value. If the salesperson were to suggest a higher fair market value than the CMA and adjustment worksheet indicate, the result would be an overpriced, unsalable listing. All the effort that went into preparing the CMA would be wasted.

When presenting the CMA the setting should be carefully chosen. A small table or the end of a large dining table is preferred for negotiation by many experienced salespeople. The salesperson should be close enough to the owners to point out items as they read them on the CMA. The owners should be positioned so that they can look at the salesperson and he or she at them, but also in such a way that they cannot easily look at one another. In this way the salesperson maintains maximum control of the sellers by both conversation and visual contact.

The salesperson should explain the amount of work that went into the preparation of the CMA, including the visual inspections he or she made of the chosen comparables. In that way the sellers soon realize that the fair market value they will ultimately hear was arrived at carefully and with great thought. Directing the sellers to their copies of the CMA, the salesperson can explain the procedure. Good strategy would be to begin with the comparable with an adjusted price lower than the fair market value finally established on the subject property. The second comparable should be one with an adjusted price a little higher than the subject fair market value. Last would be the comparables with adjusted prices closest to the fair market value of the subject property. The salesperson should always use the phrase, "This comparable sale would indicate that the fair market value is . . ." and never, "I think your house is worth. . . ." The sellers can argue with the salesperson's opinion, but it is difficult to argue with the facts on the CMA before them.

It is not necessary for the salesperson to read every item on the CMA form, as it could make for a dull presentation and bored and confused sellers. One should, however, present enough of it so that a point in the presentation is reached where it is natural to say, "Based on these comparables do you agree that your house has a fair market value of approximately_____?" (Name the actual figure.) If the sellers' reaction is negative, the information in Sections 2 and 3 should be reviewed to prove what happens with houses that are priced higher than the competition.

Although the salesperson determines the fair market value and the list price, the sellers should be made to feel as if they had arrived at the fair market value; it is easier for them to accept a price they think they set rather than one set by someone else. This may require several reviews of the CMA information to reinforce what has already been presented.

If the sellers fail to agree on a realistic price that will attract an offer, the salesperson should suggest that they get an FHA, VA or independent appraisal. Some salespeople suggest that the firm's sales staff come in to inspect the house and give their opinions; this action is unwise, because it generally tends to weaken the listing salesperson's position, as it appears that he or she is not sure of the conclusions based on the CMA.

If faced with the situation of having to accept an overpriced listing or not getting the listing at all, the salesperson often is tempted to accept the overpriced listing rather than see it go to the competition. At times, accepting an overpriced listing may be justified; for example, when the seller *must* sell the property within the term of the listing because of certain circumstances. In this case the salesperson knows that a price reduction will be granted so that a sale can take place. However, a salesperson must never accept an overpriced listing without the seller's complete understanding and acknowledgment that it *is* overpriced. Each overpriced, expired listing earns the broker and the firm a reputation that could cost many times more dollars than the loss of one listing. This is especially true in cases in which a for-sale sign has been on the property for the term of the listing. Removing a for-sale sign rather than replacing it with a sold sign is a signal to the entire community that the real estate firm did not do the job.

After the fair market value figure has been agreed to by the seller, a listed price can be established and entered on the CMA. It is important not to establish the list price, which is the higher amount, until the fair market value is firmly fixed in the seller's mind. To establish the agreement on the fair market value and to avoid future dispute, the seller should be asked to initial the fair market value figure. If the seller disputes the fair market value at a later date, the salesperson may then produce the initialed copy of the CMA from the files.

Handling objections. At this point, when asking for a signature on the listing agreement, the salesperson can expect to hear more objections than at any other point in the presentation. Any temptation to skip over some lengthy parts of the contract must be overcome, as it is the broker's or associate's responsibility to be sure that the clients have full understanding of the document they are about to sign. Common sources of objections that can be anticipated at this point include the type of listing, the amount of commission and the term of listing. Objections may also be raised to using a for-sale sign, giving a house key to the broker's office or holding an open house. Rather than being nervous or apologetic about these objections, the salesperson should learn the proper responses. Every objection handled successfully brings the parties that much closer to the close.

A few basic techniques will become second nature as the salesperson learns to use them and sees how well they work.

1.   Answer a question with another question.

2.   Concentrate on the benefits.

3.   Present two positive alternatives from which the client may choose.

4.   Express understanding of or apparent agreement with the objection before countering it.

Three possible objections and ways to handle them are presented here:

Objection to the type of listing may be expressed. The salesperson should always ask for an exclusive-right-to-sell listing, as explained in Chapter 3. The client may object by asking, "What if I sell the place to my neighbor? Do I still have to pay you a commission?" To counter this objection with a question the salesperson should ask, "Do you want to sell your home to your neighbor?" Most often the client's answer is no and the matter can be dropped. If not, and the client persists, the salesperson should not apologize but simply say, "Yes, under this agreement the full commission is due my office when the house is sold."

Objections to the amount of commission may arise. The client's friends may have told them of another broker whose fee is only five percent, while the fee in question is six percent. Concentrating on the benefits, the broker or salesperson might ask, "Wouldn't you prefer to list the property with an office that will bring you top dollar quickly because the commission provides a budget adequate to cover all marketing possibilities?" If the seller continues to try to negotiate the commission, the broker or salesperson should continue to emphasize the quality of service offered in exchange for the fee charged.

Objections to the For-Sale sign often occur. This objection can be countered by an expression of agreement or sympathy with the homeowner's plight. The salesperson can appear to agree by saying, "I can understand that you might not want to be reminded that you are leaving this fine home by seeing a sign on your front lawn." Then, he or she should concentrate on a benefit: "But our statistics show that 60 percent [or whatever the firm's records support] of our buyers came to us as a result of seeing our signs in the area. I am sure you would not want to lose this excellent source of buyers for your home."

Many other objections can be handled in a similar way by using these few simple techniques. Minimum space has been devoted in this book to techniques for canvassing, handling objections and closing, but there are many excellent books, tapes, films and seminars in which one can learn these techniques from seasoned experts.

Preparing to Show the Property

When the salesperson has given the clients a copy of the listing, along with any related material such as business cards, a few more minutes should be spent advising the client how to prepare the house for showing and to plan for the immediate marketing of the property.

Major repairs required to make the property more salable should have been discussed with the client prior to determining the fair market value, as such conditions should be reflected in the fair market value figure. Minor negative conditions that are merely cosmetic in nature may be covered at this time. Untrimmed bushes or uncut grass, a wall covered with crayon marks, or a ceiling stained from an old, repaired leak should all be corrected as soon as possible. The client should also be advised to open drapes and shades, to remove clutter that makes rooms appear to be smaller than they are, to empty overflowing garbage pails, and to attend to any other household chores to make the home more appealing. RNMI has published a pamphlet entitled "You Can Help Sell Your Home Faster for the Best Price" that offers excellent suggestions to the seller.

After the salesperson feels confident that the house will be presented in as positive a manner as possible, he or she should explain to the client the initial stages of the marketing procedure. Items to be covered include use of a lawn sign giving visual notice that there is a house for sale; availability of a key or lockbox so that staff and prospects can be shown the home immediately, even if the homeowner is not available; fixing a time for a tour of the home for the staff and the members of the MLS, if there is one; and deciding upon the date for an open house. Open houses will be discussed in detail in Chapter 10.

COMMUNICATION AND CONTROL

After a new listing is acquired, all sales associates in the office should be notified and a checklist should be prepared for the property.

Communication

There are at least three ways to spread the word to the staff. The notice can be entered in a centrally located *message book,* where messages for all salespeople are entered, or distributed by whatever intra-office communication is available to all associates, such as the "Flash" listing notice. (*See* Figure 6.2.) A *chalkboard* may be placed in the staff room or whatever area is used where it can readily be seen by the sales associates. A *phone squad* can be enlisted by means of a planned list: A designated person calls a group of people, each of whom, in turn, calls on a similar-sized group.

The telephone pyramid enables one person to call five people who each call five more people. The message reaches 25 people in a short time. This method is especially effective if the listing is brought into the office late in the day when salespeople may not be in the office or may be calling in for messages.

The phone squad also may be used to transmit other important messages, such as the cancellation of a meeting or a price reduction of a listing. It should be organized so that key people in the office can be notified of the message and they, in turn, can contact the associates on their phone lists. This gets the message out in the fastest possible time, avoids placing the burden for all the calls on one person and conveys messages on weekends, when secretaries or receptionists are not available. If the office staff is small, however, the listing salesperson might easily handle the communications on each new listing.

The Checklist

The well-organized checklist lists all the things to be done on acquiring a new listing. Of course, each office must prepare its own checklist so that it includes what must be done, according to office policy and local MLS procedures. Figure 9.6 is an example of such a checklist.

Inventory Control

A control system should be set up that covers every phase of the marketing process from inception of the listing to closing. A good control system provides enough information so that in an emergency any salesperson could take appropriate action to handle the emergency.

Methods of control are many and varied. The broker may use any or all of the following suggestions or design his or her own system.

The Ledger Method

Recording a new listing in a ledger book, rather than in another type of book, has many advantages. The pages are prenumbered, allowing a

---

FIGURE 9.6   Listing Checklist

1: Distribute listing to staff

    a.   message book
    b.   chalkboard
    c.   phone squad.

2. Enter in ledger book (Figure 9.7). Be sure to put NAME IN INDEX with page number. Give name, address, date listing taken and termination, price, type of listing, commission split, and salesperson's initials.

3. Record in file. Fill in as much information as possible on data sheet (Figure 9.8). On tab put NAME of client and phone number. Staple copy of signed listing on right side of folder.

4. Verify mortgage information with bank or have homeowner write letter requesting this information.

5. Sign. Record on sign list.

6. Keys (or lockbox on property)

    a.   make keys
    b.   assign code number
    c.   record in key log.

7. Write ads. Be sure to indicate the ledger number and name of owner.

8. Send copy of listing to multiple-listing services.

9. When listing is published by MLS, check for accuracy.

10. Arrange tour; record reactions.

11. Send "thank you for listing" letter.

12. Review comments after tour and discuss with client.

---

permanent code number to identify each listing. The book is strong, easy to handle and not bulky. It will survive all the use it gets while it is current; when completed, the old book can be stored in little space. The primary purpose of the ledger book is for advertising control. The preprinted number becomes the advertising code number of each listing; the dates and papers in which it is advertised, as well as the number of responses received on each ad, are recorded here. Figure 9.7, a copy of an actual ledger page, shows several items of information, including the name of the owner; address of the property; owner's address, if other than the listed property; type of listing; term of listing; listing salesperson's initials; and columns for advertising information, such as date ads

FIGURE 9.7   Advertising Ledger Entries

MR & MRS MAURICE DARROW
2009 CRAWFORD AVENUE
HILLSDALE, N.J. ————— 14

2

TYPE OF LISTING	LISTING SALESPERSON	INCEPTION DATE	EXPIRATION DATE		LIST PRICE / REDUCTION			
ER	ELI	4/10/81 —	10/16/81		89,900 —			
			6/25/81		87,000 —			

		AD COPY #	PAPER	DATE	CALLS	S.P.
		1	REC	4/13		
		4	REC	4/14		
		1	REC	4/16	1	ELI
		4	NYT	4/19		
		4	REC	4/23	1	TOM
	PICTURE HOUSES		MAG	5/3		
		4	DAILY	4/28	1	DORIS
		1	REC	5/1	1	PETER
		1	NYT	4/27		
5/4/81 DABO * SOBECK		1	REC	5/7	1111	GILDA CRAIG WENDY
5/11/81 BACK ON		4	REC	5/7		PULLED
5/17/81 DABO SOBECK						

SOURCE OF CLIENT:

SOURCE OF BUYER:

* DEPOSIT ACCEPTED BY OWNER

Made in U.S.A.

were placed, name of paper or periodical, identifying number of the copy used, number of calls received on the ad and initials of the salesperson receiving each call.

The File

Each listing should have its own file or file envelope. The name and phone number of the client should appear on the tab along with information that must be made known immediately to any salesperson looking at the file, such as "house not to be shown unless accompanied by listing salesperson" or "co-ops not to be given except with permission of client." This procedure eliminates errors that often are made when the information is not readily available. Additional information, such as correspondence, is inside the folder, clipped together in chronological order with the most recent piece of correspondence on top. All contact with the client, attorneys and others, whether by phone or in person, should be recorded by date on the folder itself or on a communications sheet kept in the file for that purpose. Proper documentation has often served brokers very favorably if investigated by the Real Estate Commission. The initials of the person entering each memo should be included so that the listing salesperson can refer to that person with any questions.

With the combination of these two elements—the ledger page indicating ad placement and response and the file folder containing a record of all contact with the client—the broker has a permanent record that proves the client was served diligently by the broker. Should the client ever question the broker's diligence, such record-keeping would support the broker's position.

Files should include control sheets covering every phase of the listing; these sheets should be prepared in advance. This advance preparation saves time the salesperson would otherwise spend during processing the listing. Figures 9.8 through 9.12 are examples of these control sheets.

The files should be maintained with the sheets always in the same place for finding specific information efficiently. The data, comment and co-op sheets, for example, can be stapled inside the left file cover. Original listings, "Tell-20" forms, and changes in status, such as price reductions, can be stapled inside the right file cover. The "Tell-20" form is an especially valuable day-to-day record that is used to tell people in the neighborhood about the listing. The form allows for a permanent record of solicitations and serves as a progress chart for the listing. It includes columns for name, address, phone, date mailed, date phoned, date of personal contact and remarks.

FIGURE 9.8 Data Sheet

```
ADDRESS: _____          PRICE: _____

SELLER'S NAME: _____          LOCK BOX # _____

ADDRESS: _____          KEY# _____

PHONE # _____ BUS# _____          # OF KEYS HD-  WW-

DATE LISTED _____ EXPIRATION DATE ____          MLS LISTING# _____

LISTED BY: _____ S.P. MLS # _____          LEDGER# _____

SIGN ON PROPERTY   YES    NO    DATE SIGN INSTALLED _____

SELLER'S ATTORNEY: _____  PHONE# _____

ADDRESS: _____

        _____

        _____

***SPECIAL SHOWING OR APPOINTMENT ARRANGEMENTS: _____

_____

*************************************************************
*************************************************************

SALES PRICE: _____ COMMISSION AGREEMENT: ____ GROSS COMMISSION _____

LISTING OFFICE: _____ SELLING OFFICE: _____

MLS CODE# _____ MLS CODE# _____

SALESPERSON: _____ MLS# ____ SALESPERSON: _____ MLS#

OFFICE PHONE# _____ HOME PHONE# ____ OFFICE PHONE# _____ HOME PHONE# ____

ADDRESS: _____ ADDRESS: _____

DABO CONFIRMATION# _____ DATE _____

BUYER'S NAME: _____ ATTORNEY'S NAME _____

ADDRESS: _____ ADDRESS _____

        _____          _____

PHONE# _____          PHONE# _____

DATE FORMAL CONTRACT SIGNED: _____  COPIES TO: SELLER    BUYER
                                         BUYER'S ATTY ___ SELLER'S ATTY ___ MTG.CO
DEPOSIT TAKEN: $ _____ WHERE IS DEPOSIT? _____ DATE DEPOSIT TAKEN

MORTGAGE COMMITMENT DATE: _____ BANK OR MTG. COMP. _____ REP. _____
REQUEST FOR RELEASE OF ESCROW GIVEN TO PjS ON: DATE _____

CLOSING DATE: _____ TIME: _____ PLACE: _____
BCMLS CHECK# _____ AMOUNT _____ DATE _____ OTHER CHECK# _____ AMOUNT _____ DATE _____
```

FIGURE 9.9   Sales Associates Comment Sheet

	DATE	COMMENT
BELINFANTE, J.		
CAVALLO, H.		
COOPER, J.		
FABIAN, M.		
FITZPATRICK, F.		
FINKLER, M.		
FREEMAN, R.		
GIUCA, T.		
KELLY, D.		
KWATKOSKI, L.		
LEALE, C.		
LUSTIG, D.		

FIGURE 9.10   Prospect Comment Sheet

S.P.	DATE	PROSPECT	COMMENTS

FIGURE 9.11   Inspection Report

Report of Inspection or Showing to: _____
                                        Listing Salesperson

From: _____ Property Inspected: _____
          Salesperson's Name   *Owner's Name*

Date: _____   _____
                              Address of Property

Comments: _____

_____

_____

_____

_____

What will make this house sell? _____

                              Probable Selling Price $ _____

Keys

At least three keys should be made for each property in case of loss or when several associates use the key. Each property should be given a key code number. All keys to a property should be tagged with that number, rather than with the address. In case of loss, no one finding the key would know the address of the house to which it belongs. A key board with numbered hooks for all keys should be hung in a private place in the office. Keys for new listings can be assigned any number that becomes available; they need not be assigned in sequence. When a lockbox is attached to the property, a duplicate key should always be available at the listing office. Keys have disappeared from lockboxes or the entire lockbox has been known to vanish. Remember, readiness for all emergencies is good business practice.

Names of clients should be listed alphabetically in a key log kept near the key board, with the code number of each key recorded by client name. Any special instructions for key use would also be entered in the key log, as nothing but the code number should be on the tag.

FIGURE 9.12 Co-Op Sheet

Name of Broker	SP	Date	Sol	Unsol	Com + Split	Name of Broker	SP	Date	Sol	Unsol

Name of Broker: office (branch if any) and person spoken to
SP: initials of sales associate who gave co-op out
Date: date co-op given
Sol: check (———) if broker *solicited* the co-op
Unsol: check (———) if broker did not solicit the co-op but was offered it
Com + Split: record both here

A sign-out book at the reception desk should be used whenever a salesperson takes a key out of the office. In this way there is always a record of who has taken the key and whether it has been returned.

When a property is sold or taken off the market, the keys should be removed from the key board and the entry in the key log and key log index crossed out. The file should then be marked to show whether keys were returned to the owner, turned over to the purchaser or otherwise disposed of.

Signs

The use of yard signs poses two control problems for the busy office. The first is to keep a record of the inventory and distribution of signs as a supply item, so that signs will be returned to the office when no longer in use, and to ensure that a supply of fresh signs and coordinate parts (frames, inserts, stakes) is always available.

The second problem is carrying out office procedure regarding the distribution of prospects who are produced by the signs. This is of particular importance when an office is structured to give those prospects to the listing salesperson.

A sign list showing the listing salesperson of each property should be posted where it is readily accessible to the person receiving a prospect call. The list must be updated constantly and kept in sequence for easy identification. An effective tool for this purpose is the strip index, available at commercial stationers. A removable strip should contain the location (town or area) of each property, its street address, name of owner, name of listing salesperson and whether it is a for-sale or sold sign. The listed price should not be included because it encourages the person answering the phone to reveal this information to the prospect before obtaining an identification and making an effort to secure the prospect.

Information about placing a sign on the property should be given to one responsible person in the office and that person, whether secretary or manager, should maintain the list. When a sign is no longer on the property, this should also be reported and the entry removed.

The listing salesperson should be required to report the return of signs to the office before a transaction is considered closed or a commission paid. This will enable control of both the sign list and the inventory.

SUMMARY

Accumulating and maintaining an inventory of listings takes time, money and knowledge and is essential to the success of the real estate broker. An established broker with a good track record can rely on repeat business from satisfied buyers and sellers and on reputation, among other things, to serve as a constant source of listings. Novice brokers must work diligently to master proved listing techniques, including farming, personal contacts, direct mail relocation services and FSBOs. Even more important, they must develop a plan to handle listings in the most productive manner so that the listings will sell quickly and bring a profit to the broker rather than remain unsold for so long that the marketing costs exceed the profit.

After the listing has been obtained, a procedure for its control must be followed. By using the forms and other methods described in this chapter, the history of each listing is readily available to the broker. This serves two purposes. First, proper control systems make it possible to determine if a fast sale occurred because of a lawn sign, an open house, swift dissemination of listing information to cooperating brokers or a list price competitive with the marketplace. Second, they provide the means of communicating with the client during all phases of the marketing process.

A competitive list price is usually the primary factor in facilitating a fast sale. Therefore, establishing the competitive price is most important. The preparation of a complete, accurate competitive market analysis is best accomplished by the two-appointment method of obtaining a listing, as it provides the broker with the time necessary to thoroughly research and analyze all data to make conclusions as to the fair market value. However, the one-appointment approach has proven a reliable method to some, depending on area, tradition and the market conditions at the time.

If the listing does not sell quickly, it usually moves into that phase of marketing that requires structured advertising. Advertising is discussed in Chapter 10, along with the controls a broker can use to make certain that this costly item is handled in the most productive manner possible.

DISCUSSION QUESTION

Prepare a presentation binder.

10 Advertising and Promotion

INTRODUCTION

If listings are the "lifeblood" of the real estate brokerage business, then the advertising and promotion of those listings is the "heartbeat" of the company. One of the main reasons an owner gives an exclusive listing to a brokerage firm is because that owner feels that he or she does not have the expertise or resources required to expose the property to the greatest number of prospective purchasers. In other words, that owner *thinks* that he or she is employing an expert to market their property professionally.

Undoubtedly, the broker has an advantage over the homeowner because the broker has the ability to establish a well-rounded marketing policy for his or her firm. This policy should include three areas of involvement—institutional advertising, specific (or merchandise) advertising and public relations. Institutional advertising is designed to promote the image of the broker and his or her firm. Specific advertising is the marketing of a particular property. Public relations is the involvement in one's community, for example, in civic organizations and the like.

However, whatever marketing policy is established, the most important thing to remember is to be consistent. Regardless of the number of times one advertises, the type of advertising used or the media chosen to get the message across, all should be planned so as to accomplish one objective: to make the firm and its product known in the marketplace—that area from which the firm expects to draw business. This task is best accomplished by developing a style or theme and using it in all types of marketing. In terms of impact on the public and maintaining the firm's image in the community, frequency of advertising is not nearly as important as the consistent use of an identifying theme in all the firm's advertising and promotion.

This chapter is devoted to demonstrating proven ways of employing all three areas of marketing to accomplish one's goal of becoming the premier firm in his or her marketing area.

INITIAL EXPOSURE

Too often one thinks of the newspaper as being the primary vehicle of calling the public's attention to a company and/or the new listings offered. This is not necessarily the case. A variety of other forms of communication that are far less expensive and offer immediate exposure, beginning with the listing contract itself, should not be overlooked. A number of them will be presented here.

The Listing Contract

The first place in which any information appears about the property to be sold is the listing contract. This contract includes the description and a list of the amenities of the property. This description is circulated to the broker's sales associates and, if the broker is a member of an MLS, to the sales associates of all other member brokers. In effect, the listing contract is the first time the property is advertised. It should be written accurately and clearly to attract the attention and favorable response of the salespeople who will be offering the property for sale. Furthermore the broker who develops a reputation for accuracy of information and for listing the inventory at fair market value will discover that his or her listings are the first to be offered to potential buyers.

Listing forms are becoming more and more standardized as a result of computerization and leave less opportunity for the exercise of originality and writing skill; nevertheless, they usually contain a "remarks" section that allows space for marketing the property's assets. It is beneficial to use wording that will capture the interest of salespeople when they first read the listing. Although the information must be factual, alternative choices of wording usually are available.

If a picture of the property is to be published with the information sheet, great care should be taken to present the house attractively. Removing garbage cans and debris from the curb and front lawn, moving cars from the driveway and from in front of the home, closing garage doors and putting window shades and drapes in uniform position all help to produce a good picture of the house.

The Tour for Sales Associates

After having produced the neatest and most descriptive listing sheet possible, the broker should arrange for sales associates to tour the newly listed property immediately. Most salespeople have a backlog of prospective customers with whom they keep in contact. Very often that brand-new listing is just the right house for a prospect who is still looking. The salesperson who sees it as soon as it comes on the market can frequently effect an immediate sale to this particular prospect. Salespeople should be encouraged to maintain weekly contact with all prospects and to contact a prospect immediately if the new listing appears to meet that prospect's requirements.

For-Sale Signs

The judicious use of for-sale signs is another popular means for giving wide exposure to a property listing. However, there are a few do's and don'ts that should be observed in the use of such signs.

- Do design the sign to convey only three messages, i.e., What, Who, and How.
  What—Is the property for sale, for lease, build to suit or what?
  Who—Who is offering the property? This is shown by the name of the firm, distinctive logo and colors.
  How—How can a prospect find out more about the property? A telephone number is generally sufficient. Some companies allow a small rider sign to be attached showing the name of the listing agent together with the agent's phone number. (This may not be permitted in all areas of the country.)
- Do abide by municipal and other regulatory body regulations concerning type, size and wording permitted.
- Do observe the wishes of the homeowner and/or the homeowners association as to where and how to place the sign. (Some planned unit developments or condominiums do not allow signs in the common areas.)
- Do replace the for-sale sign with a "Sale Pending" or "Sold" sign when appropriate.
- Don't install the sign on the property until all information regarding that listing is properly distributed to the firm's sales associates.
- Don't nail the sign to a fence, tree or side of the building unless the building is in such a dilapidated condition that it will not demean the property any further.
- Don't design the sign with so much lettering that it distracts the reader from the main message.

Sale pending signs are used in many areas to indicate that a deposit has been taken but the transaction is not yet firm nor has title passed. The sold sign is usually used after the transaction is firm (all contingencies met) or when title passes. There are two schools of thought as to the advisability of putting up a sale pending or a sold sign quickly. One is that potential customers might not call, thus losing buyers for other properties or as "back-ups," should the pending sale fall through. On the other hand, the impact on the neighborhood of having a broker's for-sale sign replaced (especially if in a relatively short period of time) by a sale pending or sold sign can be of great value in attracting other listings.

Phone Calls

The use of the Tell-20 form discussed in Chapter 9 is another way of bringing a new listing to the attention of people who are not actively looking. It is a form that serves as a reminder to tell 20 (or 40, 60 or 80) people about the new listing. This can be done by either telephoning neighbors in the vicinity of the home or sending them a handwritten note or prepared flyer. Remember that any kind of solicitation must be done in such a manner as to comply with town ordinances, real estate commission rules and antidiscrimination laws.

ADVERTISING

Advertising can be of two general types: institutional or specific (property) advertising. As already defined, institutional advertising is designed to build confidence in the broker and his or her firm. Specific advertising is designed to sell a specific property.

Although some brokers depend on institutional advertising alone, to the exclusion of property advertising, it is unlikely that a broker could survive through specific advertising alone. The real estate business requires the use of certain tools that are institutional, such as business cards, stationery and signs. Therefore, before deciding if the thrust of the advertising will be institutional or specific or a combination of both, the broker should review the available choices for real estate advertising: mass media, direct mail, outdoor, novelties and printing.

Mass Media

The media include television, radio and the newspapers. The decision as to which of these to use depends upon the cost, what the competition is doing and the number of people reached per advertising dollar. The new broker can obtain many publications from RNMI, as well as tapes of radio commercials and other advertising aids.

In certain areas, TV and radio advertising is very expensive. The broker who is affiliated with a franchise, however, can share in the franchise's local and national advertising at a fraction of the cost of individual advertising. The practicality of television or radio advertising for a particular office is usually determined by the extent to which the broker's firm serves the market area. Where a real estate broker effectively serves the major portion of the radio or TV audience, these media can usually be defended as cost-effective. Where only a small portion of the station's audience is served by the firm, however, the broker would be paying for too much wasted coverage. The advent of cable TV has provided another vehicle for brokers to get their message across to the public. Some have found this to be extremely effective.

Newspaper advertising, although also expensive, may be far less costly if you compare it to the readership and buyer inquiries it produces. The broker should review all the newspapers published in his or her service area, dividing them into four classifications: metropolitan dailies, regional dailies, weeklies (or semiweeklies), and shoppers (free distribution).

As a general rule of thumb, metro dailies attract the transferee and regional dailies attract the upgrader. The weeklies and shoppers, although they attract the local upgrader, are used more often for institutional advertising and as a source of listings than to attract prospective buyers. The distinction between the metropolitan and regional papers is becoming less sharp, mainly because of the general upgrading of quality of the regional and large local dailies.

An excellent source of prospects at relatively little cost is local house magazines. *Homes* magazine, based in Connecticut, is a biweekly publication featuring pictures and descriptions of properties, usually listed by the counties in which they are located. Brokers in Bergen County, New Jersey, for example, submit pictures of and ad copy for their listings along with their logos. The listings are published in a magazine titled *Bergen County Homes.* The company places these in supermarkets, motels, banks, etc., in Bergen County, where they are free to all. There are a number of such magazines throughout the country.

The broker should check the circulation of the newspapers considered. Most papers will supply an ABC (audit bureau of circulation) report to substantiate their circulation figures, as well as information on the demographic characteristics of their readers.

The three styles of newspaper ads are classified, display and classified display. The principal differences among them are placement, size and purpose. (*See* Figure 10.1.)

FIGURE 10.1   Examples of Newspaper Ads

Classified Display

IT'S "OPEN HOUSE" WEEKEND

...You are cordially invited!

Sun., May 3rd. 1-4:30 PM

House Description	Address	Directions
$99,000 Cape Cod, 3 BR, 2 baths, 2 zoned Gas H/W heat 80x104 property	811 Riverdell Rd. Oradell	North on Forest Ave., right on Spring Valley Rd., right on Riverdell Rd. to #811
$102,900 Victorian Colonial 75x160, low taxes, LR, DR, MEIK, 4 BR, 1½ baths, laundry	269 Maple Ave. Oradell	Kinderkamack Rd. to Ridgewood Ave., east to 269 Maple Ave.
$129,900 Ex. Ranch, 100x104, LR, DR, EIK, 5 BR, 2 baths, finished basmt.	222 Spring Valley Rd. Park Ridge	Grand Ave., Montvale, south on Spring Valley Rd. to #222
$122,900 Williamsburg, ¾ acre, LR, DR, Kit., 3 BR, 2 baths, fin. FR w/fplc.	614 Mew Street River Vale	River Vale Rd. to New St., east to #614
$114,900 Immaculate Mother/ Daught. LR, MOD EIK w/DR, 3 BR, 1 bath, APT: LR/KIT/BR full bath, screened porch	150 Old Lafayette Ave. Washington Township	Lafayette Ave. (extension) south on Ridgewood Rd. to 150 Old Lafayette Ave.
$149,000 Dutch Col., 9 rms., 3 BR, 1½ baths, LR w/fplc., fantastic Great Rm.	74 Dean Street Westwood	Westwood Ave. east to 74 Dean Street
$119,900 50 Ft. B/L, 75x100, LR, DR, MEIK, 3 BR, 2½ baths, FR, DEN	15 Burger Place Westwood	South on Lafayette Ave. to 15 Burger Place
$124,900 New England Colonial 125x180, LR w/fplc., DR, FR, ¾ BR, 2 baths	43 Benson Ave. Westwood	Westwood Ave. east to Dean St., left on Benson Ave. to #43

For more information call:

SIGN OF SERVICE
Joan m. Sobeck INC
REALTORS ®

666-1606
330 Broadway
Hillsdale, N.J. 07642

666-0705
287 Kinderkamack Rd.
Westwood, N.J. 07675

Classified

WESTWOOD   DUTCH COLONIAL

WHERE DREAMS COME TRUE

Imagine a Garden Room, 25 x 26 feet, with beamed ceiling, skylight and a Brick Floor. Relax! Entertain! Write! Listen to Beautiful music...this room (and the entire house) lends itself to Happy Moments!! The Kitchen is a Country Charmer, the Dining Rm. formal, The Liv. Rm. cozy w/FPLC and Bookcases. There's even a small Library for very private Times. 3 Bdrms., 2 Bath units and a covered Slate Patio...all nestled on a pretty piece of prop. and a winding country street. Owners don't want to leave, but they must. Offered at $134,900.

Joan m. SOBECK, Inc.
REALTORS

666-1606   666-0705

the REALTOR for ALL REASONS

There are **24 Reasons** to buy or sell thru **Joan m. Sobeck, inc.**
(and we back them up in writing)

The **24 Reasons** are spelled out in our Brochure
"CONSUMER SERVICE STANDARDS"
Call or stop by for your complimentary copy.

SIGN OF SERVICE
®   **Joan m. Sobeck**   ⌂
REALTORS

666-1606   666-0705

Display

Classified.   Any advertisement that appears in the columns set aside in newspapers for classified advertisers is a classified advertisement. These ads appear in uniform typography under such fixed headings as Houses for Sale, Farms, Estates, Acreage or Business Properties. In large city papers the ads are usually subclassified by counties, by communities within the county, and by state. No illustrations are used. By effective use of white space, varying line widths, varied spacing between lines and other devices, a classified ad may be made attractive and unique. The ads are closely read by those who turn to them, and their appearance, once they have attracted the reader, is irrelevant if the wording of the copy does not result in an inquiry.

Display.   Advertising matter not included in the classified section is called display advertising. Display ads have an attention-getting quality obtained through the skillful use of display type, photographs, artwork and space. Display type is usually a large-size type. Different sizes and styles of type are used in display ads, as well as varying line widths and spacing between the lines.

Classified display.   Advertisements in the classified columns of a paper using some display advertising characteristics, such as artwork, logos and photographs, are termed classified display ads.

Although one might hastily conclude that the classified ad is specific advertising, the display ad institutional and the classified display a combination of both, this is not completely true. Strictly classified advertising can also be institutional in effect if the firm's ads are numerous or distinctive enough to catch the reader's eye. Prospects frequently say they have gone to a particular office because they have seen many of its ads or they have seen the broker's name advertised, rather than because of specific ads.

Direct Mail

This form of advertising includes announcements of new salespeople to the firm, introductions of new residents to a neighborhood, copies of ads published, offerings of new listings, postcards, flyers, newsletters, and so forth, mailed directly to homes or businesses in the area served. It can be very expensive, so the mailing message should be carefully chosen and sent to those apt to be interested in that message. The discussion in Chapter 7 of cost effectiveness of direct mail in recruiting salespeople is also generally applicable to advertising by direct mail.

Outdoor Advertising

Billboards, taxi signs, bus signs, auto signs, for-sale signs and sold signs all fall into this category. In some communities the name of a local broker is advertised on attractive trash cans placed in shopping centers or on benches provided at bus stops.

Novelties

Novelties include literally hundreds of items on which a broker can have the company name imprinted, from combs to sponges, key rings to growth charts, calendars to balloons, rulers to bottle caps. Novelty items are especially useful as giveaways when farming an area. These items should be consistent with the broker's other advertising in color, if possible, and certainly in logo and print style.

Printing

Letterheads, envelopes, business cards, contracts, flyers, forms and brochures are printed items that reach the public eye. These should be so distinctively designed that they will do an advertising and promotional job as well as convey the basic message. Whether the printed material is an elaborate brochure or simply the return address on an envelope, it should convey the image of the office. Therefore, it is wise for a broker to invest in a professionally designed logo or graphic that is distinctive and readily recognizable. The use of color increases the cost but the increased effectiveness often makes the expenditure worthwhile. Obviously, much of this printed matter reaches the public through direct mail or other forms of advertising.

Another highly effective form of printed advertising that is becoming increasingly popular is the direct mail newsletter. John Cyr, one of the authors, reports the effectiveness of such a medium.

> Because of my interest in writing I tried developing my own newsletter to send out to about 350 of the more important decision makers and leaders in and around our city. The newsletter followed a format of interspersing chatty items about events, places, and persons in the community with commercials describing properties for sale.
>
> After several years of producing such a piece among my peers I found my business increasing to the point where I no longer had time to write and produce it, and therefore had to cease publication.
>
> I intend to start it up again but this time with the help of a professional ad agency and a regular addressing and mailing service. That is, if my time and increased production will allow it.

If one does not have the time or writing skill to create his or her own newsletter, there are various companies that publish them. These usually can be personalized by putting the firm's logo in a space reserved on the first page. Salespeople often use their pictures, too. This is done by the publishers; when the newsletter is received, all one has to do is put them in envelopes and mail them.

Public Relations

Community activities, or public relations, are every bit as important to the success of a company as any method of advertising. It can also be the least expensive. A friendly handshake, a smile and a bit of conversation do not cost any money and are excellent ways of advertising one's company and inventory. If one thinks of a real estate firm in a community as being a sort of quasi-public utility with a heavy stake in the welfare of that community, then a solid, well-planned public relations program is definitely a major requirement.

Also, if one follows the philosophy that the broker is the figurehead of the firm and that the community activities in which he or she engages reflect on the entire company, then such activities should be exemplary in nature to reflect the finest of images. Some of those public relations activities should include:

- Participation in the local board of REALTORS® as well as in state and National Associations;
- Active membership and participation in the local chamber of commerce;
- Church and other civic organizations; and
- Youth organizations.

Press releases. Local papers are usually eager to receive press releases but it is most important that the release be written in a clear, neat and factual manner. Figure 10.2 shows a sample press release for submission to a newspaper.

The release should be typed for easy reading, double spaced for editing and on one side of the sheet only. Authorities differ on whether the phone number of the person submitting the release must be clearly visible. That person should be readily available for contact. "For Immediate Release" or specific release date and reference to an accompanying photo, if any, should be clearly typed across the top. The pages should be numbered and the word "more" written on the bottom of each page that is followed by another. At the top of the second page should be typed "Add 1," at the top of the third page "Add 2," and so on. At the end of the last page, the # sign indicates the end of the article. The release must be factual—no editorializing. The most important information always should appear in the first paragraph or two. This is not difficult if the writer remembers the "five Ws": who, what, when, where and why. If the

FIGURE 10.2   A Sample Press Release

FOR IMMEDIATE RELEASE WITH PHOTO   _____Date_____

To: ___Name of paper___
        _____Address of paper_____   Photo Caption: Joan m. Sobeck, Bergen
Attention: _____   County REALTOR®, is shown presenting
From: ___Name of firm___   to a group of REALTORS® at Crestwood
        ____Address of firm____   Village Adult Community in Whiting,
        ____Phone # of firm____   New Jersey, a program for assisting
                                                retiring New Jersey homeowners in
                                                planning for their retirement.

REALTOR® SOBECK SPEAKS ON RETIREMENT PLANNING

In a recent meeting with a group of New Jersey REALTORS® held in Whiting, New
Jersey, Joan m. Sobeck, President of Joan m. Sobeck, Inc. REALTORS®, reported
to those assembled that planning and preparation for retirement are very serious
matters. "The decisions that must be made cover many areas," commented the Bergen
county REALTOR®. "The prospective retiree should make a thorough assessment of
his or her medical condition and requirements, family ties and commitments, the
emotional impact of leaving friends and familiar surroundings, and the financial
consequences of changing a present residence for a retirement home."

REALTOR® Sobeck urged other REALTORS® to train their staff in these matters and
pointed out that the REALTOR® and REALTOR-ASSOCIATE® staff at Joan m. Sobeck, Inc.,
is fully prepared to provide the necessary advice and assistance relative to the
residence choice and decisions. She added that the firm has embarked on a media
campaign to bring the firm's services fully to the attention of Bergen County
residents and suggested other REALTORS® do the same in their marketing areas
of the state.

#

lead paragraphs tell *who* did *what, when* and *where* it was done and *why* it was done, the basic purpose of the release will have been accomplished.

News column. One additional combination form of institutional, product and public relations advertising is the periodic news column that can be inserted in a publication of some sort. The periodical can be the local newspaper, a shopping news organ, the chamber of commerce publication or a magazine targeted for a city, county or portion of the state. Figure 10.3 illustrates the kind of column that John Cyr reports has been effective in his local business community, as published in the Stockton Chamber of Commerce monthly bulletin.

ADVERTISING CONTROL

Advertising is usually the largest item in a broker's budget. Nationally, a typical broker spends anywhere from 5 to 25 percent of the company dollar on advertising. Some exceed 25 percent. Advertising is more than an ad in the classified section of a newspaper. It encompasses all of the media just described, in their broadest aspects. The broker must review all available advertising media and decide in which areas to spend the money allocated for advertising from the company dollar. Furthermore, he or she must decide whether the advertising will be specific, institutional or a combination. A review of the basic media indicates that mass communications, direct mail, outdoor, and printing can be both institutional and specific advertising, whereas novelties are strictly institutional in effect.

To determine the cost of each prospect call generated by classified advertising merely requires dividing the amount spent by the number of calls during the same period. It is not unusual for each call to "cost" $75 or more. If these calls are not converted to buyers or sellers (classified advertising is a good source of attracting future clients), the money spent on this type of advertising can far exceed the returns. It is more difficult to determine accurately the cost of calls on institutional advertising because there is no specific property to identify and such calls usually are a result of a combination of the broker's institutional ads.

Two obvious reasons for maintaining good intraoffice advertising procedures therefore, are to determine which ads pulled prospects best, and to decide where to spend the advertising dollar. Other less obvious but just as important reasons include obtaining price reductions, extending listing contracts, saving time, maintaining good broker-client relations and making the sale.

With advertising as the broker's major expense and the prime vehicle for projecting the firm's image in the community, the broker should

FIGURE 10.3   Two News Columns

OUR MONEY WHERE OUR MOUTH IS!

John Cyr, Realtors has long been a strong supporter of downtown Stockton real estate. We were located in our offices at 840 N. El Dorado Street for 25 years as Tenants of an investment that our late President, "Pete" Crowl put together for an investor.

This month we have moved into new quarters at 630 N. Sutter Street in a building we own jointly with 3 other investors. This move takes us even closer to the Central Business District.

Staying in the CBD (Central Business District) has paid off well. As the other real estate brokerage firms move out to the newer areas in the North, we find our share of the downtown market to be constantly increasing.

For example, this firm has participated in the sale and leasing of many such properties including:

* Major portion of the old Pepsi Cola Plant.
* Original Breuner Bldg., 601 E. Main Street.
* 3 warehouses in the Fite-Oates Ind. Park.
* 225 S. American
* 423-435 S. San Joaquin St.
* 645 E. Main Street.
* 745 N. Broadway
* 729 E. Weber Avenue.
* Block on E. Charter Way and Aurora and many others.

If you wish to participate in an investment in the resurging Stockton Downtown, then give us a call. Whether you want to buy or sell you will find us ready to help— at 630 N. Sutter Street— 466-5311.

John E. Cyr, President;
John E. Cyr, REALTORS®Inc.
630 N. Sutter Street;
466-5311;

REALTOR®

Meet Mayor Bradley

Here's your chance to hear the leading contender for the governorship of California, when Mayor Bradley speaks at the 2nd annual Outlook Conference. On February 20th, there will be a repeat performance of last years conference with an entire new cast. Last year was so well received and so highly acclaimed that your Chamber has decided to make it an annual event.

This year it is being presented a month earlier to give business-folks an opportunity to make business plans geared to the economic outlook as envisioned by a group of experts.

This year's conference has someone for everyone including: Clark Wallace, President of the National Association of Realtors; Tim Wallace, Director of the Giannini Foundation U.C. Berkeley; Tom Paton, President of Blue Shield and California Chamber of Commerce; Oscar Wright, Small Business Advocate State of California; and Bill Popejoy, President of American Savings.

The Conference is from 8:30 to 2:00 P.M. and includes luncheon. There is room for only 500 at the luncheon and first paid first accomodated! You can reserve a table for 10 at the luncheon for your staff or group of associates by sending in a check for $250 to the Greater Stockton Chamber of Commerce. Otherwise single tickets are $25.

Be sure you don't miss this year's Conference as it is one of the few opportunities you will have to hear these nationally known experts talk to you directly about the problems and opportunities facing your business in the coming year. Don't miss it!

John E. Cyr, AFLM
John E. Cyr, Realtors®Inc.
840 N. El Dorado
Stockton, CA 95202
466-5311

REALTOR®

devise a system for keeping tight control of advertising procedures. A system to control the use of the advertising dollar should be designed to fit the operating style of the office, yet be effective. Good advertising policies should be established for the tasks of writing ads, recording and processing ads, maintaining an ad book and keeping records of results. These procedures will be described here.

Writing the Ad

Although some firms employ an advertising agent or copywriter to write the ads, in many cases it is the listing salesperson or someone in the office who is assigned to compile the information and write all the ads. When the listing salesperson writes the ads, he or she should be encouraged to gather basics for the ad copy while actually getting the listing information, so that impressions that will later "paint a picture in words" will not be forgotten.

For example, a salesperson, while in the house taking statistical information for the listing contract, might note "how good the coffee smelled as it perked on the new harvest gold electric range in the cheerful kitchen that could seat eight comfortably." In the absence of a written reminder of this impression, the salesperson, attempting to write an ad back in the office, might be able to think of nothing more to say than "Elec. kit. w/new stove."

After a couple of years of trial and error and coming to the realization that most salespeople could not write a decent ad, one of the authors developed an "ad copy form" that lists the main features of the property and successfully extracts the special features and benefits. Without ever having seen the house, a respectable ad can be written from the information on this form. (*See* Figure 10.4.)

The popular "AIDA" formula—Attention, Interest, Desire, Action—is featured in almost every textbook on advertising. One should strive to include these elements in every ad, whether classified, classified display or display. One or more thorough training sessions should be devoted to this proven method of ad writing.

Attention and interest are often synonymous. However, in the strictly classified ad, attention is usually achieved through the headline, although it can also be achieved through the use of white space or unusual use of type. Interest is accomplished by the wording of the first few lines of the body of the ad. Figure 10.5 is an example of an ad with an attention-getting headline and an interesting first few lines. In classified display and display advertising, interest may be generated by the headline and attention by the layout or illustration. Figure 10.6 is an example of this type of ad. Desire must be created throughout the body of the ad so the reader's interest is not lost.

FIGURE 10.4   Ad Copy Form

CLIENT'S NAME: _____   SP.: _____

ADDRESS _____   LED. NO.: _____

TOWN: _____   AGE: _____

LIST PRICE: _____   LIST DATE: _____

STYLE: _____   EXT.: _____

ROOMS: _____   DR: _____   FAM. RM.: _____

BR: _____   E-I-KIT: _____

BATH: _____   FULL: _____   HALF: _____

FINISHED BASE: _____

FPLC: _____   WHERE: _____   TYPE: _____

GARAGE: _____   CENT. AIR: _____

POOL: _____   DESCRIBE: _____

PROP. SIZE: _____

ITEMS INCLUDED:
WALL TO WALL: _____   SELF CLEAN. OVEN: _____
REFRIG: _____   CENT. VAC.: _____
WASHER: _____   INTERCOM: _____
DRYER: _____   OTHER: _____

SPECIAL INSTRUCTIONS AS TO ADVERTISING COMMITMENTS:
_____
_____

WHAT MAKES THIS HOUSE DIFFERENT FROM ALL OTHER HOUSES ON THE MARKET AT THIS TIME? (USP—UNIQUE SELLING PROPOSITION)
_____
_____

WHO DO YOU SEE BUYING THIS HOUSE?:
_____

LIST AN INDIVIDUAL FEATURE AND DESCRIBE THE BENEFIT OF THAT FEATURE TO A BUYER:

SPECIAL FEATURE: BENEFIT:
_____
_____
_____
_____

1-Year Homeowner's Warranty Included: _____ Yes   _____ No

FIGURE 10.5 An Ad with an Attention-Getting Headline and Interesting First Few Lines

TIRED OF
HOUSING AROUND?

Walk into this extra large 3 bedroom ranch and walk into luxury family living at an affordable price. ALL BRICK CONSTRUCTION provides extra value and low maintenance. LARGE MASTER BEDROOM with walk-in closets allows creative furniture arrangements, including your over-sized waterbed. SPACIOUS COUNTRY KITCHEN makes entertaining a pleasureable experience while family and friends play peek-a-boo through the DOUBLE ALL BRICK FIREPLACE. Many more custom features, so STOP HOUSING AROUND. CALL PETE WESTHORP and get all the details at 451-8200 or 452-8836.

NORTHGLENN, INC.   451-8200

FIGURE 10.6 An Ad with Attention-Getting Layout and Illustration

ITS A JUNGLE
OUT THERE

Inflation . . . Recession . . . High Interest Rates . . .
Increasing Housing Costs . . .
All-Time High Mortgage Rates. . .

Steeple Hill Condominium,
Hoffman Estates, Has a Survival Kit.
Affordable Housing, Low Monthly Assessments
Below Market Interest Rates,
Ownership Tax Benefits.
Two and Three Bedroom Condominiums Starting at
$35,600

Steeple Hill Condominium

555 Heritage Drive, Hoffman Estates, IL 60194
(312) 885-4555

Northwest Tollway (I-90) to Route 53 go South to Higgins (72)
Then West 2½ Miles on Higgins Road

The property must be described clearly and precisely and in such a way as to create a mental picture. When an ad paints a picture in words for the reader, he or she will want to see the property.

Keeping in mind that the property can be sold to only one buyer, the ad writer should visualize the person who is most likely to buy this property and write the ad for that buyer. For example, if a house features five bedrooms and an in-ground swimming pool plus a darkroom, one ad should be written to attract the large family that enjoys swimming or vacationing at home and another to attract the photography buff.

In addition to attracting the reader's attention and interest and instilling a desire to see the property, a good ad must make it easy for the reader to do what the ad intended—that is, see the property. Give the reader a name and number to call for an appointment or, if the ad is for an open house, give the reader the address and directions. Tell the reader what to do so it will be easy for him or her to act.

A basic rule of ad writing, besides the AIDA formula, is to write the body of the ad first, then pull from it a single salesworthy feature, often referred to as the USP (unique selling proposition), and make this the headline. In times of tight financing the USP often is the financing terms available. It should be noted, however, that statements concerning financing terms, interest, payments, and the like must conform to truth-in-lending laws and, in some cases, to state regulatory laws.

Persuasive words should be used in ad writing. Research indicates that these include: *save, money, you, need, results, easy, safety, love, discovery, proven* and *guarantee.*

Maintaining or improving one's lifestyle also is important and is often the primary factor in a decision. Examples of popular phrases that can be used in describing lifestyles are: *privacy, easy maintenance, conveniences nearby, safe neighborhood, easy commuting, showplace* and *comfort.*

Before spending time and money on ads, whether classified or display, it should be remembered that every ad must have a purpose; if the purpose is not achieved the time and money are wasted. Obvious purposes or objectives are to sell the property, obtain listings, bring a steady flow of traffic into the office and create and maintain a good public image for the firm. Other objectives, less obvious but also important, include publicizing individuals within your firm, thereby increasing associates' pride and loyalty and reducing staff turnover; announcing additional services the firm offers, such as rentals, financing, property management, retirement and transferee counseling; and remaining competitive in the industry.

More than one ad should be written for each listing so that they can be alternated and written to attract different types of buyers. In an active market the property might sell so quickly that more than one ad might not be needed. However, if it appears that extensive advertising is required, it is suggested that four ads be written. Two should have large headlines and signatures and be fairly long and descriptive; the third should be a three-line ad that may be used in composite advertising. The fourth should be a five- or six-line ad resembling principal-only (PO) or for-sale-by-owner ads. Its purpose is to be seen by readers who follow only PO ads. Even though the ad contains the broker's name at the end, properly identified, if sufficient interest and desire have been created, the reader usually responds even though it is not a principal-only ad. This type of ad is frequently the best puller.

Recording and Processing the Ad

As each new listing is brought into the office it is recorded on its own numbered page of a ledger. The number of that page becomes the advertising code number of that listing and remains the code number until the listing is sold. After the ads are approved, they are typed and identified by code number and copy number. Three copies of each ad are made: one for the listing file, one for filing in a binder and one for the advertising agent, if the broker uses one. Even if the broker and salespeople write their own ad copy, the services of a local advertising firm are often used to place ads in the various papers and compile all billing. When the advertising agent has a number-coded duplicate of all ads, it is easy to make requests for ad placement; the salesperson merely has to identify the ad by code number and ad copy number.

The ledger, discussed in Chapter 9, is used primarily for advertising control. The dates of papers in which the ad appears and the number of times each ad is run are recorded in the ledger. This record is usually maintained by a person who has been placed in charge of scheduling ads and who is also responsible for calling them in to the advertising agent. An example of a ledger page is shown in that chapter. (*See* Figure 9.7.) Periodically, a list of the calls that result from ads should be posted to the ledger along with the name of the salesperson who received each call.

As mentioned early in this book, good office procedures enable the broker to determine the type of ad that attracts prospects and thereby know where to spend the advertising dollar. The ledger book is a good, fast source for this information. In addition, it indicates which salesperson received calls on a particular ad so that the broker can determine the status of those calls. Saving time and maintaining good broker/client relations can also be a direct result of the ledger book. For example, if a client phones to complain about lack of advertising, the broker quickly can refer to the ledger book. Assuming the ads have been scheduled properly, he or she will be able to read an effective ad schedule to the client and may even choose to photocopy the page and send it to the client. A client generally is impressed when, within 30 seconds of his complaint, the broker says to him: "Mr. Client, your property has been advertised 1-2-3-4-5-6-7-8-9-10-11 times [counting out loud is very effective] in 1-2-3-4 different newspapers, alternating four different kinds of advertising copy. Furthermore, we have received two calls on ad copy number 1 on [dates] and three calls on copy number 4 on [dates] and we are, therefore, going to concentrate on those two ads for a while and not on the others."

Depending on what the ledger page tells the broker, he or she will check with the salespeople regarding their follow-through on calls, re-write ads that did not pull, or advise the client that prospective buyers are not responding because the client's house is not competitively priced in comparison with other similar homes, thereby leaving the door open for a price reduction.

The history of the listing contained on one ledger page can do more than any other procedure to extend a listing, reduce a price or get an offer accepted.

Ad Book

The ad book, generally a three-ring binder, contains copies of all ads, both as they were submitted and as they appeared in print. The ads for each listing are typed on one page and this page is placed in the back of the book in order by advertising code number. Ads placed on all listings each day are recorded in front, one page for each day of the month. Ads are recorded by price, town, ledger number, copy number and the name of the paper in which they appeared. As salespeople begin their floor duty, they should check the ad book to see what listings have been advertised that day so they can have the listings handy when the calls come in. A secretary or someone who is on floor duty when the newspapers are delivered clips the ads and pastes them next to the entry, already recorded on the ad page for that day, marking in red any errors in the ad. This enables immediate corrections of the error with the advertising agent. When the bill comes at the end of the month a check against the red notes in the ad book is made to obtain credit, sometimes substantial in amount.

Master Annual Charts

At the end of each month, the total number of new prospect calls for that month should be recorded on a master chart that shows the number of calls each salesperson received and the source of each. Sources should be specific as to newspapers, for-sale signs, personal referrals, walk-ins, telephone directory, or any other source of prospects the firm has. Master charts enable the broker to get a complete year-by-year picture of advertising effectiveness.

OPEN HOUSES

An open house is held for three purposes: to sell that particular property, to sell another property more suited to the buyer's needs and to attract listings. As mentioned earlier, only those houses priced at fair market value should be used to obtain listings. This is because potential listers, viewing an overpriced house during an open house inspection, tend to get an inflated idea of what their own homes are worth. Furthermore, neighbors usually watch the marketing progress of the overpriced house, becoming disillusioned with the listing broker when the house does not sell.

If the broker's primary objective is to bring exposure to a new listing by holding an open house, he or she may do so even for an overpriced or marginally marketable property. A broker who decides to hold an open house on an overpriced listing should be aware of the risk of turning away listings that might have resulted from the marketing of that property.

When, after careful exploration of the advantages and disadvantages, a broker decides to hold an open house, he or she should do so with careful preparation and diligent follow-through. The following is a suggested procedure to use in preparation for an open house.

Planning (On Your Mark)

1. Plan and discuss with owners to get informed consent and cooperation. Arrange for owners to be away from house during open house.
2. When advertising, set up a schedule far enough ahead so advertising can be properly prepared and placed with regard to newspaper deadlines. (To do this properly, as many as ten days may be required.)
3. Schedule staff coverage (list of salespeople responsible). For security reasons, two salespeople should cover whenever possible.
4. Invite neighbors (an excellent source of leads). Send out as many invitations as the neighborhood warrants. Let the neighbors know the owners will be away. The curious will be intrigued by an opportunity to inspect the house.

Bring with You (Get Ready)

1. An appropriately dressed salesperson.
2. Guest book (properly headed with salesperson's name, address and phone number) and pens to encourage guests to sign.
3. Flags, a great attention getter, and signs, where permitted, should include an open house sign and a for-sale sign. Place

them in front, to be visible from as far as possible up the street in both directions. The salesperson's parked car should not block view of signs. Directional signs and tackers should be placed on poles leading in from main roads. Always get permission from the property owner to place signs if public space is not available.

4. Set of backup listings to discuss with guests who are not interested in subject property.

5. Offer-to-purchase agreements.

6. Mortgage payment book.

7. A sufficient supply of office brochures.

8. Office souvenirs or giveaways if available.

9. Business cards to hand to prospects; do *not* depend on card attached to brochure.

10. Key to house.

11. Deodorant spray to eliminate odors (scented candles are nice, even if there are no odors).

Preparing the Subject Property (Get Set)

1. Turn on the lights.

2. Open shades/drapes.

3. Remove clutter.

4. Arrange soft background music.

5. Prepare fireplace and light fire if weather permits.

6. Have coffee prepared for serving.

7. Turn on air conditioner.

8. If you must smoke, ask owner's permission and locate ashtray.

9. Say goodbye to owners; reassure them.

10. Park away from best parking, leave plenty of convenient space for guests.

Showing the Subject Property (Go!)

1. Don't read or display anything other than real estate material.

2. Keep TV off.

3. Place a picture of house in alternate season on display.

4. Have printed information available concerning warranties on appliances, utility bills and proximity to schools and transportation.

5. Greet people at the door.

6. Accompany people through the house. *Do not leave them alone.*

7. If customers want to see any other house suggested by you, *call your office* and *arrange* for someone from there to meet them and take them or replace you at your position while you take them. (Make sure your replacement is there before you leave.)

8. Have each prospect sign the guest book.

9. Treat every guest as a *listing prospect.*

Before Leaving

1. Turn off *all lights* and any air conditioners when you leave, unless owners have instructed otherwise.

2. Lock all doors and close all windows.

3. Remove signs, guest book and all items not previously on property.

4. Tidy up; empty ashtrays.

Follow-Through

1. Return items (signs, brochures) to office or leave in convenient place at property if first day of a two-day open house.

2. Record names in prospect book. Indicate if source was newspaper ad, sign or invitation to neighbors.

3. Report to owner, by phone call or in person; follow report by photocopy of guest book page with letter to owner. (Listing salesperson is responsible for this.)

4. Do prospect follow-up as usual.

5. Send thank-you note to everyone who attended.

MLS AND THE COOPERATING BROKER

The listing broker, as the agent of the seller, may decide to either distribute or co-op the listing information to other brokers. In an area where there is an MLS, the broker can "co-op" through the service. In either situation, the listing broker has created a subagency and afforded the client more exposure than could be had if the listing remained in one office only. The agent, however, must be careful not to use any form of cooperative arrangement as an excuse to abandon the client and count on someone else to sell the property. The responsibility for marketing and servicing the listing remains with the listing broker. The marketing approach should be as thorough as if this were the only office working on the listing.

Any rights the subagent has are derived from the agent (listing broker) *with permission*. If the listing broker chooses to give the subagent the right, for example, to advertise, present offers or negotiate with the client, that agent must realize that he or she is responsible for the subagent's actions.

In the case of advertising, one might think that multiple advertising is good for the client. However, multiple ads that appear in the same paper on the same date over the signature of several different offices may denote that a home is unmarketable: It is not selling, so everybody is advertising it. An even worse situation arises if the information is different in each ad. This can easily happen because of a time lag between the listing broker's acquisition of pertinent information, such as a price reduction or tax change, and the dissemination of this information to subagents. The listing broker must be careful not to give away his or her rights and control of the listing.

MAINTAINING CONTACT

Contact should be made between the agent and the client on a regular basis, certainly not less than once a week. The client will know that the listing is being serviced and that the agent is interested; the client's trust in the chosen broker will continue.

A second reason is to determine any changes in the status of the listing that could affect its marketability, such as occupancy date, increased or decreased taxes, seller's willingness to hold a mortgage, price adjustment, inclusion of items not originally included on the listing agreement, damage to the property or improvements made to the property. Any change should be in writing, signed by the client and immediately forwarded by the listing broker to subagents.

A third reason is to communicate to the client the reactions of prospects and other agents who have seen the property. Frequently, the listing broker is embarrassed to contact the client for a variety of reasons: no calls on ads, no showings, no offers. There is no reason for embarrassment if the broker properly prepared the CMA before putting the property on the market. If, at the owner's insistence, the property was not listed at the suggested CMA value, it leaves room for the client's acknowledgment that the listing is at a price above the agent's recommendation. The listing broker or salesperson should be embarrassed only when, finally having to make contact for whatever reason, he or she faces a client who asks, "Where have you been? I haven't heard from you in months!"

SUMMARY

After an agency is accepted, the broker must do everything in his or her power to effect a sale. The initial exposure for the new listing includes the listing contract, which is circulated to staff and cooperating brokers, a tour of the new listing by sales associates and a for-sale sign. However, there also must be a well-rounded marketing policy for the firm. This includes institutional advertising, specific (or merchandise) advertising and public relations, any of which can be instrumental in effecting a sale of the property.

Because institutional advertising is designed to build confidence in the REALTOR®, it will attract prospects to the firm who then can be shown available properties. Institutional advertising includes display ads, novelties, newsletters and news columns. Specific advertising is designed to bring a specific property to the attention of prospects and includes classified ads, for-sale signs and open houses. Public relations is press releases and one's personal involvement in the community. Public relations can reflect a highly favorable image of the entire firm, thus attracting prospects to that firm.

The actual writing and designing of ad copy often is done by the broker/manager or a staff person assigned to this task. There are various forms and guidelines available to accomplish this. However, more professional and technical assistance is usually required when using radio or TV.

Because advertising is usually a firm's greatest expenditure, tight controls must be maintained to determine if the dollars spent are bringing in the desired results—prospective buyers and sellers. To sell properties and still show a profit to the company is the real challenge for the professional.

DISCUSSION QUESTION

Mentally walk through a house with which you are familiar (a listing you now have on the market or your own home). Complete the ad copy form in this chapter and write down any impressions that will "paint a word picture." From this information write two ads, one long with a heading and signature and the other a five or six liner similar to a principal-only ad.

11 Turning Prospects into Buyers

INTRODUCTION

What many property owners who try to sell their own property do not realize is just how much expertise the payment of a commission buys. From the day the sales agent gathers all pertinent information needed to present a listing properly until the day the listing is sold, there are many steps in the marketing process that require special attention and background knowledge.

For example, when owners start out to sell their properties without benefit of engaging the services of an expert they usually have zero number of prospects. If listed with an energetic, experienced brokerage firm, there can be as many as five or ten prospects per agent just waiting for that listing to come along. Multiply those numbers by all the members of an MLS and one can see the true importance of gathering and disseminating the proper information about a property's attributes among them. In addition, there is the inestimable value of the abilities of all those agents to properly qualify prospects and turn them into serious buyers.

FINDING PROSPECTS

Finding prospects for a new listing is an acquired talent. Unless the sales associate already has prospects' names on file, or until they respond to a newspaper ad or a lawn sign or walk into a real estate office and announce, "I want to buy a home," they must be sought out. Brokers and their associates have to learn to recognize circumstances that create prospects. For example, a birth announcement indicates a growing family and the possible need for a larger home. A corporate move into an area means that transferees are arriving who need housing. Deaths and retirements may create a need for smaller, less expensive housing; a promotion may lead to the desire for a more prestigious home; professionals who graduate from colleges and universities need professional office locations.

A salesperson may have to search actively for prospects for a listing that does not sell easily because of its location; one example would be a home on a busy intersection in the center of town. The broker should take a good look at such a listing and try to determine to which kind of buyer it would appeal. Marketing then should be directed at that buyer source, using one or more of the advertising methods discussed in Chapter 10.

Although the source of prospects is important when trying to attract prospective buyers for a particular home, it ceases to be important once the prospect is a reality. Whether the lead resulted from a newspaper ad, a sign inquiry, an open house or a personal referral, the same basic techniques, with minor initial variations, are used in the next step: qualifying.

THE QUALIFYING PROCESS

The prospect who calls about a newspaper ad usually knows price, basic description and locality of the property, although he or she usually has not seen it. Initial conversation with this type of prospect should be limited to obtaining the name and phone number and making an appointment.

Prospects who respond to signs, on the other hand, have seen the exterior of the property but do not know the price or interior layout. Information that might discourage the prospect from inspecting the interior of the property should not be given. The broker's primary objective is to make the appointment.

The prospect who has been referred to the broker by another party probably does not know the specific property exists. Although one usually cannot anticipate what type of home or even what price range this prospect is seeking, this information should not be gathered over the phone. Making the appointment to meet the prospect is always the best choice for a first step.

Whatever the source and the extent of knowledge the prospect has about the property he or she ultimately buys, qualifying the customer is the second step. There are two types of qualifying. One is to determine the prospect's needs and desires; the other is to determine financial capabilities.

Potential buyers often do not have a well-formulated idea of their own needs and desires. Even when they do, their desires are frequently not expressed well enough for the broker to anticipate what they would be likely to buy.

"Buyers are liars," a common saying among real estate people, is far from true. It only *appears* that the buyer was lying when the home finally chosen is totally unlike what he or she seemed to be looking for—or what the broker *thought* the purchaser was looking for. When this happens, it is usually a result of poor communication. Perhaps the prospective buyers did not really know what would satisfy their family needs, and thus were unable to communicate these needs adequately to the broker. It is also possible that the broker was unable to empathize with the prospect and truly understand the prospect's needs. Lack of empathy on the part of brokers or salespeople is probably the most significant reason why prospects are not converted into buyers and why the saying "buyers are liars" has become popular.

Qualifying Needs and Desires

Visiting prospects in their own homes is an ideal way to gain insight and establish rapport. The visit enables the salesperson to observe the prospects' lifestyle and learn whether they want to continue or change that lifestyle in the new home. Wherever the initial interview takes place, the professional can usually determine the prospect's needs by following a few basic steps.

Ask questions designed to elicit answers that will indicate what the prospect's needs really are. Such questions should include where and how buyers plan to travel to their jobs (indicating need for proximity to transportation or job location), the type of entertaining preferred (indicating a preference for formal indoor or casual outdoor facilities) and recreational tastes (indicating the need for areas that offer tennis courts, golf courses or swimming facilities).

Listen! Salespeople frequently talk so much that prospects do not have an opportunity to express their feelings or even talk with each other. Conversation between prospective buyers, if salespeople take time to listen, is often all that is needed to decide which homes to show.

Never assume that you know what a buyer means. "Privacy" might mean three acres of forest to one prospect; to another it might mean a 50-by-100-foot lot with a five-foot garden wall. "Near schools" might mean across the street from the school to one, within bus distance to another. "Lots of land" might mean privacy or space to have horses. To a couple moving from an apartment, "lots of land" may merely mean a small garden patch for geraniums. It is most important, when qualifying the prospect for needs and desires, to ask probing questions diplomatically and then listen carefully to the answers.

Qualifying Financially

Financial qualifying is extremely important and necessary *early* in the qualifying process. Without financial capability to purchase a home, everything else is wasted. It is not suggested, however, that the first questions asked of a new prospect should concern finances. Asking "How much can you afford to spend?" or "What do you earn a year?" immediately after an introduction may well lose a new prospect. Some amount of informal chatting, which is really qualifying for needs and desires, should be done first.

When the move is made into the area of financial qualifying, it can be done in good taste without diminishing the results. "What had you planned as an initial investment in your new home?" is far better than "How much can you put down?" "The investment on this home is approximately $1,600 a month, requiring an annual income of approximately $71,000. (This is based on a house selling for $200,000 with a $50,000 down payment and an interest rate of 10 percent for a 30-year term. The $1,600 includes $250 a month taxes and $50 a month insurance.) Is this within your range?" is less abrasive than "How much do you make?"

Prospects should never be asked, "What price home are you looking for?" This question almost always produces a deliberate understatement. The salesperson then has an expressed barrier to overcome, in the form of an implied agreement—a question that already has been answered. It is much better to limit questions to income and financial commitments. For accuracy and convenience some brokers choose to use a financial calculator to determine mortgage payments, amortization, etc.

The various types of financing available in the locality should be covered and kept current in the firm's training program. For the purpose of this chapter, remember that the broker should never predetermine the type of financing for a particular prospect. Many financial possibilities are available to today's homeowner. These, combined with a creative approach to financing, should be explored in detail before casting aside any prospect. Because one has no money to put down, or another's assets are tied up in stock, neither should be dismissed as a prospect. These are only two of the many reasons that apparent lack of finances prevents sales from being made. A more open approach to financing might mean more consummated transactions.

Discrimination

During the qualifying process a salesperson is most vulnerable to being accused of discrimination. At this time extreme care must be given to presenting all terms accurately and exactly as one would in the case of a nonminority prospect. It is not unusual for a homeowner to reject a minority buyer on the basis of price offered, closing time or financial qualifications when he or she would accept the same terms from a nonminority buyer. Many times salespersons find themselves in the position of having to "educate" sellers about their responsibilities under the law. Under no circumstances should salespersons or brokers permit themselves to be caught up in this subtle form of discrimination. The Civil Rights Laws and the Affirmative Marketing Agreement are discussed further in Chapter 14.

Determining Closing Costs

Closing costs should be determined as early as possible in the financial qualifying process because the amount of money a prospective purchaser needs to close includes both down payment and closing costs. When financing is through VA, the buyer is limited to paying one percent of the loan amount (a "point") as a loan fee. Any additional loan fees (points) required by the lender may be paid by the seller. Closing costs to the buyer on other insured loans usually run higher than for conventional financing.

Thus the funds the buyer has to reserve for closing may reduce the available down payment to the point where he or she must either qualify for a larger mortgage loan or seek a lower-priced home. This is particularly true in the case of the first-home buyer, who usually is totally unaware of closing costs.

The cost of each closing item, as well as the types of items involved, vary from area to area and from time to time. Therefore, a lengthy list of closing items and their costs would not be meaningful here. The salesperson or broker must know exactly what is involved for each locality and type of financing, so as to accurately advise purchasers about closing costs.

Maintaining Control

During the initial contact with a prospect, whether on the phone or in person, it is crucial that the broker maintain control of the situation. He or she is the expert, the professional. He or she should know the market area and be able to determine quickly what properties are available that would satisfy this prospect's needs. Once a broker shows almost every house on the market, hoping that something will click, or spends precious hours showing properties without knowing how much the buyer can carry financially, he or she has lost control of the situation and the prospect. *Selective showing* is the mark of the competent broker or associate.

PRESENTING THE PROPERTY

Once it has been determined which properties in inventory best meet the prospect's needs, desires and financial capabilities, a number of these properties should be chosen for showing. Although quite obviously the prospect will buy only one property, it is wise to choose several to show. There are two reasons for this procedure. First, if the prospect does not care for the target house, the broker will want to have others ready for showing. Second, it is generally good to show the prospect several properties before the chosen property to lead the prospect into the property that best meets his or her needs, desires, and pocketbook. Many real estate sales trainers suggest that four properties be selected, with the preferred property being third on the list. The first two properties are for the purpose of whetting the prospect's appetite so that he or she will fully appreciate the third. If the prospective buyer does not make a move on the third showing, there is always the fourth as a backup to reinforce the good value and appropriateness of the third.

Making Appointments

Once the broker has determined which properties will be shown, appointments should be made with the owners. When appointments are made, there are a few points to remember that will make the entire tour and demonstration of each property a lot easier. First, rather than establish an exact time for the appointment, the time should be kept flexible: Between 2:45 and 3:15 is better than 3:00 P.M. precisely. In that way, if a prior showing is either delayed or accelerated, the homeowner will not be annoyed. Annoyed homeowners do not make for relaxed showings and the prospect should always feel relaxed in the home he or she is going to purchase. Another point is to make certain the property will be shown at its best. Although this should have been covered when the listing was accepted, a reminder to the homeowner to put on lights, open drapes or put Fido in the pen is usually extremely helpful. Of course, if the property to be shown is vacant, the broker or listing salesperson should inspect it in advance so that any negative conditions may be corrected before the showing.

Demonstrating Property

Each salesperson develops his or her own style when demonstrating property to prospective buyers but the style should always be developed with selling in mind. Discuss negative features early in the demonstration and, if possible, before arrival. It is better to say, "This next house backs onto the railroad, but there are only two trains daily and its price is right," than to arrive and have the prospects discover the railroad. The salesperson who shows property without a plan, moving from room to room saying "This is the living room," "This is the kitchen," "This is the den," and so forth, is not a salesperson but a guide. The prospect buys despite the efforts of this salesperson, not because of them. Following are some suggestions for the salesperson to use when showing the property.

When the outside aspect of the property is favorable, give the prospect an opportunity to appreciate it by pausing or parking across the street. Allowing a prospect to walk to the front door of the right house may be just enough to create a favorable attitude.

Use questions that encourage a positive response as often as possible and appropriate. The observation "This is an impressive approach, isn't it?" used with a prospect whom the salesperson has qualified as needing a home to impress people, could start the momentum toward a decision to buy.

The tour should begin at the main entrance, assuming that this is the most favorable approach to the house. In a multistory home, it is wise to go upstairs first and work down. If the owner has not been counseled prior to the appointment to switch on lights, pull back curtains, or do whatever else needs to be done to present the house at its best, the salesperson should do so during the showing.

Encourage prospects to visualize themselves in the home, using positive cues and open-ended questions such as "How many people do you entertain on special occasions?"

Always watch for signs that show interest, such as quiet discussions between husband and wife on rearranging the furniture.

Make the house come alive by questions that relate to the use of each room. "Do your boys do their homework in their rooms or at the kitchen table?" will force the prospect to react. Even a negative reaction provides more information for the qualifying process, provided the salesperson stops to *listen* and does not keep up a nonstop chatter all the way through the house.

Reserve a special obvious feature for last. This gives the prospect an opportunity to "discover" it. Prospects are more impressed if they discover a good feature themselves than if it is pointed out by salespersons.

Pick a special room and sit down. Suggest to the prospects that they be seated or, if it seems appropriate, leave them alone for a while in an attractive room where they can chat comfortably. If they are interested in the property it is important that they have an opportunity to have some time to "absorb" it. If, on the other hand, there appears to be no interest, don't make the mistake of "overselling." Move on to another property where these techniques can be put to good use.

Answering Objections

Just as objections are raised by clients during the course of listing a property, so objections are raised by prospects interested in purchasing a home. Objections are raised at all stages of the sales transaction: during the initial call to the office, in the qualifying stage and at the close. Objections raised during the initial call or contact between prospect and broker usually concern either the area in which a specific house is located or features of the house.

Area objections include not wanting a particular location because it lacks "prestige," is not in a "good" school district or is not connected to city sewers or water. These and other reasons may preclude the prospect's being shown a house in a particular town even though the house might be perfect in almost every other way.

Typical objections concerning *features* of the house are: "too small bedrooms," "not a large enough lot," "no fireplace," and so forth. These kinds of objections may cause the salesperson to pass over a particular house that is in just the right location. It is always a good idea to qualify the prospect further on each objection. A prospect requesting four bedrooms really may need three bedrooms and a den, or three bedrooms and a guest room.

Usually it is not the feature itself that is important; it is the prospect's need and intended use for the feature. One way to counter objections is to concentrate on the benefit, not the feature. In qualifying, and later in showing the property, the broker or salesperson must always be alert to the need or desire that underlies each requested feature.

Objections to features, or to the lack of them, are frequently best answered with questions. For example:

Buyer: I don't want to see a house without a pool.
Broker: The particular house I had in mind is priced several thousand less than comparable homes that do have pools, and it has a perfect site for a pool. Wouldn't you rather purchase a home where you could use the money saved to install a pool exactly to your specifications?

Buyer: The house you have advertised is in the area I want, but it has only three bedrooms. I need four bedrooms.
Broker: This house has a large study that could be easily used as a fourth bedroom. Why do you feel you need a fourth bedroom?

During the showing of property the prospect may say a number of things that are demeaning to the property. In many cases this may not mean the prospect does not like it; it may be his or her way of trying to soften up the selling agent for a lower offer. One of the authors has consistently stressed, "I would rather have a prospect who finds fault with the property, pointing out objections I can counter, than one who goes through the property agreeing to everything nice I say about it but who will not be pegged down to a commitment; or, worse yet, a prospect who says nothing during the showing so I have no way of knowing if it suits him or not."

It is axiomatic that when a prospect raises objections about a specific property he or she has been shown, that prospect is ready to be "closed." It is actually difficult to close a sale without objections because, without objections, there is no communication.

THE CLOSE

The term *to close* is not to be confused with a *closing*, meaning the passing of title. In this chapter, *to close* means to bring the prospect to the point where he or she agrees to buy the property.

Closing is a much-abused word, open to wide and varied definitions. This book defines closing as "the ability of the salesperson to elicit a decision on the part of the prospect that has a beneficial effect on all parties involved."

It would be wonderful if every buyer was ready to buy and did not need to be closed. However, the professional salesperson is well aware that the majority of his or her prospects prefer not to make major decisions on their own. A consummated real estate transaction is usually based on a series of minor decisions that carry the prospect to the major decision of buying the property. Therefore, the professional salesperson determines the prospect's wants and needs, finds a suitable property and leads the prospect through the series of minor or "trial closes" to the major decision. If this process is done correctly, the buyer never has to be faced with the major question, "Do I want to buy the home?"

Techniques

The following sections cover some of the most common closing techniques and give examples of each.

Alternate choice. Prospects who answer questions that require a thinking decision confirm that they are being led along to the close. This technique is one form of what is commonly known as a *minor trial close.* For example, if the prospect comments on the condition of a home that needs painting the salesperson might say, "Mr. Prospect, would you do the painting yourself or hire someone to do it?" Either answer indicates that the prospect is seriously interested in the house. (Note: If the prospect looks the salesperson in the eye and says "You're nuts. I wouldn't live here on a bet," he is being shown the wrong house. The salesperson should get moving!)

Tie down.   This technique is used to develop a "yes" momentum. This is done by ending a sentence with a question that demands a yes answer, often isolating an objection at the same time. For example, standing in the living room, the prospect might say, "This is a large room." The professional salesperson, taking advantage of this opportunity, should respond, "Yes, this is the largest living room we've seen today, isn't it?"

Feedback.   Feeding an objection back to the prospect in the form of a question is another good minor-trial-close technique. For example, the prospect states, "It costs too much!" The salesperson responds, "It costs too much?" The prospect then has to explain the objection or drop it; either way the salesperson wins.

Porcupine, or hot potato.   Answering a question with a question is a way to maintain control of the situation. Too many times a salesperson, when asked a question, jumps right in and tries to answer it without fully understanding why it was asked. For example, the prospect asks, "Can we move in next month?" The salesperson replies, "Would you be interested in taking possession of the home in 30 days?"

Ben Franklin, or balance sheet.   If introduced at the right moment with a practiced style, this technique is often effective when used with prospects who want to buy but cannot bring themselves to make and announce the final decision. This is often expressed by a prospect's use of such an expression as, "I'm just not sure it's the right thing to do," without accompanying it with a specific objection.

At this point the salesperson should assure prospects that their feelings are understood and appreciated and that many others have felt the same way. This should be followed with a tie-down sequence, such as, "If it's the wrong choice you want to avoid it, don't you?" (Wait for a "yes.") Then: "But if it's the right thing to do you'll want to proceed, won't you?" (Again, wait for agreement.)

The salesperson then proceeds by saying something along these lines: "Mr. Prospect, most people will agree that Benjamin Franklin was a very wise man, and the story is told that when he found himself in a situation such as yours, not sure of what to do and wanting to make the right decision, he would take a piece of paper and make two columns. At the top of the first column he wrote 'Yes' and at the top of the second he wrote 'No'; then he wrote all the favorable reasons in the 'Yes' column and the negative reasons in the 'No' column. When he was finished he counted up both columns and the decision was made for him. Why don't you try that?"

Prospects should be helped to review and list all affirmative factors, such as large rooms, built-ins and convenience to shopping. When it comes time to list the negatives, the prospects should be left to do it for themselves. When the prospect is finished writing, the salesperson should count up both columns (if the house is the right choice, there will be more affirmatives than negatives) and point out quietly and gently the result by use of another tie-down such as "The answer is pretty obvious, isn't it?" If the prospect agrees, the sale is made.

Trial close.   A technique to gauge the prospect's interest in a particular home is called the *trial close*. For example, the salesperson states: "The sellers are interested in leaving the appliances. Do you think you would like to have them?" If the answer is "Yes," the prospect is interested in the home. It is time to close in earnest.

Assumptive close.   Salespeople and sales trainers in real estate and other fields often talk about the *assumptive close* without ever clearly defining it. This is probably because this close is not so much a technique as it is an overall attitude on the part of the salesperson.

The questions "When would you like possession?" "Where would you put your piano?" "Would you do the painting yourself or hire a decorator?" are all forms of the assumptive close if used by a salesperson who projects the belief that the prospect is making the affirmative decision about buying.

The Direct Approach

Sometimes one does not have to go through any of the aforementioned methods of getting a signature on the dotted line. Sometimes a simple question, such as "Well, shall we go back to the office and see how we can arrange for you to buy this lovely home?" will suffice. The old cliché is still true: "Many a sale is killed by the jawbone of an ass." The wise agent instinctively knows when to stop talking and start writing.

Always Be Closing

Professional salespeople live by this simple ABC: *Always be closing*. They continually use one or more closing techniques to get feedback from prospects and lead them through to the major decision. The most important thing to remember is that closing is not a specific function or procedure in itself. It is a vital part of a salesperson's presentation, from the time he or she first meets the prospect through the successful completion of a transaction.

The broker or salesperson must be able to close to convert an ad into an appointment, to handle objections or to get the deposit. A salesperson can be the most knowledgeable individual in the business, but without the ability to help the prospect reach a decision that is good for everybody, he or she is not a professional salesperson. From the very first contact with the customer there is only one major objective: writing the contract.

THE OFFER

Regardless of whether or not the state real estate commission laws or other rules require a written offer to purchase, it is advisable for all offers to be in writing. A written offer carries much more weight than an oral one. Psychologically it seems to encourage the seller to consider the offer more carefully than if an oral offer had been submitted. If the terms are not exactly what the seller wants, he or she will be more likely to make a counteroffer to a written offer. Since the broker's obligation to the client is to sell the property quickly at the highest fair market value, prospects should always be requested to put offers in writing. An oral offer often results in no sale, whereas even a low offer in writing can frequently be negotiated to terms and price agreeable to the client.

Caveat about Contracts

Brokers must know the laws of the state in which they practice regarding the handling of contracts. These laws vary from state to state. In California, for example, it is legal for a broker to draw up any and all contracts required in the sale, purchase or leasing of a client's property. In Texas, brokers must use forms published by the Texas Real Estate Commission. In some other states an attorney may be required to draw up the necessary papers. In any event, if a client suggests that he or she prefers an attorney's services, by all means encourage it.

Three Types of Offers

Offers are generally tendered in three different ways: receipts, conditional binders, and contracts.

Receipts are documents, usually signed by the buyer and the broker, that in effect acknowledge that the broker has received earnest money (also called deposit, initial payment or down payment) and is authorized to submit an offer of an agreed-upon price, terms and conditions to the seller. In some states, such as California, the deposit receipt is a binding contract, as all contingencies are included. In other parts of the country, terms or special contingencies are rarely set forth in detail in a receipt and it is generally inferred that a formal contract will be drawn if an agreement is reached.

Conditional binders are documents that are drawn with some detail regarding terms and contingencies. They become binding *contracts* when signed by both parties if they contain all essentials of a contract for sale of real property, that is, if they are entered into freely by competent parties, are for an agreed-upon legal purpose and are supported by consideration.

Essential Elements of a Contract

Four essential factors must be present in a valid real estate sales contract.

Description of the property. A formal description is not essential for legal validity if the description effectively identifies the property. A street address may be sufficient in some cases, as may the statement "my house and lot near the waterworks," if the seller has only one house and lot that fit the description.

Consideration. This phrase indicates that the purchaser agrees to pay a certain price and the seller agrees to convey title to the described property.

Date of closing. This item may be an agreed date or a determinable date, such as, "30 days from issuance of a mortgage commitment."

Signatures. All parties to the transaction must sign to make the contract binding.

Terms, personal property included and contingency clauses also may be itemized in the contract.

Contingency Clauses

Contingency clauses state that the contract is either void or voidable upon the happening (or nonhappening) of a stated event, such as failure to obtain a mortgage commitment, an unsatisfactory termite inspection, an unsatisfactory professional home inspection, buyer's failure to sell present home or almost any other condition to which both parties agree.

The difference between a conditional binder and a contract with contingencies is not always apparent. The conditional binder is usually called such because it contains clauses that render it cancellable at the whim of a nonparty; for example, "subject to approval of buyer's parents" or "subject to attorney's approval." This enables the buyer, or in some cases the seller, to cancel simply because he or she has reconsidered. However, binders and deposit receipts can effectively be contracts that are enforceable against the signers. It is the contents, not the name given the document, that control the effect and legal enforceability of any document. All terms and conditions should be set forth when an offer is written or the offer should state that terms and conditions will be set forth later, thus making the offer conditional.

All contingencies should have a cutoff time. In the case of home inspections or approval by a third party, the cutoff should be within a reasonably short time so that the property is not off the market for too long a period. It is also usually in the best interests of the client to eliminate optional contingencies before the seller signs the contract. Such conditions as "subject to Great Aunt Bessie's approval," "subject to the grand piano fitting in the 10 × 12 den" or "subject to driving the route from the house to buyer's place of business during the rush hour" are examples of conditions that should be satisfied before the contract is signed.

The Seller's Needs

At the point when the buyer makes an offer, the salesperson very often forgets which party is his or her primary client, sometimes identifying with the wrong party. (*See* Chapter 3.) The contract should be drawn as tightly as is legally and morally possible and at the highest price the buyer is willing to pay. Once the broker submits an offer at a lower price—with knowledge that the buyer is actually willing to pay more and without disclosing this fact—the broker has violated the fiduciary relationship with the seller (assuming the seller is the broker's primary client).

When the offer is drawn, the seller's plans must also be considered, such as where he or she is moving and when and his or her need for the proceeds of the sale. If a seller cannot give occupancy for four months because he or she has no place to go until that time, it is foolish to draw an offer asking for occupancy in one month. If the seller needs the total amount of equity to invest in another home, it would make no sense to draw up an offer providing for the seller to carry the mortgage.

Once again it becomes clear how important it is to be in constant touch with the seller. Many sales have been lost for the seller-client because the broker did not have current information. If the possession date changes on the house the client is purchasing or a recent inheritance enables the client to carry a first mortgage, these facts are crucial to a sale.

Spirit of Goodwill

During negotiations between buyers and sellers, as well as those between listing and selling brokers in a co-op sale, a spirit of goodwill and cordial relationships must continually be maintained. True, oftentimes a listing broker may be chagrined to find another office presenting him or her with an offer on what the listing broker considered a choice listing and one he or she had high expectations of selling alone. This feeling may express itself in a less-than-enthusiastic presentation of the offer to the owner. This is wrong. To make the MLS work efficiently in any city, the total cooperation and energetic pursuit of mutual objectives must always come first. Any offer should be presented in the same spirit, whether it is the listing agent's or from someone else.

One must remember this: *A truly successful sale is only one in which all parties come away happy!*

PRESENTING THE OFFER

The Listing Office's Responsibilities

The NAR Code of Ethics and most real estate commission rules put the responsibility of marketing the property on the listing agent. When an offer taken by a cooperating broker is to be presented, it is the listing agent's responsibility to present the offer, although the cooperating broker has a right to be present. In preparing to present the offer the listing agent must first become familiar with all matters that could affect the sale, such as the buyer's financial abilities. The most practical approach is for the selling agent to be present when the listing agent presents the offer to the client. In this way any questions concerning the buyer can be answered on the spot by the selling salesperson and any negotiating can be done right from the client's home. By agreement between the listing broker and the cooperating broker, however, the cooperating broker may actually present the offer in the absence of the listing office's representative.

Groundwork for the Presentation

Before making an appointment to present the offer, the listing agent should determine, if possible, whether the offer is at fair market value but less than the seller wants. If it is, the agent should take along any documents necessary to reinforce fair market value: the original CMA, the comparables used, current homes on the market and comment sheets previously received from other prospects. In this way, if the seller refuses the offer, the agent can show that the offer is consistent with the CMA and all other data.

If the offer is not the best one the seller-client can expect, the listing agent should try to determine whether this particular prospect will meet the seller's price and terms; the seller is entitled to receive fair market value. Also, if the selling agent has any knowledge or indication that the buyer made a low offer, intending to raise it if necessary, he or she must tell the client that the buyer has indicated that he or she might raise the offer. It should be suggested to the seller that a counteroffer be made, which should encourage the buyer to accept or come back with his or her best offer. Once a counteroffer is made, however, it constitutes a rejection of the offer, thus releasing the buyer from any obligations set forth in the offer. The client cannot make a counteroffer and expect to hold the buyer to the original offer.

When phoning for the appointment, the broker or salesperson should determine that all decision-making parties (owners of record) will be present, so that the decision becomes a unanimous one, thereby eliminating more than one presentation of the offer.

It usually is advisable for the appointment with the client-seller to be made by someone other than the salesperson who will be presenting the offer. This procedure avoids the possibility of the broker or salesperson being asked to disclose the amount and terms of the offer over the phone. Because an offer presented by phone is much easier to reject than one presented in person, all offers should be presented in person.

Presentation

Remember that when an offer is presented, the client is usually anxious and quite nervous. Unless the price and terms offered are exactly what he or she expects, it is not wise to divulge too quickly the negative aspects of the offer. By telling the price first if it is too low, or stating one of the terms if it is not what the client wants, the salesperson may well create a defensive wall that may make it impossible to continue the presentation. Negotiations, on the other hand, might well have resulted in an acceptable offer to the client.

The sales agent must set the stage for the presentation. When first in the home of the client, the broker or salesperson should establish rapport by spending a brief time on pleasantries such as weather, health or children. The sales agent should then tell the sellers a little about the buyers: where they come from, their family and how much they like the house. The next step is to carefully go over the positive points in the offer. For example, if the price is too low, it should not be mentioned immediately; the sizable down payment, a possession date the seller requested, or the fact that the buyers did not ask for inclusion of any special items should be introduced. On the other hand, if the price offered is good but the occupancy date is not desirable, the agent should avoid immediately divulging the occupancy date. After reviewing the positive, strong points in the offer, the sales agent must of course tell the client about the negative, weak points. Very often, realizing that there is so much in the offer that is positive, the client will find a way to accommodate the buyer on the negative points or will counter with a compromise that might be acceptable to the buyer.

NEGOTIATING

Unless everything is exactly to the seller's expectations, there will be negotiations. It is during this crucial period of negotiating the offer that professionalism and skill are essential. At this moment of decision for the client, even if up to this point the broker has done everything according to the book, the client will certainly raise objections. These usually are merely a defense mechanism to postpone having to make a decision. Nevertheless, the sales agent must be able to answer them.

Objections

The most common objections a seller raises concern price, closing date, possession, items included and financing. The techniques recommended earlier in this chapter to handle buyers' objections can also be guidelines for handling sellers' objections. In addition, the broker may reiterate information previously conveyed to the seller during the listing process. This approach presupposes that the agent has done the homework effectively and kept in continuous contact with the client with constant feedback.

Client Feedback

An invaluable tool for effective marketing of a property is to feed back to the client all reactions to the property previously received from both salespeople and prospects. If the broker or salesperson did a good job of listing the property by preparing an accurate CMA and offering constructive advice and suggestions to the client as to the fair market value, pricing and preparing the home for showing, these reactions should reinforce what the broker already has said. Just as repetition is essential in training, so is it essential to tell the client repeatedly about drawbacks that are making the home hard to sell. These comments can be conveyed quickly and easily to the broker, listing salesperson or whoever is responsible for relaying the information to the seller when an inspection report, as shown in Figure 9.11, is made available to the staff.

The Counteroffer

Objections raised by the client that cannot be reconciled can sometimes be handled successfully by modifying the objectionable parts as a counteroffer. For example, if the offer is $75,000 and the seller will accept $76,000, the figure can be changed to $76,000 and submitted as a counteroffer. If the buyer wants a washing machine to be included in the sale and the seller does not want to include it, "washing machine" can easily be struck out. Since the offer to purchase is no longer binding on the buyer once any change has been made in it, the counteroffer must be returned to the buyer.

If the buyer agrees, both parties must initial the changes. If some, but not all, of the changes made by the seller are agreed to by the buyer, the buyer should initial those he or she does approve. Through this process of offer and counteroffer, the sales agent narrows the differences until the terms of the contract are agreeable to all parties. There must be a complete meeting of the minds and unequivocal acceptance of all terms by all parties before the agreement is binding. Both parties must initial *all* changes.

If many changes are made, they soon can make the contract look pretty messy. Therefore, it often is advisable to replace the altered contract with an entirely new, clean document in which the changes are clearly spelled out and contingencies eliminated wherever possible. Remember, the simpler the contract, with the fewest changes and rewording, the easier it will be to interpret if a disagreement develops.

During the negotiating process, even if many counteroffers and counter-counteroffers are made, the broker or salesperson should follow several basic techniques: (1) maintain good personal relations with cooperating agents; very often the greatest problems encountered in negotiating are between brokers, who become emotionally involved, each trying to get the "best deal" for his customer or client; (2) avoid creating hostility between the principals; buyers and sellers who are on cordial terms are much more apt to agree on terms of the contract; and (3) skillfully handle any and all objections as they arise.

The Fully Executed Agreement

Each time a party signs an agreement or initials a change, a copy should be left so that the party is aware of what has been signed. This procedure is recommended by the NAR Code of Ethics. It is imperative that everyone in the real estate business follow this procedure. It avoids any misunderstanding on the part of the buyer or seller and avoids any recriminations that are likely to follow. In almost every jurisdiction, real estate rules or statutes require that parties be given fully signed copies either immediately or within a fixed number of days—usually not more than five—after agreement has been reached. It is important to remember that delivery of a contract is a prerequisite to enforceability.

Once perseverance has led to a fully executed agreement, the broker should immediately secure from the seller such documents as deed, survey, mortgage, title policy and any others needed to draw the formal contract or that will be helpful in the title search. The sales agent should verify that the buyer has ordered any required inspection of the property and should take any steps necessary to see that all other contingencies included in the agreement are met. It is most important to see that a mortgage application is completed and that all other data necessary to obtain financing are provided to the lending institution as quickly as possible.

A prospect converted to a buyer does not accomplish the final goal, which is a satisfactory sale for the client and a commission for the broker. Until all contingencies are met, enabling title to be transferred, there is no sale. Salespeople must be able to guide a prospect through all the stages before the sale can be completed.

SUMMARY

Ideally, prospects who could be converted into buyers would be readily available through newspaper ads, for-sale signs, open houses or referrals. However, more often that not, the sales associate must actively seek out the buyer by determining the type of person he or she might be and then directing the marketing to that type of person.

When the prospective buyer is on the scene, the qualifying process commences. The buyer's needs and desires must be determined, which can best be accomplished by asking questions and listening to the answers. One must never assume that one instinctively knows what a buyer means. Financial qualifying also is necessary at this time so that affordable properties can be presented to the buyer. During this process it is essential that all financing options be disclosed to all prospective buyers so that no claim of discrimination can be made. The salesperson also must make certain that sellers do not reject prospective minority buyers on the ground of financial terms if those terms would be acceptable from nonminority buyers.

Although each salesperson develops his or her own style when demonstrating a property, there are basic guidelines one should follow. These include a discussion of negative features early in the demonstration, beginning the tour at a point where the first impression will be a favorable one and ending by pointing out a special feature or going to a particularly attractive room where the buyer can relax and absorb the surroundings.

One must become skilled in the techniques of answering objections and "closing," many of which have been discussed in this chapter. Although laws and customs vary from state to state, it is advisable for all offers to be in writing, whether they are receipts, conditional binders or contracts. The actual presentation of the offer usually requires doing one's homework, such as bringing documentation to support the offered price, if it is, in fact, reflective of fair market value. The associate must be particularly skilled in maintaining goodwill and cordial relations between the buyer and the seller during the presentation and especially so during the negotiations and counteroffers that usually follow. One must avoid any animosity that might prevent a sale.

DISCUSSION QUESTION

Using your own home as a case study, do the following:

1. List all the reasons why you think someone should buy your particular property rather than someone else's.
2. Formulate a description of the party or family who would be the logical purchaser for your home and explain why.
3. Make a list of all the objections a buyer might find in your property and then provide arguments to counter those objections.

12 Financing Strategies

INTRODUCTION

There is no more important function of the real estate broker in arranging the sale of real property for his or her clients than to provide competent advice on how the sale (or purchase) is to be financed. Unless the purchaser is to pay all cash for the property, which eliminates any problems (and is somewhat rare), then the buyer is often at a loss about how to proceed with the financing. If the sales agent is also uninformed, then the sale easily can collapse.

While all aspects of real estate financing cannot be adequately covered in one simple chapter of any book, the information provided herein should give a broker and/or sales associate the basics needed.

REAL ESTATE AND THE MONEY MARKET

Certainly no other activities of the business world affect the real estate brokerage business as much as the fluctuations of the money market. To understand all the underlying forces that cause those fluctuations would require a college course in economics, but this chapter presents some of the basics.

It is necessary to realize that regulation of the money market is a function of the Federal Reserve Bank, familiarly known as the *Fed,* a quasi-governmental agency whose directors are appointed by the President of the United States. It is up to the Fed to regulate the money supply for the nation; this regulation, in turn, affects the raising and lowering of interest rates; and interest rates more or less regulate real estate activity.

241

For example, if interest rates go up, then real estate brokerage activities slow down because fewer buyers can afford the monthly payments. Conversely, if interest rates go down, the business activity is spurred as more buyers enter the market for homes. Watch for news articles that describe what the Fed is doing with the money market. Is it increasing or clamping down on the money supply? Is it raising or lowering the interest rates?

By watching for those simple signs one can forecast with some degree of accuracy how brokerage business activity will be moving, up or down. One of the factors the Fed closely watches is the rate of inflation. If it looks as if inflation is getting stronger (rate is going up), then the Fed will begin to exercise curbs on the money supply, which has the effect of raising interest rates, which then curtails real estate activity. If inflation remains low and relatively stable, then interest rates too should remain somewhat stable.

The study of economics and the money supply is a fascinating one; because it has such a dramatic effect on one's livelihood, a broker is well-advised to take a college course in economics.

THE IMPORTANCE OF FINANCING

The Needs of the Buyers

Financing must be tailored to meet the needs of each particular customer. Special needs may consist of a low cash down payment, a tax shelter of income-producing properties, estate growth, smaller monthly payments to fit a budget, the use of leverage, use of current assets to produce higher income, holding the property for anticipated appreciation and subsequent tax benefits or providing a secure investment for retirement income. It is up to the broker or the associate to know which tool of financing, coupled with which source, will be most apt to satisfy each particular need.

For several reasons, purchasers of real property often prefer to use as little of their own cash as possible for the down payment. One of these reasons is that during times of high inflationary pressures, it is considered prudent to buy any investment by using as few of today's *more valuable* dollars as possible, paying off the balance some time in the future with *less valuable* inflationary dollars. Another is that the principle of *leverage* dictates that an investor in real estate can frequently derive greater benefits from the equity investment dollar by borrowing a large portion of the purchase price. Finally, through the use of borrowed funds investors can control a much larger amount of real property than if they were forced to pay all cash for each parcel.

The Needs of the Sellers

The easier financing that has become available since World War II is largely responsible for today's tremendous turnover in real property. Obviously, as the buyer's ability to purchase real estate increases when borrowed funds are more readily obtainable, the seller's chances of selling property more quickly and at a better price also increase.

Sometimes the seller is asked to aid the buyer in financing the sale. He or she may be asked to carry a loan for all or a part of the purchase price, depending on the availability of funds from other sources. Sellers are also sometimes asked to pay *points*, or loan fees, to help facilitate a sale. The seller must be thoroughly convinced in such cases that it is in his or her best interest to participate in the financing to sell the property at a more advantageous price.

THE BROKER'S ROLE IN FINANCING

Qualifying the Buyer

Because of the importance of financing to both seller and buyer, the broker who lacks knowledge of how to finance transactions is at a distinct disadvantage in the real estate business. When faced with the task of qualifying a prospect to match him or her with a home purchase, the broker must first establish what resources the buyer has to effect a purchase. The broker must ask the potential buyer some rather pertinent and personal questions about:

- Cash, or other liquid assets available for a down payment and/or closing costs;
- Earnings, to qualify for a particular-sized monthly payment;
- Employment history and future prospects; and
- Credit rating.

The broker must ascertain such facts as tactfully as possible, of course. It would be useless to show a prospect a $100,000 home if he or she had $5,000 for a down payment, earned $20,000 per year, had been on a job for six months and had a poor credit rating.

In qualifying the prospect's financing resources the broker must be aware of all possible means of financing. Each particular case presents particular problems. By ferreting out such problems ahead of time, the broker can then proceed more effectively in attempting to solve the problems. Some typical cases follow:

PROBLEM EXAMPLES

Problem: The prospect has a considerable amount of cash but went through bankruptcy a few years earlier and has a bad credit rating. *Solution:* Find a property with an existing loan high enough to be assumed so the buyer does not need new financing, for which he may not qualify.

Problem: The buyer has very little cash, a good job, a good credit rating and is a veteran of the Vietnam War. *Solution:* Find a home that can be purchased on a VA loan where the seller is agreeable to paying points to help finance the loan.

Problem: The buyer is selling an FHA-financed home in a distant community from which she is being transferred. She has some cash, a good job and good credit experience. *Solution:* Find her a home that can be financed through a new FHA loan.

Problem: The prospect wants to purchase a small farm in a rural area where banks make loans at only 50 percent of value, yet he has only a small down payment. *Solution:* Prevail on the seller to carry back a loan secured by a second deed of trust on the property for the difference between the buyer's down payment and a new 50 percent loan from the bank. Failing that, investigate the possibility of obtaining for the buyer a no-down-payment Farm Home Administration loan (made in rural communities).

These examples show how a sound background in financing techniques can help to create transactions that might otherwise be lost by a broker or salesperson. It would be safe to say that fully 50 percent of the transactions that have originated in general brokerage offices are made possible only because unusual financing arrangements have been devised. A broker who does not have the ability to do this may easily keep potential business volume down by that 50 percent.

FINANCING TOOLS: PROMISSORY NOTES
AND SECURITY DEVICES

Tools of financing, those legal instruments that may be used to pledge real estate as the security for the repayment of an obligation, are usually used in conjunction with a promissory note. While a promissory note is the *evidence that a debt is owing,* a security device is an instrument that ties that evidence to a legal instrument attaching the real estate as security.

The three types of promissory notes in general use today are the straight note, the self-amortizing note with interest included and the amortized note with level principal payments.

Security devices, the instruments that pledge real estate as security for a loan, come in several forms. The most frequently used are mortgages (both first priority and junior liens), deeds of trust (first priority and junior liens), installment sales contracts (contracts of sale, land contracts, short- or long-form contracts with power of sale), wraparound (all-inclusive, overriding, overlapping) mortgages or deeds of trust, variable rate mortgages (VRMs), adjustable rate mortgages (ARMs), renegotiable rate mortgages (RRMs), annuity mortgages, shared appreciation mortgages (SAMs) and deeds given in lieu of a mortgage.

Straight Note

This note requires interest to be payable at stipulated periods of time, with the entire principal balance due and payable at the end of a specified period. An example of a straight note is a promise to pay a bank $10,000 at the end of one year with an agreement to make payments on the interest monthly. If the interest is eight percent per year, .08 × $10,000 equals $800 for the year's interest. Divide the annual interest of $800 by 12; the monthly interest payment is $66.67. The final payment for the twelfth month would be $10,066.67.

Interest-Included, Self-Amortizing Note

This note is most commonly used in today's normal real estate transaction. It is an amortized note, with constant level payments on both principal and interest computed on the decreasing balance. A monthly mortgage calculator booklet, or amortization schedule, is invaluable to the real estate broker for calculating the amount and number of payments required to pay off a stipulated amount in a required period of time.

An example of an interest-included note is a promise to repay the $10,000 to a bank in equal monthly installments of $100 per month, including interest at eight percent per year. Reference to an amortization schedule for a $10,000 loan at payments of $100 per month, including interest at eight percent, shows that it would take 168 payments, or roughly 14 years, to amortize the loan completely. (The word *amortize* comes from the Latin root that means death or to die; hence, an amortized loan principal slowly dies as it is being paid off.)

Amortized Note with Level Principal Payments Plus Interest

In this type of note interest is computed on the unpaid balance for the previous period, while the principal payments stay the same. An example of an interest-extra note is a promise to repay a loan of $10,000 at the rate of $100 per month on the principal plus the interest due on the balance for the preceding month. In this case the loan would be paid off in 100 months ($10,000 ÷ 100), or eight years and four months. The payment for the first month would be $166.67: $100 on the principal and one-twelfth of the eight percent annual interest on the $10,000 ($66.67). The next payment would be $166.66; $100 is applied to the principal, thus reducing the interest to $66 (one-twelfth of the eight percent annual interest on the $9,900 balance). Each month the payment to interest is thus reduced by approximately 67 cents, until the entire loan is paid in full.

Learning to use the calculator. While most simple loan terms can be quickly and simply calculated with the use of a monthly amortization schedule that is readily purchased in any office supply store, a good broker who expects to handle more than simple house transactions would be well advised to learn how to use a hand-held calculator for more complicated financing. Several of the NAR Institutes offer one-day seminars in use of multiple-function calculators. After a person learns how to use such an advanced machine, he or she will not want to be without it again.

Mortgages and Deeds of Trust

A mortgage is essentially a two-party agreement between the borrower (mortgagor) and the lender (mortgagee). Its use as a financing device is common in many parts of the country.

In the event of default, the lender must initiate court action to foreclose on the mortgage and recover the property. In some states the borrower then has a year's time to redeem the property by paying all back principal payments, interest accumulated, back taxes and court and carrying costs incurred by the lender. It is this right-of-redemption period that makes the mortgage unpopular in some areas. In other states, including New York and New Jersey, there is no statutory right of redemption. The right of redemption in those states is cut off (foreclosed) on entry of a judgment of foreclosure, usually extended by the court to date of sheriff's sale—a period of about 30 days. Possession of the property that is being foreclosed on is ordered in the same judgment.

A deed of trust is a three-party transaction among the borrower (trustor), the lender (beneficiary) and the trustee. To ensure repayment of the loan, the trustor signs a form of deed to the trustee with the instructions that if he or she does not live up to the terms of the agreement with the lender, the trustee is to sell the property to the beneficiary or a higher bidder.

If a borrower defaults in payments under a deed of trust, the lender initiates a foreclosure action by asking the trustee to file a notice of default. The borrower usually has three months in which to cure that default by bringing the payments current (plus any accrued interest, late charges and attorney costs). Should the borrower fail to cure the default, the trustee has a specified number of days, usually less than 30, in which to advertise the property for sale in a local publication. The ad must stipulate the time and place where the sale is to take place. Any interested buyers are invited to attend. At the sale the lender bids the amount that is still owed, including all costs of foreclosure. Anyone who overbids the lender has bought the property. Any amount over the lender's bid is paid to the former owner. At this time transfer of title is absolute and the sale is final. There is no grace period for right of redemption. This is why lenders in many parts of the country prefer to use the deed of trust as a security device.

These are the general differences between the mortgage and deed of trust, but there are many other ramifications in the use of either instrument. A person in doubt about which instrument to use should consult an attorney.

Junior deeds of trust or mortgages.   The difference between a first mortgage or deed of trust and a second or third (junior lien) is the sequence of recording. The first deed of trust or mortgage is recorded first, a second is recorded second, and so on.

At one time, lending institutions looked askance at making a second mortgage; they believed their security was considerably less than on a first mortgage—perhaps rightly so. If they held a $50,000 loan on a property appraised at $65,000, they were lending almost 77 percent of value. With an 80 percent top loan limit, they would not lend an additional $10,000 on a second mortgage. However, because of the inflationary economy, property worth $65,000 a few years ago could easily be worth $130,000 today. The $50,000 loan balance now is only 38 percent of value. As long as their top lending policy is 80 percent of value, there is no reason (other than the borrowers' inability to repay) why banks or other financial institutions cannot make another (second) loan of $50,000 and still stay within the 80 percent overall limit. So the equity loan (second mortgage) business has been very active in recent years as values have increased.

In the case of a foreclosure with more than one deed of trust or mortgage against the property, each lien is satisfied according to its priority. For instance, if the property sells at foreclosure for $10,000 and there is an $8,000 first deed of trust and a $2,500 second deed of trust, the holder (beneficiary) of the first receives $8,000; the holder under the second trust must be satisfied with $2,000.

Special clauses.   Each security device contains many special clauses designed to protect the security and interests of the lender. The study of real estate financing covers all of these clauses in more complete detail than can be offered in this chapter. Certain clauses, however, may or may not be included, depending upon the special circumstances surrounding the sale or loan. Use of any of these clauses—subordination, acceleration or due-on-sale (call), alienation or release—may seriously affect the transaction and carry over to future transactions, should the loan be assumed. Therefore a broker must be aware of them and familiar with their effects.

A *subordination clause* is primarily used to indicate that the holder of the first deed of trust or mortgage is willing to subordinate this loan—that is, let it become a junior lien—to a new first loan at some future date under certain specified circumstances. For example, if a man bought a parcel of land for future development that he partially paid for with a purchase-money deed of trust payable to the seller, that purchase money deed of trust contains a clause (subordination) in which the seller agrees to subordinate his first deed of trust to a new loan from an institutional investor, the proceeds to be used for improving the property.

Acceleration is a generic term for a clause that protects a lender if a borrower is reducing, or "wasting," the value of his or her property. As used in real estate lending, accelerate means to cause the loan to become immediately due and payable on the happening, or nonhappening, of a specific event or obligation. For instance, if the borrower does not pay the taxes when they become due, the loan may be accelerated (called).

An *alienation clause* is a form of acceleration clause. To *alienate* in real estate means to dispose of, possibly to sell, the property. If there is such a clause in the mortgage or deed of trust, a certain act immediately triggers the acceleration clause. An alienation clause is also often termed a *due-on-sale,* or "call," *clause.* It is used to ensure that lenders will retain control over who receives the benefit of their financing of the property.

The *release clause* is used primarily in connection with "blanket" mortgages or deeds of trust. A blanket mortgage is one that covers more than one parcel of property, such as a loan on a multiple-lot subdivision or a loan in which several buildings are pledged as security. The release clause in the blanket mortgage stipulates the terms and conditions under which the lender will release part of the security. For example, in the case of a subdivision loan, each lot may be released to the buyer upon payment of a specified amount.

Prepayment privileges.   Mortgage loans are not automatically prepayable by the borrower unless the loan documents specifically provide for such prepayment. The reason for this is that a loan is a contract; the lender has a right to expect that the investment will earn a return for a fixed and agreed-upon period of time. Prepayment makes it necessary for the lender to process a new loan to keep this capital earning, thus incurring additional expenses and exposing the investment to the fluctuation of interest rates in the money market.

Most mortgage loans granted today contain either a negotiated *prepayment privilege* or one that has been set by state legislative action. These clauses often permit the borrower to pay a percentage of the principal each year above normal amortization without penalty and to pay a small penalty of part of a year's interest for the privilege of paying off the loan in full. FHA loans carry prepayment penalty clauses that are seldom enforced. VA or GI loans have no such prepayment penalty.

Any prepayment penalty can usually be eliminated by inserting the words *or more* in that part of the note describing the method of repayment. For example, the sentence may read "to be paid in installments of $100 *or more* per month, until the entire balance is paid in full."

Contracts of Sale

If a mortgage or deed of trust contains an alienation or due-on-sale clause and the owner wishes to sell the underlying security but leave the present loan or loans in place, he or she may resort to the use of either a *contract of sale* or an *all-inclusive* mortgage.

The contract of sale is usually a two-party contract, much like a mortgage. The main difference between the sales contract and a mortgage is that the sales contract usually is not recorded; therefore, the title to the property is not changed on the official records. The theory is that if the title is not officially recorded, the lender under the first mortgage (containing the due-on-sale clause) does not have knowledge that the property has changed ownership and therefore will not call the loan. Due-on-sale clauses will be discussed later in the chapter.

Because title does not change hands, the contract of sale is a dangerous form of security device for both the unwary buyer and the seller. If the seller fails to make payments on the existing loan or engenders some other form of lien against the property, the borrower under a contract of sale may suffer considerable damages and expense in trying to get such liens removed. In addition, if a contract of sale is used to circumvent a due-on-sale clause, it is the broker's responsibility to make sure the buyer is aware of the consequences of using such an instrument. If the holder of the first loan should learn about the alienation of title to the real property at some later date, that lender may call the loan, causing the new owner considerable distress.

The best thing to remember when considering the use of a contract of sale, whether the broker represents the buyer or the seller, is to seek the advice of a competent real estate attorney.

The "Wraparound" Mortgage (or Deed of Trust)

This type of financing is called by several names, including *all-inclusive, overriding* or *overlapping*. Probably the most familiar of the names used is the *wraparound* mortgage or deed of trust. Such an instrument enables a borrower who is paying off an existing mortgage or trust deed loan to obtain additional financing from a second lender. The new lender assumes payment of the existing loan and gives the borrower a new, increased loan at a higher interest rate. The total amount of the new loan includes the existing loan as well as the additional funds needed by the borrower. The borrower makes payments to the new lender on the larger loan and the new lender makes the payments on the original loan.

A wraparound mortgage is frequently used as a method of refinancing real property or financing the purchase of real property when an existing mortgage cannot be prepaid.

ALTERNATIVE MORTGAGE INSTRUMENTS

As explained earlier, the fluctuating money market can cause considerable problems to lenders and borrowers alike. During inflationary periods lenders find themselves with huge portfolios of low-interest-bearing mortgages while at the same time they are required to pay out considerably higher dividend rates. The resulting dislocation of funds requires the lender either to charge higher interest on new loans or to stop lending for a period of time. To overcome this disproportion, a number of new forms of lending instruments have been devised.

Variable-Rate Mortgages

Variable-rate mortgages become popular when market interest rates are volatile. They include a formula in which the interest rate on a loan is tied to a national financial indicator, such as the consumer price index. During times of high interest costs the rate on a borrower's loan may be increased according to a specified formula. Should interest rates fall, the lender is required to reduce the interest rate on the loan. There is a high degree of risk to the borrower, who may not be able to handle inconveniently timed changes in payment schedules.

Renegotiable-Rate Mortgages

The *renegotiable-rate mortgage* is another technique for adjusting payment schedules and interest rates. Long-term loans of up to 30 years are established with monthly payments designed to reflect the required amortization amounts but the call dates included in the contract can specify three, four or five years, to force borrowers to refinance at these times to meet the balances due. At the time of refinancing, the lender has an opportunity to reexamine the condition of the collateral as well as the borrower's financial position. The lender is also able to adjust the interest rate to reflect market conditions and to charge new loan placement fees.

Other Innovative Loan Programs

A number of other innovative forms of mortgage instruments should be mentioned here. Inasmuch as this is not a textbook on financing, space does not allow for lengthy explanations of how they work. By placing a call to a knowledgeable mortgage loan broker or savings and loan association executive, the astute broker can probably learn which of the following forms of financing are in vogue and available in the area.

Graduated payment mortgage (GPM) is a 30-year fixed-rate loan designed to help young people who cannot qualify for a loan to buy a home today. They make lower payments initially, and the payments—but not the rate—rise over a five- or ten-year period, presumably as incomes rise. Negative amortization is necessary during the early year(s) of the loan.

Reverse annuity mortgage (RAM) is a fixed-rate loan designed to provide an additional source of income for older homeowners who use their equity as security for a loan. The lender pays the homeowner x dollars per month for a certain number of years, say 15 or 20, or until a specified event, such as the owner's death or sale of the property. Then the entire loan balance becomes due and payable, from either the proceeds of the sale, the estate or the borrower. Interest is charged on the amount loaned while interest is being credited on the loan proceeds left in the institution.

Flexible loan insurance plan (FLIP) is a plan that provides for monthly mortgage payments reduced by as much as 15 to 25 percent during the first five years of home ownership. Amount of payments is then increased for the balance of the loan. Interest rate is fixed at a specific level throughout the life of the mortgage. The benefit of the FLIP is that it allows young families to qualify for more mortgage financing than they can immediately afford by virtue of lower monthly payments during the first five years. At the end of this period, when family income is greater, payments then level off for the balance of the mortgage.

Other plans.   There are a number of other sophisticated forms of financing that cannot be fully covered in this book, including the SAM, or shared appreciation mortgage, the lender participation loan, open-end loans, sales and leasebacks, compensating balances, balloon payment mortgage and stock equities.

PRIVATE SOURCES OF FINANCING

Assumption of Existing Loans

One of the best methods for financing a real estate transaction is to have the purchaser assume the existing loan and pay cash for the balance. Then, if necessary, the present owner may be convinced to carry back a portion of the needed down payment.

Assuming a loan should not be confused with buying a property *subject to* the existing loan. There is a difference. In assuming a loan the buyer enters into an agreement with the lender to pay the amount due under the existing loan, becoming obligated for the full amount due. In many instances an assumption requires the approval of the lender, in which case the buyer must qualify financially.

In buying a property subject to the existing financing, the buyer takes no personal liability for the loan. Therefore, should the new owner default, the lender must look to either the property or the original signer of the note for payment.

Due-on-sale clause.   It is of primary importance for the broker to know if the loan can be assumed. There may be an alienation clause in the original loan agreement that prohibits anyone from assuming the loan without the consent of the lender. The effect of the due-on-sale clause is to give lenders the prerogative to say who can or cannot assume their loans and at what rate of interest. The loan may have been made at an interest rate favorable to the original borrower. If the prevailing interest rate at time of sale is higher, the lender is certainly going to expect the new owner to pay the higher rate to assume the existing financing.

Secondary financing.   If the existing financing can be assumed but is still not large enough to make up the difference between the purchase price and the buyer's down payment, it may then be possible to persuade the seller to carry secondary financing to help with that difference.

Here is an example of how such a transaction works:

Sales price	$50,000
Existing assumable first loan	−25,000
Buyer's cash down payment	−15,000
Amount needed to finance	$10,000

A possible solution is a second loan from the seller for $10,000.

Tax Advantages for the Seller

The favorable tax rules governing the sale of homes remain intact under the Tax Reform Act of 1986 (TRA '86), with some minor changes.

If you sell your home at a profit, you can defer paying any tax on the gain as long as you buy another home within two years that costs at least as much as your old home sold for. The tax is not eliminated but it can be deferred indefinitely—*if* you reinvest the profits in a new home each time you move. Under this rule, the home you buy and the home you sell must qualify as your principal residence, not a vacation home.

If you buy a cheaper home than the one you sold, you will have to pay taxes on the profit. Your tax bill may be slightly higher under the new law because of the changes in capital-gains tax treatment.

If you are age 55 or older, you may be entitled to a one-time exclusion from tax of up to $125,000 of gain on the sale of a principal residence. (The exclusion is $62,500 if you are married and filing a separate return.) This exclusion can prove especially beneficial for elderly people who decide to sell their home and move into a smaller, less expensive home, move in with a relative or move into a rental apartment. Under these circumstances, the deferral rules would not apply, but the one-time exclusion can shield part or all the profit from tax. In addition to meeting the age requirements, you must have owned and lived in the home for three of the five years prior to the sale of the home to qualify for the exclusion.

Prior to the TRA '86 there were certain tax advantages available to the seller if he or she elected to take part of the purchase price in two or more years. Such tax advantages, termed installment sale reporting, originally were conceived as a relief to sellers: They could dispose of real estate and, sometimes, personal property by paying capital gains tax in installments as received, thereby avoiding the payment of tax that might exceed the total amount of cash received. However, TRA '86 somewhat mitigated such tax advantages. Only in rare and more complicated transactions can one now derive any advantages from the use of the installment sales method.

Capital gains, installment sales reporting and other tax information as described herein are subject to frequent change by law and regulations. All decisions involving current tax laws and IRS regulations should be made with the help of an accountant or a tax attorney.

Institutional Financing Sources

Institutional financing is the name applied to financing obtained from institutions rather than from individuals. Such institutions include both savings and commercial banks, savings and loan associations, insurance companies, real estate investment trusts (REITs), other trusts and pension funds. Each of these institutional lenders is controlled and supervised by various agencies of the local, state and federal governments. The state where the institution is located, as well as whether the institution is state or federally chartered, determines the amount of money that may be loaned in various categories, the loan-to-value ratio employed and the interest rates that may be charged.

When commercial properties are financed, probably the first source of funds to explore is the investor's own banker. A purchaser of commercial property has usually established a line of credit with a bank, which will either finance the transaction or refer the investor to an alternate source of funds, such as an insurance company or a trust fund.

To finance residential properties, local savings and loan associations are probably the best source. Savings and loan associations were originally conceived and structured for just this purpose, so they welcome applications for residential loans. Savings and loans are also a source of money for some commercial ventures, depending on the size of the institution, the location and whether it is state or federally chartered. Each state has a regulatory body that strictly controls the operations of savings and loan associations chartered within its jurisdiction. Federally chartered institutions are governed by a federal regulatory body, not by state agencies. It is important that a broker knows the difference, as it may well affect financing decisions.

Insurance companies, while conservative in their approach to residential financing, are an excellent source of money when they are in the market. They frequently require a larger down payment or smaller loan-to-value ratio, but they also often are satisfied with a slightly lower interest rate than are savings and loan associations. Inquiry of local representatives of such companies as Prudential, New York Life, Equitable Assurance Society or Occidental Life will familiarize the broker with their current residential loan policies.

Mortgage loan brokers are usually the representatives of several sources of funds, such as trust funds, pension funds and real estate investment trusts. While such financing sources are primarily interested in the larger and more lucrative real estate developments, they can often be persuaded to finance tract developments and both off-site and on-site improvements. In some parts of the country mortgage loan brokers control and process most of the VA or FHA and other insured or guaranteed loans as a convenience for the lending institutions.

Because of the diverse regulations governing these institutions it would not be appropriate to attempt to list all the practices required by each one. However, it is imperative that a broker become completely familiar with the lenders' requirements in his or her area and have this information always available.

SUMMARY

Most purchases of real property require some type of financing and the terms of this financing usually become one of the most important contingencies in the contract. A primary responsibility of the broker is to be knowledgeable about the financial options available so that the transaction will reach a successful conclusion. He or she should also be aware of the effect the economy and a fluctuating money market have on real estate. High interest rates usually mean slow real estate activity because owning a home becomes less affordable to the consumer. On the other hand, low interest rates make more prospective buyers eligible to qualify financially. An era of soaring inflation usually dictates smaller down payments so that the larger balance of the loan will be paid off in tomorrow's less valuable dollars; mortgage assumptions and seller financing become more frequent when short money supply and high interest rates make many home buyers ineligible for the more conventional loans.

The first step is to thoroughly qualify the buyer. Rarely will two cases be exactly alike, but by knowing the buyers' total financial picture, the broker is better able to find suitable financing. Since the late 1970s and continuing into the late 1980s, a variety of innovative financing plans have sprung up that give more people the opportunity to purchase homes. Because these plans and the accompanying formulas used in the qualifying process are so numerous and varied, it is wise for the broker to be knowledgeable in the use of a financial calculator to avoid spending many hours trying to find the best plan for the buyer.

When borrowing money to purchase real estate, both a promissory note and a security device usually are used. Many of these have been defined in this chapter. As with so many aspects of real estate, financing methods and the types of instruments used vary by geographic boundaries and custom. Therefore, brokers should become totally familiar with the terms of all financing plans offered by banks and mortgage companies in their market areas. Brokers should regularly update their knowledge because financing changes daily.

DISCUSSION QUESTION

You have been showing Mr. and Mrs. Worth homes all afternoon and they have finally decided on a $150,000 home that perfectly suits them. You go back to your office to write up the contract. Mr. Worth has told you that he is being transferred from another city where the sale of their home is in escrow. They must move within the next 60 days. He is still with the same company and has a good credit rating. That is all you know about him. As you sit together at your desk, Mr. Worth says to you, "We like that last home you showed us. We want to buy it, so how do we go about it?" What do you say to Mr. Worth?

13 A Blueprint for Closing

INTRODUCTION

As mentioned before, the word "closing" is rather generic in nature, having a number of different connotations in the real estate business. It can mean the time when the buyer says, "Yes, we'll buy the property under the terms and conditions agreed on" or it can indicate the time and process when all parties to the transaction meet and sign the final legal documents or it can refer to that moment when the deed is recorded and title actually passes.

The smooth transition of a real estate sale depends on the proper structuring of each stage of closing, beginning with the sales contract and ending with recording the deed and passing the consideration to the seller.

If the sales contract is vague or incorrectly drawn, the transaction will be in trouble from the start. That is why it is so important to make sure that all requirements and responsibilities of all parties are properly documented and unequivocally agreed upon.

LEGAL REQUIREMENTS FOR A VALID CONTRACT

At the first type of closing, when the buyer and seller have reached a meeting of the minds on every detail involving the sale, it is essential that the broker draw a sales contract that binds all parties and tries to meet every eventuality.

Should a transaction reach a point where one or both parties want to be released from the contract and the differences cannot be resolved, then it behooves the broker to negotiate releases and try to settle the dispute over the deposit paid.

Barring a satisfactory settlement between the parties, the escrow holder of the deposit should hold the money until the court tells it whom to pay and how much. That is why the broker must determine that the agreement is right for both parties and that all loose ends to the contract are neatly tied.

First, because of the statutes of frauds, the contract must be in writing if it ever may have to be defended in a court of law. (An oral contract may be valid between the parties to it but it is not easily defended in court if there is no written evidence of some sort as proof.)

Second, it must contain the names of the parties to the contract (and they must be legally able to perform).

Third, it must contain an identifiable description of the property, all contingencies and "subject to's" agreed on and, finally, the signatures of the parties to be bound.

RESPONSIBILITIES FOR TITLE CLOSING

A real estate contract that is specific in every detail can make the difference between a smooth and a difficult completion of a transaction. In many cases it makes the difference between ultimately closing the title and having no closing at all. The parties to the contract (the buyers and the sellers) are directly involved and their responsibilities are spelled out in the contract.

Others, however, such as brokers, attorneys and title insurance companies, are indirectly involved. Once retained, these professionals should be bound to perform as diligently as the buyers and sellers because of the ethical, moral and legal responsibilities inherent in their positions. If only one of all parties involved in a real estate transaction does not perform, the transaction may well not close, leaving a buyer without a property, a seller without a sale, an attorney with an unhappy client, an escrow with a pile of worthless papers and a broker without a commission.

Broker's Responsibilities

The broker is responsible not only for disclosing defects but for overseeing the contract through every stage and every contingency. Other parties involved should not be depended on to monitor the contract; the buyer might not understand the importance of taking immediate steps to satisfy contingencies; the seller might not appreciate the urgency of making the house available for inspections; the attorneys might be involved in other seemingly important matters; the title company might have a backlog of paperwork, with this particular transaction on the bottom of the pile. The broker is usually compensated for the time, money and knowledge already invested in a particular transaction only on the passing of title. It is therefore essential that he or she keep control of the situation at all times.

In transactions where there is both a listing and a selling broker, this responsibility is often shared. The actual responsibility each assumes usually depends on custom in the area and their own working relationship. It must be remembered, however, that both the REALTOR'S® Code of Ethics and recent court cases have put the ultimate responsibility on the listing broker for follow-through on the contract. The listing agent may not walk away from the sale and leave the selling broker to complete the transaction. If a problem arises, the listing broker may well be faced with the question, "Why didn't you know about this?"

Buyer's and Seller's Responsibilities

The buyer's main obligation under the contract is to pay the purchase price by acquiring the necessary financing. The seller's main obligation is to provide clear title—or at least a title acceptable to the buyer—and a deed to the property. Until recently, the buyer also had the sole responsibility of determining any physical defects in the property. For example, if after taking title to the property a buyer discovered that the house was infested with termites, he or she had no recourse against the seller. The doctrine of *caveat emptor,* "Let the buyer beware," applied. Recently, however, courts have ruled in favor of buyers who were sold homes with inherent defects that were known to the seller or the broker or both and were not disclosed to the buyer. Disclosure has become an important part of real estate contracts, even if the word is not in the text of the contract itself. The broker should bring this matter of disclosure to the attention of the client, who may still think, "Let the buyer beware." The national trend of extending real estate agents' liability to defects about which they *should* have known is reflected in recent court cases. The broker should, of course, divulge any known, concealed defects in the property, as discussed in Chapter 3.

Use of Attorneys, Title Insurance Companies and Escrow Companies

In earlier times it was the practice in this country for attorneys (and, in some cases, brokers) to assume the responsibility for all phases of the transfer of title in a real estate transaction. The attorney was expected to examine the public records, order and examine the survey or make a physical examination of the property and issue a certificate of title that set forth his or her opinion of the validity of the title being transferred. Responsibility for the accuracy of this certificate was borne by the attorney.

As part of this procedure of certifying title, the attorney or the broker assumed the responsibility for attending to the details of the transaction, such as clearing funds, arranging financing and recording documents. Recently, however, the increased tempo and complexity of real estate transactions has created a division of responsibility for carrying them through successfully. This division is not clear-cut; it consists of overlapping functions and responsibilities, depending mostly on custom and usage as they have developed locally. It is, therefore, important that every broker know the procedure and assignment of responsibility in the area in which he or she functions, and have a general understanding of real estate practices elsewhere.

Attorneys occasionally still make their own searches of the public records, but generally this function is performed by title searchers who work for a fee or salary for either attorneys or title insurance companies. Title searchers prepare an abstract of title, which consists of condensations or actual copies of all recorded documents relating to the property that is the subject of the contract. This abstract is prepared from public records usually kept in the office of the county clerk or the registrar of deeds. Titles of these officials may vary from place to place, but in every county one or more persons are charged with the responsibility for keeping these records in a form that provides access for title searchers. Until recently these records and copies of them were made by hand. The first change in method occurred when photostating was introduced in making the record copies but abstracting was still done by hand. More recently the increased availability of photocopy equipment has to a large extent eliminated the need for hand copying or abstracting. In some places the records are kept on microfilm, enabling use of condensed storage techniques. Such record systems usually provide electronic indexing and automated copying.

Using the abstract of title, either the buyer's attorney or the title insurance company's title examiner prepares a preliminary report of title. The preliminary report points up any problems in the validity of the title to be conveyed. When the preliminary report is prepared by an independent attorney, it is countersigned by the title insurance company. This confirms that the insurance company will issue an insured certificate when any listed defects are cleared up. The countersigned preliminary report is usually referred to as the title binder.

This preliminary report is sent to the seller or the seller's attorney. Necessary responses are then made or actions taken to remove the legal defects in the title.

Once this has been done, settlement takes place in a mutually agreed on site where the buyers, sellers, brokers, attorneys for the parties, mortgagee, mortgagee's attorney and sometimes a representative of the title insurance company are present. The actual transfer of title then takes place, requiring the execution of documents and closing statements. This process will be covered in greater detail later in this chapter.

The two major kinds of closing procedures used in the United States are direct closing and escrow closing. Direct closing, the older of the two methods, is a procedure whereby attorneys or other representatives of the parties to the transaction, including buyer, seller, mortgagee and sometimes others, work in concert toward a settlement time and place. Each of the parties or a representative is expected to keep in communication with the others so that any differences between them can be resolved either prior to or at the settlement.

Escrow is used as a closing procedure for two reasons. It simplifies the settlement meeting itself, which can be very crowded and cumbersome in a direct closing, and it eliminates the possibility of liens attaching to the property between the time of contract and the time of settlement or closing. In an escrow closing, the parties also execute an agreement called an escrow agreement at the time the contract is entered into, which sets out the obligations of the parties and permits the escrow agent, a neutral third party, to carry out the legal necessities of the transaction. The fee the escrow agent receives for this service may be paid by one of the parties or shared, depending on the agreement between them or the accepted practice in the area.

At the time the escrow agreement is entered into, the sellers execute a deed to the buyers, which is recorded. Recording eliminates the possibility of additional liens attaching during the course of the settlement procedure. The escrow agent then proceeds to the next steps: determining the status of the title and processing the necessary mortgage and documents. If the title is determined to be unacceptable, the buyers then execute a deed of the property back to the sellers, terminating the transaction. If the title is satisfactory and other conditions of the escrow agreement are met, the escrow agent turns over the proceeds to the sellers, completing the transaction. All of this can be done with neither party present when title is actually conveyed. While escrow is the common practice in some parts of the United States, in others it is nonexistent; in some areas it is available as an optional procedure.

Another variation of the escrow process is practiced in the western states. In this process one of the brokers to the transaction opens escrow, either with a title company that has an escrow department or with a separate escrow firm. The specific company chosen depends on the preferences of either the seller or the buyer or, in the absence of preference, by agreement between the brokers. Each party places in escrow instructions for the escrow holder to follow. The buyer presents his or her money, mortgage loan papers and any other documents required. The seller places the deed to the property in the hands of the holder. When all instructions have been met in a satisfactory manner, the escrow holder closes the transaction, that is, gives the money to the seller and records the deed in the name of the buyer. All other instructions are also carried out simultaneously, such as recording the deed of trust; paying off the previous loan; prorating taxes, rents and insurance premiums; and paying any bills authorized by either party. In California and some other states, licensed brokers are allowed to prepare any and all documents relating to their own transactions.

SATISFYING CONTINGENCIES IN THE CONTRACT

A contingency is a possible want whose outcome, at the time of signing the contract, is uncertain. The most common contingencies include the mortgage, home inspection and pest control inspection. Every contingency in a contract should have a cutoff date so that the party responsible for satisfying that particular contingency has a specific time period within which to perform. Usually the contract provides that if the contingency is not met (satisfied) or waived (deleted), either party has the right to declare the contract null and void. Because there is no firm transaction until all contingencies have been met, steps should be taken immediately on signing the contract to satisfy them. At this point the broker can be especially effective in helping to see that contingencies are met by their due date by offering his or her services, such as opening the house for an inspector or appraiser, assisting the buyer in filling out mortgage applications or hand-carrying papers between attorneys and banks.

Financing

Financing is probably the major contingency in most contracts and the most important single obligation the buyer has, unless he or she is going to pay cash. As discussed in Chapter 12, many types of financing are available to the buyer. The financing contingencies should be specific about the exact type (conventional, FHA, VA), term (number of years to pay off the mortgage loan), interest rate and date within which the buyer must obtain the mortgage. The broker should see that the contract is drawn to provide financial terms that are compatible with the current market. If this is done, the mortgage loan is usually obtained and the contingency date is met.

There are times, however, when the market suddenly changes and the stated type or amount of loan or interest rate is no longer as readily available. In such cases, the broker should help the buyer and seller renegotiate the financing terms to those that are currently obtainable or agree to extend the mortgage contingency date to allow the buyer more time to shop for a mortgage loan.

Most mortgage commitments only remain in effect for a fixed period of time. If the settlement or closing is not scheduled to take place during that time period, an extension of the commitment will have to be arranged. Mortgage commitments themselves also frequently contain contingencies, such as termite inspection, credit check or the receipt of municipal or federal compliance certifications. For these reasons the broker should carefully review each mortgage commitment.

Inspections

There are several kinds of inspection contingencies that buyers request or that are required by law. They will be discussed in this section.

Home inspection.   Often referred to as an engineer's inspection, this contingency requires that the premises be examined by a party designated by the buyer. This inspection is done to satisfy the buyer as to the physical condition of the premises, including the operating condition of the heating, plumbing and electrical systems; the soundness of construction; the condition of appliances; and potential radon levels.

Pest control inspection.   This inspection is performed by a qualified exterminator. It includes an inspection for active infestation of termites or carpenter ants, as well as certification of damage from prior infestations. In some areas the inspector also checks for dry rot, fungi or water damage.

Municipal code compliance.   This qualification requires a certification from the building inspector or an equivalent municipal officer that the premises and its intended use are in compliance with building codes and zoning requirements.

Health code compliance.   This certification covers purity of water supply, if privately provided, and the proper design and functioning of waste disposal systems, including septic systems.

Federal flood control.   Most mortgage commitments require verification that the property is not in a flood zone or has flood insurance if it is. The regulations vary from state to state, but for both insurance and regulation purposes property is certifiable as either within or outside the flood hazard zone, as established by the combined action of both state and federal governments and their surveying teams. Certification can be by a designated official in the area or by private qualified persons from official maps. Legislation has made available reasonably priced insurance for property owners in designated flood hazard areas. Concurrently, state and local governments have instituted controls over construction in these designated areas.

Buyer presettlement inspection.   Since the buyer is entitled to receive on the day of transfer of title that which he or she bought on signing of contract, it is usual for the buyer to inspect the property immediately before the closing. This inspection avoids possible recriminations afterwards and ensures a satisfactory transfer. The broker or his or her representative should be present at this inspection.

SEARCHING AND CERTIFYING THE TITLE

While ownership of land is transferred through the act of granting or the symbolic transfer of ownership, its legal effectiveness is conditional on public notice. During the Middle Ages, *granting* took the form of handing over a few blades of grass and some sod; *notice* was taking physical possession personally or through servants or family members. Today, however, the granting must be in the form of a written document and the notice in the form of entry into public records.

The purpose of recording a document is to announce to the world (theoretically) that the document exists, thus putting all persons in the world legally, if not literally, on notice of that fact. Every state and county has a system of filing and indexing documents and assigns the task to someone, either a county clerk, register (or registrar) of deeds or recorder. The documents that are recorded are limited in many cases only by the ingenuity of both lawyers and laypersons, but generally they fall into the categories of deeds, mortgages, leases and contracts.

Chain of Title

The chain of title, which is the history of a parcel of land, is searched to establish the deed ownership of record as revealed by the public records. Although statutes of limitation usually do not require a search to go beyond twice the time provided in the statute, a search could reveal the chain as far back as the entry of the state into the Union or even to grants from a king. Gaps in the chain are then filled in by a public record of death, resulting in probate of a will or, where there is no will, descent of title.

The use of title insurance has expedited establishing a chain of title, since the chain established in a prior search of the same property can be used. In such cases the title insurance company issues a *back-title certificate,* which agrees to honor as valid a search that continues the chain from the point at which this company last certified it.

Common flaws that soon become apparent in a chain of title include the existence of easements and liens. Easements show up early in the search because they are granted by the owner and are, therefore, documents recorded as deeds. The easement differs from a deed in that it does not transfer title but grants a right to the grantee to use all or part of the land for a purpose, such as permitting utility companies to run pipes or electric wires across property or allowing the crossing of property for access to adjacent land. When easements are examined to find their effects upon the title and the value of the property, all the wording of the easement and its possible effects must be considered.

A lien is a right given by law to certain classes of creditors to have their claims paid out of the property of the debtor, usually by means of a court-ordered public sale. Liens often have the capacity to become breaks in the chain of title unless attended to (usually by payment). The existence of a lien makes the title both unmarketable and uninsurable, unless sufficient funds are placed in escrow to pay the lien.

Liens take many forms and vary from state to state. The most common types are prior contracts, mortgages, taxes, mechanics' liens and judgments.

In understanding the effect of the recording statutes, it is important to distinguish between *constructive notice* and *actual notice,* although the effect of both is usually the same. Actual notice, as the name implies, is the real knowledge of a fact that has been learned by a party.

Constructive notice, on the other hand, is created by law; it makes it impossible for a person to deny knowledge of any matter concerning such notice is presumed to have been given by recording a document.

The law further has created as a part of constructive notice a presumption that the person knows what could have been ascertained by reasonable inquiry. Thus the rights of a party in possession of property are presumed to be known by a purchaser. That is, the law says that a purchaser has constructive notice of the rights of a person in possession because the purchaser could have asked under what right the person is in possession of the land. The inquiry might have ascertained the existence of an unrecorded lease or purchase contract or even an unrecorded mortgage; the law lays on the purchaser the duty to inquire. If the purchaser fails to inquire, he or she is presumed to have knowledge. This presumption is also defined as constructive notice.

Survey

A survey is a civil engineer's report made for a particular client and purpose in the form of a drawing of the location and size of a parcel of property and the location and size of buildings, easements and physical aspects of the land. The engineer is responsible to the client for its accuracy. Because a subsequent purchaser does not have the right to rely on a survey made for a previous owner, mortgagees and title companies usually require a new survey for each transaction. However, the cost of a new survey can sometimes be avoided, if the mortgagee and title company agree to use a survey affidavit. In this case the seller certifies that the survey accurately depicts present conditions, and becomes legally liable for any inaccuracies in the survey.

Description of the Property

An essential element for a legal real estate contract is an adequate description of the land being conveyed. Although the courts of most states have accepted a street address as being sufficient to locate or identify a parcel of real estate, it does not serve as a legal description. Three basic methods of describing real estate that are accepted by a court of law are: metes and bounds, rectangular survey system and subdivisions. Brokers should be aware of all local real estate practices regarding legal descriptions.

The Torrens System

In some states the previously described recording system is supplemented, but not replaced, by a system of land title registration called the Torrens system. This registration offers an owner the opportunity to register his or her title to land by filing a court application reporting the facts of the title and all liens. The court then holds a hearing at which all interested parties are invited to present any claims. If the ownership is proved, the title is registered; title is then transferred by endorsement and delivery of a duplicate certificate of title and a deed or mortgage to the registrar.

Title Insurance

In the typical settlement procedure, title insurance is issued. It may be either a mortgage policy or a fee policy. For the former, the premium is based on the amount of the mortgage. For the latter, the premium is based on the selling price. A title insurance premium, unlike other insurance premiums, is paid only once and covers the life of the policy.

The policy insures the owner, in the case of the fee policy, or the lender, in the case of the mortgage policy, against any loss because of a defect in the title. (This possible defect may be disclosed at any time during the life of the policy.) Banks and other lenders almost invariably require the borrower to provide a mortgage policy. Purchase of a fee policy is optional but usually advisable. Its cost is based on the excess of purchase price over the amount of the mortgage and is usually not excessive. Because premium costs tend to be similar among title companies, there is little advantage in shopping except in very large transactions.

SETTLEMENT

Whatever form is observed by local custom, the settlement always includes two facts: (1) the execution of documents that carry out the expressed intent of the parties as set out in the contract and (2) the presentation of statements approved by the participants setting forth the financial resolution of the transaction. Many of the documents and closing statements of the title and mortgage closings in a typical transaction are referred to in this chapter. Most forms vary locally; examples can be found in the files of every office. Usually, the documents that formalize the passing of title and create evidence of liens for money loaned are prepared by attorneys, but lenders, escrow officers and even brokers may perform this service in some jurisdictions where it does not constitute unauthorized practice of law. The broker who prepares deeds or mortgages and the accompanying documents must be extremely careful, because he or she is required to do so as skillfully as a lawyer would.

The *closing statement* (sometimes called a "settlement" statement) is a written form of financial accounting of the transaction entered into in the contract. Generally in the form of a balance sheet, it is prepared with the concurrence of all parties or their representatives, sometimes with all parties present. The example shown in Figure 13.1 will be referred to throughout this section of the chapter. The closing statement shows a record of how payment will be made and the division of responsibility for payment of those items that are adjusted between the parties. All adjustments are made as of the day of closing, unless otherwise agreed between the parties. A change of adjustment date is often agreed on, for example, when possession is not delivered simultaneously with the closing. In some areas adjustments are commonly prorated, using an arbitrary 360-day year with an assumed 12 months of 30 days each. The amounts by which the end results differ usually are not significant.

All entries on the closing statement shown in Figure 13.1 originate in an imaginary contract for a residence with a sale price of $65,000. Down payment and other amounts have been negotiated in reaching the contract agreement. Numbered lines in the statement are presented and explained in the following pages.

While it is understood that practicing brokers will be thoroughly familiar with the items in the statement, the discussion here serves an educational purpose. It can be used as a procedural guide to instruct the broker's associates in accepted techniques; it serves as a guide for those not entirely comfortable with the multitude of details to be handled in

FIGURE 13.1 Closing Statement

PREMISES: 911 W. Washington Avenue, Washington Twp., New Jersey

SETTLEMENT DATE: 11/3/XX	BUYER'S STATEMENT		SELLER'S STATEMENT	
	DEBIT	CREDIT	DEBIT	CREDIT
1. Purchase price	$65,000.00	$	$	$65,000.00
2. Earnest money deposit		100.00	100.00	
3. Additional deposit				
4. Survey	150.00			
5. Title insurance/ fee policy	215.65			
6. Title insurance/ mortgage policy	10.00			
7. Drawing deed			50.00	
8. Recording deed and mortgage	35.00			
9. Cancellation of existing mortgage			10.00	
10. Pay off existing mortgage			16,908.30	
11. Interest on existing mortgage			16.68	
12. Judgment			1,790.85	
13. Prepaid taxes, prorated	354.60			354.60
14. First mortgage proceeds		55,000.00		
15. Brokerage fee			3,900.00	
16. Insurance, prorated	205.80			205.80
17. Second mortgage proceeds		7,000.00	7,000.00	
18. Escrow for disputed mechanic's lien			580.00	
19. Rent adjustment/garage	4.50			4.50
20. Security for rent		45.00	45.00	
21. Attorneys' fees	650.00		350.00	
22. Buyer's subtotals	$66,625.55	$62,145.00		
23. Balance due from buyer		4,480.55		
24. Seller's subtotals			$30,250.83	$65,564.90
25. Balance due seller			34,814.07	
26. Totals	$66,625.55	$66,625.55	$65,564.90	$65,564.90

connection with every housing purchase; and it provides a checklist to assure the associate that each item has been settled and no loose ends remain to disrupt a smooth, satisfactory closing.

1. Purchase price, being due from the buyer to the seller, shows as a debit to the buyer and a credit to the seller.

2. Earnest money, previously paid to the seller, is a credit to the buyer and a debit to the seller. If held by a broker or an attorney as escrow, it is not a debit to the seller; it is included in item 25.

3. Additional deposit, if any, is handled the same as item 2.

4. Survey is the buyer's obligation unless agreed otherwise; debit buyer $150.

5. Title insurance policy cost is usually borne by the buyer but in some places is paid for by the seller and in other instances the fee is split 50-50 between buyer and seller. In any event the fee is based upon a charge per thousand dollars of the purchase price. In the foregoing example the fee is $3.33 per thousand.

6. Title insurance/mortgage policy is nominal if a fee policy is purchased, because the premium is included in item 5. The buyer gets both for the cost of the greater, plus a processing fee if purchased together. Debit buyer $10.

7. Drawing deed, a seller's cost, is a debit to the seller.

8. The recording cost of deed and new mortgage is borne by the buyer; debit $35. The cost of this item varies from state to state.

9. Cancellation of existing mortgage is a seller's cost. The amount usually is nominal.

10 and 11. Payoff of existing mortgage is the seller's cost and is calculated on a per diem rate. At nine percent the rate is $4.169. Payment is likely to reach the mortgagee by mail two days after closing: November 5 is payoff day. Four days' interest is due.

12. A judgment against the seller was paid to convey clear title. Debit seller $1,790.85.

13. Real estate taxes (actual, not estimated) are divided by 365 to find the tax per day. The seller is responsible for taxes to the day of closing. In this case, all taxes for the year had been paid by the seller. November 3 is day 307 of a 365-day year. The buyer is therefore liable for the balance for 58 days at $6.114 per day. Debit buyer and credit seller $354.60.

14. Proceeds of the first mortgage, $55,000, are paid to the escrowee. The seller, obligated to repay it, receives credit for the amount of the mortgage. Credit buyer $55,000.

15. Brokerage fee is paid, in most cases, by the seller.

16. Existing homeowner's policy is transferred from the seller to the buyer. The policy, with an anniversary date of May 15, costs $389.15 for one year. This total is divided by 365, giving a per diem cost of $1.066.

May 15 is day 135 of the year and November 3 is day 307. Subtraction (307 − 135 = 172) shows that the seller has used 172 days of the insurance policy. Multiplying 172 by $1.066 (per diem cost) shows the seller has used $183.35 worth of insurance out of the $389.15 premium. The seller is entitled to a credit of $205.80. Debit the buyer this amount.

17. Second mortgage proceeds: Seller takes back a second mortgage of $7,000; seller is debited this amount.

18. A mechanic's lien against the property is reported in the search of records. The claimant demands $580 but the seller says all but $100 is paid. The parties agree that $580 will be held in escrow by the escrow officer to be turned over to the seller when the lien is satisfied. Debit seller $580.

19. Garage rental to a neighbor at $45 per month is unpaid for one month. Seller is entitled to three days' rental. Per diem is calculated by dividing the monthly rental by 30, or $1.50; three days × $1.50 equals a $4.50 credit to seller; debit the buyer, who will receive the rent payment.

20. Garage tenant has posted security of $45. The obligation to return this at the end of the rental term now passes to the buyer as a landlord. The security is transferred by crediting $45 to the buyer and debiting the seller the same amount.

21. Attorney's fees are a debit for each party.

22. To determine the additional amount the buyer must pay, the debit and credit columns are totaled.

23. Subtraction determines that $4,480.55 additional must be credited to balance credits with debits. Payment of this sum balances the account.

24. To determine the amount left to be paid by the seller, the seller's debit and credit columns are added.

25. Subtraction of seller's debits from seller's credits determines that the sellers will leave the closing with a check from the closing escrow officer in the sum of $34,814.07.

26. Although debits and credits balance (equal) each other for both buyer and seller, buyer's and seller's figures do not match because the statement includes items that solely involve one or the other.

Other adjustments, such as fuel adjustments in the case of oil or coal, are computed by measuring the amount on hand and calculating at the most recent price paid. The amount is credited to the seller and debited to the buyer. When the fuel is gas or electricity, delivered by a metered utility, the meter is read concurrent with the closing and no adjustment is necessary. Water and other metered services are handled similarly. Where services are not metered but are billed chronologically, adjustment is made on a per diem basis, as for taxes, item 13.

As indicated earlier, this closing statement is used in escrow closing and in other closings where all funds are cleared through a single trust account. The closing attorney or other presiding party collects item 23 and the first mortgage proceeds (14) and any other funds being held in escrow; the attorney pays out the balance due seller (25) and other disbursements (items 4, 5, 6, 10, 11, 12, 15 and the actual recording and cancellation fees in 8 and 9), holds the $580 in item 18 until it is released to seller, and keeps what is left as the closing fees.

THE FEDERAL REAL ESTATE SETTLEMENT PROCEDURES ACT (RESPA)

RESPA was created to ensure that the buyer and seller in a residential real estate sale or transfer have knowledge of all settlement costs. RESPA requirements apply when the purchase is financed by a federally related mortgage loan and when the transaction involves a new first mortgage loan. RESPA provides that loan closing information must be prepared on a special U.S. Department of Housing and Urban Development (HUD) form, the "Uniform Settlement Statement," designed to detail all financial particulars of a transaction. A copy of this form is illustrated in Figure 13.2. RESPA is administered by HUD.

BROKER FOLLOW-UP AFTER THE CLOSING

Nothing is more damaging to a broker's image than to appear to have taken the commission and run. The last picture the buyer and seller have of the broker should not be of the commission check being put into his or her hand. To avoid this, the broker or salesperson should remain in the picture even after the settlement. There are many ways in which the broker can be of assistance to both buyer and seller immediately following settlement. If the seller is leaving the area, most of the broker's assistance will have been offered before settlement, such as referring the seller to a reputable broker in the area he or she is moving to, providing a list of moving companies and arranging for utility readings and shutoff. If the seller remains in the area, however, both the seller and the buyer should be offered postsettlement assistance by the broker. This not only reinforces a good image of the broker but is the basis of future business for the broker and his or her firm.

Occupancy

There are many items of information the new homeowner will need or will benefit from when he or she moves into the newly purchased property. Obviously, the first item is to receive all available keys to the house,

FIGURE 13.2 Uniform Settlement Statement

1401—PAGE 1 HUD-1
OMB. No. 2502-0265 (Exp. 12-31-86)

HUD-1 UNIFORM SETTLEMENT STATEMENT

ALL-STATE LEGAL SUPPLY CO.
One Commerce Drive, Cranford, N. J. 07016

A.
U.S. DEPARTMENT OF HOUSING AND URBAN DEVELOPMENT

SETTLEMENT STATEMENT

B. **TYPE OF LOAN**

1. ☐ FHA   2. ☐ FmHA   3. ☐ CONV UNINS
4. ☐ VA   5. ☐ CONV INS

6. File Number: 7. Loan Number:

8. Mortgage Insurance Case Number:

C. NOTE: This form is furnished to give you a statement of actual settlement costs. Amounts paid to and by the settlement agent are shown. Items marked "(p.o.c.)" were paid outside the closing; they are shown here for informational purposes and are not included in the totals.

D. NAME AND ADDRESS OF BORROWER: E. NAME AND ADDRESS OF SELLER: F. NAME AND ADDRESS OF LENDER:

G. PROPERTY LOCATION: H. SETTLEMENT AGENT: I. SETTLEMENT DATE:

PLACE OF SETTLEMENT:

J. SUMMARY OF BORROWER'S TRANSACTION		K. SUMMARY OF SELLER'S TRANSACTION	
100. GROSS AMOUNT DUE FROM BORROWER:		**400. GROSS AMOUNT DUE TO SELLER:**	
101. Contract sales price		401. Contract sales price	
102. Personal property		402. Personal property	
103. Settlement charges to borrower (line 1400)		403.	
104.		404.	
105.		405.	
Adjustments for items paid by seller in advance		*Adjustments for items paid by seller in advance*	
106. City/town taxes to		406. City/town taxes to	
107. County taxes to		407. County taxes to	
108. Assessments to		408. Assessments to	
109.		409.	
110.		410.	
111.		411.	
112.		412.	
120. **GROSS AMOUNT DUE FROM BORROWER**		420. **GROSS AMOUNT DUE TO SELLER**	
200. AMOUNTS PAID BY OR IN BEHALF OF BORROWER:		**500. REDUCTIONS IN AMOUNT DUE TO SELLER:**	
201. Deposit or earnest money		501. Excess deposit (see instructions)	
202. Principal amount of new loan(s)		502. Settlement charges to seller (line 1400)	
203. Existing loan(s) taken subject to		503. Existing loan(s) taken subject to	
204.		504. Payoff of first mortgage loan	
205.		505. Payoff of second mortgage loan	
206.		506.	
207.		507.	
208.		508.	
209.		509.	
Adjustments for items unpaid by seller		*Adjustments for items unpaid by seller*	
210. City/town taxes to		510. City/town taxes to	
211. County taxes to		511. County taxes to	
212. Assessments to		512. Assessments to	
213.		513.	
214.		514.	
215.		515.	
216.		516.	
217.		517.	
218.		518.	
219.		519.	
220. **TOTAL PAID BY/FOR BORROWER**		520. **TOTAL REDUCTION AMOUNT DUE SELLER**	
300. CASH AT SETTLEMENT FROM/TO BORROWER		**600. CASH AT SETTLEMENT TO/FROM SELLER**	
301. Gross amount due from borrower (line 120)		601. Gross amount due to seller (line 420)	
302. Less amounts paid by/for borrower (line 220) ( )		602. Less reductions in amount due seller (line 520) ( )	
303. **CASH (☐FROM) (☐TO) BORROWER**		603. **CASH (☐TO) (☐FROM) SELLER**	

FIGURE 13.2 (Continued)

1401—Page 2 SETTLEMENT STATEMENT HUD-1 ALL-STATE LEGAL SUPPLY CO., One Commerce Drive, Cranford, N. J. 07016

L. SETTLEMENT CHARGES

	PAID FROM BORROWER'S FUNDS AT SETTLEMENT	PAID FROM SELLER'S FUNDS AT SETTLEMENT
700. TOTAL SALES/BROKER'S COMMISSION based on price $ @ % =		
Division of Commission (line 700) as follows:		
701. $ to		
702. $ to		
703. Commission paid at Settlement		
704.		
800. ITEMS PAYABLE IN CONNECTION WITH LOAN		
801. Loan Origination Fee %		
802. Loan Discount %		
803. Appraisal Fee to		
804. Credit Report to		
805. Lender's Inspection Fee		
806. Mortgage Insurance Application Fee to		
807. Assumption Fee		
808.		
809.		
810.		
811.		
900. ITEMS REQUIRED BY LENDER TO BE PAID IN ADVANCE		
901. Interest from to @ $ / day		
902. Mortgage Insurance Premium for months to		
903. Hazard Insurance Premium for years to		
904. years to		
905.		
1000. RESERVES DEPOSITED WITH LENDER		
1001. Hazard insurance months @ $ per month		
1002. Mortgage insurance months @ $ per month		
1003. City property taxes months @ $ per month		
1004. County property taxes months @ $ per month		
1005. Annual assessments months @ $ per month		
1006. months @ $ per month		
1007. months @ $ per month		
1008. months @ $ per month		
1100. TITLE CHARGES		
1101. Settlement or closing fee to		
1102. Abstract or title search to		
1103. Title examination to		
1104. Title insurance binder to		
1105. Document preparation to		
1106. Notary fees to		
1107. Attorney's fees to		
(includes above items numbers;)		
1108. Title insurance to		
(includes above items numbers;)		
1109. Lender's coverage $		
1110. Owner's coverage $		
1111.		
1112.		
1113.		
1200. GOVERNMENT RECORDING AND TRANSFER CHARGES		
1201. Recording fees: Deed $; Mortgage $; Releases $		
1202. City/county tax/stamps: Deed $; Mortgage $		
1203. State tax/stamps: Deed $; Mortgage $		
1204.		
1205.		
1300. ADDITIONAL SETTLEMENT CHARGES		
1301. Survey to		
1302. Pest inspection to		
1303.		
1304.		
1305.		
1400. TOTAL SETTLEMENT CHARGES *(enter on lines 103, Section J and 502, Section K)*		

CERTIFICATION

I have carefully reviewed the HUD-1 Settlement Statement and to the best of my knowledge and belief, it is a true and accurate statement of all receipts and disbursements made on my account or by me in this transaction. I further certify that I have received a copy of the HUD-1 Settlement Statement.

_____ Seller   _____ Borrower

_____ Seller   _____ Borrower

The HUD-1 Settlement Statement which I have prepared is a true and accurate account of this transaction. I have caused the funds to be disbursed in accordance with this statement.

_____ Settlement Agent   _____ Date

WARNING: It is a crime to knowingly make false statements to the United States on this or any other similiar form. Penalties upon conviction can include a fine and imprisonment. For details see: Title 18 U.S. Code Section 1001 and Section 1010.

garage and any other outbuildings. The broker can best make certain this transfer is made by tagging keys with an office key tag or placing them in an office-identified pouch. Another help is an initial utility reading and hookup in the new owner's name. The procedure for this is different in different areas; some utility companies will turn off, start up and take readings only on authorization of both seller and buyer. The broker should know the procedure in his or her area and offer to take care of as many of the details as possible.

Municipal service information is important to a buyer new to the area. This knowledge can do much to make the transition pleasant. Although buyers frequently ask about schools before deciding on an area, they rarely get down to specific information such as exact places and times for school bus pickups, school menus (often printed in advance in local publications or sent out by bulletin from the school) or PTA schedules. It is a nice touch for the broker to make this information available to the new homeowner.

Sanitation procedures also vary with different areas. The new owner should not have to ask neighbors or find out by accident the scheduled garbage pickup days, that trash cans are expected to be put at the curb or that the municipality requires that trash cans be lined with plastic bags. All of this information can and should be provided by the broker.

A list of painters, carpenters, plumbers, electricians and other skilled persons a new homeowner might need may also be provided. A calendar of the area's civic and cultural activities is usually of interest to newcomers. In other words, the broker and the firm can become their own "welcome wagon"—an important part of institutional advertising.

Because it is the nature of many salespeople to move on to other transactions after they have received their share of the commission from the broker, the broker might want to provide a simple checklist (Figure 13.3) for his or her salespeople to refer to after a settlement to be sure that everything has been done. Also useful is a commission verification form (Figure 13.4) that incorporates all of the loose ends as well as postsettlement follow-through. The latter is a two-part form to be filled out when the transaction becomes firm (when all contingencies in the contract have been met) and completed when the settlement takes place. When verifying a firm transaction, the salesperson will complete certain sections of the form that will remind him or her of certain responsibilities at each stage, such as putting up a sold sign, removing lockboxes and sending out appropriate mailings. When the transaction has closed and the commissions are ready to be disbursed, the salesperson completes the form. At that point he or she verifies the amount of commission due and again completes reminder sections to tie up loose ends and begin the steps for follow-through, such as removing the sold sign, returning the

---

FIGURE 13.3 Postsettlement Checklist

---

1. Deposit commission check.
2. Submit commission disbursal statement.
3. Make closing entries in file.
4. Report closing to MLS and cooperating brokers.
5. Close out key entries and distribute keys.
6. Return valuable documents (deeds and so forth).
7. Update lawn signs.
8. Prepare follow-up tickler for seller.
9. Prepare follow-up tickler for buyer.
10. Thank-yous (attorneys, banks, buyer, seller, others).
11. New home gift.
12. New neighbor introduction (written consent needed).
13. Press releases and advertising.
14. Terminate service agreements.
15. Schedule personal follow-up visit.
16. Ask for referrals.

---

keys, providing a gift and sending out mailings to the neighbors introducing the buyers (with the buyers' permission).

The salesperson who is diligent in closing out the transaction file and making preparations for future contact with buyers and sellers is laying a firm foundation for future business and additional public identity, both for the firm and for himself or herself.

SUMMARY

The first step to the successful closing of a transaction is when the original sales contract is drawn! To avoid problems and possible lawsuits, the contract of sale *must* be in writing and be specific in every detail.

Brokers, buyers and sellers all have responsibilities under the contract: the buyer to pay the purchase price and obtain the necessary financing, the seller to provide clear title and a deed to the property and the broker to monitor the progress of the transaction as it moves through each state and contingency. Until recently, those were the parties' basic responsibilities, with the buyer having the sole responsibility for discovering any physical defects about the property. The courts have reversed this, however, ruling in favor of buyers who were sold homes with inherent defects; thus, "disclosure" by both brokers and sellers has become a most important part of the contract.

Closing procedures vary throughout the country, with the two major kinds being the direct closing and the escrow closing. The entire process

FIGURE 13.4   Salesperson's Statement for Disbursement of Commissions and Closing Follow-Through

The following transaction is firm and will close about _____ or closed on _____ (date)

Buyer: _____ Source of contact _____

Seller: _____ Source of contact _____

Address of Property _____ Town _____

Selling Price _____ Total Commission _____ % or $ _____

SELLING OFFICE   LISTING OFFICE

Name _____ ____ % $ _____   Name _____ ____ % $ _____

Less MLS Fee	$ _____	Less Unreimb. MLS	$ _____
Less Connie Reade	$ _____	Less Referral Fee	$ _____
Less Referral Fee	$ _____	Less _____	$ _____
TOTAL DED.	$ _____	TOTAL DED	$ _____

Balance $ _____   Balance $ _____

Selling S.P. _____ ____ % $ _____   Listing S.P. _____ ____ % $ _____

  (Name)   (Name)

Deductions _____ $ _____   Deductions _____ $ _____

Name _____ $ _____   Name _____ $ _____

Name _____ $ _____   Name _____ $ _____

Total Deductions $ _____   Total Deductions $ _____

I am entitled to receive _____ I am entitled to receive _____

as selling salesperson.   as listing salesperson.

Permission for SOLD SIGN has been requested from Seller and *agreed* to or *refused* (circle one).

Permission for SOLD SIGN has been requested from Buyer and *agreed* to or *refused* (circle one).

I HAVE COMPLETED THE FOLLOWING:

A: Intros written and mailed to: (List last names of people.)

_____ _____ _____ _____

_____ _____ _____ _____

_____ _____ _____ _____

B: GIFT ORDERED _____ (Date) _____

    (Type of Gift)

C: CLIENT FOLLOW-UP FORM IN (duplicate attached)

D: I have asked the buyers and sellers to refer me to their friends, neighbors, and business associates for sales and listings. They have referred me to:

_____ _____ _____ _____

_____ _____ _____ _____

_____ _____ _____ _____

These are my customers *if* they call as a result of *my* contact with them.

E: KEYS WITHDRAWN FROM KEY LOG: Given to new owner or returned: _____

F: LOCKBOXES REMOVED _____

G: SIGN REMOVED. Returned to Office and noted in Message Book _____

Firm Date _____ Signed by _____

Closed Date _____ Signed by _____

FOR OFFICE USE ONLY   Gross Payment Anticipated

Gross Commission Received _____ $ _____

Listing Fee to Other Broker	_____	$ _____
MLS Fee _____		$ _____
Referral Fee _____		$ _____
Sell S.P. _____		$ _____
Sell S.P. _____		$ _____
Total _____		$ _____

has evolved from one where an attorney or broker handled all phases of the contract to one where many others, with expertise in areas such as searching the title and arranging financing, become involved. The broker must be familiar with the procedures followed in each of his or her market areas so that appropriate contracts can be prepared and contingency negotiations expedited.

The major contingency in most contracts is the financing. However, many others commonly are found, including home inspections, pest control inspections and municipal and health code compliance, to name just a few. The legal effectiveness of home ownership is conditional on public notice, which is done by recording a document in public records. Such documents include deeds, mortgages, leases and contracts. To assure clear title to property, its history is searched and surveys made.

The settlement, or closing, always includes the execution of documents that carry out the intent of the parties to the contract and statements approved by the participants that set forth the financial resolution of the transaction. A closing statement that gives a financial accounting of the transaction is provided at the closing as a checklist.

The broker's responsibility does not end at the closing table; it should extend beyond in the form of postsettlement services. A gift and a visit are also appreciated by both the buyer and the seller and leave them with the impression of a broker who really cares as opposed to the broker who walks away from the closing table with his or her commission and is never seen again.

DISCUSSION QUESTION

Choose a listing to your liking in your local MLS and pretend that you are going to buy it. Draw up a sales contract that contains all of the terms and contingencies you would like to see in that agreement. Then take the agreement to an escrow officer and ask that officer to evaluate the agreement and see if you have covered every aspect of the purchase required for him or her to complete the closing without further complications.

14

The Public Sector's Impact on Real Estate

INTRODUCTION

Long ago the poet John Donne said, "No man is an island." That fact holds true for the real estate market too. It is not an island unto itself. Activity in the real estate market is extremely sensitive to governmental activities related to the four major areas of the real estate profession: brokerage, property management, property financing and the bundle of property rights involved in ownership. In this chapter the focus will be on effects of government action on these four areas.

As with most other forms of human endeavor, the government has surrounded the real estate industry with controlling laws and regulations. Because the laws and controls have not always been in the public interest, they require an alert and informed real estate profession. The real estate business is highly susceptible to both ill-intentioned and well-meaning meddling. Therefore, as government controls continue to proliferate, it becomes increasingly evident that members of the real estate profession must be fully aware of these regulations. They should be able to judge which potential legislation would be harmful to the real estate industry and private property owners.

Organized real estate professionals have traditionally been influential in spearheading legislation beneficial to the public interest. They have also been instrumental in improving the image of the real estate industry in the public eye. As shall be seen in this chapter, however, many laws currently on the books actually work against the public interest.

THE CONCEPT OF SOCIAL PROPERTY

There appears to be a concept growing in popularity across the country that real estate is not a commodity that is freely owned and controlled, within certain limitations, by individual citizens. Rather, it is thought of as a natural resource. All people of the country are considered under this theory to have a voice in its control and development. This is the concept of *social property*. The basic concept is that society as a whole should say what is to be done with the nation's real property. Property rights of the individual are considered subordinate to this concept. Such legislative controls currently affect streams, lakes, forests, swamps, deserts and ocean shorelines, although controls might easily extend to private farms and homesteads.

No-Growth and Other Community Considerations in Land Development

A practice becoming increasingly popular with local governments is instituting a no-growth policy. A noted land economist once termed this program the "last-one-in-slams-the-door" policy. It stems from the desire many people have to preserve the status quo of a community without regard for the wishes and rights of others.

Certainly, there are some valid reasons for restricting growth in a community, for example, to forestall serious shortages of water or sewer facilities. While these reasons may be valid in the short term, such shortages can often be overcome; the doors to the community could be opened again to newcomers. The proponents of no-growth often end up deploring the rapid rise in real estate prices in their community, not realizing that the economic law of supply and demand creates the very problem of local property inflation they deplore, with supply severely limited by the enforced building curtailment.

Revitalization of Urban Facilities

The efforts to revitalize the cities have taken on new urgency. Many social problems that infect the cities can be directly attributed to the deterioration of the inner cities. This is brought about by unsightly physical blight, financial losses in property values, moral and spiritual erosion and the waves of human despair as evidenced by riots, vandalism and ever-increasing criminal activity.

Urban renewal legislation was first enacted by the federal government in 1949, with emphasis on slum clearance and the creation of new housing. Later the concept was broadened to include redevelopment of downtown business sections. Early urban renewal projects consisted mostly of tearing down old buildings and building new ones on those sites. This resulted in a serious waste of resources: potential historical landmarks and rehabilitable buildings.

Urban revitalization is hardly a new idea. Whether it is called urban renewal, redevelopment, rehabilitation or revitalization, within the past few decades there have been several "save-our-cities" movements. The waves of slum clearance and urban renewal projects during the fifties and sixties are typical examples. For the most part, however, these programs met with only limited success. Some were dismal failures.

In the seventies there was a dramatic shift in the American attitude toward change. Instead of tearing down and building anew, the approach shifted to one of how to save and rehabilitate valuable buildings: the still savable housing stock, historically significant buildings and examples of earlier cultural heritage, restoring all this to a useful role in the community.

This new attitude has opened up many new avenues of specialization, profit and altruistic endeavors for the real estate broker inclined to this interesting aspect of the business.

There is also a whole range of financing devices and programs offered by the Department of Housing and Urban Development (HUD) that may be obtained from the local office of the Federal Housing Administration. The federal government is intensely interested in revitalizing the cities and a sincere effort by a broker or firm in this regard is generally welcomed with open arms.

GOVERNMENT ACTIVITIES AFFECTING REAL ESTATE BROKERAGE

Antitrust Activities

Several years ago the federal government concentrated on curtailing the antitrust activities of manufacturers. Recently, attention has turned to the service industries, with real estate activity in the forefront. There are four general reasons for this special attention.

1. The idea that the real estate industry is of concern purely at the local and state levels has now been discarded. The political strength of the NAR is being felt on a national level.

2. Economists in the federal government realize that the real estate business is assuming major proportions in the country's economy. With the NAR membership now over 700,000, it appears to be a prime target for possible antitrust violation harassment.

3. The fact that the real estate industry has been assuming the mantle of professionalism, akin to the American Bar Association

or the American Medical Association, makes some people suspect it is trying to avoid competition through such association.

4.   With inflation a major concern and a hot political issue, it is natural for the federal government to take a hard look at service industries that might try to control price competition for services.

Under the Sherman Act, price fixing is considered a major violation. Once a group of brokers has been found guilty of collaborating for the purpose of setting commission schedules, they no longer have any defense and punitive action is taken. This applies in the case where a board of REALTORS® or an associated MLS merely suggests a recommended fee schedule.

In fact, any fee schedule (other than an in-office memorandum) printed by any organization is suspect as price-fixing and liable for heavy penalties. The Supreme Court has taken the position that any communication among competitors regarding pricing or fee structuring is extremely dangerous and should be carefully avoided.

Antitrust investigations into the powers of associations also have had recent effect in real estate. One of the objectives of a real estate association is to promote the high ethical standards of its members. It is sometimes necessary for that association, through one of its local associations, to expel a member for not adhering to such standards. When it comes to real estate boards or MLSs, any expulsion or rejection from membership may be tantamount to putting a broker out of business. As a California court observed, "Membership in the board with its attendant advantages including the multiple-listing system is of substantial value to any real estate broker's opportunity to fully practice his trade."

In the case of *Grillo* v. *Board of REALTORS®*, a New Jersey broker applied for admission to the local board as a necessary prerequisite for using the MLS. After being rejected several times, he went to court to seek damages and to get a court order giving him access to the multiple listings. He succeeded on both counts, as the New Jersey court said, "His knowledge of available properties is the broker's chief stock in trade. Listings are equivalent to the news items of the Associated Press. . . . Without goods to sell, the businessman cannot survive. The restrictions which defendants have placed in the way of a nonmember obtaining and using listings may drive that nonmember from the field of real estate selling."

Rulings in California have resulted in several boards of REALTORS® entering into consent decrees agreeing not to withhold multiple listings unduly from brokers who are not board members. Some courts elsewhere, however, have upheld membership in the board, if not discriminatory, as a requirement for access to the multiple listings.

Consumer Rights—Written Disclosure

The requirement of written disclosures regarding the condition of real estate being purchased, signed by both the broker and the seller, certainly is one of the major advances for the consumer in recent times. Such a disclosure, when signed by the seller, in many instances relieves the broker from being accused of misrepresentation or of nondisclosure of problems.

Most states require that if a licensed real estate broker or salesperson is the principal in a transaction, as either a buyer or seller, this fact must be made known, by written disclosure, to the other party. (In many states there also is a regulation that requires salespeople and brokers acting in the capacity of salespeople to make written disclosure to their supervising brokers if they enter into a transaction to buy or sell real property, a business opportunity or a mobile home.)

In an Idaho case, *Funk* v. *Tifft,* real estate broker Tifft offered certain property to prospect Funk. The purchaser signed an offer to purchase on certain terms and conditions, which Tifft delivered to the owner. While the owner was thinking it over, the broker decided that he would like to buy the property. The broker contacted the owner and offered to buy on better terms than Funk had offered, and the seller accepted. When Funk found out what had happened, he sued. The court held that the real estate broker had violated his fiduciary relationship with the prospective buyer. The court pointed out that a licensed real estate broker has a duty to treat all parties to a transaction fairly.

A broker should never purchase one of his or her own listings without giving disclosure of all terms of the transaction to the seller, giving any prospective buyer the first right to buy. Handling it any other way may cause the broker serious problems with both the court and the licensing authorities.

As discussed in detail earlier, new requirements regarding disclosure of latent defects—regardless of whether the broker knows or should have known of them—are coming into effect.

New Trends in Escrow Procedure

In states that use the escrow process for the final closing of real estate transactions there appears to be a growing trend in legal procedure. For example, the policy of "steering" is becoming increasingly objectionable, and even is illegal in some states. *Steering,* as used in this context, is the practice of a broker, seller, buyer or lender requiring that the transaction be placed in escrow with a specifically named escrow or title company. In many cases in the past, brokers and/or lenders who owned controlling interests in escrow or title companies made such a demand part of the sales or lending agreement.

The Real Estate Settlement Procedures Act (RESPA)

Although in some states it is legal, the practice of paying a finder's fee to someone who refers a client to a broker is at best a questionable, even unethical, practice. Section 8a of RESPA provides that "No person shall give and no person shall accept any fee, kickback, or thing of value pursuant to any agreement or understanding, oral or otherwise, that business incident to or part of a real estate settlement service involving a federally related mortgage loan shall be referred to any person." The terms *settlement services* and *federally related mortgage loan* are broadly defined under this act. Settlement services are defined to include any service provided in connection with a real estate settlement (closing), including, by way of express example, "services rendered by a real estate agent or broker." Federally related mortgage loan is defined to include any loan— other than a temporary one—secured by a first deed of trust or mortgage on residential property of from one to four units, which is: (1) made by a lender insured or regulated by an agency of the federal government; (2) made, insured, guaranteed or assisted by any federal agency; (3) intended to be sold to FNMA, GNMA, or FHLMC; or (4) made in whole or in part by any creditor who makes or invests more than $1 million per year in residential real estate loans.

Although this section has been interpreted to mean that it is not illegal for one licensee to pay another licensee a finder's fee, it does explicitly apply to kickbacks to nonlicensees, such as attorneys, surveyors, banks and mortgage companies.

The Status of For Sale Sign Limitations

Many communities have from time to time attempted to limit, restrict or even ban the use of for sale and sold signs within their jurisdictions. However, a decision by the U.S. Supreme Court may have laid to rest all such future attempts.

In a landmark decision made May 2, 1977, in the New Jersey case of *Linmark Associates, Inc.* v. *Township of Willingboro,* the court handed down a unanimous decision of eight justices that struck down an ordinance enacted by the Willingboro Township. That ordinance prohibited the posting of for sale and sold signs on residential property with the exception of model homes.

The court held that the effect of the ordinance had been to "stem what is perceived as the flight of white homeowners from a racially integrated community." The ordinance was declared unconstitutional on the grounds that it violated the First Amendment by impairing the flow of truthful and legitimate commercial information. In the court's own words:

Persons desiring to sell their homes are just as interested in receiving information about available property as are sellers of other commodities. Similarly, would-be purchasers of realty are no less interested in receiving information about available property than are purchasers of other commodities.

Income Tax Deductions as They Relate to a Broker's Expenses

The very nature of the business gives the real estate broker more than usual opportunities to deduct travel and education expenses because anywhere a broker travels, he or she can legitimately be considered to be engaged in real estate activity. Searching for parcels of land for a client, traveling to other parts of the state in hope of obtaining a specific listing or attending a beneficial educational seminar (even if it happens to be in Hawaii) are all legitimately deductible expenses. However, the following rule must be kept in mind: "Away-from-home travel expenses are deductible if the primary purpose of the trip is the pursuit of real estate business and the expenses are ordinary and necessary." These are some of the primary rules one must observe.

1. If a broker is not away from home, no expenses are considered travel expenses.

2. Travel expenses include the costs of getting to and from the business destination and include most living expenses while there, as long as one is away from home overnight.

3. Entertainment expenses do not qualify as travel expenses, even if incurred away from home. They are considered as entertainment expenses. Entertainment expense rules must be observed.

4. For expenses to be deductible, the travel must be shown to be of primary importance to the broker's real estate business, although it is not necessary for the travel to have culminated in a successful transaction.

5. Some trips may be for both business and pleasure. If the trip is primarily for business, then all expenses are deductible. If the trip is primarily for pleasure, then only those expenses that relate to business are deductible and it is necessary to prorate the travel expenses between the two activities.

6. Travel expenses incurred in attending conventions, seminars and other meetings beneficial to one's business are deductible. If one attends for social or political reasons (or for any other personal reason), the expenses do not qualify.

7. Travel expenses to a convention or business meeting in a resort area are not disallowed simply because it is a resort area as long as the broker can prove his or her attendance was necessary and beneficial to business and that the primary purpose for attending was business.

8. The Tax Reform Act of 1986 made changes in the tax laws relating to attending conventions, seminars or meetings. A broker who is

considering attending such functions is wise to consult his or her CPA for advice on travel expense deductions. (This rule applies for any and all deductions that may be considered.)

9. Deducting travel expenses for a spouse is generally suspect. The distinction is whether the spouse's presence is *absolutely necessary* (deductible) or just *helpful* (nondeductible).

The cost of travel, meals and lodging is deductible if one travels away from home to obtain qualifying education. Four tests can be applied to determine the allowability of such deductions:

1. Does the seminar provide the kind of education the broker needs to maintain or improve real estate expertise?

2. Are the total number of classroom and study hours sufficient to qualify as a bona fide educational experience?

3. Are instructors fully qualified to teach the subject and is the material that will be studied of the quality required?

4. The broker must obtain a certificate of attendance or retain a program or other evidence of attendance.

Under TRA '86 the amount of deductions allowable for business meals and entertainment expenses is reduced by 20 percent. For example, if you pick up the tab for a business dinner for $50, only $40 will be deductible. The change also applies to meals and beverage costs incurred in the course of travel away from your tax home.

Exceptions to the new rule will be made for meals furnished to employees as part of their compensation.

Meals served as an integral part of a convention, seminar, annual meeting or similar business function are deductible in full. However, this exception applies only for the years 1987 and 1988. In addition, the exception applies only if more than 50 percent of the participants at the banquet meeting are away from home, at least 40 persons attend the banquet meeting, and the meal event is part of the meeting and includes a speaker.

The bill also changes the substantiation requirements. Under the new rules, no deduction will be permitted unless business is discussed during or directly before or after the meal. An exception is made if you are eating alone while away from your tax home on business.

Under TRA '86, no deduction will be allowed for nonbusiness conventions, nonbusiness seminars or similar meetings. (A nonbusiness meeting is any meeting not deductible as a Section 162 expense. As a real estate agent or broker, most meetings you attend are business meetings and therefore deductible under Section 162.) The change will hit the nonbusinessperson attending conventions and seminars. Investors are a good example. No longer will they be able to attend conventions and seminars and deduct the costs on their tax returns.

(The foregoing and other tax information contained in this book is furnished by Richard Robinson, CPA and chief tax consultant and instructor for the REALTORS® Land Institute. Additional information or a subscription to his *Real Estate Tax Education Letter* may be obtained by writing to him at 501 East Main Street, Fredericksburg, TX 78624.)

Again, as with all information regarding a person's income tax liabilities, a broker should consult his or her tax consultant or attorney to make certain that deductions are being handled properly.

Civil Rights and Affirmative Action in Marketing

Two major federal laws prohibit discrimination in housing in the United States. The Civil Rights Act of 1866 requires that "All citizens of the United States shall have the same right, in every State and Territory, as is enjoyed by the white citizens thereof to inherit, purchase, lease, sell, hold, and convey real and personal property." In the case of *Jones* v. *Mayer,* decided on June 17, 1968, the U.S. Supreme Court held that the 1866 law prohibits "all racial discrimination, private as well as public, in the sale or rental of property."

In Title VIII of the Civil Rights Act of 1968, known as the Federal Fair Housing Law, Congress declared a national policy of fair housing throughout the United States. The law makes illegal any discrimination based on race, color, religion, sex or national origin in connection with the sale or rental of housing. The law further requires that all people be treated equally and under the same terms and conditions.

A broker who engages a salesperson who discriminates for reasons of race, color, religion, sex or national origin is equally guilty with that salesperson of violating the law. Furthermore, Article 10 of the NAR Code of Ethics requires that "the REALTOR® shall not deny equal professional services to any person for reasons of race, creed, sex, or country of national origin. . . ." The consequences of any act of discrimination are serious. Such acts can result in loss of license, expulsion from the board of REALTORS®, civil damages and penalties and, in some cases, criminal prosecution, fines and/or imprisonment. Further information on this subject may be found in various handbooks on affirmative marketing and in the brochure *What Everyone Should Know about Equal Opportunity in Housing,* published by the National Association of REALTORS®, Chicago, IL 60611.

The Affirmative Marketing Agreement negotiated between HUD and the NAR was adopted in late 1975. It provides for various outreach and advertising efforts to inform minorities of housing availability, regardless of its location or source of financing. One means of accomplishing this is to have every local board of REALTORS® appoint an Equal Housing Opportunity Committee to meet on a regular basis with the local Community Housing Resources Board (CHRB). This board consists of members of the community, chosen by invitation and approval of HUD, who represent the major religious, racial and civic groups within that community.

Using such voluntary measures and complying with them should greatly enhance the chances for minority groups to find adequate housing in neighborhoods of their choice. Better-balanced communities will be created, which may well minimize the need for busing to achieve school desegregation, thereby easing tensions. Greater awareness of the civil rights laws will also result, reducing incidences of noncompliance and discrimination.

State Governments' Involvement in Real Estate Education

As mentioned in Chapter 2, many states are taking a greater interest in upgrading the educational requirements of the real estate practitioner. Besides requiring extensive courses of study to qualify for a real estate license, many states now are passing laws requiring additional hours of continuing education before a license renewal is issued. Contact your state's real estate commission for current information on the status of continuing education in your state.

GOVERNMENT ACTIVITIES AFFECTING PROPERTY FINANCING

Changes in Interest Rates

Probably no single factor affects the health and activity of the real estate brokerage business as do interest rates. When interest rates are high, buyers and developers have a tendency to defer buying real estate and borrowing money. When interest rates drop, buyers are back on the market in droves. It therefore behooves the smart real estate broker to watch the money market and the direction in which interest rates are moving.

As seen in Chapter 12, it is often government policy to use interest rates as a means of curbing inflation. The rates are raised when the nation's economy is growing too fast and lowered when it is sluggish. Policymakers accomplish this by using the Federal Reserve bank to increase the rediscount rate, the rate at which member banks may borrow money from it, thus causing banks and other lenders to raise their prime rates accordingly.

In the short run, from a broker's point of view, inflation may seem to do little damage to the real estate brokerage business because of the public's consuming desire to buy as much real estate as possible as an inflation hedge, together with the fact that brokerage commission rates are usually based upon a percentage of the sales price. However, any thoughtful person can realize that inflation harms the economy of the nation as a whole, especially the segment of the public who live on fixed incomes.

Redlining

Redlining is the name given to lending institutions' practice of discriminating against certain areas in deciding where they will place loans, based on a consideration of conditions, characteristics or trends in the neighborhood or geographic area. Literally, it is the practice of drawing a red line on the map around a certain neighborhood where the lender refuses to make home loans. Ironically, this practice was first initiated by the FHA, an agency of the federal government.

In an effort to counteract redlining, the federal government passed the Home Mortgage Disclosure Act in 1975. This act requires all institutional mortgage lenders with assets in excess of $10 million and one or more offices in a given geographic area to make annual reports by census tracts of all mortgage loans the institution makes or purchases. This law enables the government to detect lending or insuring patterns that might constitute redlining.

Truth-in-Lending

A federal law designed to protect consumers who enter into credit transactions is known as "Truth-in-Lending." By imposing disclosure obligations on creditors and by giving consumers the right to rescind credit contracts in certain circumstances, the act attempts to enable consumers to compare credit terms offered by various lenders. The consumer thus avoids the uninformed use of credit and is protected against inaccurate and unfair billing by creditors.

The act, formally titled the Federal Consumer Protection Act, is enforced by the Federal Trade Commission but a consumer also may bring civil action against a noncomplying creditor. Unless a broker is more or less constantly involved in arranging for credit, the effects of this act are not of considerable importance to him or her.

The Fair Credit Reporting Act

The Fair Credit Reporting Act is designed to protect the consumer against the abuses of personal credit reports by vendors and credit reporting agencies. Basically this act gives the consumer the right to:

- Notification when adverse action is taken against him or her on the basis of a credit report;
- Knowledge of the source of the report and/or agency compiling the report;
- Knowledge of the information contained in the report;
- Confidentiality of the file, to be used only for permissible purposes;
- Reinvestigation of disputed entries;
- Procedures to assure reasonable accuracy, including elimination of obsolete data; and
- Advance notification of an investigative report.

Like Truth-in-Lending, the Fair Credit Reporting Act is enforced by the Federal Trade Commission. The consumer also has the right to civil action if his or her rights are violated or interests adversely affected by the abuse of a credit report. The act does not apply if the report is obtained to extend credit for business purposes or for some form of business entity, such as a partnership or corporation.

Brokers sometimes become involved in the collection and transmittal of credit reports as a service to their clients. This activity could give rise to legal problems. To avoid such problems, brokers should stay out of this area of collecting, transmitting or using credit reports. It is much better to let the lessor, seller and mortgagee obtain their own credit reports, warning them of their obligation should they make a decision adverse to the interest of the person being investigated.

GOVERNMENT ACTIVITIES AFFECTING PROPERTY OWNERSHIP

"Bundle of rights" is a term used by appraisers to describe the source of inherent value in a parcel of real estate. It is apparent that the more uses to which a property can be put (the larger the bundle of rights), the more valuable that property can be to the owner. Conversely, the fewer uses to which the property can be put, the less valuable it is. For example, a parcel of land that is zoned solely for agricultural uses and cannot be rezoned will be valued only for what it can produce agriculturally. Its value will be considerably less than that of a vacant lot in an adjoining community that is zoned for various commercial uses.

Each time a new law is passed in a community that affects or restricts the uses of property, another right is removed from the bundle and the value is diminished accordingly. Therefore, such political actions as the downzoning of property from a higher to a more restrictive use contribute to lowering the value of the properties affected. Sometimes such actions also have the side effect of raising the value of other adjoining properties not so affected.

Communities use these means to regulate and restrict the growth of the community. The zoning of land is determined by the local planning commission or zoning board, which is generally appointed by the governing body of a community. Since the governing body is elected by the town's citizens, it is they who have the last word as to the value of the property there.

The first lesson of real estate control is: The more supportive and less restrictive the public sector is to the housing market, the more activity will occur in that market.

A second lesson is this: Those who influence the selection of politicians in a community control not only the land-use policies of that community but also the volume of real estate activity therein. As an example, if the voters of a community are successful in electing a city council favorable to growth, then growth in that community will ensue. Community development and growth can no longer be left to chance.

Zoning

The right to apply precise zoning to each individual parcel of land within its jurisdiction is accorded a municipality and any other subdivision of the state through the police power of that state.

Police power is the exercise of the sovereign right of the government to promote order, safety, health, morals and the general welfare of society within constitutional limits. Under the U.S. Constitution, police power exists because it is based on the duty of the state to protect its citizens and provide for the safety and good order of society. This concept antedates the Constitution.

While the possession and enjoyment of all rights are subject to a reasonable exercise of police power, the courts in exercising their function may decide what actions constitute a reasonable exercise of police power. The courts must always weigh the extent to which police powers override legitimate individual rights. Therefore, a person can go to court over what he or she may feel to be an unjust use of police power. The courts have the last word.

For example, a party might be denied the right to build an apartment house in a strictly single-family residential neighborhood. Local property owners, through fear that the apartment dwellers might introduce an undesirable element into the community, would tend to support such zoning. In such a case the party might find recourse in the courts on the grounds of "exclusionary zoning." Even so, exclusionary zoning must be proved to be an inequitable use of the police power of the state.

In his book *Land Use Without Zoning* (1972), Bernard H. Siegan speaks out strongly against the efficacy of the zoning process. The author, an attorney, contends that those concerned with the quality of life, housing and local environmental conditions must attempt to eliminate zoning as one of the principal barriers to housing production and thereby allow the real estate market greater opportunity to satisfy the needs and desires of consumers. Presenting studies that show zoning is unnecessary either to maintain or protect property values or to aid in planning, which is its principal justification, he claims on the contrary that it has an adverse effect on both. The author adds that by impeding the production of housing, zoning inevitably impedes the achievement of better housing and better housing conditions.

Siegan is especially harsh on the zoning process in his claim that one group in the population, local politicians, have been allowed to gain dominance over land use despite their lack of competence and awareness of social needs. He also goes on to point out that several cities in Texas, notably Houston, have rejected zoning as a means of controlling the use of property within their jurisdictions. Houston developers control the use of their property through deed restrictions, leaving the powers of planning to the private sector, thus eliminating the unwieldly and costly department of city planning.

A number of factors seem to forecast a change in the government attitude towards zoning, at both local and national levels. Expanding populations, social problems within the cities, increasing land and development costs, the usurping of valuable agricultural land by suburban subdivisions, scarcity of land, environmental controls, urban transportation problems and the decreasing resistance to condominiums and planned-unit developments have combined to exert pressures and bring about changes in zoning considerations.

Federal courts have rendered decisions dealing with attempts to exclude housing developments, especially where it is alleged that the municipality has sought to use zoning to exclude people for racial reasons. Although the courts traditionally have been slow to move in any manner that will upset the present system of zoning, more recently they have been more aware of zoning's effect on the need to provide housing for all income brackets. They have the ability to fashion new approaches to problems as they arise, albeit a bit slowly. As the aforementioned pressures increase, the federal courts must and will respond in an enlightened manner.

Environmental Impact Reports

Many states, counties and cities have passed laws requiring an environmental impact statement before approval is given for new developments of any kind. Such laws at times seriously retard community growth. In California a large petrochemical plant that Dow Chemical wanted to build was finally abandoned because of an onerous number of studies and permits required by the state. Although the results pleased some of the environmentally conscious members of the public, a serious loss of employment was felt in an area that badly needed it.

Environmental concerns have often been used as an excuse to deny or restrict development for other than ecological reasons—economic and racial exclusion, for example.

Environmental reports can be costly and time-consuming. However, there is much to be said in favor of imposing such requirements on developments that might drastically affect the ecology of a sensitive area. But such reports should *not* be used as a means of restricting legitimate growth or helping to shut the door on newcomers.

INDUSTRY'S ANSWER—INVOLVEMENT

One of the advantages of a trade association is the synergistic effect it can exert on the politics of a city, state or nation. A broker who does not take advantage of and support such an association evidently is not yet convinced of the beneficial results the industry attains through such support.

Support is needed on the local level in fighting city ordinances detrimental to the interests of individual property owners; supporting election of candidates sympathetic to real estate interests; and searching out and convincing brokers and associates to devote their time and efforts to serve on city councils, commissions and local advisory boards.

By the same token, industry participation in the election campaigns of state legislators and officials is needed to help stem the erosion of property rights so vulnerable to attack.

Political Action Committees

The NAR and most state associations and local boards of REALTORS® have political action committees (RPAC) that raise money for candidates who will give a fair hearing to the champions of property rights. It is important for real estate practitioners to realize that the best way to stifle attacks on property owners' rights is to defeat at the polls legislators who are opposed to the best interests of real estate.

A good example is the California Association of REALTORS® (CAR). CAR is the third largest organization in California; only the government employees' union and the teachers' association are larger. The CAR has the potential for constructive action on an enormous scale. By throwing its weight behind the efforts of local boards, the CAR defeated transfer tax ordinances in Huntington Beach and Santa Barbara, attained tax limitations in Marin and Santa Cruz counties, overthrew a city council in Berkeley. Similar victories have been achieved by New Jersey, and other state associations can cite similar accomplishments.

Legal Action Funds

One of the most potent weapons a political action group can muster is a legal fund. Currently having insufficient funds to provide the presentation of the necessary legal arguments is not a valid reason to bypass involvement in any issue that adversely affects the real estate industry in a state.

Requests for legal action fund money through the NAR (or through the appropriate state organization) usually are first brought to the attention of the funds' trustees through the local boards in the state. They, in turn, petition for support on behalf of either a member involved in the litigation or the board itself. When a petition is made for funds, trustees usually review the relevant documents, listen to the attorney representing the party seeking assistance and make a determination as to whether the case would have an adverse or a positive impact upon the real estate industry as a whole.

In the past few years such funds have been used in litigations in many areas. In one case the right of a broker to recover a commission was validated where the seller of a property removed the property from the market. In an audit of another board of REALTORS®, the State Board of Equalization took the position that sales tax must be charged on the distribution of the MLS books. With support from the Legal Action Fund the position of the State Board of Equalization was altered to one in which it acknowledged that MLS books would, if they met certain minimum standards, be exempt from sales tax. This action saved MLS members throughout the state many thousands of dollars.

In an audit of the San Francisco Board of REALTORS® the Franchise Tax Board of the state and the Internal Revenue Service sought to remove that board's tax-exempt status. With fund support the San Francisco Board was able to uphold the validity of its nonprofit, tax-exempt status. Another fund is currently lending financial support on an appellate case seeking to limit the scope of city licensing ordinances as applied to real estate brokers. Such funds are useful in helping to stamp out fires wherever they break out, as the real estate industry and its participating members are harassed by government agencies from many different directions.

SUMMARY

The real estate industry is obviously much more complex than it was several decades ago. Government regulations and programs constantly seem to be attempting to make inroads on this bastion of the private enterprise system. Although such regulations and programs were undoubtedly designed to meet a problem, often they create grater and more far-reaching problems than the original.

For example, no-growth policies within a community may prevent water or sewer shortages but they also cause local inflation and restrict people from purchasing a home in a community of their choice; urban renewal seemed an excellent idea but had limited success during the first two decades after it was initiated in 1949 because buildings were demolished to build new ones rather than rehabilitating existing buildings, thus saving valuable housing stock; rent control ordinances have caused the economic decline of cities; and the Tax Reform Act of 1986 has drastically changed the deductions and other benefits that encouraged much building and real estate investment.

Many of the new developments in the law, however, have worked in the best interest of the consumer. For example, in California in 1978, a constitutional amendment known as Proposition 13 established a constitutional limit on property tax levies that cannot be changed by the legislature or by local governments.

Disclosure has become a common word in real estate language and includes giving notice if one is a licensee and also if one is acting as the buyer or the seller. It also requires disclosure, by both the broker and the seller, of any latent defects known or suspected in the property being sold. Antitrust laws have made price fixing a major violation. Not only were printed fee schedules eliminated but also any communication among competitors regarding fees. The Truth-in-Lending Law and the Fair Credit Reporting Act enable the consumer to compare credit terms and guard against credit report abuses. Legislation outlawing redlining has provided financing in areas where it was formerly denied. Civil Rights laws have made it illegal to discriminate and have led to REALTORS® adopting Affirmative Marketing Agreements pledging equal service to all, thus furthering the elimination of steering and discrimination.

In the long run, however, legislation negatively affecting real property and its use constantly is proposed. It is essential that the broker, who depends on the preservation of private property rights and a healthy real estate market for his livelihood, be cognizant of such impending legislation and actively oppose it. Much negative legislation has been postponed or defeated through the establishment of Political Action Committees and with money that has been contributed to candidates who will listen to the REALTORS'® position. It is through such concerted and cooperative action at the local state and national levels that the industry will survive.

DISCUSSION QUESTION

Make a list of all laws and regulations that affect real estate transactions and developments in your state, county and community. These would be laws and regulations concerning growth regulations, environmental considerations, general plan requirements (if any) and zoning, to mention a few of the areas.

15 Beyond Residential Brokerage

Successful real estate brokerage is a matter of the three I's: intelligence, initiative, and integrity.

—Marvin Starr, Attorney

INTRODUCTION

The Internal Revenue Service classifies real estate ownership in three groups or categories, according to purpose: for personal use, for inventory and for use in a trade or business or for the production of income.

The primary concern of this book has been the basic principles of opening and staffing a real estate brokerage office engaged chiefly in dealing with properties held for *personal use,* residential properties. The successful broker, however, will be called upon from time to time to deal in real estate for owners in the other two classes.

Real estate is owned for inventory mostly by those in the business of developing lots and tract homes from raw land or by those who buy and sell properties as a business. These owners are generally considered to be *dealers* or speculators. Some real estate brokers also buy and sell property for their own account; they are generally considered to be dealers and are required to pay income taxes at ordinary rates on the profits from such dealings.

Ownership of real estate for use in a trade or business or for the production of income categorizes a person as an *investor.* This class of ownership once received special treatment from the IRS in income tax calculations and costs. However, since the Tax Reform Act of 1986 (TRA '86), such is no longer the case. An investor no longer has means of saving on income taxes that are unavailable to owners in the other two categories.

This chapter focuses on some of the more advanced concepts of dealing in property for use in a trade or business or for the production of income—in other words, investment properties. These concepts include such fields as selling investment properties, leasing commercial property, developing and brokering industrial property, managing property and counseling. These fields are all interrelated, as will be shown. The opportunities available for increased income and personal satisfaction are limited only by a person's willingness to learn and become an expert.

THE NINE MAJOR ADVANTAGES OF INVESTING IN REAL ESTATE

As a basis of knowledge for these more advanced activities it is important to have a wide perspective of the advantages and disadvantages of owning and investing in real estate. In this section these advantages and disadvantages are listed and explained in somewhat abbreviated form.

High Rate of Return on Investment

Despite the general belief that real estate is not as lucrative as other forms of investment, the irrefutable facts show that it usually is. Granted, an ill-considered investment in any field can be a setback; real estate is no exception. When certain rules are followed, however, it is fairly easy for a prudent investor to do better in real estate than in most other forms of investment.

One of the first rules to observe is that if a prime property investment does not return at least two percent over the prevailing bank interest rate in the mortgage market, the investor should not buy it. For example, if the bank is willing to make a loan on a property at an interest rate of ten percent, the return on the overall real estate investment should be at least 12 percent. This means the total investment should pay at least 12 percent, resulting in a much higher rate of return on capital invested. Therefore, if a person purchases a property for $100,000 with $30,000 cash down and a $70,000 bank loan, then collects 12-percent return on the total investment of $100,000, the figures would look like this:

Return of 12% × $100,000	$12,000 gross annual return
Interest ($70,000 @ 10% per annum)	− 7,000 gross interest
Return on $30,000 invested	$ 5,000 gross return

A $5,000 return on $30,000 invested capital amounts to 16.6 percent, a good return by anyone's standards.

Note that the two percent differential is merely a rule of thumb, and it applies to *prime properties only*. Other factors affecting the investment include age of the improvements, deferred maintenance (lack of proper upkeep), physical depreciation, weakness of the tenant and economic obsolescence (changes in market conditions). These factors may call for a much higher spread than two percent over current bank lending rates.

Other forms of investment, such as stocks, bonds, savings accounts and mutual funds, usually yield less than two percent over current bank interest rates. They seldom yield more except in cases of higher-risk offerings.

Shelter Resulting from Interest and Depreciation Deductions

Interest paid on the loan received to purchase a parcel of income property may be deductible from taxable income. Hence, if a person is in the 28-percent tax bracket, 28 percent of the interest paid is "tax savings."

Depreciation, as it refers to real estate investing, is based on the government's theory that everyone who invests in an asset is entitled to the return of capital invested. When a person invests $10,000 in a savings account, that person is entitled to the return of that $10,000 plus any interest it has earned. So it is with an improvement on real estate. Investment in the land is not depreciable because theoretically land does not depreciate in value; only the improvements depreciate. Hence any investment made in real estate that has improvements on it entitles a person to a return of the cost of those improvements.

Depreciation of Real Estate Under TRA '86

It once was the custom to depreciate improvements on a parcel of real estate over the term of its expected life. For example, if an old apartment house was expected to be in service for another 25 years, then the value of that property was divided by 25 to give the depreciation deduction for each year.

However, under the new rules, residential rental property will be depreciated over 27.5 years (regardless of its life expectancy) and nonresidential property over 31.5 years. Only the straight line method may be used. (The straight line method divides the value of the improvements by the number of depreciable years, either 27.5 years or 31.5 years.)

These new rules serve to diminish the value of the depreciation deduction for tax shelter purposes on a real estate investment. However, there is still some value inherent in the process. For example, if a person buys an apartment house for $250,000 and $50,000 is allocated to the value of the land, then $200,000 is allocated to improvements and is depreciable over the 27.5-year period. That $200,000 divided by 27.5 years will provide a deductible expense of $7,272 annually for 27.5 years, which, multiplied by the top tax rate of 28 percent, means a cash savings on income taxes of $2,036 each year. No other form of investment furnishes this kind of tax savings!

A Hedge Against Inflation

If a person purchases diamonds or wheelbarrows in times of inflation, the value of those commodities will rise enough to enable that person later to sell them at a higher price, thereby hedging the value of the money against inflation, or keeping up with the declining value of the dollar. But neither diamonds nor wheelbarrows—nor most other commodities—will produce an income while the investor is waiting for their value to rise. In fact, these investments usually incur storage expenses while waiting. A well-chosen real estate investment, however, should not only rise in value with inflation but should also provide the investor with an income while doing so.

For example, if a $100,000 property is purchased with $30,000 down and a $70,000 bank loan, and requires annual *principal payments* of $1,107 in the first year of the loan, the return-of-cash income computations would look like this:

Total purchase price	$100,000
Cash down payment	30,000
Bank loan	70,000
Return on investment (after expenses, before payments)	$ 12,000
Payments to repay loan in 20 years at 10% interest ($1,107 + 7,000)	8,107
Net income from investment after expenses and payments	$ 3,893

The example shows that while the investment is paying for itself, it is also providing the owner with a return of $3,893 on the $30,000 cash down payment originally made ($3,893 ÷ 30,000 = 12.9% yield on the cash invested). Few other forms of investment can do that.

Further, if a person purchases a well-chosen property, he or she can be sure its increasing value will keep up with, and often outdistance, the climbing rate of inflation. For example, during the inflation and recession of 1974–1975, the stock market fell by at least 40 percent (Dow-Jones Industrial averages fell from the 1,000 level to around 600). At the same time the prices and dollar values of real estate doubled and, in some areas, even tripled.

As the cost of living goes up, so do the prices of and the income from real estate investments. Increased construction costs automatically pull up the value of existing improved properties. As the cost of new construction rises, the rents that must be charged to support investment in those new projects must also rise. At the same time, rents on existing investments will also rise, although perhaps to a slightly lesser degree. Therefore, the advantage of hedging against inflation through real estate investments is a real and important one.

Leverage for Increased Earnings

Effectively using leverage is probably one of the least understood but most important benefits of investing in real property. The principle of leverage is based upon the investor's ability to utilize borrowed funds to increase the yield from his or her investments.

A simple example of this principle was illustrated earlier in this chapter by the $100,000 investment that returned 12 percent on the overall investment but actually produced a 16.6-percent yield on the money invested. This spread was brought about through the use of borrowed funds. At first it sounds absurd to borrow money and pay the bank a high rate of interest and yet increase the yield on the purchase by doing so. Yet this is exactly the way leverage works, to the advantage of the real estate investor.

Forced Savings from Equity Buildup

Another distinct advantage of real estate ownership is equity buildup. Equity is the owner's share in the property after deduction of the mortgage loan balance from the fair market value. A person who buys real estate with borrowed funds is required to make periodic payments to principal and interest on that loan. The part of the payment that is applied to reduce the principal balance of the loan is termed *equity buildup* because it increases the owner's share of ownership (equity) while reducing the principal amount of the debt.

The money to make those payments frequently comes from the income generated by the property. In essence, the property is paying for itself while increasing the value of the forced savings account (equity). This ability of a real estate investment to provide an investor with a cash flow and at the same time pay for itself and increase the asset's value is truly unique and remarkable.

Tax Deferment

A provision of the Internal Revenue Code (Section 1031) allows the owner of a property to dispose of that property and acquire another in a tax-deferred exchange without paying tax on the capital gain. The person who uses this method carefully can build quite an estate without the constant drain of capital gains taxes on the profits from each transaction.

However, there are a number of rules and regulations that guide a person through the intricacies of this process. It is thus important that a person understand the rules of tax-deferred exchanging before attempting to defer capital gains taxes in this manner.

Tax Breaks for Those Who Own, Maintain and Improve Property

For instance, a person in the 28-percent tax bracket who spends $10,000 painting an investment building will have an expense deduction of $10,000 to apply as an offset against earnings. The government gets $2,800 less from that taxpayer (28 percent of $10,000), while he or she is actually increasing the value of the property.

Equally important, an improvement such as painting will undoubtedly add to the building's value when the owner is ready to sell. As an added benefit, in most cases the taxpayer is required to pay at most only 28 percent of this additional value in tax at the time of sale. Further, by improving the property with a capital expenditure as opposed to a maintenance expense, the taxpayer can add the cost of such improvements to the tax basis (book value) of the property and depreciate that cost over the estimated life of the improvements. This practice enables the taxpayer eventually to recover the cost of the capital improvement. Because other forms of investments do not involve this kind of expense and capital outlay deductions, they cannot offer the taxpayer the same tax advantages.

Equities: A Source of Tax-Free Capital

An investor proceeding with an investment program must be sure at all times to avoid becoming insufficiently invested. This means keeping close watch on the loans and equities of the properties. When an equity becomes large enough, it may be time to refinance and use the *new tax-free funds* as down payment on another property. By refinancing properties as they increase in value and using the proceeds from such loans to purchase another property, the investor can actually increase the number of his or her holdings without using any other capital, and without having to pay taxes on the new capital.

For example, suppose a potential investor owns a home purchased a number of years ago for a modest price of $15,000 that is now worth $60,000. With a loan balance of $7,000 there is a $53,000 equity. By refinancing or obtaining a second loan on the property, the investor can release at least $40,000 in capital to use as a down payment on another property.

However, one must not be misled into believing that all interest payments on a home refinancing loan are deductible. The TRA '86 specifically bars a taxpayer from deducting interest on refinanced loans if the refinancing was done after August 1986. This prohibition does not apply if the proceeds are used for legitimate educational or medical expenses.

Personal Psychological Satisfaction

Finally, an investment in real estate can satisfy the owner's security needs because real property is solid and tangible.

Inherent pride of ownership is manifested in most people by the manner in which they care for their property. To be successful in real estate investing, it is essential for the investor genuinely to like his or her properties and be proud of them. Without pride of ownership, properties tend to deteriorate in appearance, in usefulness and, eventually, in value.

Another personal need fulfilled by real estate ownership is the need to have a sense of stability in one's investments. There is nothing like a well-chosen and well-cared-for parcel of income property to satisfy that need. Unlike the stock market, which rises and falls based on whispers and rumors, or the bond market, which seldom pays enough on the investment to keep even with inflation rates, real estate investments properly conceived and structured keep sailing along on an even keel, paying a good return on the investor's money, keeping pace with or staying ahead of inflation. To reinforce this point, two good questions to ask are:

- Would you sell your stock today for what you originally paid for it?
- Would you sell your real estate today for what you originally paid for it?

The answers to both questions, in most cases, are fairly obvious.

Finally, one of the greatest sources of satisfaction in investing in real property is the investor's opportunity to have a hand in guiding his or her own destiny. One retains a great deal of control over one's investment. An owner can raise rents, borrow against the property, sell it, trade it, or change its use. These things cannot be done with securities. The average stockholder has little to say about how a major corporation is run. There is nothing one can say or do if one does not like the manner in which one's money is being manipulated, other than sell the stock.

FIVE POSSIBLE DISADVANTAGES OF REAL ESTATE INVESTING

For the nine major reasons listed, real estate outshines all other forms of investments. The reader who is aware of them can find many areas for further study. Like all investments, however, real estate has some drawbacks. It would not be fair to concentrate only on the advantages without at least discussing certain disadvantages as well. The broker who is aware of these disadvantages is in a better position to advise individual clients whether or not real estate investing is the wise choice for them.

By comparing the nine major advantages of real estate investing with the following five possible disadvantages, the prospective buyer is better able to determine if he or she is suited for, and wants to get into, the complicated world of real estate investments.

Liquidity Is Limited

It should be obvious that most properties cannot be readily sold for cash within a few hours as stocks or bonds can. It may take days, weeks or months before an owner can find a buyer ready, willing and able to purchase the property for a satisfactory price and favorable terms.

This limited liquidity is often considered a disadvantage. It is true that an owner in a financial bind (because of either economic conditions or personal disaster, who has real estate as his or her only resource and not enough equity to borrow against) may find it necessary to sell immediately to the highest bidder at a loss. Nevertheless, if real estate is priced at market value, the time it takes to dispose of it is remarkably short.

Management Is Required

Seldom does a realty investment appear that does not involve management to some degree. The successful investor can overcome these problems by planning and constructing his or her investments in such a manner as to anticipate possible problems in advance and avoid management as much as possible. This may be accomplished by writing the most advantageous leases and by instituting sensible budgeting, sound renting practices, and long-term planning of investment strategies.

If a potential investor is a person who cannot help worrying over small management problems, real estate may not be for him or her. It takes an investor who is willing to trade some worrying for the lucrative returns involved to become a success at real estate investment.

Investors Need Expertise and Advice

The problems discussed so far point out the need for dealing with and through a broker with sufficient expertise to advise a client properly. An investor who does not know the real estate investment market must rely on the services of an expert. There is plenty of good counsel available— from real estate counselors, knowledgeable brokers, attorneys or certified public accountants, all people who are well equipped to guide an investor through the intricate details of investing. Nevertheless, some investors resent paying for such services and are not capable of structuring their own investments correctly. These people should probably find fields other than real estate investment.

Risk Is Involved

There is no doubt about it; risks are involved in real estate investing. As with all forms of investments, the higher the risks, the greater the rewards. That is one reason why real estate offers a higher return on the investment. Risk can be substantially minimized when investors avail themselves of the most competent counsel available. Knowing where to buy, how to buy, how to attract the best tenants and how to tie tenants down with good leases or rental agreements can take a lot of the risk out of such ventures. Risks are simply part of any investment with which one must learn to contend.

Physical Work and Mental Effort Are Required

As with risk, the more physical work and/or mental effort involved in an investment, the higher the return one should expect from that investment. If the return on investment does not cover the expense of hiring professional management or maintenance help, then perhaps it is not a good buy, unless the investor is prepared to personally provide those services.

Likewise, if the investment takes a considerable amount of work and worry on the part of the investor, then the returns must be exceptionally high to compensate for the extra effort or the investment is misplaced. On the other hand, if the investor has very little capital invested but is willing to make up for it by applying considerable "sweat equity" to get started, the investment may be well placed.

A conscientious broker hoping to attract a strong investment clientele is well advised to be completely familiar with all of these advantages and disadvantages to help clients weigh them carefully. In this way clients will not suddenly discover they have become enmeshed in activities for which they are not suited.

THE EXCITING WORLD OF INVESTMENT BROKERAGE

Many brokers are content to deal mostly in residential brokerage and they continue to grow and prosper in such business. There are, however, interesting challenges in the investment field. There is no limit to the opportunities that may open up to the aspiring investment broker. Other advantages include:

- Minimal Saturday, Sunday or evening work;
- Clients (usually business people) who can recognize and appreciate the importance of a broker's efforts and do not question the right to a commission for such efforts;
- The continuing client-broker relationship that evolves from being instrumental in improving the economic position of such clients; and
- The self-gratification and esteem derived from gaining a name in the community for providing expert and valuable investment advice and services.

What an Investor Looks for

Study of the nine advantages and five disadvantages of real estate investing should tell a broker what the investor needs to build confidence in his or her real estate counselor. Without this background knowledge the broker cannot hope to develop the "stable" of investors that makes the investment field so lucrative and enjoyable.

Investors usually go to their attorneys, accountants, bankers or business acquaintances for advice about which real estate broker to consult. An impeccable reputation in the community in which these advisors reside is necessary to engender the kind of recommendations a broker needs. Careful husbanding of that reputation pays off in constantly increased business and confidence from the business world.

Three Types of Investors

Most investment brokers will agree that there are three general types of investors with whom they deal: the *dynamic* investor, the *passive* investor, and the *prudent* investor. The amount of surplus funds one has, how deeply one wants to get involved in management, how fast one wants to increase holdings and one's willingness to take risks determine the general type of investor.

The dynamic investor.   A person who starts out with relatively little cash but tremendous motivation and a willingness to work hard, take greater risks and be satisfied with less direct cash benefits in favor of longer-term equity buildup may be considered the *dynamic* investor. The dynamic investor uses all the tricks and sophisticated techniques available for increasing his or her estate as fast as possible.

The passive investor.   If the investor has a great deal of surplus funds along with the goal of conserving those funds as much as possible, he or she will have little interest in taking any great investment risks. Investment purchases will be made with security and safety of principal in mind. For example, he or she will look for long-term leases with high-quality, low-risk tenants and be satisfied with less income because of lower risks and fewer management problems. Because he or she is more affluent and owns more properties, this type of investor also will need to employ qualified, competent advisors and managers. This kind of investor may be termed a *passive* investor.

The prudent investor.   Somewhere in between these two categories there is a place for what may be termed the *prudent* investor. The prudent investor is willing to take those risks that he or she deems prudent, weighing them carefully against expected benefits. This person knows that some investments will involve loss, but expects those losses to be more than compensated for by the fruits of wiser investment decisions.

To illustrate the differences among the three types of investors, one can examine how each type would probably view a particular offering: an old, run-down warehouse, vacant and rat-infested, but for sale at a very modest price, for cash.

The dynamic investor would have neither the cash nor the time to wait for such a property to change in use or possibilities. The passive investor would not be interested because the risk of holding the property for an indeterminate length of time with little or no immediate income forthcoming is too great. This person would have neither the time nor the inclination to explore other possibilities.

The prudent investor, on the other hand, might make a serious study of the property to determine the demand for and scarcity of cheap warehousing in the vicinity. He or she would either know or make a study of the community to determine the availability of improved competing sites in the area. Upon finding the warehouse could be rented at low rates until a much more profitable use developed for the site, the prudent investor might well buy it and hold it for higher eventual returns.

Risks in themselves are not necessarily bad. They are just another factor to consider in weighing the viability of an investment and comparing it with the investor's philosophy as passive, dynamic or prudent. Figure 15.1 illustrates this theory graphically.

After an investor has been successful as a dynamic investor for a period of years and has accumulated a number of questionable investments, he or she may then start to consolidate those investments by selling them off, exchanging them for more conservative properties or upgrading them with better tenants and/or cosmetic improvements. He or she also will start to become more selective and discerning in choices of additional properties, thereby moving toward the prudent category. Likewise, as the prudent investor becomes older, more cautious and more

FIGURE 15.1   Categories of Investors

Dynamic Investor	*Prudent Investor*	*Passive Investor*
Takes risks.	Weighs risks.	Takes no risks.
Is low on funds.	Has substantial funds.	Has ample funds.
Accepts management.	Accepts or employs management.	Employs management.
Willing to expend considerable physical and mental efforts.	Willing to do mental work.	Not willing to do physical or mental work; hires people to do it.

affluent, he or she often has the inclination to move into the passive, or conservative, classification.

FIVE AREAS OF INVESTMENT EXPERTISE

While most people think of real estate brokerage simply as the listing and selling of real property for property owners, there are actually many variations of this activity. The five general areas of expertise commonly found are selling, leasing, development, management and counseling.

Selling Investment Property as a Brokerage Activity

Selling real estate generally is considered to be the major function of a broker. In its most basic form a sale is accomplished by first obtaining a signed exclusive-right-to-sell agreement and working through to a signed contract of purchase acceptable to the seller. It is not always this simple, however, especially in selling investment real estate. A seller might have income tax problems that require the sale to be structured in a certain way: a tax-deferred exchange, an installment sale, a sale and leaseback or one of several other methods. A buyer might have problems financing the sale and need some seller participation. In addition, buyers often have other contingencies or stipulations that must be met before they are willing to complete a purchase. Examples might include inspection by a qualified agency, rezoning for a specific use, obtaining a certain type of financing or approval by an outside authority.

Thus, selling investment real estate is not always a simple matter. It requires all kinds of knowledge to satisfy the needs of each party.

Leasing as a Brokerage Function

There are probably 15 or 20 different kinds of leases that may be used in the development of a real estate investment. In fact, the leasing of real property is an entirely separate specialty. Whole books and entire courses on leasing are offered to train investment-minded brokers. A person whose interest leans in that direction should take advantage of the educational offerings provided in his or her area. A comprehensive understanding of leases and their uses and ramifications is an essential addition to an investment broker's kit of tools.

Real Estate Development as a Specialty

One of the most interesting, rewarding and exacting branches of real estate investing is the development of investments from the ground up. A potential user often comes to the broker looking for a specific type of building or other improved property in which to locate and operate a business. If the broker finds there is no such property on the market for lease or for sale, he or she may know of an active group of investors who are willing to provide such a facility—if the lease terms are acceptable. This broker has two choices. One is to tell the customer there is nothing available in that particular kind of property, letting the customer walk out the door and straight to a more enterprising person who can deliver a property. The second choice is to discuss a "build-to-suit" project with the customer. This is really what developing is all about—taking raw land and providing space for a user—whether it is apartment houses, commercial space, industrial buildings or a single-purpose facility of some kind.

The practitioner who is interested in developing real estate needs a wide range of technical real estate knowledge. From the time the developer negotiates for the land to the time the final lease or rental agreement is signed, a continuous stream of problems is encountered. The investment broker must be capable of solving each problem as it arises. With the more recent emphasis on planning, zoning and environmental controls, these problems continue to multiply.

Real Estate Management

Management, with all its concomitant problems, is frequently seen as a disadvantage of owning investment real estate. The enterprising investment broker can eliminate this objection by creating a property management department. Such a department feeds off the efforts of the other departments and at the same time provides business opportunities for them.

If a firm had developed an apartment house complex for a client, for example, the transaction would have involved the land purchase, financing arrangements and possibly the management of the facility after completion. In such cases, when the client wishes to sell the property, the most logical brokerage firm to sell it is the managing firm, *if* that firm has done a creditable job of managing. Thus the logical progression of specialization for the investment broker goes from selling to developing to leasing to managing—and thence to counseling.

Counseling as a Field of Specialization

There are two types of real estate counselors: those who call themselves counselors but in the true sense of the designation are not and those who actually are real estate counselors, entitled to display the designation ASREC (American Society of Real Estate Counselors). Anyone can call himself or herself a counselor. Many brokers do this with little regard for the true meaning of the word. A true real estate counselor is a professional. He or she is not paid by commissions but in much the same manner as an attorney, doctor, appraiser or others who receive compensation commensurate with their knowledge, expertise, experience and time devoted to the counseling process. Their fee is not conditioned upon the outcome of their deliberations or advice but only upon the soundness of that advice and counsel. Good counselors thrive and prosper while inexpert ones gradually drop out of the profession.

To learn more about this form of real estate professional endeavor one should write to the Society of Real Estate Counselors at NAR headquarters in Chicago.

THREE STAGES OF REAL ESTATE INVESTING

As one expert succinctly phrased it, "The time to make a profit on an investment is not when you sell it but when you buy it!" This observation points up the importance of the first stage of real estate investing, acquisition.

The Art of Acquisition

There are three methods a potential investor may employ to search out a suitable investment for his or her portfolio.

1. Search the classified ads of the daily newspapers for properties advertised that may fit his or her requirements. Then travel from office to office following up on the leads encountered.

2. Go to a knowledgeable, well-recommended investment broker and ask that person to search for such an investment among the firm listings, listings of the local MLS and listings available through affiliation with investment-minded groups of brokers organized for that purpose.

3. Employ the service of an investment specialist with the guarantee that the buyer will pay the broker's fee for finding him or her a satisfactory property.

The final method, the least frequently used of the three, guarantees the buyer that the broker will be acting as agent. This means that the broker works solely in the buyer's best interest instead of the seller's, as required by the fiduciary relationship of the exclusive listing agreement. This is a sophisticated form of the acquisition process that, on the surface, appears to be more costly because the buyer must pay a commission. Nevertheless, it often proves to be the opposite when the broker-agent is a shrewd enough bargainer to be able to justify the fee and more. In such cases there is no question of which party's best interests the broker is representing.

The art of successful acquisition is so complex and so fraught with sensitive strategic maneuvering that most buyers are well advised to use the service of a third-party negotiator, the investment specialist. That is why skilled negotiators are much in demand by banks and developers of large-package properties. Their ability to probe the motivation of the owners of sought-after properties and utilize that knowledge to the advantage of their clients is often worth many times the fees they are paid.

Management: The Second Stage of Ownership

As Lloyd D. Hanford, Sr., CPM, once wrote, "Real estate is a living thing and a going business requiring uninterrupted attention if benefits are to accrue and avoidable losses be eliminated. Owners must never lose sight of the fact that the higher net income from real estate is justified partially because of its demand for constant care."

Too many owners of real property consider real estate a cow to be milked until it is dry and then abandoned. This attitude is reflected in huge sections of many cities where properties have been abandoned. Such areas require extensive redevelopment efforts, usually with the help of federal funds, to make them once again usable.

The eventual goal of owning investment property is to dispose of it at a profit. Although this disposition may not take place during the lifetime of the owner, it will occur eventually. The condition of the property directly determines the amount of profit engendered. Every investor should realize that once he or she has acquired a property, he or she also has acquired a responsibility for keeping that property in the best possible condition if maximum profits are to be realized. Reserves must be set up for roofing, painting, heating and cooling equipment, furniture and any other maintenance or improvements that contribute to income from the property. Leases or rentals must be watched and constantly updated.

Operating expenses must be kept to the minimum but repairs must be made as soon as required. This is all part of good management.

Such management can be performed by a capable owner who is willing to assume the physical work and mental effort required or it may be contracted out to a real estate management firm that is qualified and equipped to handle such properties.

Disposition: The Third Stage

While it is said that the time to make a profit on a real estate investment is when you buy it, it is equally critical that a person know how to dispose of the property in the manner most beneficial to that person's interests.

The motivation for selling is most important. Income property is usually disposed of for one of the following reasons:

- Too much responsibility and management chores;
- Desire for a bigger, more lucrative investment;
- Personal reasons, such as ill health or divorce; or
- Profit taking.

Whatever the reason for disposition, there is an equal and opposite reason for not wanting to sell. The reasons for not wanting to sell must be ascertained and counterbalanced. For instance, the party who is tired of management may be reluctant to sell because he or she does not know how to use the proceeds to find a comparable income. In this case, a skilled negotiator may suggest some form of investment that does not require management but still earns a satisfactory return. This might take several forms: an owner carryback loan at an interest rate commensurate with the previous net income from the real property; stock in the company acquiring the property equal in value to the sale price; or tax-free bonds, mutual funds or blue-chip common stocks. To convince the owner to sell, therefore, the skilled negotiator must be familiar with most other forms of investments in which the seller can invest the proceeds.

For the owner of a property who wants a larger property but hesitates to sell because of the capital gains tax, an exchange may be the answer. A three-way tax-deferred exchange vehicle can often be used to accomplish tax savings and still enable the acquisition of a larger property. A negotiator must be aware of these possibilities and know how to arrange such a transaction.

An owner may want to sell but not want to pay the entire capital gains tax in one year's time. The negotiator might suggest the installment sales method of spreading the tax over a longer period of time.

The matters of disposition, acquisition and management are of equal importance. It is up to the knowledgeable broker to be able to overcome objections to selling by figuring out a method that will accomplish the seller's objectives.

INVESTMENT MARKET ANALYSIS

Complete familiarity with state and federal income tax laws and regulations as they affect real property transactions is an absolute must for the broker who hopes to be a successful dealer in investment properties. As may be ascertained from the earlier parts of this chapter, rarely is an investment property sale contemplated or consummated in which the income tax consequences are not a major consideration. In any analysis of a real property investment, the information that will affect such taxes must be clearly provided.

Traditional Methods of Investment Analysis

Traditionally, real estate brokers have used one of four methods for analyzing an investment property. These are: factor times gross income, monthly rental as one percent of value, return on net operating income (NOI), and return on cash invested (cash on cash).

Factor times gross income. The *factor-times-gross-income* method is a rule-of-thumb method, highly unreliable but persistently used by less knowledgeable practitioners. This method purports to give an investor the value of a property offered by multiplying the gross income from the property by an *x* factor derived from the *x* factor of similar properties sold. For instance, suppose a property returns $850 per month. Multiply $850 by 12 months, which gives a figure of $10,200 gross annual income. Because other similar properties sold for eight times their gross annual income, one is supposed to use an *x* factor of eight. Multiplying the gross income of $10,200 by eight, one gets a supposed property value of $81,600. This system is fallacious because there are too many variables affecting the value of the property that are not taken into consideration when comparing it with other properties sold. Such variables include age of the property, strength of the tenants' rent or leases, condition of the property and whether the rents are at market, above it or below it.

Monthly rental as one percent of value. Another rule-of-thumb method, and the next least reliable one, is used by the old-time investment broker and might be labeled *monthly rental as one percent of value*. It is based on the supposition that a property should bring in at least a ten-percent return on the purchase price. Therefore, if a property rents for

$850 per month, its value is supposedly $85,000. This is computed by multiplying $850 per month by ten months, equaling $8,500, or ten percent of $85,000. The other two months' income are earmarked for taxes, insurance and other expenses incurred by the property. This method is unreliable because it also does not take into account the many variables affecting value.

Return on NOI.   The return on NOI is a slightly more accurate method. It is one of the more popular of the traditional forms of analyzing an investment still in use today. Figure 15.2 is a form that shows how to arrive at a value using this method. Any property's percentage of return on NOI is compared by the investor with the ideal return he or she expects from an investment. For instance, if the NOI shows a return of 10.5 percent on the asking price and the investor wants a 12-percent return, the price is obviously too high. On the other hand, an investor who is satisfied with a ten-percent return may decide to buy the subject property at the offered price. This method is used only when no debt service is contemplated.

Return on cash invested.   When a loan on the property is involved, and the investor is concerned only with the percentage of return from the actual cash invested, a slightly different formula is used. This also can be derived from the calculations on the investment analysis form in Figure 15.2.

The Modern Method

Today, sophisticated brokers and investors use the *internal-rate-of-return* method, calculating the rate at which *all* future cash flows will be discounted so the net present value will equal zero. An even more refined method, the *adjusted internal rate of return,* is defined as that rate that will discount future cash inflows to equal cash outflows that have been discounted at a specified rate.

The typical investor wants a return on the investment over and above the full return of invested capital. In general, this return on invested capital is expressed as an annual rate. In the case of borrowed funds, the rate of return on the borrowed funds accruing to the lender is termed the interest rate. The return on that portion of the investment that represents the borrower's equity is termed the equity yield rate. When the two interests are combined in real estate (borrower's and lender's), the rate of return on the entire property is called the *discount rate.*

The calculation of the *rate of return,* or *yield,* from an investment is an important measure of that investment's worth because it provides a basis for comparing a specific investment to alternate investments. Because rate

FIGURE 15.2 Computations for Return-on-NOI Method

PROPERTY INVESTMENT ANALYSIS

Description _____ Address _____

1. Asking Price 1
2. Comparative market value 2
3. Loan balances   1st 3
4.   2nd 4
5.   3rd 5
6.   Other (furn., etc.) 6
7. Total loans commitment or assumable 7
8. Equity value down payment 8
9. Acquisition costs (loan, title, escrow fees) 9
10. Total cash investment (8+9) 10
11. Scheduled annual GROSS INCOME 11
12. Vacancy allowance (actual has been   %) 12
13. EFFECTIVE GROSS INCOME (11-12) 13
    ANNUAL OPERATING EXPENSES:
14. Real estate taxes 14
15. Insurance 15
16. Water 16
17. Electricity 17
18. Gas 18
19. Rubbish and garbage removal 19
20. Advertising 20
21. Licenses 21
22. Telephone 22
23. Management (lodging, cash, owner's time, prof'l fees) . . . 23
    Maintenance and repair
24. Pool service 24
25. Elevator maintenance 25
26. Gardener 26
27. Other 27
28. Other 28
29. Other 29
30. TOTAL EXPENSES (14 through 29) 30
31. NET OPERATING INCOME (13-30) 31
32. Annual principal payments (will increase) 32
33. Annual interest payments (will decrease) 33
34. Total payments (32+33) 34
35. Net income after debt retirement service (31-34) 35
    (i.e. net cash flow results from property)
36. Net cash flow plus equity gain (32+35) 36
37. Net income after interest (31-33) 37
38. *Estimated depreciation 38
39. Taxable income from property if any (37-38) 39
40. Loss applicable to other income if any (38-37) 40
41. Income taxes if any (%) 41
42. Net income after income taxes and debt service (35-41) 42
43. Tax savings from other income if any 43
44. Total cash flow (or spendable) 42+43 44
45. Inflation protection and increase in value -   % 45
46. Total annual dollar benefits (32+44+45) 46
*** RETURN ON TOTAL INVESTMENT (31÷2) . . . .
*** RETURN ON TOTAL CASH INVESTMENT (37÷10) . . .
*** SPENDABLE ON EQUITY (44÷10) . . . .
  * DEPRECIATION DETAILS:
        Method   : _____
        Term   : _____
        Land   : _____

of return is calculated from data relating only to the specific investment, that is, initial investment plus estimated future cash flows from the investment, the method is known as the *internal rate of return.*

The internal rate of return on an investment also may be more easily defined as the *rate of discount* at which the present worth of future cash flows is equal to the initial capital investment. This sophisticated method is rather difficult to use unless one has taken a concentrated course specifically designed for teaching this method, such as the course offered by the REALTORS® National Marketing Institute called Commercial-Investment Division Course A, "Fundamentals of Real Estate Investment and Taxation." Another excellent, even more sophisticated course in this area, offered by NAR's REALTORS® Land Institute, is called "Land Return Analysis." This course is presented periodically throughout the United States. The space limitations of this book do not permit further exploration of this complex but intriguing concept.

ALTERNATIVE MARKETING METHODS

Selling real estate directly is not the only method a broker may employ to help principals dispose of their real estate profitably. Other strategies include exchanging, installment sales, syndication and condominium conversion.

Exchanges

There are three principal reasons why parties might want to exchange their property rather than sell it. The first is to get rid of an unsalable property, or trade "down and out." For example, an owner who has been having difficulty disposing of an unwanted property agrees to exchange it for a smaller property owned by someone who could use the property but has no funds to buy it. The principal thus takes the smaller property (or properties) in trade, plus perhaps a mortgage back for the difference, in the expectation of selling the smaller property. A second reason is to defer the capital gains tax, according to the provisions of Section 1031 of the Internal Revenue Code. A third reason is to acquire more depreciable property. Exchanges are treated differently for tax computations according to the reason for owning the real estate. As mentioned earlier, the IRS classifies real estate ownership into three groups: personal use, inventory or production of income or use in a trade or business.

Property held for inventory purposes.   Inventory property, lots and tract homes developed by a developer or any properties bought and sold by a real estate *dealer* are not eligible for special treatment under long-term capital gains tax-deferred exchanges. Real estate brokers, unless they can prove they are not dealers, are not allowed capital gains treatment. They must pay ordinary income tax rates on any profit from the sale or exchange of any real property. In some instances a broker can qualify as both a dealer and an investor on separate properties. However, professional tax advice is required to accomplish this successfully.

Because a dealer may not depreciate inventory property there is little tax shelter advantage in owning speculative property.

Property held for the production of income. People who own property for the production of income or for use in a trade or business are classed as *investors* by the IRS. Investments have a tax shelter advantage because they may be *depreciated* over their estimated useful life.

Depreciation, the return of capital, is distinguished from *yield,* the return *on* capital invested. Other terms should also be defined to clarify the following discussion. *Basis* is the book value of the property: Cost – Depreciation + Improvements = Basis. *Gain* on a sale is the adjusted sale price less the basis.

It is possible under some circumstances to avoid capital gains taxes altogether. Section 1031 of the Internal Revenue Code provides for nonrecognition of all or part of the gain realized on the exchange of property held for productive use in a trade or business or held for investment. To qualify, the exchange must be solely for *like kind,* to be held for similar purposes. A tax-deferred exchange of investment property thus has the following requirements:

There must be a bona fide exchange. Deeds must actually change hands and do so in the proper sequence. One cannot avoid taxation by selling a property and buying another within a prescribed time period, as with a personal residence. Exchange must involve like-kind property, that is, investment property for investment property. It cannot involve exchange of a personal residence for investment property or (with some exceptions) inventory property for investment property or a personal residence.

Any property that is not investment property is *unlike* property. This includes all *personal* property, such as cash, stocks, bonds, cattle, boats and cars. If such *unlike* properties are involved in an exchange they are considered *boot* and can be taxed.

The technique of exchanging is used constantly by well-informed brokers; it can become extremely complicated as well as profitable. It is not unusual for an expert to put together a string of transactions that involves anywhere from three to dozens of properties exchanged in very complicated procedures.

Installment Sales of Real Estate

Before the enactment of TRA '86, computing an installment sale for tax reporting was easy and straightforward. But the requirements of the new law have taken a simple computation and turned it into an accountant's nightmare.

The members of Congress believed the installment sales method was "inappropriate" for dealers of ordinary income property and for the sale of certain business and rental income property. After all, they said, the reason for the installment sale method was to help the seller who was unable to pay tax currently because he or she received little or no cash from the sale. But what happened, they continued, was a situation whereby the taxpayer received cash by borrowing on the property—and extending his or her credit line by the presence of installment obligations among his or her assets. To prevent this, TRA '86 includes a major modification that requires a seller to recognize gain on installment sales to the extent to which he or she has been able to receive cash from borrowings related to installment obligations.

The bill limits the availability of the installment method of accounting to real estate by:

1. Disallowing the use of the installment method with respect to a portion of certain installment receivables, based on the amount of the outstanding indebtedness of the seller. This is called the "Proportionate Disallowance Rule."

2. Granting an election to taxpayers selling certain timeshares and residential lots if they agree to pay interest on the deferred tax liability. By doing this, taxpayers will not be subject to the new rules.

Farm properties, personal use properties and other properties selling for $150,000 or less are excluded from these changes.

The proportionate disallowance rule. The use of the installment method by persons who regularly sell real property and for certain sales of business and rental property is limited, based on the amount of outstanding indebtedness of the person. The limitation is applied by determining the amount of the person's *allocable installment indebtedness* (AII) for each taxable year. This amount is then treated as *payment* immediately before the close of the taxable year.

Here is how you figure AII:

1. Divide the face amount of the seller's applicable installment obligations that are still outstanding at the end of the year by the sum of:

a. the face amount of *all* installment obligations; and

b. the adjusted basis of all other assets of the seller.

2. Multiply the quotient from Step 1 by the seller's average quarterly indebtedness.

3. Subtract any AII attributable to applicable installment obligations that arose in previous years.

Applicable installment obligations are any installment obligations that arose from the sale of the following properties after February 28, 1986:

1. All real estate held as "dealer" property, including homes sold by builders and developers;

2. Real estate (except farm property) used in the taxpayer's business *or held as rental income property*. However, the selling price must be more than $150,000. If the selling price is not more than $150,000, the sale will not be subject to these rules.

Example: During 1987 you sell a rental property for $360,000 and take back an installment note for the entire price. The property was sold at a profit and you received no payments in the year of sale.

The adjusted basis of your assets (not counting the $360,000 note) totals $1,240,000 as of December 31, 1987, and your average quarterly indebtedness for 1987 is $800,000. Your AII for 1987 is $180,000.

Step 1

Face amount of all installment obligations	$ 360,000
Adjusted basis of your assets, not including the $360,000 installment note	$1,240,000
Total	$1,600,000

Step 2

Face amount of applicable installment obligation	$ 360,000
Divided by total from Step 1	$1,600,000
Quotient	22.5%

Step 3

Average quarterly indebtedness	$ 800,000
Multiplied by quotient from Step 2	22.5%
This is your AII for 1987	$ 180,000

Result: Even though you received no actual cash payments on the installment sale in the year of sale, you would recognize a payment of $180,000. Your recognized gain would be your gross profit percentage multiplied by your $180,000 AII.

The first $180,000 of actual payments received by you from the buyer would not result in recognition of additional gain. Payments in excess of $180,000 would count as "regular" installment payments and would result in recognition of gain.

(The foregoing tax information has been furnished by Rich Robinson, CPA, of Fredericksburg, Texas. Rich is tax consultant and nationwide lecturer for the REALTORS® Land Institute. He also has available a newsletter, as well as tapes and books on the subject.)

Syndication as a Marketing Tool

A syndicate is an association of individuals united for the development of an investment enterprise. A group of 50 people who contribute $100 each to buy a $5,000 lot is just as much a syndicate as two people who contribute $250,000 each to invest in a $500,000 property.

A simple example of the use of a syndicate might involve a property listed for sale for $20,000. It appears to be an excellent buy at this price, having the potential for a substantial increase in value. The problem is that the seller wants cash, perhaps a reason why the property is a good buy. An enterprising broker sees the potential and gathers together four people to purchase the property for $5,000 each. Each purchases an undivided one-fourth interest. That broker has just put together a syndicate. A good listing with poor terms has frequently been sold through "creative syndication."

There are some potential problems hidden in this example that must be anticipated if the broker is to advise clients properly. For instance, one must consider how members of the syndicate should take title: as tenants in common, as a partnership, as a trust or as a corporation.

If one investor dies or declares bankruptcy, there must be provisions for (1) his or her portion of the tax, loan, insurance and other payments; (2) the effect of the encumbrances of one party's liens; and (3) the effect of probate of one party's estate.

The question of the legality of creating a syndicate without first obtaining a permit from the commissioner of corporations (state or federal or, in some cases, both) frequently arises, even though the syndicate may not be in the form of a corporation.

These are only some of the questions that should be settled for all parties to the syndicate. Although the possibilities for creating brokerage business through the use of syndicates are almost limitless, the process is open to many legal implications. The broker who decides to include such a marketing device in his or her bag of marketing tricks is well advised to make a comprehensive study of all the ramifications of using this method before plunging into it full scale.

Condominium Conversions

This is a highly sophisticated (and profitable) marketing tool for the broker willing to devote the necessary time and effort to learning how to do it.

A condominium is a property divided into fragmented ownerships, giving each owner a right to use and occupancy of a specific portion of that property. For example, a high-rise apartment house may be converted to a condominium where each dweller receives a deed to a specifically described apartment dwelling (a space in the air) together with some ownership rights to the common areas (hallways, garages, gardens, pools and surrounding lawns).

Condominium conversion, not only of apartment houses but also of office buildings, industrial complexes and recreational developments, enables the owner to sell individual units to either present occupants or newcomers. An example of the profitability of such a venture can be found in the case of a 100-unit apartment house having a market value of $1.2 million if sold as one unit. By subdividing that apartment house into a condominium and marketing the individual units separately for $25,000 per apartment, the owner has raised the sales proceeds to $2.5 million for these same apartments.

Condominium conversion is subject to many legal restrictions. Hardy and patient is the owner of such a facility who is willing to spend the time, money and frustrating effort it takes to complete such a conversion successfully. A broker who is assisting such an owner had better be well prepared and schooled in converting. Condominium conversion can be a lucrative form of brokerage because of all the commissions generated by the individual sales of the units.

COUNSELING: THE ULTIMATE REAL ESTATE PROFESSION

While a real estate broker may become accomplished in such specializations as exchanging, syndication, condominium conversions, land developments or commercial leasing, counseling takes a special kind of expert who is well versed in all of these areas. Such an expert is acknowledged as a real estate consultant. A consultant is concerned with helping his or her clients accomplish their goals—usually to attain maximum wealth within a minimum period of time.

Helping clients achieve their goals may involve general restructuring of the client's investment program, such as selling some properties, buying other properties, revising leasing policies (adjusting rents to apply to current market rates) and developing some assets into higher and more profitable use. If a client asks a consultant to search out and find suitable property, the consultant does not participate in commissions on any sale. Remuneration is entirely dependent on the value of the advice to the client. Basically, a consultant solves problems for his or her clients. For services rendered, the consultant charges a fee.

A consultant may be employed by an owner of many diversified realty investments, a buyer or potential buyer of real property, another broker who needs the consultant's expertise to help conclude a complicated transaction or a major corporation with varied and diverse real estate interests that has no in-house experts to identify and solve its problems.

The advantage of employing a consultant is that a client has an expert with an impartial view working in his or her behalf. Because the consultant is paid on an hourly basis, rather than from commissions, he or she has no financial stake in a transaction. A consultant can dissect and analyze transactions with an entirely dispassionate view. Consultants may not always have total expertise in all areas. Thus part of the value is the consultant's advice in recommending a qualified expert.

RESPONSIBILITIES OF THE BROKER TO THE COMMUNITY

There is more to being a real estate broker than just earning a livelihood. If a broker is to fill the role of a professional in the community, he or she must recognize all of the responsibilities owed to that community, such as to:

- Help preserve the valuable resources of the community;
- Contribute to the orderly growth of the community;
- Help everyone with the means to do so find a home in the area in which he or she wants to live;
- Cooperate with the city, county, state and federal governments to ensure the success of programs designed to assist taxpayers and property owners;
- Resist and help defeat proposed legislation unfavorable to the best interests of taxpayers and property owners;
- Encourage and aid minorities in their efforts to move to the areas of their choice;
- Take a leadership role in as many community activities as he or she is capable of, both physically and financially; and
- Present an image of solidarity, honesty, reliability and integrity, as befits a representative of an honored profession.

While the main body of this book has been devoted to the nuts and bolts of becoming successful in residential brokerage, this chapter has concentrated on those broader areas of opportunities open to individuals who want to do more than sell houses.

SUMMARY

Although the primary concern of this book is about residential real estate and the basic principles brokers should follow when opening and staffing residential offices, there are times when brokers will represent those who invest or speculate in real estate. Frequently, brokers themselves will become investors or speculators.

Since the passage of TRA '86, investors no longer enjoy the special treatment once afforded them. However, there are still many advantages of real estate investing. The nine major advantages are explained in this chapter. Five possible disadvantages also are covered.

For a broker to cultivate a "stable" of investors, he or she must be familiar with both the advantages and the disadvantages of investment real estate. Equally important, to ensure referrals from other professionals, the broker must establish and maintain an impeccable reputation in the community.

There are three general types of investors: the dynamic, the passive and the prudent. All investors fall into one of these three categories, depending on their amount of surplus funds, the depth of their involvement in management and their willingness to take risks. Investment real estate is more than the listing and selling of real property. It also includes leasing, development, management and counseling. The very nature of these specialties leads to more intricate transactions. With investment real estate the broker will be required to structure financing and consider (and sometimes try to change) zoning, among other things.

Throughout the three stages of real estate investing, the knowledgeable broker can play a vital and productive role in the acquisition, the management and the disposition of the property. This knowledge must include complete familiarity with state and federal tax laws and regulations affecting real property. The modern method of investment analysis, the use of internal-rate-of-return, replaces the traditional methods, which included factor times gross income, monthly rental as one percent of value, return on net operating income and return on cash invested.

Although one usually thinks that the direct sale of real estate is the way to dispose of property, frequently other strategies are used. These include exchanging, installment sales, syndication and condominium conversion.

The consultant is the epitome of the real estate professional. If a broker aspires to become a consultant, it behooves him or her to spend the long years of study and preparation it takes to become an expert in all the disciplines of brokerage, appraising and development.

This book mainly addresses the way to become successful in residential brokerage. However, it also emphasizes the importance of knowledge, service and integrity. The ultimate type of broker will recognize his or her responsibility to the community in which he or she earns his or her livelihood and will take a leadership position in upholding the rights of private ownership for all people.

DISCUSSION QUESTION

Make a list of the nine Institutes, Societies and Councils of the NAR and briefly describe the functions and areas of expertise of each.

16

Trends and Impacts: The Changing Industry

INTRODUCTION

Real estate brokerage keeps changing. Sometimes the changes are almost imperceptible; other times they are abrupt and radical. The year 1986 was a signal year of major changes in the industry. There were many new laws, rules, regulations and ways of doing business promulgated throughout the nation.

These new developments have taken two major directions, which may be summed up in a few words: consumerism and correction of abusive tax shelter practices. Some of the major changes that will drastically affect the business during the coming years are:

- Tax Reform Act of 1986;
- New laws regarding consumer protection;
- Increased uses for the computer;
- Trend toward appraiser certification and licensing;
- Development of marketing sessions by professionals;
- New developments in finder's fee exceptions; and
- Trend toward licensing reciprocity among states.

TAX REFORM ACT OF 1986 (TRA '86)

The proliferation of abusive tax shelters has been a major concern of legislators and the administrative branch of the government for some years. TRA '86 addresses this concern and will go far in eliminating opportunities for further abuses of tax shelters.

325

The legislation that was passed by Congress alters the basic design of the tax laws that created tax-advantaged investments. In the case of real estate the primary focus of the bill is to reduce the fundamental benefits of so-called tax-shelter deferral of income. In addition, the bill decreases depreciation benefits, repeals or restricts certain business credits, limits deductions and repeals many incentives for low-income housing.

Furthermore, one of the key elements of a tax shelter, the possibility of converting ordinary income into capital gains, also is eliminated by treating all gains on disposition as ordinary income.

In general, the new law will have the effect of making economic rather than tax considerations the determining factor in guiding investment decisions. In other words, an investment must show a good return (or yield) on the money invested without the benefit of any tax-shelter manipulations. Cash flow and appreciation in value will once again be the major items to consider when investing. In return for the loss of the tax-shelter provisions, the average taxpayer will enjoy a lower tax rate of no more than 28 percent of his or her income during the coming years.

Another effect of TRA '86 on the real estate business will be the increased use of the *Section 1031 tax-deferred exchange* provisions of the tax laws, which have not been changed by TRA '86. Many investors will probably prefer to exchange their properties for bigger and better ones rather than sell and pay the new high capital gains tax. This will create incredible opportunities for real estate professionals who are well versed in this type of transaction.

Reporting Real Estate Transactions to the IRS

For any sales closing after December 31, 1986, all real estate transactions involving one- to four-family real estate must be reported to the Internal Revenue Service by the *person responsible for closing the transaction*. If the person responsible for closing the transaction is other than the real estate broker, then that person must file such information returns. If there is no other person acting as the closing, or settlement, agent (such as an attorney or title company), then the real estate broker is the responsible party.

It is evident from this new law that this is just the tip of the iceberg. Eventually the IRS will attempt to get laws passed that will require all real estate transactions, *regardless of size or category*, to be reported by the real estate broker. If this happens it will place an undue, totally unfair burden on the real estate brokers of this nation.

NEW LAWS REGARDING CONSUMER PROTECTION

Every year another law or two is passed by various state legislatures to raise ever higher the walls that protect consumers from unscrupulous practitioners. The latest law changes affecting real estate in some of the states are described here because such legislation enacted in one state eventually becomes law in most of the other 49 states, in one form or another.

Ethics into Law

On August 25, 1986, the California Department of Real Estate succeeded in having an Ethics and Professional Conduct Code incorporated into state law that applied to all licensees. This was a radical departure from previous practice, when ethics were left up to the jurisdiction of organized real estate, i.e., the NAR, the California Association of REALTORS® and local boards of REALTORS®.

However, the legislature felt that because only about 125,000 of the nearly 400,000 licensees belonged to such organizations, there were not enough ethical restraints placed on the majority of the licensees in the state. Hence, the ethics code was passed.

In addition to establishing a state code of ethics, the real estate law reinforces the measure by requiring that a licensee, to renew his or her license, also must take 45 hours of continuing education each four years, including three hours of legal aspects of the Ethics and Professional Conduct Code. All courses and seminars accredited for the 45 hours must include a written examination to be passed by the participant.

Trend Toward More Complete Agency Disclosure

Many states now require disclosure by the licensee of which party—the buyer or the seller or both—he or she represents. The following is a synopsis of the actions of various states regarding this disclosure.

California. Requires real estate brokers acting as listing and selling agents to (1) provide sellers and buyers with a prescribed disclosure form containing general information on agency relationships in real property transactions and (2) specify in the contract between parties whether the listing agent represents solely the seller or both the buyer and seller. The obligation of a buyer or seller to pay compensation to a real estate agent is not necessarily determinative of the agency relationship. The disclosure form is to be provided (1) to the seller prior to entering into the listing agreement and (2) to the buyer as soon as practicable, but prior to execution of the buyer's offer to purchase.

Florida. Requires disclosure in the sales contract that "the person procuring the sale of real property is the agent of the seller of the real property, if such is the fact, and that the person procuring the sale of the real property will be paid by the seller on completion of the sale, if such is the fact."

Hawaii.   The new law includes, as a ground for suspension or revocation of license, "When the licensee fails to obtain on the contract between the parties to the real estate transaction confirmation of who the broker represents."

Maine.   Requires that the selling licensee shall provide a written statement to each prospective buyer disclosing which party or parties the listing and selling licensees are representing, prior to showing any properties to that prospective buyer. Licensees employed by prospective buyers shall provide notice at the initial contact with a seller or with the seller's agent that the licensee is acting as the buyer's agent.

Minnesota.   A new section of the licensing law entitled "Disclosure Regarding Representation of Parties" requires an affirmative written disclosure in the purchase agreement, acknowledged by both buyer and seller, of who represents whom.

Oregon.   Proposed legislation combines oral and written disclosure, though no prescribed disclosure form is required. Oral or written disclosure must include (1) whom the licensee represents; (2) what, in simple terms, the client should or should not expect from the licensee; and (3) how the licensee will be compensated for services rendered.

Colorado, Missouri, Nevada, New York, South Carolina, South Dakota, Texas, Vermont, Washington and Wisconsin all have similar laws or regulations. Mississippi, Nebraska, Pennsylvania and Utah are in the process of enacting similar rules and regulations.

License Law Changes Enacted by the Various States in 1986

By reviewing many of the new license law changes, one may get a better perspective on the direction in which the legislation affecting the real estate industry is going.

Alabama.   Licensees are required to complete 12 clock hours of approved course work to renew their licenses on an active status. Licenses are renewed every two years.

California.   Educational requirements for brokers and salespersons were modified as follows: (1) Broker educational prequalification requirements increased from 18 to 24 units; (2) prequalification requirements for an original salesperson license became three units in Real Estate Principles or its equivalent; (3) within the first 18 months following initial issuance of a salesperson license, completion of six additional units in real estate courses are required, these courses to be selected from a list of courses used for broker prequalification. (Completion of such courses by salespersons would count toward a broker's educational requirement.)

Colorado. Amended Broker's Act requires an additional 24-hour prelicensing course in Colorado Law and Colorado Contract Preparation. Licensing requirements for out-of-state brokers and salespersons were eased. Such persons licensed in other states now need to take only the course in Colorado Law and Colorado Contract plus the local portion of Colorado's examination to meet all educational and testing requirements.

Georgia. Increased prelicense education for salespersons from 24 hours to 60 hours. Decreased the 80 hours of postlicense education required of salespersons in their first two years of licensure to 30 hours required in the first year of licensure. Express legislative authority has been given licensees to complete contract forms prepared by legal counsel.

Hawaii. Deleted residency requirement for taking Hawaii real estate examination.

Kentucky. Beginning April 1, 1987, all licensees must carry errors and omission insurance; the Commission will offer group policy or it can be obtained through your own insurer. A new law also clarified property management exemptions from licensing.

Louisiana. Made changes in Timeshare Act.

Iowa. Passed a Timeshare Act.

Maine. Rent/lease activities exempted for real estate brokerage license requirements.

Minnesota. Prelicense requirements after January 1, 1987: (1) 90 hours prelicense classroom training for salesperson; (2) 30 additional hours in first year as salesperson. Continuing education after July 1, 1987: 15 hours per year (replaces 45 hours every three years).

New Mexico. Enacted Timeshare Act.

Tennessee. Repealed "inducements" provision. It is now legal to offer gifts.

Vermont. New law mandates four hours of continuing education for brokers and salespeople over a two-year period.

Wisconsin. Fee-splitting: permits licensees who legally engage in the practice of real estate in a foreign country or in a territory or possession of the United States to share commissions. The Education Act created a new inactive license at reduced renewal fee; increased salesperson's prelicense educational requirements from 30 hours to 45 hours and broker's from 60 hours to 90 hours; created a one-year experience requirement for broker applicants; eliminated mandatory continuing education; removed designated cemetery broker.

The foregoing should give one a good idea of how the states are progressing individually and collectively toward a more professional approach to the real estate industry.

A more comprehensive look at states' requirements in licensing and education can be obtained by writing to: Stephen J. Francis, Executive Vice President, NARELLO, P. O. Box 129, Centerville, UT 84014-0129. Request a copy of the National Association of Real Estate License Law Officials *Digest of Real Estate License Laws in the United States and Canada for 1986*. The price of the digest is $30.

Mandatory Disclosure to Home Purchasers

This book already has gone into the matter of mandatory disclosure statements required from the sellers of real property or their agent. Consequently, it is only briefly touched on here because it serves to illustrate a significant trend in the real estate business that will have an increasingly strong impact as time goes on.

The trend is definitely away from the old concept of *caveat emptor* and toward increased responsibility on the part of the sellers and their agents for making sure buyers are well protected. The old ploy of selling a residential unit in an "as is" condition no longer relieves the seller of the responsibility for disclosing all defects in the property known to him or her.

INCREASED USES FOR THE COMPUTER

More and more real estate practitioners are adopting computers to use in their offices. Brokers who do not become adept at computer usage may well find themselves hopelessly lost in the business world of tomorrow.

In fact, the authors can foresee the day when all realty offices will be hooked up to a central computer and will be able to communicate with each other and the NAR headquarters at all times of the day and night through their office terminals. The technique and hardware are already available; it is only a matter of putting all the pieces together.

TREND TOWARD APPRAISER CERTIFICATION AND LICENSING

For the first time legislation has been passed effective on January 1, 1988, that establishes legal standards for the performance of real property appraisal services when the client specifies that a certified appraisal is desired. The standards are based on guidelines established by major appraisal organizations and may be enforced through civil action, injunction or other equitable relief. The use of a "Certified Appraisal" is not mandatory; but users expect that when the designation of "Certified" appears on an appraisal the report was prepared in accordance with statutory standards.

Since the law was passed, eight real estate appraisal organizations have reached basic agreement on a program to establish such standards for appraisals and requirements for education, experience and examinations for the nation's 250,000 appraisers.

The program, proposed by the American Institute of Real Estate Appraisers, would set up a qualification-and-enforcement structure similar to that of the accounting profession. As in the certified public accounting system, appraisal certification would be voluntary. Uncertified industry members would not be prohibited from calling themselves appraisers or from performing appraisals.

The self-regulatory system, which is expected to take from two to three years to implement, was initiated in response to congressional findings of widespread abuses in the industry and demands for reform. After a lengthy investigation, a subcommittee of the House Government Operations Committee concluded that "faulty and fradulent real estate appraisals are a serious national problem that have caused taxpayers, lenders, and insurers billions of dollars."

The committee issued a report calling for qualification and certification requirements for appraisers, testing and review of their work and a disciplinary process.

Only two states—Nebraska and Oregon—license appraisers. A few other states require that appraisers have real estate sales licenses. In other states anyone can be an appraiser. Reports are that legislation is expected to be introduced in Congress in 1987 empowering federal regulatory agencies to establish uniform requirements and to discipline appraisers guilty of abuse. Brokers in the nation who engage in making appraisals for a fee should look ahead toward certification and, eventually, licensing requirements.

DEVELOPMENT OF MARKETING SESSIONS BY PROFESSIONALS

As the real estate business becomes more sophisticated and real estate investors and other buyers become less bound by geographic restraints, a new form of real estate marketing has emerged and is being practiced.

This technique is being used more and more, primarily by the REALTORS® Land Institute and the Commercial-Investment Division of the REALTORS® Marketing Institute as a means of providing more widespread exposure to members' listings.

Marketing sessions are essentially meetings of brokers and their associates in which the members "pitch" their listings to each other in the expectation that one or more of them will have a buyer for the property. Such sessions are held on the national (mostly in conjunction with the NAR national conventions), regional and state or local levels.

The practice of holding marketing sessions has become an excellent method of encouraging cooperation among practitioners throughout the nation. It is not uncommon for a billion dollars' worth of properties to be exposed to the marketers with the result that many millions of dollars in sales are transacted. This has the potential of becoming a much more popular selling technique, as more and more professionals become aware of its possibilities.

NEW DEVELOPMENTS IN FINDER'S FEE EXCEPTIONS

In 1986 the Supreme Court of Hawaii, in a case entitled, *Property House, Inc.* v. *Kelley,* chose not to recognize a "middleman" or "finder" exception to the real estate broker's fiduciary duty to inform both the buyer and the seller of real property that the broker is acting as the agent of each party. Further the court found that by (1) entering into a listing agreement with the sellers and (2) soliciting purchasers, Property House, Inc. (PHI), had acted as a real estate broker, even though PHI was not involved in the actual negotiations between the parties.

In this case, PHI, a licensed real estate broker, entered into an agreement with Kelley to sell two hotels. Thereafter, without the knowledge or the written consent of Kelley, PHI entered into a separate and secret agreement with a prospective purchaser to act as his agent with respect to the purchase of the two hotels. After the buyer submitted an offer that met Kelley's terms but was nevertheless rejected, PHI brought an action against Kelley to collect a brokerage commission.

PHI sought to collect its commission by establishing that it was acting merely as a finder or middleman because it had not been involved in the actual negotiations between the seller and the prospective purchaser. PHI had to rely on this theory *because it had acted as an undisclosed dual agent,* which deprived it of a right to compensation from the seller under the listing agreement.

Hawaiian real estate law allows finder's fees to be paid to "one whose employment is limited to bringing parties together so that they may negotiate their own contract. The law also states that "the middleman, unlike a broker, is in no fiduciary relationship to his principal nor under any obligation not to receive compensation from the opposite party to a transaction" but does owe a fiduciary loyalty to the party that engaged him or her to sell the real estate, namely the listing agent. As PHI had not lived up to that fiduciary relationship, the court ruled it was not entitled to either a commission or a finder's fee.

TREND TOWARD LICENSING RECIPROCITY AMONG STATES

Many states offer the opportunity for licensed agents in other states to obtain licenses in their states if a reciprocity agreement exists. Such reciprocity is generally based on the fulfillment of each state's licensing requirements to insure protection of the citizens in their state from unscrupulous practitioners.

There are many examples of reciprocity agreements among licensing departments of the various states. An inquiry to one's own state's real estate commission is necessary to find out to which states one can apply for a reciprocal license. As more and more states raise their licensing standards to match those of the more advanced states, the practice of reciprocity should become more prevalent. Perhaps someday a real estate licensee in one state may be eligible for licenses to practice in all 50 states.

SUMMARY

It is evident from the information in this chapter that there are new laws, rules and regulations promulgated each year that affect the real estate brokerage business.

As time goes on, one probably will witness other and tighter controls placed on the actions of real estate practitioners. The authors view such heavy emphasis on controls over the business with mixed emotions. It is often exasperating to find that we continually must take time out from our busy schedules to study the new regulations as they are churned out by our various state legislatures.

However, the establishment of so many onerous laws does make the public more aware of the need for professional help in solving real estate problems. Many of the laws make it almost impossible for the layperson who sells only one or two properties in a lifetime to keep up with the restraints placed on the acquisition and disposition of real property. Hence, the need for the professional real estate broker and sales associate to keep educated and abreast of all the legal developments concerning their livelihood.

As John Cotton, a former president of the NAR, often said, "Young man, don't knock the problems involved in buying and selling real estate. If it weren't for those problems the public wouldn't need you!"

DISCUSSION QUESTION

Obtain from your local board of REALTORS® or state association a list of legislation affecting real estate brokerage that recently has been passed by your state legislature. Discuss in class why it may have been necessary to adopt such laws.

Policy Manual
for John Cyr, Inc., REALTORS®

This manual is designed to contain definitions and explanations of the policies and procedures to be followed by all employees and independent contractors engaged by the firm in the conduct of its business. Note that salaried employees can be required to adhere to a firm's policies and procedures but independent contractors can only be encouraged to do so.

It is also intended as a repository for useful and helpful information, which may be utilized in solving the problems that arise from time to time in the handling of real estate transactions.

This policy manual is prepared for a loose-leaf binder so it may be revised, amended, and improved to keep pace with change. It remains the property of the company and is on loan to each new person who becomes affiliated with us. Anyone leaving the company shall be required to return it.

CONTENTS

A Message from the President
A Word About John Cyr, Inc., REALTORS®
Guidelines for Policies and Procedures
Common Real Estate Law Violations

A MESSAGE FROM THE PRESIDENT OF
JOHN CYR, INC., REALTORS®

Welcome to John Cyr REALTORS®

We are a vigorous, aggressive, expanding organization, one of the largest of our kind in San Joaquin County. We are dedicated to continued growth through satisfactory service.

Our reputation has been accepted, and a respect for fair dealings has been established for John Cyr REALTORS®. This is the greatest asset you will have going for you as we work together. We trust that you too will honor that reputation and guard the respect we engender, so that we both may thrive as a result of it.

The people you will be working with are the finest colleagues you can find anywhere. Each one started in real estate exactly as you are starting. Each one has faced and solved some of the very problems you will be facing. Their experience can be invaluable to you. Please listen and learn from them, since we know they will be more than willing to help you. If you sincerely apply yourself to your new tasks, we know you will be a success! Many others before you have done it!

John E. Cyr

A WORD ABOUT JOHN CYR, INC., REALTORS®

John Cyr REALTORS® is a California corporation governed by the laws of this state. We are members of the National Association of REALTORS®, the California Association of REALTORS®, the Stockton Board of REALTORS® and its affiliated multiple-listing service. In addition, we are members of the REALTORS® National Marketing Institute and the REALTORS® Land Institute, which are affiliates of NAR.

We are governed by the Code of Ethics (and the Golden Rule embodied therein) of the National Association of REALTORS®.

John E. Cyr is president of the corporation and its chief executive officer. He holds the following professional designations: Graduate, REALTORS® Institute (GRI); Certified Residential Specialist (CRS); and Accredited Land Consultant (ALC) of the NAR.

Joan Cyr, his wife, is secretary-treasurer of the corporation and handles the payment of commissions and bills. She is a major stockholder of the company.

Phyllis Bertrand is office manager and escrow officer, and she handles all details of processing listings and sales, from inception to close of escrow. She is also secretary and assistant to the president.

GUIDELINES FOR POLICIES AND PROCEDURES

All members of the sales department can contribute in important ways to the success of the firm as a whole. For the smooth running of company operations, you are encouraged to:

1. Attend a sales meeting each Monday morning at 8:30, unless otherwise excused. Salespeople working Saturday and Sunday will be encouraged to take at least one full day off per week for relaxation, and at least one Sunday off per month.

2. Attend the multiple tour each Wednesday morning. (Residential Associates only)

3. Keep your appointed floor day. Once a week, each salesperson will be asked to stay in the office and to take and handle all real estate calls for that day. The office hours are from 8:30 A.M. to 5:00 P.M. Monday through Friday. (See Item 37, Telephone Procedure.)

4. Maintain at least 5 but preferably 10 current exclusive salable listings at all times. (See Item 10, Farming.)

5. Service these listings by writing ads for the paper, posting signs (both for sale and sold signs), getting *all* of the information required, holding the house open for inspection Saturdays, Sundays, and evenings whenever possible, and keeping the owners constantly informed as to your efforts.

6. Help your fellow salespeople whenever possible. Over the years we have found that salespeople can make more money for themselves and for each other by maintaining a cooperative attitude.

7. Keep advertising expense within reason. All advertising will be placed by the sales manager. All personal advertising must be approved by the sales manager. Each salesperson's monthly expense should not exceed $100.

8. Be loyal to your firm and fellow workers. If you don't feel everything is just as it should be, tell the sales manager—not the other salespeople or the public!

9. Maintain a neat personal appearance, and keep your car and your desk as neat as possible. Remember that you are judged by the public. A dirty car or messy desk does not reflect proper working habits. Help keep the office looking professional.

10. *Farming.* A territory of approximately 500 homes will be available for each salesperson to work and develop. It is a good practice to visit each house once every three months. By following these procedures, you should be able to maintain the required number of listings and minimum income.

11. Strive for an income of at least $2000 per month. It costs the company approximately $500 per month for each desk supplied. An apprentice salesperson is expected to be earning $2000 after six months' work. Earning less than that shows a definite lack of those qualities needed to be successful as a real estate salesperson.

12. Maintain as much contact with the public as possible by joining civic and fraternal organizations and keeping in touch with previously satisfied customers and prospects.

13. *Drinking.* Stay away from the office and customers when you have been drinking. You may never know how you might offend with liquor on your breath. If you must drink during working hours, do not represent the company in any way. Continued overindulgence will not be tolerated.

14. Follow up with a phone call or letter whenever you contact people in other cities.

15. Submit all letters to your sales manager for approval before mailing.

16. Make all your appointments so they will not interfere with floor duty or office meetings. If is extremely important to keep all appointments on time. It is rude and disrespectful to be late. If you find that you will be late, call and inform the client what time you will arrive.

17. Make it a practice to phone and verify all appointments in the morning for the rest of the day. It is much better to have time to plan if a client cannot make the appointment than to wait until the last minute to find out.

18. *Always check in and out.* We cannot serve our salespeople adequately unless they keep the office informed of their whereabouts. It is the duty of all salespeople to keep in close contact with the office and they should not be out of contact for periods longer than two hours. Remember to notify the office where you may be reached and when you will return.

19. *Keys.* There is a key board provided in the office on which keys are kept for properties that are listed with the office for sale or rent. When you remove a key, immediately put your business card on the empty hook. Return all keys immediately after the showing and remove the business card at the same time.

Any salesperson or broker from any other office who is given a key shall have his or her business card placed on the hook from which the keys was removed and must return the key promptly after the showing.

After using the keys, leave your business card in a conspicuous spot in the home being shown so the owner or tenant will know who has been in the house. Further, check all doors and windows to determine that they are securely fastened or locked, since our office's possession of these keys represents a major responsibility that we have assumed.

Repeated carelessness in leaving the doors to a property unlocked will be grounds for cancellation of your contract with us.

20. *Tours.* One morning each week, except Wednesday, Saturdays, and Sundays, we will view the properties listed. On Wednesdays, the person assigned to attend the multiple tour will attend it. He or she will report back at the Thursday meeting on the properties that were viewed. All other salespeople are urged to attend the multiple tours whenever possible.

21. *Desk space.* Each salesperson will have desk facilities available. Please be considerate and use your own desk, not those of your fellow salespeople.

22. *Contributions.* It is our policy to contribute to charitable organizations in the name of the firm. From time to time each associate may be encouraged to make a separate contribution to a special charitable organization.

23. *Ethics.* The matter of proper ethics shall govern all aspects of this firm's operations. The staff shall familiarize themselves with the REALTOR® Code of Ethics.

24. *Stenographers.* So that all salespeople may receive as much secretarial help as necessary, they should not require secretarial help for those things they can do themselves. The policy regarding stenographers will change from time to time, and questions regarding the proper use of the stenographers should be directed to the sales manager.

25. *Closed transaction records.* The firm maintains a filing system for all closed transactions, cross-referenced for ease of use. These files are for reference work only. Under no circumstances should the file be removed from the office, nor should any of the papers in the file ever be removed. Feel free to consult them any time you wish; they are a fine source of listings and prospects.

26. *Automobile insurance.* Each salesperson must furnish an automobile and pay all expenses for it and shall furnish the sales manager with a memorandum showing

name of the company with whom it is insured, the policy date, type of coverage, and limits and liability for personal injury and property damage.

27. *Health insurance.* It is the policy of this firm to make the California-Western States Life Insurance Company, or an equivalent health insurance program, available to all employees and independent contractors.

28. *Withholding taxes and Social Security.* It has been established by contract that all real estate salespeople in this firm are independent contractors. They do, however, work under the supervision of the broker as required by rules and regulations of the State of California.

29. *Expenditure of office funds.* The management shall not be liable to the salespeople for any expenses incurred by them or for any of their acts, nor, except as otherwise stipulated in the policy manual, shall the salesperson be liable to the management for office help or expense.

30. *Who may obligate the broker.* No personnel of this firm may obligate the firm to any expense without the specific approval of the board of directors. Salespeople shall have no authority to bind this firm by a promise or representation, unless specifically authorized in a particular transaction. However, expenses for attorney's fees, revenue stamps, title insurance, reports, and the like must, by reason of some necessity, be paid from the fee. Expenses that are incurred in the collection of or an attempt to collect the fee shall be paid by the parties in the same proportion as that used for division of the fee.

31. *Legal expense.* If you find yourself involved in any transaction that results in a dispute, litigation, or legal expense, you are expected to cooperate fully with the firm. Expenses connected with such a dispute will be shared in the same proportion as fees would normally be shared.

32. *Change of address.* Please notify the office immediately of any change in home address or telephone number.

33. *Settlement of disputes.* Any controversy between a salesperson and another office or with a salesperson of another office must be turned over to the sales manager of that department in this office for arbitration or immediate action.

We all want harmony in the office. It is the policy of this firm that any dispute between salespeople will be settled by an arbitration board. The arbitration board will consist of the board of directors, with the sales manager acting as chair. After both sides of the dispute are heard, there will be a secret written vote and the majority vote will decide the issue. All personnel agree by virtue of their contracts to abide by such decisions. This also applies to any decisions on disputes with other offices that are settled by the Arbitration and Ethics Committee of the local Board of REALTORS®.

34. *Fees.* This firm renders a professional service for which we charge a professional fee set by the company, from time to time as conditions warrant.

Division of fees is completely outlined in the office fee schedule, issued by the sales manager and covered in the contractual agreement with each employee. Salespeople will be paid their share of the fee as it is received. It is the policy of this office to accept no notes in lieu of a fee, except upon the approval of the sales manager.

In cases where two or more salespeople work together in listing or selling a property, their names should go on the listing sheet or deposit receipt together with a notation regarding how the fee will be shared.

Fees received from the sale of an office listing made by an outside broker will be retained in full by the office unless special arrangements have been made between a salesperson and the firm before any work is done towards the sale by the salesperson.

35. *Termination.* Upon termination of a salesperson's association with the office, all equipment, supplies, and reference material belonging to the office must be returned.

Any transaction that the salesperson closes, but upon which fee has not been received, will be his or her transaction, and the fee will be paid in the regular manner even subsequent to the severance date. The same procedure will apply to any transaction that may be closed at any time after the salesperson leaves the firm, provided the salesperson has been instrumental in making the sale. Deferred fees due salespeople will likewise be paid promptly when received. Real estate listings credited to the salespeople during their terms of service become the sole property of the office upon severance. When salespeople leave, their listings will be assigned to another salesperson, who will receive the listing fee in full when the property is sold.

It is necessary under the law for a salesperson to obtain an authorized release and transfer signature from the office before leaving in order to submit it to the State Real Estate Commissioner's office before joining another office.

Any transactions started or revived by other salespeople of the organization with office prospects after a salesperson has left the office are to be considered new transactions and the departing salesperson will have no interest in them.

The association created under the terms of this manual may be terminated by either party hereto, at any time upon written or verbal notice given to the other, but the rights of the parties to any commission that accrued prior to said notice will not be divested by the termination.

The salesperson shall not, after said termination, use to his or her own advantage, or that of any other person or corporation, any information gained for or from the files of this firm.

36. *Buying and selling property for your own account.* The office does not object to salespeople's buying or selling real estate as individuals or as members of a syndicate.

A salesperson who is buying individually must inform the owner of his or her role as a principal. Any salesperson buying or selling for him- or herself will pay to this firm 25 percent of the fee. However, all such transactions must be discussed with the real estate sales manager before the papers are signed to complete the transaction.

In the case of an employee or officer selling real estate for his or her own account, it will be the policy of the firm that the salesperson selling for said employee will receive the usual salesperson selling share of the fee and the firm will receive a flat 25 percent of the fee. The balance of the fee may be retained by the salesperson or officer, including the listing fee.

In the case of a salesperson or officer who buys a property, he or she is entitled to the salesperson's normal fee. The firm will receive 25 percent of the total fee. No credit towards a bonus will be paid to any salesperson—independent contractor or officer—participating in such a sale.

Permission must be obtained from the sales manager for any personnel to charge advertising to the firm on this type of transaction.

Participating in purchase of trust deeds is also welcomed; however, special care must be taken to guard the good name of the firm.

37. *Telephone procedure.* Avoid poor public impressions and many frayed nerves by following these instructions:

A. The receptionist is to answer when the telephone rings. If there is no receptionist, the floor person is to answer. In the event the floor person is busy, another salesperson may answer.

B. When answering the phone, watch the buttons a moment to see which one is flashing, then push that button *before* picking up the receiver.

C. Say "John Cyr Realtors" and give your name when answering a call. If the call is for someone else, say "Just a moment, please" and push the hold button. Then push the com'l button on your phone and dial the desk number of the phone you desire. When that person answers, say "Take line 1 (2 or 3) please," referring to the line on which the call came in.

D. When someone dials your desk, *please* push the com'l button and answer the call. Do not push any button but the com'l when the bell at your desk phone rings. Then push the button corresponding to the number of the line given you on the com'l and answer with a pleasant "Hello" or give your name.

E. When you start to make an outgoing call, please see that the line you choose is not busy or ringing with an incoming call. If a call is coming in and you pick up that line to call out and then, hearing no dial tone, you hang up, you will lose the call. If you should pick up a line and hear no dial tone, please answer the incoming call. Please extend to others the courtesy of making sure a line is open before dialing.

F. All long-distance calls must be approved in advance by the sales manager. When the call is approved, fill out a long-distance phone call form, providing adequate information on the purpose of the call and the transaction to which it applies.

G. Restrict your personal calls to those absolutely necessary and then keep them as short as possible. This rule applies to both incoming and outgoing calls. Lines *must* be kept open for business calls.

H. It is important *not* to inform the caller if the salesperson is at home. We are a professional sales organization and spend our days working.

I. It is important to take the caller's name and number correctly. Repeat to the caller both name and number.

38. *Credit reports.* Credit reports will be ordered only by the sales manager. Salespeople will direct all requests for these only through the sales manager.

39. *Signing documents.* No personnel of this firm will sign a statement, document, or paper of any kind for any person other than themselves. The only exception to this rule will be in case of a written statement on file with the corporation and signed by the client in which specific functions are outlined. Any violation will result in dismissal and recommendation to the Real Estate Commissioner for the removal of the guilty party's license.

40. *Licensed salespeople* and *department managers* other than officers of the company will work under real estate salesperson licenses. Anyone wishing to obtain a broker's license may do so at his or her own expense; however, said broker shall sign an associate broker contract with the company. All license fees shall be paid by the individual, except in the case of officers.

41. *Membership in local Board of REALTORS®.* All brokers and salespeople of this company must hold paid-up memberships at all times in the local, state, and national boards, and must adhere to the regulations of the multiple-listing service.

The yearly dues for a broker, REALTOR®-salesperson member in the board will vary. All salespeople affiliated with the company shall pay their own dues.

The fee for processing a listing in the multiple-listing service is $15. All listings of residential property, which is defined as up to four rental units on up to five acres, must be listed in the MLS unless the owner refuses and then signs the necessary withhold slip.

42. *Grooming and dress.* It is not our policy to regiment personnel in their own grooming habits, but it is urged that all personnel be well-groomed and dress in a neat and professional manner. Men should wear suits and ties or sportswear. Women should wear tailored suits, sport outfits, or other professional attire.

43. *Policy on smoking.* This firm has absolutely no objection to your smoking in the office and on the job. However, smokers are prone to forget that the habit is some-

times objectionable to nonsmokers. Therefore, we wish to caution smokers to be considerate to their customers and their fellow workers.

When working with nonsmokers in a small room like a conference room, private office, or sales meeting, a smoker should be able to refrain from indulging until the meeting is over. It can't be more than an hour of sacrifice and would certainly eliminate a serious source of annoyance for perhaps five or six other persons.

Also, we consider it rude for an agent, when showing property, to smoke in a car with prospects who are nonsmokers, or to carry a lighted cigarette, pipe, or cigar into another person's house. Many people object to the smell of tobacco in their own home even if they aren't at home at the time the smoking occurs. So enjoy smoking, but please do not smoke if it makes other people uncomfortable!

44. *Procedure on joint sale with another REALTOR®.*

A. If we are the listing brokers in the sale, we expect to do the following:

1. Present all offers to the seller, but the selling salesperson or broker may accompany us if he or she wishes.

2. Notify MLS of the hold.

3. Select the title company in which the order is to be placed.

4. Order the termite inspection from a company of the owner's choice.

5. Reserve the right to approve the lending institution's charge for any loan fees to be paid by the sellers.

6. Draw the seller's escrow instructions.

B. If we are the selling brokers, we expect to do the following:

1. Accompany the listing salesperson or broker when presenting our offers.

2. Choose the lending institution for the buyer's loan—subject to the approval of the loan fees by the seller.

3. Draw the buyer's escrow instructions.

45. *Fee controversy.* It is the policy of this company that no employee shall discuss a fee-split controversy with any of the principals in a real estate transaction.

If there are any differences of opinion on how any fee is to be divided, discussion of that difference shall be confined to the parties involved and the officers of the corporation. The most important part of our work is to see that any sale is developed and followed to its final and satisfactory conclusion. Muddying the waters of the closing by arguing over the fee only serves to create additional problems and may cause loss of the sale. *ANY DEVIATIONS FROM THIS POLICY SHALL BE CONSIDERED GROUNDS FOR IMMEDIATE CANCELLATION OF CONTRACT.*

Any calls from ads or signs shall be referred to a member of the department advertising the property. For instance, a call on a residential listing shall be referred to a residential salesperson and a call on a farm listing shall be referred to a farm salesperson.

For the purpose of this section, types of transactions are defined as follows:

Commercial property: any property that is zoned CR, C1, C2, C3, or CM.

Industrial property: any property zoned M1 or M2.

Rental-income property: apartment houses or rental-income property with more than four units.

Farm or ranch property: raw land not zoned specifically for industry.

Residential-income property: duplexes, triplexes, or four-unit buildings. Any R3-zoned property will be assigned at the discretion of the sales manager.

Residential property: single-family dwelling.

Mobile home: set up in park.

Rural residence: rural home on less than five acres.

If a salesperson of one of the departments obtains a prospect for a different type of property than his or her department handles, that salesperson may sell in the other department; however, if help is requested from a member of that other department, the two should arrive at a clear understanding of how any fee is to be divided *before* any work is done or help is given. The sales managers of the departments involved should then be notified immediately of the arrangement.

In the event of a controversy over a fee split between the salespeople the problem shall be turned over to three officers of the corporation, who, after hearing all sides to the controversy, shall decide on how the fee is to be divided and *that decision shall be final.* (See Items 33 and 34.)

46. *Procedure for submitting offers.*

A. *When it is your own listing.* Have a third party call the owners and make an appointment to see both of them together. If after you have made the initial presentation you have not been able to get anywhere with them and you feel you need some help, then call the sales manager and set up another appointment for them to meet you and the clients for further discussion.

B. *When it is a John Cyr salesperson's listing.* Call the listing salesperson and say you have an offer on the listing and state the terms. Ask if they want you to present it, or to go along and help present it. If you wish to go along, you have every right to and can insist upon it. However, many times the *listing salesperson* is in a better position to talk to the people, having already gained their confidence and knowing what has previously transpired in the way of offers and price discussion. It is only common courtesy to notify the listing salesperson of your offer as soon as you get it; however, if it appears expedient to present that offer yourself without the listing salesperson because you cannot locate him or her right away, then go ahead and contact the owners.

C. *When it is another office's multiple listing.* Notify the sales manager that you have an offer on ABC Realty listing. He or she will either ask to present it to the other office or tell you to go ahead and submit it to the other broker or salesperson for presentation.

47. *Fees shared between departments.* The firm encourages salespeople to specialize in one department. This practice is based on the proven success of such specialization and the better service to our clients made possible by it.

Nevertheless, we have not tried to rule out activity in other departments entirely. Salespeople who list property in a department or branch office area other than their own should share the listing with someone in that department or office who will be responsible for servicing the listing. In the absence of any agreement *in advance,* the firm will assume a 50/50 split between the person who got the listing and the one who serviced it. We shall also assume that in order to qualify as the procuring cause of the listing, a salesperson must physically bring together the seller and the servicing salesperson. This means that if you intend to split a listing fee based only on a name referral or a phone referral, you should state so and agree immediately and inform the sales manager of your department and/or office. The same prior agreement should be reached when working with someone else on the sale of any property. Any agreement with which the salespeople involved are satisfied will be fine with us.

48. *Referral system.* We are members of Nationwide Referral System. Membership allows us to refer our clients to other offices throughout the United States and collect a referral fee. Incoming referrals will be assigned on a rotating basis.

49. *Education.* We encourage salespeople to attend classes and seminars.

50. *Procedures when obtaining listing or transaction numbers from branch office.*

The original listing or original deposit receipt must be delivered to the branch office the same day it is obtained from the client and the listing number or transaction number is assigned. In the case of an evening transaction, the listing is due the following day.

All listings must be checked and approved by the sales manager before delivery to the branch office. An additional $15 listing fee is required by the board if a listing is returned for insufficient information.

All deposit checks or cash must be delivered to the branch office on the same day they are received from the prospective buyer; if it is an evening transaction, it is due the following day. *No deposits* are to be retained by the salesperson. This practice protects the salesperson, the client, and the company; it is in accordance with the law.

COMMON REAL ESTATE LAW VIOLATIONS

Section 10176 is concerned with actions of a real estate licensee *while engaged in the practice and performance of any acts within the scope of the California Real Estate Law.* Section 10177 applies to situations in which the person involved was not necessarily acting as an agent or as a licensee.

Section 10176 (a) *MISREPRESENTATION.* The licensee must disclose to his principal material facts that his principal should know. Failure to do this is cause for disciplinary action. A large percentage of the complaints the commissioner receives allege positive or negative misrepresentation by the salesperson or broker.

Section 10176 (b) *FALSE PROMISE.* Although it may seem a false promise and a misrepresentation are the same, they are not. A misrepresentation is a false statement of fact. A false promise is a false statement about what the promisor is going to do in the future. A false promise is usually proved by showing the promise was impossible of performance and the person making the promise knew it was impossible.

Section 10176 (c) *MISREPRESENTATION THROUGH AGENTS.* This section gives the commissioner the right to discipline a licensee who misrepresents or makes false promises through other real estate agents, and also for a continued and flagrant course of misrepresentation.

ETHICS AND PROFESSIONAL CONDUCT, REAL ESTATE REGULATIONS (CALIFORNIA STATE STATUTE Article 2785)

CODE OF ETHICS AND PROFESSIONAL CONDUCT. In order to enhance the professionalism of the California real estate industry, and maximize protection for members of the public dealing with real estate licensees, the following standards of professional conduct and business practices are adopted.

(a) *UNLAWFUL CONDUCT.* Licensees shall not engage in "fraud" or "dishonest dealing" or "conduct which would have warranted the denial of an application for a real estate license" within the meaning of Business and Professions Code sections 10176 and 10177 including, but not limited to, the following acts and omissions:*

---

*The remainder of the policy manual should be specific to your state, incorporating the license law and rules and regulations.

Glossary

Abstract of title A documented search of public records for all items pertaining to subject property to date. (*See also* Chain of title; Title company.)

Acceleration clause A clause in the note or deed of trust causing the entire balance to become due and payable should a default in one of the provisions therein be triggered.

Accrual method An accounting system that records income when earned and expenses as incurred.

Ad valorem tax Tax "according to the market value" of subject property.

Affirmative Marketing Agreement (AMA) An agreement designed by the Department of Housing and Urban Development and NAR, whereby REALTORS® agree to provide equal service and housing opportunities to the public.

Alienation clause A specific clause in the note and/or deed of trust that states that should the property be sold or transferred in any manner, the entire balance of the note shall be immediately due and payable. (To alienate is to transfer.) A form of acceleration clause. (*See also* Due-on-sale clause.)

All-inclusive deed of trust A deed of trust that includes one or more deeds of trust that have priority over the all-inclusive deed of trust.

American Institute of Real Estate Appraisers (AIREA) The institute of NAR solely devoted to the advancement and education of real estate appraisers.

American Society of Real Estate Counselors (ASREC) One of the nine institutes, societies and councils of NAR dedicated to the advancement and education of the counseling specialty of real estate brokerage.

Amortization tables Tables that show what rate of payment is needed to retire a principal balance of a note at a stipulated rate of interest and over a certain period of time.

Amortized note A note payable in full over a specified time period and at a specified rate of interest.

Appraisal The valuation of property, using three basic approaches: market data, income, and replacement.

Appreciation in value The increase in value a property may sustain over a given period.

ARMS Adjustable rate mortgages. Mortgages (or deeds of trust) with a floating interest rate tied to some specified economic indicator, such as the Federal Home Loan Bank cost of funds.

Basis An accounting term referring to the adjusted book value of a property.

Beneficiary under deed of trust The party to whom the principal amount of the loan is owed.

BFOQ Bona fide occupational qualification.

Board of REALTORS® A local jurisdiction governing the activities of member REALTORS® in a given geographic area; concomitantly a division of a state Association of REALTORS® as well as the National Association of REALTORS®.

Brainstorming A method of group discussion in which participants are encouraged to suggest any and all solutions to the problem being considered, regardless of how incongruous it may seem, and criticism is discouraged.

Broker One who buys and sells for another or arranges contracts of various types for a commission.

Broker's inspection Personal inspection by the broker listing the property for sale to duly note any and all defects inherent therein.

Building codes A licensed real estate practitioner is generally required to know the basic requisites of his or her local building code and be able to spot any infraction thereof. All incorporated cities and most counties in the nation are required to have a set of building codes that must be adhered to by anyone constructing any kind of dwelling or other type of improvement on a property.

Bundle of rights An ownership concept covering all the rights to owning real property.

Buyer presettlement (preclosing) inspection Inspection by the buyer when the transaction is about to be culminated and title to be passed, so that the buyer may be satisfied that all conditions of the purchase have been met.

Buyer's agent Usually the practitioner who is working primarily on behalf of the buyer's interests (as opposed to the seller's agent or a dual agent).

Callback reports   The reports a sales associate is required to make (in some offices) describing the results of a meeting with a prospective seller or buyer.

Carryback loans   A loan the seller is carrying for the buyer secured by a mortgage or deed of trust on the property he or she is selling.

Cash flow   The return from an investment's income after all expenses and loan payments have been deducted.

Cash method   An accounting system that records income as received and disbursements as made.

CCIM   Certified Commercial Investment Member (of the REALTOR® National Marketing Institute). The designation awarded to members who have completed a prescribed course of study and completed other requirements.

Chain of title   A document that contains all recorded instruments affecting a particular property dating back to the beginning of record-keeping for that jurisdiction. (*See also* Abstract of title; Title company.)

Closing costs   All costs involved in a transaction that must be paid either by the buyers or by the sellers, depending on the custom in the area.

Closings   Any one of three different times occurring during a real estate transaction: (1) When the buyer and seller reach a meeting of the minds over the terms of a transaction and sign preliminary documents attesting to that fact. (2) When the buyer and seller, as well as any other entities involved, such as attorneys, brokers and escrow officers meet and sign documents allowing title to be transferred to the new owners and the consideration for purchase to change hands. (3) The actual recording of the deed and transfer of title and funds. (*See also* Settlement of transaction.)

Closing techniques   Various methods that can be used to convince the buyer and/or seller they are doing the right thing by agreeing to the terms of the transaction placed before them.

CMA   Comparative (competitive) market analysis. A form used by real estate practitioners to help show the sellers of a property how their property compares in price, terms and condition to similar properties that have either sold or are up for sale in the general area.

Code of Ethics   The code to which all REALTORS® (members of a local board of REALTORS®, state association of REALTORS® and the National Association of REALTORS®) must subscribe and swear to follow to retain membership.

Commission   Generally figured as a percentage of the sales price paid to the broker or brokers who effect the sale of a property. There is no "legal" rate of commission and such fees are arrived at through negotiations between seller and agent.

Company dollar   The amount a broker realizes in income after all commissions have been deducted from the gross amounts received.

Conditional binder   A sales agreement that contains certain conditions that must be met before it becomes unconditionally binding on all parties.

Contingency clause   The clause in an agreement that makes the entire agreement conditional on the happening of a certain event.

Contract of sale   Contract for the sale of real property that spells out the terms of said sale and suffices for the time being to be the only documentation of the sale. It is generally used when a buyer is offering a small down payment and the seller does not plan to relinquish title to the property until the buyer has more equity in it. It is usually supplanted with a deed and note secured by a mortgage or deed of trust after the purchaser has amassed sufficient equity in the property. (*See also* Installment sale.)

Conventional financing   The usual type of financing employed in purchasing a property as opposed to government-aided financing, such as FHA- or VA-insured loans.

Cooperating broker   A broker who is working in conjunction with the listing or selling broker to effect the sale of a property.

Corporation   An entity of joint ownership in which all parties have a share (equal and unequal) but which acts in the same capacity as an individual owner. Usually governed by a board of directors elected by the shareholders.

Counteroffer   A new offer made as a reply to a given offer.

Creative financing   The use of various tools of financing to effect a desired result not accomplishable through the usual channels of financing, i.e., use of an unsecured promissory note or a second or even third deed of trust as part of the purchase price.

Credit check   The results obtained by requesting a credit report on a prospective purchaser.

CRS   Certified Residential Specialist. A designation awarded by the REALTORS® National Marketing Institute for members of NAR who have demonstrated above-average qualifications in the brokerage of residential properties.

Demographics   The study of population trends and/or buying habits of the public in a certain geographic area.

Depreciation   Loss in value from any cause. Losses in value a property may sustain through such actions as normal wear and tear, deferred maintenance and economic conditions changes in the area.

Desk cost   The cost figured by the broker for each associate's share of the overhead—usually computed by dividing the total operating expenses of the company by the number of salespeople associated with it.

Dual agency (agents)   When a real estate broker purports to represent both the buyer and seller in a transaction he or she has created a dual agency situation, which is illegal and unethical in many states.

Due-on-sale clause   The clause in the loan papers that gives the lender the right to call the loan due and payable upon the happening of a certain occurrence, such as sale of the property. (*See also* alienation clause.)

Environmental impact report   Report required in some states that shows the effects a proposed development will have on the environment of the area. Such reports study the effects on the wildlife, traffic, schools, terrain, and so forth.

Equity   The monetary share of an investment that may be considered as the owner's clear share, i.e., the difference between any indebtedness and the actual market value of the property.

Escape clause   A clause in an agreement such as a deposit receipt or agreement of sale that can release either party from the agreement if a certain happening does or does not occur.

Escrow   The procedure of placing all papers and money concerning a transaction in the hands of a disinterested third party with instructions on how such items are to be treated in the event all conditions are or are not met.

Exchange agreements   Agreements delineating the method of exchange of properties between two or more parties.

Exclusionary zoning   Zoning sometimes used to exclude multiple-family dwellings from predominantly single-family neighborhoods.

Exclusive agency listing   A listing that contains a termination date in which the owner and the broker enter into a written contract for the broker to sell the property. The broker, as agent for the seller, will receive a commission if the property is sold during the term of the listing by that broker or by any other but not if the owner sells the property independent of the broker's efforts.

Exclusive-right-to-sell listing   A listing with a termination date in which the principal (owner of the property) authorizes the agent in writing to represent him or her and agrees to pay a commission if the property is sold during the term of the listing, regardless of who makes the sale.

Executed agreement   An agreement that has been signed by all parties to it.

Existing loan   The loan already in place on the property.

Factor times gross income   An investment analysis formula for judging the worth of a piece of income property by multiplying the annual gross income by a factor derived from the ratio of gross income to the selling price of similar properties.

Farm Home Administration Loans (FMHA)   A branch of the U.S. Department of Agriculture concerned with making home loans in rural areas that lack the usual financing sources.

Farming   A system in which a sales associate is assigned a certain area or target market to consider as his or her special district in which to cultivate all of the owners there for their real estate business (also sometimes referred to as zone marketing).

FHA loans   Loans made by conventional lenders but with a portion insured by the Federal Housing Administration.

FIABCI/USA   The American Chapter of the International Real Estate Federation. (The initials are derived from the original French name.)

Fiduciary   The person named in a trust or agency agreement to act for another on his or her behalf and in the same manner as if acting for himself or herself.

First deed of trust   A mortgage security instrument that has first priority over any other voluntary financial liens on a property.

Foreclosure   The process in which property used as security for a mortgage is sold to satisfy the debt when a borrower defaults in payment of the mortgage note or on other terms in the mortgage document.

Foreclosure under court action   Foreclosure procedure that is handled in a court of law and allows the lender to obtain a deficiency judgment against the borrower. It also allows the borrower a year's right to redeem the property by paying all back monies and costs incurred to and from the date of foreclosure.

Foreclosure under right of sale (deed of trust)   An automatic procedure that allows the lender to foreclose on the property through the power of sale provision in the contract. It usually takes about four months to process and allows neither a deficiency judgment against nor a right of redemption to the foreclosed-on borrower.

Franchise   Right to operate a business under the name and operating procedures of a large, often nationwide parent company. Century 21 and ERA are examples of franchise operations.

FSBO   (For sale by owners)—A term used in the trade that refers to owners who are attempting to sell their own property without benefit of an agent.

General agent   One who performs continuing services for the principal.

General partnership   An entity of ownership in which all partners in it hold voting rights as to decisions being made and in which all partners share in the profits and liabilities as their interests appear.

GI loans   Loans available to veterans of the nation's wars that are made by conventional lenders but guaranteed by the federal government.

GRI   Graduate REALTOR® Institute. A professional designation earned by those who have successfully completed a prescribed course of study.

Health code compliance   Property that meets all standards of a local health jurisdiction.

Home inspection   Inspection of a property that is sold or for sale by an accredited building inspector to ascertain if there are any inherent defects or violations of local building codes.

Inclusionary zoning   Zoning awarded to a developer of real estate who agrees to include a certain percentage of lower to moderately priced dwellings in the development.

Independent contract　Agreement under which a real estate agent or sales associate may be working in conjunction with a licensed broker (as opposed to an employee-employer relationship).

Independent contractor　Real estate sales associate acting under contract to the broker and under self-direction, for whose income tax withholding, Social Security or unemployment insurance payments the broker is not responsible.

Inflation　Abnormal increase in the volume of money and credit that results in a substantial, continuing rise in the general price level.

Installment sale　(1) A sale that is arranged so that the buyer pays the seller a stipulated series of payments for the property. (2) An IRS term indicating that the sale may receive preferential tax treatment because the seller did not receive the total purchase price at the time of the sale. (*See also* Contract of sale.)

Institute of Real Estate Management (IREM)　That institute of NAR primarily concerned with the education and development of the management part of the real estate business.

Insured loans　Loans that insure the lender against loss, such as FHA and VA loans.

Internal rate of return　The true rate of return from an investment when expressed as a percentage and after all factors concerning that return, such as future value of present cash flow, have been taken into account. (Sometimes defined as the rate of discount at which present value of cash flow equals the initial cash investment [down payment].)

Investment market analysis　A method for determining the market for a given kind of real estate investment, such as determining the vacancy experience for office space, apartments or industrial warehouses.

Investment property analysis　A form for analyzing a real estate investment that shows the rate of return a purchaser might expect from a given investment if purchased at a given figure and with a specified cash down payment.

Junior deed of trust　Deed of trust that has a lesser claim to payment than some previous lien, such as a first deed of trust.

Law of agency　The section of statutes pertaining to the relationship that is created when one entity is authorized to act on legal matters for the benefit of another.

Legal description　A description of real estate that is unique to that property and is detailed enough for an independent surveyor to locate and identify it.

Leverage　The process whereby an investment can be burdened with a loan or loans and still provide a higher yield than if an investor had paid all cash for it.

Like-kind properties　An IRS term used in describing the limits to effecting a Section 1031 Tax Deferred Exchange. (All property in the exchange must be "like-kind property," e.g., income-producing real estate exchanged for income-producing real estate.)

Limited partnership   Syndication in which many parties can participate, except that the limited partners have no say in the operation of the venture nor do they suffer any recourse from potential liabilities beyond their initial investment.

Line of credit   A prearranged commitment from a lending institution to advance up to a specific amount of money to a customer of that bank.

Liquidity   The facility with which an asset can be converted to cash.

Listing agreement   An agreement between an owner and a broker in which the owner gives the broker the right to sell his or her property at a given price. (There are a number of different types of listings, e.g., limited, open, exclusive agency, oral and exclusive right to sell.)

Loan commitments   A commitment by a lender to loan a specific amount of money at a specified rate of interest over a certain period of time; subject to other conditions.

Lock boxes   A small, secure box affixed to a property that contains a key to that property and that only members of the MLS that issues such boxes are privy to opening, either by a key or combination lock.

Locked-in loan clause   Clause in a loan that does not allow such things as paying it off ahead of time or allowing another party to assume.

MAI   Member American Institute of Real Estate Appraisers. A professional designation. One of the nine institutes and councils of the NAR.

Metes and bounds description   Description of a parcel of real estate that depends on the description of physical characteristics. For example, "Starting at the intersection of Jack Tone Road and proceeding in an Easterly direction for approximately 1206 feet along the South Line of said road to the west bank of Bear Creek," and so on.

Money supply   A figure issued weekly by the Federal Reserve Bank indicating the amount of money in circulation in the United States during the past week. It can be expressed as M1 or M2, with different connotations for each.

Monolithic office   A single office in which all services of that company are concentrated (as opposed to a multiple or branch office concept).

Mortgage   Security device that guarantees repayment of a note by pledging the property as security. There are two parties to a mortgage: the mortgagor and the mortgagee.

Multiparty exchange   An exchange of real property where more than two properties or two parties are involved.

Multiple listing service (system)   A means by which a participating broker makes a blanket unilateral offer of subagency to the other participants and a facility for orderly correlation and dissemination of property information among members so they may better serve their clients and the public. Commissions derived from a cooperative sale under such a system are then split between cooperating brokers according to a prearranged schedule.

Municipal code compliance (*See* Building codes.)

NARELLO National Association of Real Estate License Law Officials.

NAR National Association of REALTORS®.

Net listing A listing in which the owner agrees to accept a net figure from the sale of his or her property and the broker receives as commission any monies above that amount. (Net listings are illegal in many jurisdictions.)

NOI Net operating income. A figure arrived at in completing an investment analysis form that indicates the amount of income to be derived from the property after the vacancy factor and all other operating expenses have been deducted from the gross income but before any loan payments are applied.

Notice of default A notice recorded by the trustee under a deed of trust that indicates that the trustor (borrower) is in default on the note and is in danger of foreclosure.

Office brochure A flyer devised and produced by a company that describes the services offered by that company.

100% office Office arrangement whereby the licensee rents those facilities and keeps 100 percent of the commission.

One-time capital gain credit A provision in the Internal Revenue Code that allows a taxpayer who is over 55 years of age to sell his or her home once without having to pay income tax on up to $125,000 of the profits.

Open listing A listing in which the seller gives the right to sell to any number of brokers who can work simultaneously in trying to effect a sale. Commission is contingent on the broker's producing a ready, willing and able buyer before the seller or another broker sells the property.

PACS Political action committees. Committees allowed by the federal government to collect contributions that then are used for the political advancement of candidates or causes favorable to the aims of the organization forming the committee.

Passing of title Recording a deed in the name of the new owner.

Points Fee for processing a loan—one point equals one percent of the loan amount. For example, if a loan is for $50,000 and the loan fee is two points, then the amount charged is $1,000 (2% × $50,000).

Policy and procedures manual A manual developed by a real estate broker to help guide associates in their conduct while in the broker's office. It should contain the code of conduct expected by the broker from his or her associates as well as suggested rules of procedure in conducting the business of the company.

Preliminary title report   A first report provided by most title companies that lists all pertinent facts affecting a property being considered for sale or purchase.

Prepaid interest   Interest charged by a lender before it is actually due or earned.

Prepayment penalty   A penalty charged to a borrower by a lender for paying off the principal of a loan ahead of time. Sometimes it is charged if the loan is paid off too quickly. The terms of the note and security agreement determine if it can be assessed.

Prepayment privilege   The privilege spelled out in a loan agreement that allows the borrower to pay off a loan ahead of maturity.

Presentation binder   Documents put together to help a sales associate make a presentation to owners for the listing of a property. It contains a description of the company and what it has to offer, comparative market sales, qualifications of the sales associate, and so forth.

Press release   A release to newspapers in an area telling about some event that may be of general interest to the public and that will be of some public relations value to the company issuing the release.

Processing fees   Fees charged by a bank or other lender for processing a loan.

Promissory note   The note evidencing a debt and outlining the terms under which the debt is to be repaid.

Quasi-franchise   An organization to which a company can belong that does not pose the requirements of a regular franchise.

Redlining   The illegal practice of lenders denying or restricting loans for certain neighborhoods.

Release clause   Clause in a deed of trust or mortgage that allows certain properties secured thereunder to be released from the agreement on receipt of a stipulated amount of money paid to the principal of the note.

REIT   Real estate investment trust. A form of ownership of real estate investments that is allowed in groups of, usually, 100 or more investors. This type of investment is rigorously controlled by the Securities and Exchange Commission and special licenses are required for its use.

Rent control   A practice that rigidly controls the amount of rents that a landlord can charge on his or her units.

Reserve for taxes and insurance   An amount usually set aside from the borrower's monthly payments that is used by the lender for the payment of taxes and insurance on the property as they become due. Also called a loan trust fund.

RESSI   Real Estate Securities and Syndication Institute. One of the nine institutes, societies and councils of NAR. RESSI specializes in marketing real estate through syndication methods.

Right of redemption The right to redeem a property foreclosed on through court action, usually because of default on a mortgage but sometimes on a deed of trust.

RLI REALTORS® Land Institute. A NAR institute that specializes in land use brokerage, whether it be farm, ranch or urban land.

RNMI REALTORS® National Marketing Institute. A NAR institute that specializes mostly in residential brokerage.

Role-playing A method of training sales associates in which the parties assume the roles of buyers, sellers and sales associates and learn how to enter into dialogues with each other.

ROTI Return on time invested. A term that describes how the return from time spent on a prospect should be evaluated and carefully considered in proportion to the returns expected.

Rural area That area of real estate outside the urban and suburban confines of a city or town.

S corporation A special kind of corporation allowed by law that provides all of the protective benefits of a regular corporation but also allows income and deductions to pass through to the shareholders, much the same as in a partnership.

Second deed of trust A deed of trust second in priority to the first deed of trust.

Security device A device such as a mortgage or deed of trust that is used to secure real property for the repayment of the terms on a note.

Seller's agent The agent responsible for protecting the interests of the seller—usually the listing broker—as opposed to the buyer's agent or the dual agent, who purports to act for both parties.

Settlement of transaction The time when all monies, deeds, loans and other documents are deposited in escrow and the transaction is ready for closing. (*See also* Closings.)

SIOR Society of Industrial and Office REALTORS®. An NAR institute devoted to the welfare and practices of industrial and office brokers.

Special agency An agency agreement that allows one to act for another in the pursuance of a special act, as opposed to a general agency.

Square footage The area of a given property, whether it be the land plot or the building alone. Land sales are often computed on a price per square foot. Commercial and industrial buildings also are leased by this method.

Statutory letter A means of protecting the broker's commission in cases where the listing was orally given; a notice sent by registered mail or hand-delivered to the owner within a fixed number of days after oral authorization was given.

Steering An illegal practice of channeling prospective homeowners to a certain area or lending institution.

Subagent One who acts as an agent for an agent.

Suburban area An area of land immediately surrounding a city or town and either developed or considered ripe for development.

Subordination clause A clause in a mortgage or deed of trust that permits the priority of the instrument to be made subject to another security device. For example, a land purchaser may give the seller a note and first deed of trust for the balance owing on a purchase with the stipulation that if the purchaser can obtain a construction loan for constructing improvements on the property, the seller/owner will allow the mortgage or deed of trust to become subordinate (second) to the construction loan.

Switch sheets Sheets of alternate listings kept by sales associates. Should a telephone inquirer not be interested in the property on which he or she originally called, the sales associate can then offer other properties as possibilities—hence, "switch" the prospect to something else.

Syndication A joint ownership arrangement of two or more parties to a real estate transaction. It can be two or 100 joint owners under a number of different ownership vehicles.

Tax-deferred exchange An arrangement under Section 1031 of the Internal Revenue Code that allows an owner to accept another property of like kind in exchange for his or her present holding, thereby eliminating payment of tax on the profit from the one he or she is disposing of.

Tax shelter An accounting term describing an investment that throws off tax deductions from interest and depreciation allowances.

Title company A company that specializes in searching the abstract of titles to a property and then insuring that title for a new buyer for a fee. Some title companies in some areas of the country can also handle escrow for real estate transactions.

Title search (*See* Abstract of title; Chain of title; Title company.)

Training manual The manual in a brokerage office that outlines the procedure for training sales associates.

Transfer tax The tax charged by many cities, counties and states for the privilege of transferring title to property.

Trustee under deed of trust The entity under a deed of trust that holds a form of title to the property to insure the repayment of a debt (usually a corporation formed by the lender).

Trust fund (*See* Reserve for taxes and insurance.)

Trustor under deed of trust The entity that holds an equity title to a property under trust to insure the repayment of a debt, usually called the "owner" of the property.

Truth-in-Lending Laws A group of laws enforced by the Federal Trade Commission to ensure that consumers are made fully aware of the cost of credit and are protected against false credit claims in advertising.

Two-party exchange An IRC Section 1031 tax-deferred exchange in which only two parties are involved as distinct from a three-party or multiparty exchange.

VA Veterans Administration.

Vacancy factor A percentage of the gross rent allocated as a reserve for vacancies in the tenancies (also called a vacancy allowance), usually based on previous history of the tenancy of the subject or similar property.

Vacancy survey A survey of similar investment properties to determine the history of vacancy in such units. Generally done to determine if there is a need for additional units in the area.

VRM Variable rate mortgage. The same as an ARM (adjustable rate mortgage).

WCR Women's Council of REALTORS®. A NAR institute.

Wraparound mortgage (*See* All-inclusive deed of trust.)

Yard signs For-sale signs placed in front yards by the brokerage firm that holds a listing on the property.

Zoning Laws in most cities, counties and states that stipulate the uses to which any property may be put.

Index

A

Abstract of title, 260
Acceleration clause, 248
Accredited Land Consultant (ALC), 159
Acquisition, 310–11
Activity
  daily log, 122
  monthly sheet, 120
Actual notice, 265
Ads
  book, 214
  processing, 213–14
  recording, 213–14
  writing, 209, 212–13
Advertising, 97
  budget, 207–209
  control, 207, 209, 212–14
  cooperating broker and, 217–18
  "For Sale" sign as, 166–67, 199–200
  ledger entries, 188
  listing contract as, 166
  open houses for, 215–17
  source of listings, 166
  telephone, 200
  types of, 200–207
Affirmative action, 287–88
Affirmative Marketing Agreement, 128, 287
Agency
  law of, 31–32
  relationship, 32–43
Agent
  definition, 33
  duties of disclosure, 37–38
  duties of principal, 35–36

  principal's agreements, 46
  principal's responsibilities to, 39
Alienation clause, 248
Allocable installment indebtedness (AII), 318–19
American Institute of Real Estate Appraisers (AIREA), 10, 160, 331
American Society of Real Estate Counselors (ASREC), 10, 310
Amortized note with level principal payments, 245–46
Antitrust activities, 281–82
Appraiser certification and licensing, 331
Assumptive close, 231

B

Back-title certificate, 264
Bergen Country Homes, 201
Bern, Ronald L., 109
Better Homes and Gardens, 71
Broderick Company, Henry, 71
Broker
  as administrator, 66
  association group, 71–72
  commission, 46–48
  community responsibilities, 322–23
  cooperative, 71
  defined, 1
  duties to other brokers, 42–43
  earnings, 6–8
  experience, 19–21
  income tax deductions, 285–87
  independent, 69–70
  intermediary, 3
  licensing requirements, 21–22

Broker *(continued)*
  median income, 18
  principal's responsibilities to, 39
  psychological traits, 24–25
  reputation, 140
  required courses, 19
  service, 2–3, 13
  social skills, 24–25
  specialization, 4–6
Brokerage. *See Real Estate Brokerage.*
Broker association group, 71–72
Broker-owner, role of, 66
Bundle of rights, 290
Business plan, 51–52
Buyer
  needs, 242
  presettlement inspection, 264
  qualifying, 243–44
  servicing after closing, 271, 274–75

C

Calculator, using, 246
California Association of REALTORS®, 283, 327
California Department of Real Estate, 117
Capital, 92–93
Capital gains tax, 301
Careers in Real Estate, 130
Certified Commercial Investment Member (CCIM), 159
Certified Property Manager (CPM), 160
Certified Residential Broker (CRB), 159
Certified Residential Specialist (CRS), 159
Certifying title, 264–67
Chain of title, 264–65
Chart, master annual, 214
Civil Rights Act of 1866, 287
Civil Rights Act of 1964, 133
Civil Rights Act of 1968, 33, 287
Classified ads, 203
Classified display ads, 203
Client
  feedback, 237
  maintaining contact, 218
Closing, 229–32
  and attorneys, 259–62
  broker follow-up after, 271, 274–75
  broker's responsibilities, 258–59
  buyer's responsibilities, 259
  costs, 225
  escrow companies and, 261
  procedures, 258–62
  seller's responsibilities, 259

  statement, 14, 267, 268
  techniques, 229–32
  title insurance companies and, 259–62
Code of Ethics. *See National Association of REALTORS® Code of Ethics.*
Coldwell Banker Company, 10, 71
Commission, 46–48, 107
Communication, 86, 87, 185–86, 218
Community identity, establishing, 100–101
Company dollar, 91
Compensation methods, 106–107
Competitive Market Analysis (CMA), 173–74, 235, 237
  adjustment worksheet, 176–77
  handling objections, 183–85
  listing form, 178
  preparation, 174, 181–85
  sample form, 175, 179–81
Computers, 87–90
  costs, 89
  decision to own, 89–90
  effects on brokerage, 13–14
  hardware, 89
  selection of equipment, 90–91
  software, 89
  uses, 88, 330–31
Condominium conversions, 321
Conger, Dave, 117
Constructive notice, 265
Consumer protection laws, 326–30
Consumer rights, 283
Contingency clauses, 233–34
Contract, 98
  caveat about, 232–34
  contingency clauses, 233–34
  essential elements of, 233
  fully executed, 238–39
  legal requirements for valid, 257–58
  of sale, 249
  satisfying contingencies, 262–64
"Co-op" listing, 42
Corporate chain, 71
Corporation, 67–68
  centralized management, 67
  continuity of life, 67
  limited liability, 67
  no income limitation, 67–68
  transferability, 67
Counseling, 310
Counteroffer, 238
Courtroom challenges, 47–48
Credit, 100
Cushman/Wakefield, 10

Cyr, John, 81, 207
Cyr, Inc. REALTORS®, John, 140, 155–60
  policy manual, 335–44

D

Daily work plan, 152
Deed of trust, 246–47, 249–50
  clauses, 247–48
Depreciation, 299, 317
Depreciation deduction, 299
Desk cost, 83–84, 115
Direct closing, 261
Direct mail
  advertising, 203
  as source of listing, 167
Disclosure, 283, 327–28
Disclosure statement, 40–41
Discount rate, 316
Discrimination, 224–25
Display ads, 203
Disposition, 312–13
Down-zoning, 29
Dual agency, 36–39
  duties of disclosure, agent's, 37–38
  duties of disclosure, seller's, 37–38
  inaccurate statements, 38–39
Due-on-sale clause, 248, 252

E

Easements, 265
Easton v. *Strassburger*, 37
Education
  academic, 18
  continuing, 21
  formal, 17–19
  government involvement in, 288
  professional training, 18
  of sales associates, 159–60
Ego-drive, 109, 136
Ellsworth Dobbs v. Johnson, 47
Emotional health, 28
Empathy, 109, 136
Employee status, 59–60, 65–66
Energy, 9–10
Environmental impact reports, 292–93
Equal Employment Opportunity Commission, 133
Equal Housing Opportunity Committee, 287–88
Equipment, 86–90
  communication, 86–87
  economic factors, 90
  selection of, 90–91

standardization, 91
Equitable Assurance Society, 254
Equity, 301, 302–303
Escrow closing, 261–62, 283
Esprit de corps, 28
Ethics and Professional Conduct Code, 327
Evaluation
  criteria for, 115–17
  desk cost of, 115, 116
  keeping records for, 117
  of performance, 114–18
Exchanges, 316–17
Exclusive agency agreements, 43–44
Exclusive-right-to-sell agreement, 44–45

F

Factor-times-gross-income, 313
Fair Credit Reporting Act, 289–90
Fair market value (FMV), 174, 182, 183
Farm and Land Institute, 10, 12
Farming, as source of listing, 167
Federal Fair Housing Law, 287
Federal flood control, 263–64
Federal Home Loan Mortgage Corporation (FHLMC), 284
Federal Housing Administration (FHA), 225, 289
  loans, 249, 254
Federal National Mortgage Association (FNMA), 284
Federal Reserve Bank, 241–42, 288
Federal Trade Commission (FTC), 289
Feedback, 230
Fiduciary relationship, 33, 42
Fiduciary responsibilities, 33–34
Financing, 241–54, 262–63
  broker's role in, 243–44
  government activities affecting, 288–90
  importance, 242–43
  institutional sources, 253–54
  needs, 22, 24
  private sources, 252–54
  secondary, 252
  tools, 244–50
"Flash" listing notice, 113
Finder's fee exceptions, 332–33
Flexible loan insurance plan (FLIP), 251
For Sale by Owner (FSBO) signs as source of listings, 166–67
For Sale signs, 199–200, 284–85
Franchise, 69–72
  full-, 70–71
  quasi-, 71

Franchise networks, 11
Franklin technique, Ben, 230–31
Fraud, 46
Friedman, Dr. M., 24
Funk v. *Tifft*, 283

G
Gallery of Homes, 71
GIGO effect, 90
Goals, 52–53, 105–106, 156
  planning personal, 109–11
  self-imposed and actual evaluation
    form, 120
Goodwill, spirit of, 235
Government activities
  affecting financing, 288–90
  affecting ownership, 290–93
  affecting real estate brokerage, 281–90
Government National Mortgage Associa-
    tion (GNMA), 284
Graduate Realtor Institute (GRI), 151,
    159
Graduated payment mortgage (GPM), 251
Greenberg, Herbert M., 109
Grillo v. Board of REALTORS®, 282

H
Hanford Sr., Lloyd D., 311
Health, good, need for, 28–29
Health code compliance, 263
Herbert Hawkins Organization, 71
Home Guide, 71
Home inspection, 263
Homes magazine, 201
Hot potato technique, 230
HUD (U.S. Department of Housing and
    Urban Development), 128, 287, 288

I
Inaccurate statements, 38–39
Income, 93
  distribution of gross, 92
Independent contractor, 59–60
  agreement, 62–64
  tax legislation, 60–61, 65
Independent operator, 69–70
Inflation, 8–9, 300–301
Information storage and retrieval, 14
Inspections, 263–64
Installment obligations, 319
Installment sale, 318–20
Institute of Real Estate Management
    (IREM), 160

Insurance, types of, 98–99
Insurance companies, as sources of
    financing, 254
Integrity, 26–29
Interest rates, 288–89
Internal-rate-of-return, 316
Internal Revenue Code, 11, 60, 316
Investment
  advantages of, 298–303
  areas of expertise, 308–310
  brokerage and, 305–308
  choosing type of, 306
  disadvantages of, 303–305
  market analysis for, 313–16
  stages of, 310–13
Investors, types of, 306–308

J
Johnson, Samuel, 26
Jones v. *Mayer*, 287
Junior deed of trust, 247
Junior mortgage, 247
Junior lien, 247

K
Keys, 192
Kiwanis, 101
Knowledge
  marketing, 20
  product, 20
  technical, 19–20

L
Land development, 280
Land Use Without Zoning, 292
Landlord-broker, 72
Law of agency, 31–32
Laws
  consumer protection, 326–30
  effects on brokerage, 9
  no-growth ordinances, 9
Leads, getting, 165–66
League of Women Voters, 101
Leasing, 308–309
Ledger page, sample, 96
Legal action funds, 294
Leverage, 301
Licensing
  reciprocity, 333
  requirements, 97, 328–30
Liens, 265
Linmark Associates, Inc. v. *Township of
    Willingboro*, 284

Lions, 101
Liquidity, 304
Listing
  affirmative attitude toward, 164
  avoiding overpriced, 182, 183
  checklist, 186, 187
  communicating, 185–86
  contract as advertising, 198
  co-op sheet, 193
  data sheet, 190
  file, 189
  inspection report, 192
  inventory, control of, 186
  key control and, 192
  leads, 165–68
  ledger method, 186–87, 189
  office responsibilities, 235
  production and results form, 118
  prospect comment sheet, 191
  research, 169–70
  sales associate comment sheet, 191
  sources, 165–68
  yard signs and, 194
Listing agreement
  exclusive agency, 43–44
  exclusive-right-to-sell, 44–45
  net, 45–46
  open, 43
Listing interview
  initial, 168–69
  objective, 171–73
  presentation, 174, 182–85
  presentation binder, 170–71
  second appointment, 174, 182–85
Loan
  assumption of existing, 252–54
  programs, 251
Lockbox, 192
Logos, 83

M

Management, 304, 309–10, 311–12
Market identification, 82–83
Marketing
  development of sessions, 332
  establishing firm's policy, 197
  methods, 316–21
  new listings, 221–22
  v. professional concept, 10–11
  using syndication for, 320
Market survey questionnaire, 154–55
Maslow, Abraham, 108, 109
Mass media, 200–201, 203

Meals on Wheels, 101
Meetings
  planning, 112
  sales, 111
  staff, 111
  suggested format, 112–14
  training, 111–12
  types of, 111–12
Member of the Appraisal Institute (MAI), 160
Merrill Lynch, 10
Minimum average production (MAP),
  115–17
Money market
  effects on real estate, 241–42
Monolithic office, 55–56
Monthly rental as one percent of value,
  313–14
Mortgage, 246–50
  alternative instruments, 250–51
  amortization schedules, 14
  clauses, 247–48
  loan brokers, 254
  prepayment privileges, 249
Motivation techniques, 107–111
Motivators
  ego-drive, 109, 136
  empathy, 109, 136
  goals, 109
  quotas, 109
  sales meetings, 111
  training programs, 140
Multiple-listing service, 2, 89, 164, 217–18
Multiple-office firm, 58–59
Municipal code compliance, 263

N

National Association of Real Estate
  License Law Officials (NARELLO), 3,
  21, 330
National Association of REALTORS®, 3, 5, 7,
  10, 70, 78, 90, 99, 110, 128, 129, 150,
  173, 246, 281, 287, 294, 332
  Agency Task Force, 37
  Code of Ethics, 33, 35, 42, 45, 238, 259
  financial analysis, 94
  Membership Profile 1984, 5, 6, 7, 17, 18,
    20, 21, 89
  1986 Statement of Policy, 29
  Profile of Real Estate Firms: 1984, 11, 13
  Profile of Real Estate Firms: 1985, 70
  *Real Estate Brokerage, 1985: Income
    Expenses, Profits*, 92
Negotiating, 1, 237

Net listing agreement, 45–46
New Jersey Association of REALTORS®, 62, 63, 64, 150
New Jersey Real Estate Commission, 42
Newspaper advertising, 207, 209–14
New York Life Insurance Company, 254
Nonowner/manager, 79
Notes, type of, 244–46
Notice, 34
Novelties as advertising, 204

O

Objections
    answering, 228–29
    at closing, 237
    handling, 183–85
Objectives, 52–53, 158
Occidental Life Insurance, 254
Occupancy, 271, 274–75
Offers, 232–37
    agreement, fully executed, 238–39
    presenting, 235–37
    types of, 232–33
Office
    administration, 77
    arrangement, 85
    bank connections, 99–100
    budget, 91–97
    certificate of occupancy, 98
    cost control, 97
    employee contracts, 98
    image, 83
    inspections, 98
    legal contracts, 98
    location, 80, 82
    monolithic, 55–56
    multiple-, 58–59
    100 percent commission, 72
    one-person, 54
    one-to-ten associate, 55
    physical layout, 82–85
    policy manual, 98
    records, 14, 94–95
    size selection, 54
    space area checklist, 86
Olson, Forest E., 71
100 percent commission office, 72
One-person office, 54
One-to-ten associate office, 55
On-the-job training, 142
Open house
    concluding, 217
    follow-through, 217

objective of, 215
planning, 215
preparing, 215–16
showing property at, 216–17
source of listings, 167
Open listing agreement, 43
Operating expenses, 93–94
Optimists, 101
Outdoor advertising, 203–204
Ownership
    forms of, 66–69
    of real estate, 297–98

P

Parent Teacher's Association (PTA), 101
Partnership
    general, 68
    limited, 68–69
Performance evaluation, 114–17
Personal contact, as source of listings, 116
Personnel problems, 119
Pest control inspection, 263
Points, 243
Police power, 291
Policy and procedures manual, 122
Political Action committees, 293–94
Porcupine technique, 230
Postsettlement checklist, 275
Prepayment privileges, 249
Press releases, 205, 207
Prime rate, 242
Principal-agent agreement, 46
Principal's responsibilities, 39
Printed advertising, 204–205
Procedural guidelines, 73–74
Product knowledge, 154
Production goals, 110
Profits, 141
Promissory notes, 244–46
Property
    concept of social, 280–81
    demonstration, 226–27
    description of, 233, 266
    government activities affecting ownership of, 290–93
    inventory, 316–17
    showing, 185, 226–29
Property House, Inc. v. *Kelly*, 332–33
Proprietary firms, 10
Prospects
    converting to buyer, 222
    determining needs, 223
    finding, 221–22

Prospects *(continued)*
  maintaining control of, 225
  qualifying, 222–25
  qualifying financially, 224
  real estate brokerage, 3–4
Prudential Insurance Company, 254
Psychological traits, 24–25
Public relations, 224–25

Q

Qualifying
  buyer, 243–44
  discrimination, 224–25
  financially, 224
  needs and desires, 223
  process of, 222–25
Quasi-franchise, 71

R

Rate of discount, 316
Rate of return, 298–99
Real estate brokerage
  budget for establishing, 23
  choosing a specialty, 53
  counseling as a specialty, 310, 321–22
  economic justification for, 1–3
  effects of computers on, 13–14
  effects of inflation on, 8–9
  effects of laws on, 9
  evolution of a specialty, 4–7
  government activities affecting, 281–88
  leasing as a specialty, 308–309
  monolithic office, 55
  multiple-office, 58–59
  office size, 54
  100 percent commission, 72
  one-person office, 54
  one-to-ten associate office, 55–56
  planning, 51–52
  real estate development as specialty, 309
  real estate management as specialty, 309–10
  response to change, 8–10
  selecting the right size, 54–59
  selling investment real estate as specialty, 308
  table of organization, 57
  See also Office.
Real estate
  counseling. *See Counseling.*
  development, 309
  education programs, 18–19
  as hedge against inflation, 300–301

  investment. *See Investment.*
  management. *See Management.*
  money market, 241–42
Real Estate Group Insurance Trust (REGIT), 99
Real Estate Network, The, 71
Real Estate Office Administration, 117
Real Estate Settlement Procedures Act (RESPA), 271, 284
Real Estate Tax Education Letter, 287
Real Estate Today, 114
REALTOR® Boards, 287, 327
REALTORS® In-House Training and Education (RITE™), 150
REALTORS® Land Institute, 287, 316, 332
REALTORS® Marketing Institute, 332
REALTOR® National Marketing Institute (RNMI), 12, 159, 173, 316
Reciprocity, licensing, 333
Records
  accounts payable, 95
  commission, 95
  financial, 94–95
  income, 95
  payment, 95
  payroll card, 95
  trust account, 95
Recruiting methods
  advertising, 127–29
  career nights, 129–30
  direct mail, 132
  image, 127
  "King Arthur" technique, 132
  licensing courses, 130–31
  scholarships, 131–32
  sponsorship, 131
  trial training sessions, 131
Red Cross, 101
Redlining, 289
Referral, 167–68
  fee, 12
  service, 70
  systems, 12
Release clause, 248
Relocation, 13, 167–68
Renegotiable rate mortgage (RRM), 250–51
Responsibilities in agency relationship, 35–43
Return on cash invested, 314
Return on net operating income (NOI), 314
Reverse Annuity Mortgage (RAM), 251

Robinson, Richard, 287
Roseman, Dr. R. H., 24
Rotary, 101

S

Sales associate
  acquiring, 59
  evaluating, 106
  goal setting, 105–106
  motivating, 106, 107–11
  organization, 156–58
  priorities, 158–59
  recruiting, 105, 127–33
  selecting, 59, 133–38
  self-discipline, 158
  supervising, 140
  tour, 199
  training, 105, 139–55
  training manual, 155–60
Sales management, 77–79
Sales manager
  basic functions, 104–106
  compensation, 106–107
Sales meetings, 111, 142
Salespeople
  attrition patterns, 27
  ego-drive, 109, 136
  empathy, 109, 136
  failure of, 115
  morale, 140
Sales process, 79–81
Sales production form, 119
San Francisco Board of REALTORS®, 294
Sears Roebuck and Co., 71
Secondary financing, 252
Security devices, 244–50
Selection process
  application, 133–34
  final, 137–38
  interview, 134–36
  pitfalls of, 137
  testing, 136–37
Self-amortizing note, interest included, 245
Seller
  duties of disclosure, 37–38
  financing, 243
  needs, 234, 243
Settlement, 267, 269–71
Sherman Act, 282
Showing property, 185, 226–29
  appointments, 226
  preparation for, 185

Siegan, Bernard H., 292
Signed agreement, 47
Signs, 194
"Smart Start" program, 150
Social awareness, 29
Social property, 280–81
Social security taxes (FICA), 65, 106
Society of Industrial and Office REALTORS®
  (SIOR), 10, 160
Space ratios, 83–84
Specialty, choosing, 53
Staff meetings, 111
Starr, Marvin, 297
Statute of Frauds, 31, 46
Statutory letter, 46–47
Steering, 283
Straight note, 245
Subagent, role of, 34
Subchapter S corporation, 68
Subordination clause, 248
Successful Salesman, The, 109
Supplies, office, 97
Survey, 265–66
Syndication, 320

T

Tax
  advantages for seller, 253
  breaks for real estate owners and
    investors, 302
  broker's deductions on income, 285–87
  capital gains, 301
  deferment, 301–302
  personal income, 11
  property, 11
  shelters, 11, 299
Tax Equity and Fiscal Responsibility Act
  of 1982, 60
Tax-free funds, 302–303
Tax Reform Act of 1986, 10, 11, 253,
    285–86, 291–98, 302–303, 318, 325–26
  depreciation, 299–300
Technical knowledge, 19–20
Telephone, 86–87
Termination, 114
Tie down, 230
Time management, 152–54
Title
  abstract of, 260
  binders, 260
  certifying, 260, 264–67
  closing. *See Closing.*
  insurance, 266–67

Title, *(continued)*
  insurance companies, 260–61
  search, 264–67
Torrens system, 266
Training manual, 155–60
Training meetings, 111–12
Training program
  benefits of, 140–41
  choosing instructor, 144
  choosing location for, 146–47
  classroom instruction, 142
  course content, 147–50
  factors in planning, 143–44
  ingredients, 141–52
  instructor do's and don'ts, 144–45
  methods, 141–42
  objectives, 140–41
  presentation methods, 142–43
  sales meetings as, 142–43
  sources of instructional material,
    150–51
  supplementary, 151–52
  teaching aids for, 151
  timetables, 141–42
Transactions, 3
  reporting to IRS, 326
Trial close, 231

Truth-in-Lending Law, 289
Turnover, 114, 141
Type A Behavior and Your Heart,
  24

U
Uniform Settlement Statement, 272–73
Urban revitalization, 280–81
U.S. Department of Housing and Urban
    Development (HUD), 128, 271, 287, 288

V
VA loans, 249, 254
Variable rate mortgages, 250
Veterans Administration (VA), 225

W
*What Everyone Should Know About Equal
    Opportunity in Housing*, 287
Word processing, 14
Wraparound mortgage, 250

Z
Zone marketing, as source of listing, 167
Zoning, 291–92
  exclusionary, 9
  inclusionary, 9

More Real Estate Books That Help You Get Ahead...

Detach, sign and mail today!

Name_____

Address _____

City _____ State _____ Zip _____

Telephone No. (   ) _____

Account No. _____ Exp. Date _____

Signature _____
(All charge orders must be signed.)

Qty.		Order Number		Price	Total Amount
			Real Estate Principles		
_____	1.	1510-01	Modern Real Estate Practice, 11th ed.	$32.95	_____
_____	2.	1510-	Supplements for Modern Real Estate Practice are available for many states. Indicate desired state _____	$10.95	_____
_____	3.	1510-02	Modern Real Estate Practice Study Guide, 11th ed.	$13.95	_____
_____	4.	1513-01	Real Estate Fundamentals, 2nd ed.	$22.95	_____
			Exam Guides		
_____	5.	1970-04	Questions & Answers to Help You Pass the Real Estate Exam, 2nd ed. . . .	$19.95	_____
_____	6.	1970-02	Guide to Passing the Real Estate Exam (ACT), 2nd ed.	$19.95	_____
_____	7.	1970-01	The Real Estate Education Company Real Estate Exam Manual, 4th ed. (ETS)	$19.95	_____
_____	8.	1970-06	Real Estate Exam Guide (ASI)	$19.95	_____
_____	9.	1970-03	How to Prepare for the Texas Real Estate Exam, 4th ed.	$19.95	_____
_____	10.	1970-07	California Real Estate Exam Guide	$19.95	_____
			Advanced Studies/Continuing Education		
_____	11.	1556-10	Fundamentals of Real Estate Appraisal, 4th ed.	$34.95	_____
_____	12.	1557-10	Essentials of Real Estate Finance, 4th ed.	$34.95	_____
_____	13.	1559-01	Essentials of Real Estate Investment, 3rd ed.	$34.95	_____
_____	14.	1551-10	Property Management, 3rd ed.	$31.95	_____
_____	15.	1965-01	Real Estate Brokerage: A Success Guide, 2nd ed.	$31.95	_____
_____	16.	1560-01	Real Estate Law, 2nd ed.	$38.95	_____
_____	17.	1512-10	Mastering Real Estate Mathematics, 4th ed.	$22.95	_____
_____	18.	1961-01	The Language of Real Estate, 3rd ed.	$24.95	_____
_____	19.	1512-16	How to Use the HP-18C in Real Estate	$21.95	_____
_____	20.	1560-08	Agency Relationships in Real Estate	$22.95	_____
			Professional Books		
_____	21.	1913-01	List for Success	$18.95	_____
_____	22.	1926-01	Classified Secrets	$29.95	_____
_____	23.	1907-01	Power Real Estate Listing	$14.95	_____
_____	24.	1907-02	Power Real Estate Selling	$14.95	_____
_____	25.	5606-24	The Mortgage Kit	$13.95	_____

Book Total _____
Sales Tax _____

For Fastest Service, Call Our Toll-Free Order Hotline 1-800-428-3846 (in Illinois, 1-800-654-8596)

Total Book Purchase (inc. tax, if applicable)	Shipping and Handling
$ 00.00–$ 24.99	$ 4.00
$ 25.00–$ 49.99	$ 5.00
$ 50.00–$ 99.99	$ 6.00
$100.00–$249.99	$ 8.00

PRICES SUBJECT TO CHANGE WITHOUT NOTICE

Orders shipped to the following states must include applicable sales tax: AZ, CA, CO, CT, FL, IL, MI, MN, NJ, NY, PA, TX, VA, and WI.

Shipping and Handling _____
TOTAL _____

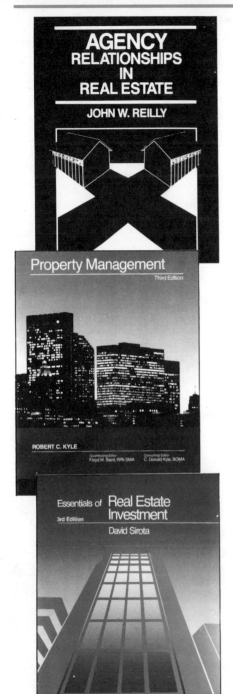

Agency Relationships in Real Estate
By John W. Reilly

This timely book explains all of the real estate agent's basic relationships with buyers and sellers of real estate—including the hot topic of "dual agency"—in clearly written, nontechnical language. The text also discusses the kinds of services offered to clients as opposed to customers, and types of agency representation a broker may choose to offer. Practical information on how to avoid misrepresentations is also presented.

Agency Relationships in Real Estate features:
- Extensive appendix on all U.S. cases involving agency
- In-text situations and examples that highlight key points
- Checklists that show the agent's responsibilities and obligations
- Quiz and discussion questions that reinforce important concepts

Check box #20 on order form $22.95   order number 1560-08

Property Management, 3rd Edition
By Robert C. Kyle, with Floyd M. Baird, RPA/SMA, Contributing Editor

The revised third edition presents management techniques for apartment buildings, co-ops, condominiums, office buildings, and commercial and industrial properties. Also features numerous sample forms, ads, and charts.

Key features added to the third edition:
- Discussion of single family homes—how they differ from apartments, vacation homes, and timeshare properties
- Section on trust relationships
- Coverage of the "intelligent building", including maintenance of automation systems and telecomunications

Check box #14 on order form $31.95   order number 1551-10

Essentials of Real Estate Investment, 3rd Edition
By David Sirota

Completely updated and reorganized, the third edition provides the most timely treatment available on an area of real estate which is constantly changing.

Third edition highlights include:
- Effects of the 1986 Tax Reform Act on the real estate investment process and its applications
- Financing and insurance topics consolidated into one chapter
- Additional discussion of defaults and foreclosures

Check box #13 on order form $34.95   order number 1559-01

Longman Financial Services Institute

LONGMAN
WHERE EXPERTS BEGIN